SHOW ME THE
EVIDENCE

Show Me the Evidence is a work of great insight and integrity about Obama administration initiatives to use scientific evidence on "what works" to guide government social spending. In a thorough and balanced account, the book depicts the vision and commitment of government officials willing to depart from the usual recipe of more spending as the answer to social problems, and to focus instead on whether money is being spent in ways that truly improve people's lives. These pages illuminate a path to effective government that transcends endless partisan debate about more spending versus less.

—JON BARON, President, Coalition for Evidence-Based Policy

The quest to insert evidence into policymaking is a long, hard slog. But Haskins and Margolis tell the tale of the fight for rigor and results like investigative reporters revealing Washington's innermost secrets. In this case, the players are working to find what works and convince elected leaders to fund and expand those programs. The stories Haskins and Margolis tell in *Show Me the Evidence* show that it's possible to convince policymakers to make decisions based on scientific fact. The more we do that, the more American citizens will see the benefits of programs that work. This insightful and engaging account of the effort to insert rigorous evidence into the policy debate shows that progress has been made. Whether the effort can be sustained across congresses and administrations remains to be seen.

—ROBERT SHEA, Principal, Grant Thornton LLC

A hallmark of the Obama administration is its evidence-based policy initiatives. *Show Me the Evidence* is a masterful examination of the challenges and benefits of using an evidence-based strategy to allocate scarce public funds for addressing the myriad social welfare concerns of the nation. The authors conducted case studies of the six evidence-based initiatives of the Obama administration, which ranged from programs to improve prenatal and early childhood outcomes to programs aimed at improving college and career training outcomes. The authors make a compelling case that by creating a space at the table for evidence, the Obama administration has changed the public funding dynamic in important ways—it has raised the bar on "evidence of promise," created greater attention to and accountability for evidence of effectiveness, and stimulated more routine use of evidence to guide program improvement. The authors also demonstrate the feasibility and power of prioritizing randomized controlled trials for generating evidence to make decisions about efficient allocations of public funds to promote social welfare.

—REBECCA A. MAYNARD, University Trustee Chair
Professor of Education and Social Policy, University of Pennsylvania

SHOW ME THE
EVIDENCE

OBAMA'S FIGHT
FOR RIGOR *and* RESULTS
IN SOCIAL POLICY

RON HASKINS
GREG MARGOLIS

BROOKINGS INSTITUTION PRESS
Washington, D.C.

Library of Congress Cataloging-in-Publication data
Haskins, Ron.
  Show me the evidence : Obama's fight for rigor and evidence in social policy / Ron Haskins and Greg Margolis.
    pages   cm
  Includes bibliographical references and index.
  Summary: "Describes development and implementation of six evidence-based social policy initiatives undertaken by the Obama administration—spanning areas such as education, teen pregnancy, employment and training, and health—that led to effective ways in the use of social science evidence to guide federal policymaking and the operation of federal grant programs"— Provided by publisher.
  ISBN 978-0-8157-2571-8 (pbk. : alk. paper) — ISBN 978-0-8157-2570-1 (e-book)
  1. United States—Social policy—21st century. 2. Evaluation research (Social action programs)—United States. 3. Obama, Barack. I. Margolis, Greg. II. Title.
  HN59.2.H38 2014
  361.6'10973—dc23   2014022510

9 8 7 6 5 4 3 2 1

Printed on acid-free paper

Typeset in Minion

Composition by Cynthia Stock
Silver Spring, Maryland

Contents

JIM MANZI

Foreword

Bloodletting was a common medical practice for thousands of years, used by the ancient Egyptians, Mayans, and Aztecs and by Europeans from the Middle Ages through the mid-nineteenth century. The practice, which appears to have arisen from the intuitive idea that illness is caused by blood and other bodily fluids being out of balance, has been supported by both sophisticated theories and widespread folk wisdom. It has now been all but eliminated from modern medicine, having been shown in well-designed experiments since the mid-nineteenth century to be useless in treating any but a small number of very specialized medical conditions.

It is easy to mock bloodletting now, but very smart people across millennia believed that it worked. Why was it so difficult to learn from experience that this practice was, for the most part, hurting the sick people to whom it was applied?

The idea of designing and executing a test to determine the efficacy of a therapeutic treatment—giving patient group A one treatment and patient group B a different treatment and then observing whether one group does better than the other—is at least as old as the biblical Book of Daniel. In the tenth and eleventh centuries both Chinese and Islamic scholars recorded therapeutic trials. In the modern West, credit for the first clinical trial is generally given to James Lind, who in 1747 prescribed multiple treatments for scurvy to British sailors aboard HMS *Salisbury* and discovered that citrus fruit was the best available remedy.

Lind was consciously applying the experimental concept of Baconian science, which had revolutionized physics over the prior century. Major discoveries were made using this method throughout the nineteenth century. However, use of the experimental method progressed much more slowly in therapeutic biology than it had in physics, because the human body is more complex than a prism refracting light or chemicals interacting in a test tube. Therapeutic experiments for many potential treatments raised debates about whether the treatment was the only thing that varied between the test and control groups.

Around 1900 several researchers hit upon the idea of randomly assigning patients to the test and control groups, resulting in the so-called randomized controlled trial (RCT). That superficially minor change turned out to be fundamental. RCTs tell us that everything must be equivalent between the two groups if assignment is purely random, subject only to sampling error. To date, medical science has conducted several hundred thousand therapeutic RCTs, and they are central to the progress of medicine.

It was natural to attempt to apply the RCT method to social interventions like literacy, job training, and prisoner counseling programs. Those programs began in the same era as therapeutic RCTs, but the method did not turn out to be nearly as important to twentieth-century social science as it was to medicine. That was because the effects of social interventions tend to be so context dependent that we usually need to run many experiments to find the conditions under which a given program works. Running multiple experiments, in turn, requires a dramatically lower cost per test. Over the past twenty-five years or so, commercial businesses have been able to reduce costs by applying information technology to routinize and ultimately automate many aspects of testing. The technology needed to apply RCTs to evaluate, improve, and target government social welfare, education, corrections, and other programs is now available. The remaining barriers are political.

One component of political resistance is simply a visceral negative reaction to "treating human beings like lab rats." A second component is the argument that using experiments to determine what program reforms will be executed reduces the autonomy, prestige, and scope of judgment of program administrators and their political overseers. A third is the contention by program administrators that although a test may have shown some success in another state or with another kind of participant population, it will not work for "my program." Because of the context dependence of most social interventions, the last argument carries great intellectual weight, but it can also be used as an excuse to retain autonomy. Ultimately, to overcome these sources of resistance, sufficient political pressure must be brought to bear by the public or other countervailing interest groups and combined with sensitive and intelligent application of testing methods.

The combination of public political pressure and behind-the-scenes political savvy was central to the transition of the U.S. welfare system from Aid to Families with Dependent Children (AFDC) to Temporary Assistance for Needy Families (TANF) in 1996. That transition, which often is described simply as "welfare reform," was one of the greatest domestic policy successes in the United States of the past twenty years. Thirty-one well-designed RCTs were executed by various U.S. states in the early 1990s to test a wide variety of potential welfare reforms, including mandatory work requirements, financial incentives to encourage work among welfare recipients, and time limits on receipt of welfare benefits. The results were clear and dramatic. Mandatory work requirements, which consistently moved people off welfare in a humane fashion when nothing else worked, became a crucial element of the TANF program.

Work requirements worked across all tested states. That is very unusual. Because even most successful social interventions work only under some conditions, testing must be conducted within various operational entities to determine where a program will work. The Obama administration has made admirable efforts to embed rigorous methods of program evaluation, ideally using RCTs, into various operational units within the federal government. If this improved approach to evaluation works, it will create for the first time a reliable feedback loop for many kinds of public programs.

Ron Haskins is perhaps uniquely qualified to evaluate the progress of the administration's effort to date. As staff director of the subcommittee that wrote much of the welfare reform bill, he was one of the handful of key insiders who managed through the political process to make welfare reform happen. He had previously been an academic specializing in social policy and program evaluation at the University of North Carolina–Chapel Hill and subsequently the senior adviser to President George H. W. Bush for welfare policy at the White House. He understands the statistical science, the policy issues, and, crucially, the nature of the political barriers to adoption of rigorous evaluation. To read this book is to read highly informed field notes on a promising new development in U.S. public administration.

JIM MANZI
Founder and chairman, Applied Predictive Technologies

Acknowledgments

A truism about writing a book is that the debts to friends, colleagues, and even strangers just pile up from the day the idea for writing a book leaps into an author's mind until the day the final text of the book is sent off to the printer. In fact—especially in a book like this one, which took well over five years to complete—it seems inevitable that by then, important debts will have long since been forgotten. Even so, we remember many.

We first acknowledge our gratitude to the 134 people we interviewed (see appendix A), almost all of whom were exceptionally cooperative. They seemed to try their best to recall everything about their involvement in their respective evidence-based initiatives and often checked e-mails, documents, notes, and other personal sources of information to try to refresh their memories. Some even had notes of important meetings that they shared with us. We couldn't have asked for more from the people we interviewed. The simple fact is that we could not have written this book without the information they gave us.

We are especially grateful to three senior officials at the research firm MDRC: Gordon Berlin, Rob Ivry, and Kate Gualtieri. MDRC played several roles in the Social Innovation Fund (SIF) initiative as well as other evidence-based initiatives, and Gordon, Rob, and Kate were generous with their time both during an interview about their experiences with SIF and afterward. They gave us valuable background information about SIF and about the Corporation for National and Community Service, the agency responsible for administering SIF. In addition, they shared a useful memo about their early involvement in briefings for federal officials on the value of random assignment designs that was written by John Wallace, a senior MDRC official, who wrote it despite the fact that he had retired.

A sometimes unfortunate fact about social science research is that investigators need money and sometimes must spend far too much time chasing it. But we were saved from that fate by the William T. Grant Foundation—in particular by Robert Granger, its president at the time, and Vivian Tseng, vice president for programs. Every aspect of our relationship with the foundation was ideal. The foundation departed somewhat from its preferred issues to fund our study, it conducted an efficient review process that resulted in approval of our grant application, it was invariably helpful when we had questions, it had modest reporting requirements, and it gave us extensions when our project took longer than we anticipated. Above all, both Bob and Vivian gave us a lot of good advice. We want to express special gratitude to Bob for a late Friday afternoon meeting at a bar in Washington in which he talked at length and with great insight about the importance of evidence and the keys to spreading its use by community-based programs around the country. Several of his insights are recounted in chapter 8 of this volume.

We feel unrestrained gratitude for the help of a number of people who took a personal interest in our project and devoted a lot of time to checking records, talking with us on the phone, writing us long e-mails, proofreading the book, reading drafts of the chapters, and giving us comments and suggestions, most of which we followed. This group of amazing friends and colleagues includes Jon Baron, Andrea Kane, Naomi Goldstein, Lauren Supplee, Seth Chamberlain, Robert Gordon, Michele Jolin, Jim Shelton, Kathy Stack, Kelleen Kaye, Martha Coven, Lance Potter, Adrienne Hallett, Allison Cole, Lily Zandniapour, Kim Syman, Evelyn Kappeler, James Wagoner, Alice Johnson Cain, Chris Spera, Demetra Nightingale, Martha Moorehouse, Beth Boulay, Allegra Pocinki, Gina Wells, Emily Cuddy, and Ross Thompson.

Our Brookings colleague Kent Weaver provided us with help and advice at every stage of the project. He helped write the initial grant application, using his insights as a political scientist to help us frame our proposal to the Grant Foundation. He also helped us construct the questionnaire that we used for all the interviews, gave us valuable comments on a book chapter that we wrote about the Investing in Innovation initiative, and generally gave us excellent advice at every stage of our project. We are enormously grateful to him.

We cannot fail to mention our colleagues at the Brookings Press who encouraged and guided us as the book moved smoothly toward publication.

Finally, Greg thanks his parents, Lewis Margolis and Linda Frankel, for their wisdom, support, and encouragement, and Ron thanks his wife, Susann, for giving us the title of the book.

SHOW ME THE
EVIDENCE

1

Introduction: The Obama Strategy for Attacking Social Problems

In the sixth century B.C., a young Jewish man named Daniel was captured by the Babylonian king, Nebuchadnezzar, to serve as an adviser. While being held in captivity, Daniel and several of his companions refused to eat the food or drink the wine offered by the king, referring to the act of eating their captor's food as "defilement." But the official in charge of the king's slaves, who was responsible for their health and well-being, told Daniel that he was afraid that the king would kill him if Daniel began to show the effects of poor nutrition, in contrast to the young men of the court, who regularly ate from the royal table. Daniel then suggested the following experiment: "Please test [us] for ten days, and let us be given some vegetables to eat and water to drink" while the other men continue to eat from the king's table. The official followed Daniel's suggestion. At the end of ten days the appearance of Daniel and his fellow vegetable eaters seemed better and "they were fatter than all the youths who had been eating the king's choice food."[1]

Daniel was intent on making a point about nutrition, but the way that he proved his point—nearly 3,000 years ago—opens whole vistas in human understanding. Two ideas implicit in Daniel's approach are crucial. First, the appeal to evidence, along with theory, is one of the two pillars of science. Why stand around arguing about abstractions when you can collect evidence to answer a question about what causes what? Second, Daniel instructs the chief chamberlain to gather a particular type of evidence: evidence from a planned experiment. If you want to understand whether A causes B, assign people to two groups, administer A to one group, and keep everything else that the groups experience as similar as possible. Then, after some period of time, measure B in both groups. If the two groups differ with respect to B, A must have caused the difference. While his experiment could be improved in many ways, especially by better measurement of outcomes and by assigning people to the two groups at random to ensure their initial comparability, Daniel was nonetheless onto something big.

Discovering the Obama Evidence-Based Initiatives

The Obama administration and the federal bureaucracy are full of Daniels. Sometime during the summer of 2010, around 18 months into the new administration, I became aware of a home visiting initiative that the administration was implementing, formally called the Maternal, Infant, and Early Childhood Home Visiting initiative. Home visiting is a health and educational intervention to help young, usually single, mothers make good decisions in their personal life and adopt parenting practices that help their babies flourish. In undertaking the home visiting initiative, the administration had decided to fund only home visiting programs that had strong evidence of success. In September 2010, Kathy Stack, a senior career official at the Office of Management and Budget (OMB) who also was a friend of mine, called to say that she had heard that I was looking into the Obama initiative on home visiting. When I told her that I was writing a brief paper about the home visiting initiative,[2] she asked if I wanted to have lunch to discuss not only the initiative but also other evidence-based initiatives that the administration was planning. I eagerly accepted. Over lunch, Kathy described the full scope of what the administration was doing and remarked that people should know more about the initiatives because they could be precedent setting. Well, I had an idea about how to let people know more about the Obama evidence-based initiatives—namely, by writing a book about them. I left our lunch determined to raise enough money to hire a research assistant and learn everything that I could about the initiatives. My initial idea was to describe how the initiatives had been conceived; how the administration got them through Congress; how "evidence-based" was defined; how the administration managed to communicate its evidence-based concept to potential program operators around the nation; how the administration ensured that money went to program operators who were using evidence-based programs; and how the administration would ensure that the programs were having the intended impacts. Eventually, the William T. Grant Foundation, which for many years had been focusing on how social science evidence informs public policy, agreed to finance my enterprise, and I was bound for the Promised Land—especially after I hired Greg Margolis, who became the legs—and, in large part, the brains—of my operation to tell the story of the administration's evidence-based ventures.

What does it mean for the Obama administration to create "evidence-based initiatives?" It means that the administration strives to be as certain as possible that federal dollars are spent on social intervention programs that have been proven by rigorous evidence to work. What does it mean to say that the programs "work"? It usually means that someone, following a scientifically rigorous version of Daniel's approach, randomly assigned people to two groups, one of which had the intervention program and one of which did not, and found that the outcome of the group that had the intervention was superior to that of the other group in one or more important ways. For example, poor and low-income mothers who participated in a home visiting intervention were found to have better outcomes in several areas than similar mothers who had not participated, depending on the particular study. Improvements included less smoking and drinking by the mothers during pregnancy, reduced rates of child abuse and harsh parenting, healthier children, lower levels of parent depression, and higher achievement test scores of children.[3]

As we began to learn more about the Obama evidence-based initiatives, a second meaning of "evidence-based" became clear. Besides striving to fund primarily programs that already had been shown to work, the administration would also insist on rigorous ongoing evaluation of nearly every program that it funded. Running what eventually became six evidence-based initiatives, administration officials in the four executive agencies (Department of Labor, Department of Health and Human Services, Department of Education, and the Corporation for National and Community Service) greatly increased the likelihood of good evaluations by requiring entities applying for federal grant funds to give detailed information on how they would evaluate their project and to set aside money in their budget to pay for the evaluation. The agencies also provided projects with technical assistance to improve the quality and implementation of their evaluations.

It gradually dawned on me that the Obama approach to increasing the impact of government social intervention programs by greatly expanding the use of evidence was an idea with very broad applications and great promise for improving social outcomes. I originally came to Washington in 1985 from the University of North Carolina on a one-year fellowship sponsored by the Society for Research in Child Development and the American Association for the Advancement of Science to learn more about how to use social science research to improve the nation's social policy, especially policies that could boost the development of children from poor and minority families. My plan was to stay in Washington for a year or two, learn through observation and participation in the policy process about the uses of social science in the formulation of public policy, and return to the university to write a book about improving policy through more frequent and sophisticated use of social science knowledge. But I was captured by Washington and wound up working as a staffer on the House Ways and Means Committee for 14 years and as a White House staffer for a year. But I never lost my

Figure 1-1. *Model of Factors That Influence Legislation*

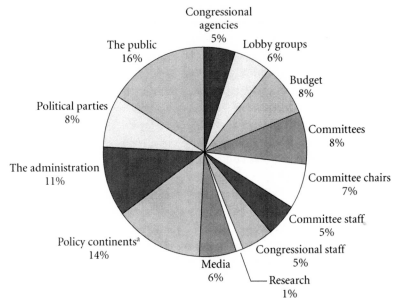

Source: Author's compilation.

a. "Policy continents" refers to the complex set of statutes, regulations, lobbying groups, congressional factions, committees of jurisdiction, and so forth that affect legislation in each area of social policy.

desire to return to scholarship, and at last—getting a little long in the tooth—I joined the Brookings Institution in January 2001 to finish my career by writing about poverty and economic opportunity. I also wanted, to the extent possible, to work with Congress, the executive branch, and congressional and executive branch agencies to use social science to improve policy. I saw then, as I do now, that a productive approach to using social science to improve policy is to conduct policy analysis, classically defined as the application of reason, evidence, and a values framework in choosing between alternative policies.[4] But the entire enterprise hinges on being able to use social science methods to determine whether social programs are producing their intended effects.

Within my first five minutes in Washington, I realized that the influence of research, program evaluation, and policy analysis on policy formulation in Congress, the administrative agencies, and the White House was tenuous at best. When I left Capitol Hill and came to Brookings in 2001, I was asked to give a talk to the Brookings trustees about how research influenced public policy. In a somewhat whimsical vein, I summarized my thinking in a pie chart similar to the one shown in figure 1-1. The pieces of the pie chart represent the factors that

I had seen determine the votes of members of Congress in committee and on the floors of the House and Senate. While the exact size of the pieces, which are proportional to their relative influence on policy formulation, varied from issue to issue, it was rare that social science research or policy analysis had much of a direct impact. The lesson here is that the U.S. government is a free-wheeling, wide-open form of democracy, conducted in many cases as a blood sport. Political philosophy, to apply a grandiose term to the simpler shibboleths by which many members of Congress operate (such as "Small government is best," "The IRS is evil," "Welfare destroys the incentive to work," "A rich country should not tolerate child poverty") trumps social science evidence on all but rare occasions. In that context, refined thinking about how research and evidence should influence policy must fight for a place at the table. The purpose of the Obama evidence-based initiatives is to pull up another chair and set a place for evidence.

While still on the Hill, I came to accept and even appreciate this messy world in which evidence would have to fight to play a role. On the other hand, it was impossible not to see that evidence was not always used in ways that enlightened debate. Consider the normal social science activity of conducting a literature review to determine what is known about how to attack a social problem. Such a review often focuses on both what is known about the causes of a social problem (such as child abuse, teen pregnancy, dropping out of school) and the effectiveness of programs designed to attack the causes. After years of reading and writing such reviews, I began to realize that even after completing thorough, fair-minded, and unbiased reviews, two equally impressive scholars might reach different conclusions in large part because of their different interpretations of the evidence. But such disagreements between scholars after careful review of the evidence were milder than and different in kind from the differences in the positions—supposedly based on the weight of evidence—often taken in the political world. In politics, evidence is typically used as a weapon—mangled and used selectively in order to claim that it supports a politician's predetermined political position. That is policy-based evidence, not evidence-based policy. This and similar problems would have to be overcome or bypassed if social science evidence were to play a more constructive role in formulating social policy. Indeed, this is the goal of the Obama administration's commitment to evidence-based policy.

The Guts of the Evidence-Based Initiatives

The more I came to understand what the Daniels in the Obama administration were up to, the more I came to see a clear, appropriate, and greatly expanded role for evidence in the policy process. Here is the essence of what could be expected from a full and vigorous implementation of the Obama approach. First, new funding for social programs would go primarily, but not exclusively, to programs that showed strong evidence of success. Let me quickly note that the requirement for evidence-based policy does not mean that the legislation authorizing spending should contain language specifically intended to ensure that the money is spent primarily on successful programs. In fact, as will be seen, it may be better to keep the legislative language about evidence somewhat loose. Later, the administration in power at the time and career professionals in the federal agencies can include definitions in regulations and funding announcements to ensure that funded programs meet well-defined standards of evidence. Evidence is constantly piling up, but legislation moves at a speed that is ponderous at best. As a result, it seems better to give an important role to administrative officials, who can stay abreast of the evidence. Second, new programs that received funding would be implemented at the state and local level and would be subject to continuous evaluation to make sure that they were having their intended impact; if they were not, the programs would be reformed until they produced the expected results or they would be terminated. Third, over the course of many years, programs that already were being funded by federal agencies would be brought under the evidence-based umbrella. Implementing this vision, federal agencies would become fanatics about continuously evaluating their programs through the use of rigorous designs. They also would insist on substantially revising or terminating programs that failed and then using the money saved to invest in programs that either already had developed or were in the process of developing strong evidence of success.

At some point, the flexibility of any administration to implement federal social programs and the extent to which it can change or terminate programs that are not working are limited by statutory provisions. Many social programs are based on statutory language that specifies who can participate in the program, how long they can participate, and what type of activities can be paid for with federal dollars. Yet in many programs the language is elastic, providing an agency at least some leeway in allocating funds. A federal agency may not be able to end a program that evaluations have shown to be ineffective, but often it may be able to use regulations and grant announcements to change the type of activities that program funds can be used to support. Similarly, often the federal agency can take money away from programs that do not meet quality measures or minimum outcome requirements.

Why would senior officials in the Obama administration invest so much energy and political capital in trying to force the federal government to change the way that it funds social programs? Here is an example of the kind of federal grant making that the administration's demand for evidence-based proposals is intended to eliminate. Consider Title I of the Elementary and Secondary Education Act, passed by Congress in 1965 and signed into law by President Johnson as part of his War on Poverty. The law has three primary goals: improving financial equity across the states; giving states incentives to participate in the federal educational accountability and testing regime; and providing funds for programs that help children, especially poor children, learn.[5] Regarding the last goal, which is the most important and the only one that we take up here, the act authorizes a host of activities by local school systems to equalize the educational opportunities given to advantaged and disadvantaged children. Over the nearly 50 years since the program was authorized, Title I has cost taxpayers around $320 billion—even more if that figure is adjusted for inflation. Yet there is only modest evidence that all that money has actually improved achievement test scores, increased high school graduation rates, increased either college entry or college graduation rates for poor or minority students, or had a meaningful positive impact on any measure of student performance.[6] If all that money had been spent on programs known to improve some aspect of educational performance, Title I could have achieved much more than it has and more poor children could have received a better K–12 education, which may in turn have increased their college enrollment rates and increased the nation's economic mobility while reducing income inequality.

Congress evidently shares these concerns about Title I. When Title I was reformed by the No Child Left Behind (NCLB) Act in 2001, the Title I accountability provisions were greatly strengthened. One of the new provisions was a mandate to the Department of Education to evaluate both the implementation and the impacts of Title I. The legislation also required the establishment of an independent review panel to provide advice to the secretary of education on how the evaluation should be conducted. An impressive panel was duly appointed, and the secretary followed many of its recommendations.

A major question faced by the panel was how to evaluate the impact of a federal program that operates in every school district in the nation. The solution proposed by the panel bears directly on the Obama administration's approach to expanding evidence-based policy. First, the panel proposed an informative design for the implementation study, which will not concern us here. Suffice it to say that as a result of the well-designed implementation study, researchers, policymakers, and school administrators now know a lot more about who is served by Title I; how the states have reported their annual assessments of performance in reading, math, and science; the reasons that states do not make good progress in student achievement; and so forth.

The panel also recommended randomized controlled trial (RCT) evaluations of a limited number of reading and math programs funded by Title I. Only an RCT based on a representative national sample of Title I schools would allow researchers to draw conclusions about the average impacts of the entire Title I program. Such a study, however, could be very expensive. Instead, the panel proposed an approach that greatly improves on previous evaluations of Title I and nicely illustrates how Obama's evidence-based principles can be applied to existing grant programs, of which Title I is one of the biggest. Given the emphasis on "scientific" studies of program impacts that is mentioned often in the NCLB legislation, the panel recommended three sets of RCTs of reading and math programs. Although conducting a "national" evaluation by conducting a series of smaller-scale RCTs of projects funded by the federal government may not allow conclusions about whether the federal program is having nationwide impacts—especially in a huge and somewhat amorphous field like K–12 education, in which there are large differences in the programs run by local education authorities across the nation—conducting small-scale RCTs will at least provide reliable information about specific intervention programs supported by the legislation. In fact, this strategy fits well with the administration's goal of using federal dollars on programs shown by rigorous evidence to produce impacts. In addition, in the long run this evaluation strategy will yield a host of effective programs from which school districts across the nation can choose to improve student outcomes.

To illustrate the strategy of using existing grant programs to develop and test effective education programs, we confine attention here to "Closing the Reading Gap," one of the three evaluation studies recommended by the panel. This longitudinal RCT was conducted in 50 schools from 27 school districts in Pennsylvania. The test was of four reading intervention programs in which "struggling readers" from the third and fifth grades participated. The schools were randomly assigned to conduct one of the four reading programs; within each school, students who were judged to be struggling readers were randomly assigned either to an experimental classroom that received one of the four reading programs or to a control classroom that received the normal school curriculum. A total of 1,042 students were identified by test score criteria to be struggling readers; 779 of those students were given permission by their parents to participate and were randomly assigned. At the end of the instructional year and at the end of the following year (one year after the end of the intervention program), students were tested on a total of seven measures: phonemic decoding (two measures), word reading accuracy and fluency (three measures), and reading comprehension (two measures). The one-year follow-up testing of the third-grade group (after students finished the fourth grade), combined across the four reading interventions, showed that students in the experimental groups outperformed control students on five of the seven reading measures. Each of the four reading programs produced at least three significant positive impacts on the seven measures. For the fifth-grade group, only two of the seven measures revealed significant positive impacts, averaged across the four reading programs, and two of the individual reading programs produced no significant impacts.[7]

School systems can draw their own conclusions about whether the impacts of these reading programs were adequate, but the point is that in contrast to the original Title I program, local administrators and the field of education now have a substantial amount of rigorous evidence about how four reading programs affected important reading skills of third- and fifth-grade struggling readers. Perhaps the districts can go on to improve the effectiveness of the four reading programs, but both the third- and fifth-grade students are at least somewhat better readers than they would have been without the program. That is progress.

An important point here—and a notable part of the evidence-based strategy—is that the local education programs participating in this study could have conducted their own research on whether their students closed the reading gap as a result of the intervention programs. In the long run, only when local programs, perhaps with help from third parties, conduct their own rigorous evaluations will the evidence-based strategy reach its full potential. A major goal of the evidence-based movement is to change the way that program operators do business so that they insist on generating evidence of the results of their programs and then use that evidence to improve or replace the programs.

The justification for using evidence to improve programs at the local level bears emphasis. Just because a model program has been shown by rigorous evidence to have impacts when used by a particular program operator at a particular site does not mean that the next program operator will achieve similar impacts. As the research in virtually every field of social intervention shows, many programs produce significant impacts when implemented by the team that developed the program, only to fail when other program operators implement the program and evaluate it using an RCT.[8] The aphorism "There is no such thing as a teacher-proof curriculum" underscores the fact that implementation is a huge issue in accounting for the success or failure of social intervention programs. Nor is the teacher the only factor that can thwart a good program. A more difficult population of participants, lack of parent cooperation, poor attendance, financial issues, and poor physical facilities are only a few of the other factors that can impair the effectiveness of good programs. Causality in social science almost always depends on many factors that are difficult to separate. In the end, the only way to know if a well-tested program is producing impacts in a new site is through continuous on-site evaluation.

When officials in the Obama administration began designing their own evidence-based initiatives, they took these lessons to heart. Peter Orszag, the first head of Obama's OMB and one of the primary early movers in the administration's evidence-based strategy, remarked in his OMB blog that research and evidence were built into the "DNA" of the Obama administration.[9] Part of that DNA is the requirement that most social programs funded by the administration use practices, intervention strategies, or programs that have been shown by rigorous research to have significant impacts on social problems.[10] There is something like an assumption chain that explains why Obama's team of evidence-based gurus expended so much energy, time, and money on its evidence-based initiatives:

—Random-assignment program evaluations can accurately distinguish social intervention programs that work from those that do not.[11]

—A substantial number of social programs have already been shown by rigorous evidence to reduce social problems.

—If federal grant funds are spent primarily to expand (or in administration parlance, to "scale up") programs that have rigorous evidence of success, the nation will make more progress in reducing its social problems.

—Continuous high-quality evaluations of social programs as they are being implemented will serve both to increase the likelihood that they will continue to be effective and to show when the programs are not working and need to be adjusted or terminated.

—If some funds are allocated to develop promising intervention programs that are not yet supported by rigorous evidence, a greater number of more effective model programs can be developed and progress against social problems can be enhanced.

One or more of these assumptions may turn out to be incorrect, but the least that can be said about the Obama initiatives is that within the next few years the results of a massive amount of research on hundreds of social programs will begin to pour in. But already at this stage—when the implementing legislation has been enacted, funds have been authorized, the six initiatives are in various stages of implementing about 700 local and state projects, and evaluations are in place—it seems safe to say that seldom if ever has there been such a broad use of social science evidence to formulate social policy and to implement and evaluate social programs. Especially remarkable is that, at least in Washington terms, this vast attempt to change the foundation of American social policy is being purchased for the relatively modest price of around $5 billion over five years.

Typically, social scientists and others who believe in trying to influence policy formulation through the use of evidence must fight to get their evidence considered in the public square. In terms of Knott and Wildavsky's classic seven-stage model for determining when research is having an impact on policy, the Obama initiatives fulfill the first six of the seven stages:

—transmitting the research to policymakers

—ensuring that policymakers and their staff understand the implications of the research

—influencing the way that policymakers think about a social problem and its solution

—using the research to guide policy development

—adopting the implications of the research by enacting a new policy that was shaped in part by the research

—using research to translate the policy into practice

—having a positive impact if the new policy delivers a benefit to citizens.[12]

Once the six initiatives had been implemented, all but the final stage of the Knott-Wildavsky standards—showing that the policy based on the research has a positive impact on the social problems addressed—had been met. That little sliver of the pie representing the role of research in policy formulation and implementation depicted in figure 1-1 has been dramatically increased by all the Obama initiatives. Research usually stands outside the policy formulation and implementation process looking in, but in the Obama initiatives research is on the inside, driving the entire process from beginning to end.

Equally important, the initiatives are forcing the use of research by a broad array of actors involved in the policy process. These include the policymakers who are formulating, debating, and funding new proposals; the administrators who are implementing the programs created by those proposals; the program operators who are implementing the programs; and the individuals (usually research specialists at universities) and research firms that are planning and conducting the many evaluations required by the initiatives. Again, the scope of actors in the policy process who are being required to adopt the administration's emphasis on rigorous evidence is remarkable.

Still, we wrote this book with the understanding that no one can claim that the Obama initiatives have been successful in Knott-Wildavsky terms because it is not yet known whether they are having a positive impact on the social problems that they are designed to address. We also wrote with the understanding that, as is almost always the case with federal and state programs, subsequent administrations and congresses might elect to repeal one or more of the initiatives or simply let them die a natural death by not renewing their funding.[13] Already, the Republican-controlled House of Representatives has voted to eliminate funding for four of the initiatives and to cut funding for a fifth. The Senate, controlled by Democrats, protected the evidence-based initiatives by refusing to go along with the House, and all the initiatives have been preserved. Similarly, the authorization of funding for three of Obama's initiatives (the Maternal, Infant, and Early Childhood Home Visiting initiative, the Social Innovation

Fund initiative, and the Trade Adjustment Assistance Community College and Career Training initiative)[14] will expire in 2014; if funding is not reauthorized by Congress, it will end.[15] The other three initiatives are funded by an annual appropriation that Congress must approve each year. Therefore, there is no guarantee that the Obama initiatives that we are studying will have a long life. On a more positive note, subsequent administrations or congresses may want to continue and even expand the initiatives, perhaps modifying them based on how the programs perform after five or six years of implementation.

In short, we come to praise the Obama evidence-based initiatives, but we make no claims that they are reducing the social problems that they attack. Only when we have evidence from rigorous evaluations can we make claims about whether the Obama evidence-based initiatives have succeeded and whether they have charted a new course for use of evidence in policy formulation.

The Foundation of the Evidence-Based Strategy: Random Assignment Designs

The Obama evidence-based strategy can work only if the field of social science has a method ready for widespread use that allows successful programs to be identified with high reliability. Fortunately, in what is social science's most important contribution to social policy, the field does have such a method: the random-assignment experiment or, more formally, the randomized controlled trial. Think again of Daniel and his basic experiment with two groups, one that received a particular treatment and another that did not. This simple method of creating two groups of convenience and subjecting one of them to a treatment must be substantially modified if social science is to give accurate answers about the effects of nutrition or any other factor that researchers want to study.

Two of the greatest threats to drawing valid conclusions from experiments are that the people who participate in the study are not representative of the particular group of people that the experimenter aims to understand or influence and that the treatment and control groups are not initially equivalent.[16] Let us say that we wanted to know the effect of a parent training program. So we go to a PTA meeting attended by 200 parents and ask the parents to voluntarily participate in our parenting program, intending to use the parents who did not volunteer as our control group. There are two main problems with this approach that will invalidate whatever results we might get. The first is that parents who attend PTA meetings are not a random sample of parents. Therefore, even if the rest of the experiment is well designed, we are limited in our ability to draw conclusions about a broader group of parents. Most parenting programs are aimed at low-income parents, who are the least likely to attend PTA meetings.

So even if the program had a big impact on the parenting style of parents who attended a PTA meeting, whether the results tell us that the program will work with low-income parents is questionable.

A second flaw in the experiment's design is even more problematic. If the parenting program is implemented with parents who volunteered serving as the experimental group and parents who did not volunteer serving as the control group, the experimenter does not know whether the groups were equivalent in the beginning; if they were not, that fact undermines any difference that might be detected between the groups at the end. It seems likely that parents who volunteered for the study would differ in several ways from parents who did not volunteer, not least in that volunteers are likely to be more motivated to help their child and their greater motivation could in turn be associated with all sorts of parenting behaviors that promote child development. It is also possible that the parents who volunteered would be more affluent, and many studies show that affluent parents engage in more parenting behaviors that are associated with positive child development than low-income parents do.[17] These include talking more to the child, avoiding corporal punishment, and involving the child in constructive activities such as music lessons, sports, and family outings.[18] All of these likely differences between the treatment and control groups bias our results in favor of the treatment group and mean that we cannot draw conclusions about whether the treatment itself caused particular outcomes. If such flawed methods are used to identify "good" programs, social science has failed in its most important policy-related mission: reliably distinguishing between successful and unsuccessful social intervention programs.

Recall that the experimenter's goal is to select two groups that are initially as close to identical as possible and then to make the treatment the only difference between the two groups. Although there is a lot of competition for the honor, the Scotsman James Lind is often credited with conducting the first clinical trial using the experimental method, albeit somewhat flawed in his case. In 1747 Lind divided scurvy-stricken crew members of the HMS *Salisbury* into several treatment groups and then tried to maintain constant conditions for all those participating in the experiment. After several days, it was clear that the group treated with citrus juice improved the most.[19] But the Lind method, though a great advance, is nonetheless flawed because there was no way to determine whether the groups were equivalent at the beginning of the experiment. The experimenter must do everything possible to ensure equivalence between the treatment and control group at the beginning or the results will be invalid. The Lind experiment may have revealed the effect of citrus juice on scurvy only because the effect is so strong. Social intervention programs, however, often produce only small impacts on those receiving the treatment; consequently, even small differences between the experimental and control groups at the beginning of an experiment could easily mask or magnify the effects of the treatment. It follows that the experiment would fail to produce an accurate indication of the treatment's effect.

In many experiments, the scientist tries to increase the equivalence of the groups by matching pairs of individuals on characteristics thought to be important to the outcome of the experiment. There is nothing wrong with this approach, as long as members of the matched pairs are randomly assigned to the treatment and control groups. But experience shows that it is impossible to anticipate all the ways in which individuals might differ that could influence the effect of the treatment. In fact, many social scientists have come to believe that there could well be differences between the groups that there is no way to detect with current methods of measurement.

Consequently, some method is needed to ensure that the experimental and control groups are equivalent at the beginning of an experiment. As explained by W. A. McCall in his path-breaking 1923 book, *How to Experiment in Education,* the solution is randomization.[20] To use McCall's own words, "groups equated by chance" will ensure equivalence "provided the number of subjects to be used is sufficiently numerous."[21] Any researcher can create equivalent groups at the outset of an experiment by randomly assigning people to the experimental and control groups, and with a sufficient number of participants in both groups, random assignment eliminates the single greatest threat to the validity of the experiment. Here's the surprising part of this method: None of the factors that could have an impact on the experiment's outcome are controlled, including factors that the experimenter does not even know about and might not be able to measure or control if he or she did. Nonetheless, random assignment ensures that these factors are equally represented in both the experimental and control groups, thereby canceling out the preexisting differences between the two groups.

Nor is producing equivalent experimental and control groups the only felicitous use of randomization. The way to solve the problem of ensuring that the results of the program evaluation apply to the group that the program is most intended to impact is to locate an available population of that group and then select both experimental and control subjects randomly from that population. In that way, if the population is selected wisely and in sufficient numbers, the researcher can be confident that the results will generalize to the entire group that the program is designed to impact and not just the sample selected for the experiment.

It was medical researchers who led the way to widespread adoption of RCTs by using this method to discover the impacts of medical devices, treatment regimens, drugs, and other medical interventions.[22] One of the first field trials using random assignment to treatment and control groups was conducted by Dr. Joseph Bell of the U.S. Public Health Service and Johns Hopkins University to determine whether the pertussis (whooping cough) vaccine was effective.[23] After inconclusive pilot work, in 1938 Bell obtained the names of children born over a three-year period in the Norfolk, Virginia, area. He then randomly assigned the children to a group that received the pertussis vaccine or a group that did not (some details of Bell's actual procedure have been left out in this description). The children in both groups were followed for 34 months to determine whether they developed pertussis. Contraction of the disease was confirmed by two doctors, neither of whom knew of the other's diagnosis or whether the children had received the vaccine. The results showed that there were 51 cases of diagnosed pertussis in the experimental group and 150 in the control group. This remarkable study, meticulously conducted and reported by Dr. Bell, illustrates how to deal with all the major threats to the validity of an experimental study. Techniques include

—ensuring that bias is minimized by using procedures that prevent either the subjects (in this case, the children) or the people who measure the experiment's outcome (the doctors who diagnosed the pertussis) from knowing who received the treatment (the pertussis vaccine); this feature of experiments is known as the double-blind procedure.

—maintaining the integrity of the random assignment by analyzing everyone assigned to the original experimental and control groups regardless of whether, due to error, they were assigned to the control group but received the treatment or to the experimental group but did not receive the treatment.

—ensuring that the subjects participating in the study are representative of the population to which the researcher wants to generalize the results.

—ensuring that outcomes are reliably measured, often by independent confirmation of the outcome measure (in the Bell example, by having two doctors, blind with respect to the group to which the children were assigned, independently make the pertussis diagnosis).

—ensuring that few subjects are lost in either the experimental or control group (minimizing attrition).

Since at least the 1940s, RCTs of the type conducted by Bell have become a staple of medical research. In *Uncontrolled: The Surprising Payoff of Trial-and-Error for Business, Politics, and Society,* a provocative book about the use of RCTs in business, medicine, and social science, Jim Manzi estimates that as of 2010, about 350,000 RCTs had been conducted by medical researchers to develop therapeutic drugs, medical procedures, and other treatments. Manzi also estimates that about $30 billion a year is spent to conduct an additional

10,000 therapeutic RCTs, with a significant portion of the cash coming from the National Institutes of Health and other federal agencies.[24] The progress of medical research in identifying effective treatments is due in large part to the reliability of RCTs in determining whether specific treatments are efficacious.[25] All those RCTs and all that money have created success after success in identifying both effective and, equally important, ineffective therapeutic interventions. The upshot is that the human condition has been vastly improved, not only in the United States but around the world.

It would be difficult to overemphasize the role of RCTs in establishing the efficacy of medical treatments, especially when properly conducted RCTs show that treatments with some preliminary evidence of success are ineffective. In fact, the medical research literature shows that around 50 percent to 80 percent of promising results from quasi-experiments or preliminary trials are overturned when tested by RCTs.[26]

The ability of the RCT to identify successful and unsuccessful treatments has enormous implications for social interventions as well. In principle, there is no reason why RCTs cannot be used to determine the efficacy of social interventions just as they have for medical interventions. Even so, the testing of social intervention programs by RCT is far behind the use of RCTs in medical science. But here, too, there has been substantial progress. The *Digest of Social Experiments* recorded that 240 RCTs had been completed and an additional 21 were in progress in 2004,[27] but many more have been conducted since then. The Institute of Education Sciences alone, created by federal legislation in 2002, has sponsored at least 175 random assignment studies,[28] and many other federal agencies are now supporting such studies. Thus, the 2004 estimate of 240 RCTs is seriously out of date. Even so, the number of RCTs conducted in social sciences, even if there have now been 1,000 or even 2,000 tests of social intervention programs, pales in comparison with the 350,000 therapeutic RCTs (an estimate that also is out of date). Not surprisingly, the rate of progress against the nation's social problems has been glacial compared with the rapid advances in treatments to improve health. The best way to attack the nation's social problems is to continue developing social programs and then subjecting them to RCTs and using the results to improve or discard the programs.

However, RCTs do not handle in a completely satisfactory way a number of issues in determining causality in the social sciences. One of the biggest issues is what Manzi calls "causal density" in social behavior.[29] The notion of causal density is simply that there are many causes for most human behaviors. Consider the experimental study of child development. The research literature shows that parents have a powerful influence on their child's development, but it is difficult to develop a succinct definition of what "parenting" means. Or even more to the point, try to design an RCT in which you change some aspect of parent behavior to study the influence of that particular behavior on children. Should you study punishment? How often the parent talks with a child? The number of different words that the parent uses? How and how often the parent criticizes the child? If we were to design a parent intervention program, we would probably have four or five parenting behaviors that we would like to study, but because they are likely to interact in complex ways, it is difficult to know which of the behaviors is having an impact even if we manipulate only one. In fact, most interventions—and all the interventions used in the Obama evidence-based initiatives—simultaneously change many aspects of the participants' environment. If there is an impact on the participants, we will usually not be able to say which aspect of the intervention produced the impact. Similarly, when programs fail, we usually do not know which particular aspect of the program is responsible. The causes of human behavior are exceptionally complex, making it difficult to know exactly what can be manipulated to produce a change in behavior.

A second issue is that years of RCT studies of social intervention programs teach us to expect modest impacts.[30] One reason that program operators question the use of RCTs is that they are likely to show no or only small impacts. Program operators might and often do raise the question of why they should go to all the trouble and expense of conducting an RCT if program impacts are likely to be small to zero. But that argument can be turned into an argument for why RCTs are so necessary. If the real world is such that most programs produce small impacts, we must evaluate those programs with a method that can detect small impacts. Well-conducted RCTs, with treatment and control groups that are initially equivalent, is the best way known to detect small effects. We return to this issue in the final chapter, but if small impacts are typical, program operators must learn to savor them—while trying relentlessly to produce bigger ones. For those who want to know whether mounting an intervention program to produce small impacts is worth the trouble, one good answer lies in benefit-cost analysis. If the value of the benefits is greater than the costs of the intervention, most economists would endorse the investment.[31]

Yet a third issue with RCTs, as noted above, is the fact that when programs are shown to produce or not produce impacts, the RCT does not identify which particular aspect of the program was responsible. Here as elsewhere in social science, identifying the cause probably will require conducting repeated experiments with modest changes in the intervention so that a series of RCTs can identify the components of progressively more powerful interventions. In order for this strategy to be effective, methods for conducting RCTs quickly and cheaply using primarily administrative data must be developed. We have some ideas about how to do that, which we take up in the last chapter.

A fourth issue with RCTs is that they often are criticized on ethical grounds.[32] The major ethical argument against RCTs is that they withhold valuable treatment from people in the control group. A reasonable response to this criticism is that the point of the RCT is to find out whether the treatment is effective or is effective with a different type of participant or under different circumstances than in previous RCTs. In all these cases, it is unknown if the treatment is effective.[33] Of course, some people would respond by arguing that "everybody knows" that programs like the treatment in question are effective—to which the appropriate response is that while everybody "thinks" a given treatment works, no one "knows" until the treatment has been subjected to an RCT. Another response, especially useful in situations in which the public would be likely to think that a given education treatment falls into the "everybody knows" category, is to point out that not enough money was available to enroll every child in the treatment, so assignment to treatment and control groups was decided by random lottery, providing every child with an equal chance of getting into the treatment group. Public lotteries are a way to demonstrate that the process of deciding who gets the treatment is truly random and that every child began with an equal chance. But researchers and evaluators must carefully and patiently explain to concerned audiences why random allocation of treatment programs is fair.

The use of random assignment in social science research and evaluation has not been without controversy. In their book, *Fighting for Reliable Evidence,* Judith Gueron and Howard Rolston review the opposition to RCTs in the 1970s and 1980s, when researchers first began to use large-scale, random assignment experiments to study social programs.[34] The charges against RCTs include claims that they are unethical because they withhold treatment from the control group and that they take too long to conduct, are too expensive, and test only one intervention at a time. In a Florida experiment featuring random assignment to test the effects of a program designed to get parents (mostly mothers) on welfare to work, the media even compared the experiment to the infamous Tuskegee study in which the U.S. Public Health Service followed black men with syphilis to study the course of the disease while withholding from them both the fact that they had syphilis and treatment for the disease.[35] Gueron and Rolston trace the fascinating history of how research companies and a few individual scholars fought the political battles—not to mention somewhat surprising battles with other scholars—to bring RCTs to their current status of being widely recognized as the surest way to determine whether a program actually produces significant impacts.

RCTs now have been used in studies of education, juvenile delinquency, preschool programs, parenting, and many other areas of social intervention. The main reason that many social scientists feel so strongly about RCTs is that they believe that a random assignment experiment is the only way to reliably establish a claim that an intervention program produces a given outcome. A recent report from the prestigious National Academies holds that

> evidence for efficacy or effectiveness of prevention . . . programs should be based on designs that provide significant confidence in the results. The highest level of confidence is provided by multiple, well-conducted randomized experimental trials. . . . When evaluations with such experimental designs are not available, evidence for efficacy or effectiveness cannot be considered definitive.[36]

Support for RCTs as the only way to establish the efficacy of intervention programs is provided by two seminal papers written by economists, one by Robert LaLonde in 1986 and the other by Thomas Fraker and Rebecca Maynard in 1987.[37] Both studies compared the results of an actual RCT with results obtained by nonexperimental methods. The LaLonde study compared the results of an RCT employment program with estimates produced by an econometric analysis; the Fraker and Maynard study compared the results of the National Supported Work Demonstration, an RCT evaluation of various approaches to increasing work among disadvantaged groups,[38] with what the results would have been if the control group had been formed by selecting subjects at random from the Current Population Survey rather than from the same group of disadvantaged people as the treatment group. In neither case were the RCT results replicated by the nonexperimental results. As Fraker and Maynard conclude: "There is currently no way a priori to ensure that the results of comparison group [as opposed to random assignment group] studies will be valid indictors of the program impacts." The LaLonde conclusion is similar except that his comparison is to econometric estimates.

The Coalition for Evidence-Based Policy, a Washington-based advocacy group, has produced a short, more-or-less nontechnical summary of the literature on whether nonexperimental designs that feature a comparison group not created by random assignment are likely to produce valid estimates of program impacts.[39] The major issue in using such designs is how to ensure that the treatment and comparison groups are highly similar at the beginning of the study, through the study design itself or through statistical controls. Based on the extensive literature on this issue, the coalition concluded that the best comparison group designs are characterized by several conditions:

—The treatment and comparison groups are similar in pre-program characteristics including demographics, pre-program measures of the outcome that the program is designed to improve, and geographical location.

—Outcome data are collected in a similar fashion for both groups.

—Program and comparison group members are likely to be similar in motivation.[40]

—Statistical methods are used to adjust for any minor pre-program differences between the groups.

Thus, claiming that RCTs are the best way to definitively establish causality does not imply that all other evidence has no value. The most important issue at stake here can be thought of in terms of probabilities. Every intervention program ever designed either did or did not produce statistically significant impacts on one or more of the desired outcomes. We want to study these interventions by using a method that will correctly answer the question of whether the intervention does or does not have an impact on important outcomes. Our claim, consistent with those of the various researchers cited above, the National Academies, the Institute of Education Sciences, and the National Science Foundation, is that the method that has the highest likelihood of providing the correct answer is the RCT. But there are quasi-experimental methods[41] that are much more likely to give us the correct answer than anecdotes or simple outcome data with no controls.

This issue may seem abstruse to many readers. But our study of the Obama evidence-based initiatives shows that the issue has an exceptionally powerful impact on the fundamental goal of evaluating federal programs that aim to reduce national social problems. The most important justification for the Obama initiatives is that most social programs are not evaluated and often those that are evaluated are assessed by unreliable methods. The Obama initiatives therefore are attempting to change the culture of the entire field of social intervention to bring rigorous program evaluation to the center of the enterprise. The administration wants to replace program evaluation by anecdote and flawed comparison group analysis with rigorous evaluation featuring random group assignment. But to dictate that this goal can be achieved only by universal use of RCTs is unwise, both in political terms and in terms of the best way to achieve change. All the Obama evidence-based initiatives make room for less-than-RCT evidence while nonetheless recognizing RCTs as the best method to establish causality. It makes little sense to make the perfect the enemy of the good.

There is one more caution about the Obama approach that we want to make at the beginning, a caution to which we return in the concluding chapter. Broadly speaking, the six Obama initiatives address a host of important social issues that face the nation, including infant development, teen pregnancy, school readiness, educational achievement, dropping out of school, drug abuse, mental health issues, and a variety of workforce issues. These issues can be arrayed on a continuum: one end represents social issues for which rigorous program evaluations have shown few or even no interventions to be effective; the other end represents social issues for which such evaluations have shown many interventions to be effective. It would be difficult to build policy for all of these issues on the assumption that federal dollars should be spent primarily on programs with strong evidence of success. Some areas of program intervention addressed by the Obama initiatives, such as using community colleges to assist workers affected by foreign trade, simply have very few model programs that have been well evaluated. As discussed later, this situation poses a serious issue for some of the Obama initiatives.

Despite the far too modest number of social science RCTs, the RCTs that have been conducted show that a number of social interventions have produced positive results in attacking important social problems. Table 1-1 summarizes eight examples of program evaluations that meet the highest standards of evidence of having socially meaningful positive impacts on important outcome measures of child or adolescent development or behavior. The impacts range from improved school readiness, with well-measured, long-term effects on performance in the public schools; improved reading performance; reduced rates of teen pregnancy, substance abuse, and delinquent behavior of youth in foster care (one of the most difficult child-rearing environments); improved high school graduation rates for troubled youth; and increased employment and earnings. With perhaps one or two exceptions, the impacts of these programs are not enormous, but all of them either have passed or seem likely to pass a benefit-cost test in which the value of the benefits received by individuals, government, or society exceed the costs of the program. These examples strengthen our view that the Obama team's vision of widespread use of RCTs to test and improve social programs has the potential to yield measurable improvement in the nation's social programs.

Methods for Studying the Evidence-Based Initiatives

The major purpose of the project reported in this book was to describe and analyze how the Obama administration enacted and carried out its six evidence-based initiatives. To gather information about the initiatives, we used three primary sources: interviews with administration officials, congressional staffers, and members of advocacy groups and other nonprofit organizations who had played some role in one or more of the initiatives; administration and congressional sources such as budget documents, reports of hearings, funding announcements, and documents from the administrative agencies conducting the initiatives; and media reports. In all, we conducted formal interviews with 134 people, including 32 congressional staffers, 66 members of

Table 1-1. *Examples of Social Programs Shown by RCTs to Succeed*

Program	Description	Impacts
Carrera Founded in 1984 by Dr. Michael Carrera and the Children's Aid Society, an organization that helps children in poverty in New York.	Sex-ed program model with a holistic, long-term focus that includes knowledge about human reproduction and sexuality and gives participants the opportunity to develop their interests and talents through education, sports, and so forth.	Female participants are significantly less likely to report having been pregnant or sexually active.
Career Academies Have operated for nearly 40 years; currently there are 2,500 Career Academies across the country.	Smaller school-within-a-school for high school students, focused on themes such as health sciences, law, and business; curriculum includes career-oriented classes and frequent visits to job sites to provide work-based experiences.	Eight-year follow-up shows impacts on annual earnings of about $2,000 per year, especially for males; men were also more likely to be married and to live with their children.
Small Schools of Choice Between 2002 and 2008, New York City closed 31 large failing high schools and began opening these smaller schools to serve roughly 80,000 students a year.	Small, academically nonselective, public high schools in New York City, with an enrollment of around 100 per grade; there are 123 of these schools.	Program has sustained positive impacts on graduation with a Regents diploma and positive effects on graduation for almost all subgroups; it also has positive effects on college readiness.
National Guard Youth ChalleNGe Has served more than 120,000 youth since 1993.	Comprehensive, long-term instruction designed to prepare at-risk youth for work and adult responsibilities.	Program has statistically significant positive effects on high school graduation/GED, employment, and earnings.
Reading Recovery Has served more than 2 million children since 1984.	Short-term tutoring for the bottom 20 percent of first graders to promote literacy skills and prevent long-term difficulties in reading through one-on-one tutoring sessions with trained teachers.	Program shows significant effects on many components of reading: alphabet, fluency, comprehension, general reading achievement.

Program	Description	Impacts
Success for All Started in 1987; currently serves more than 1,000 schools in 47 states as well as 100 schools in the United Kingdom and Canada.	Comprehensive school-wide reform for high-poverty schools that focuses on reading; includes tutoring, reading classes, and cooperative learning activities.	Program has positive effects for second-graders on passage comprehension, word identification, and word attack skills (using context and other cues to figure out word meaning); program kids were 25 to 30 percent of a grade level higher than controls.
LifeSkills Training Broad implementation began in 1995; program has served more than 3 million students in all 50 states as well as 32 foreign countries.	Middle-school program focused on substance abuse prevention that teaches self-management skills to resist peer pressure and explains the consequences of drug use.	One study found reduced rates of initiation of substance abuse (including cigarettes, marijuana, and alcohol) for high-risk teens.
Multidimensional Treatment Foster Care Established in 1983 with a focus on treating serious and chronic juvenile offenders; expanded and adapted over the years.	Trains families of severely delinquent youth in behavior management skills, emphasizing preventing conflict with peers; awards "points" as a way to earn more freedom from adult supervision for good behavior.	Studies found fewer violent offenses, fewer arrests, and fewer self-reported incidents of common violence such as hitting.

Sources: Carrera: Susan Philliber and others, "Preventing Pregnancy and Improving Health Care Access among Teenagers: An Evaluation of the Children's Aid Society–Carrera Program," *Perspectives on Sexual and Reproductive Health,* vol. 34, no. 5 (2002) (http://stopteenpregnancy.childrensaidsociety.org/sites/default/files/associated-documents/Carrera%20Summary_Perspectives%20on%20Sexual%20and%20Reproductive%20Health.pdf); Career Academies: James J. Kemple, "Career Academies: Long-Term Impacts on Work, Education, and Transitions to Adulthood" (New York: MDRC, 2008) (www.mdrc.org/sites/default/files/full_50.pdf); Small Schools of Choice: Howard S. Bloom and Rebecca Unterman, "Sustained Progress: New Findings about the Effectiveness and Operation of Small Public High Schools of Choice in New York City" (New York: MDRC, August 2013) (www.mdrc.org/sites/default/files/sustained_progress_FR_0.pdf); National Guard Youth ChalleNGe: Megan Millenky and others, "Staying on Course: Three-Year Results of the National Guard Youth ChalleNGe Evaluation" (New York: MDRC, June 2011) (www.mdrc.org/sites/default/files/full_510.pdf); Reading Recovery: Robert M. Schwartz, "Literacy Learning of At-Risk First-Grade Students in the Reading Recovery Early Intervention," *Journal of Educational Psychology,* vol. 97, no. 2 (May 2005), pp. 257–67; Success for All: Marco A. Munoz and Dena H. Dossett, "Educating Students Placed at Risk: Evaluating the Impact of Success for All in Urban Settings," *Journal of Education for Students Placed at Risk,* vol. 9, no. 3 (2004), pp. 261-277; LifeSkills Training: Daniel M. Crowley and others, "Can We Build an Efficient Response to the Prescription Drug Abuse Epidemic? Assessing the Cost Effectiveness of Universal Prevention in the PROSPER Trial," *Preventive Medicine,* vol. 62 (May 2014), pp. 71–77; Multidimensional Treatment Foster Care: J. Mark Eddy, Rachel Bridges Whaley, and Patricia Chamberlain, "The Prevention of Violent Behavior by Chronic and Serious Male Juvenile Offenders: A 2-Year Follow-up of a Randomized Clinical Trial," *Journal of Emotional and Behavioral Disorders,* vol. 12, no. 1 (Spring 2004), pp. 2–8.

the administration or the administrative agencies, 32 advocates, and 4 others. Almost all the interviews were completed between August 2011 and July 2013.[42] The name and affiliation of everyone that we formally interviewed are given in appendix A. In addition, we talked with several people on a more informal basis, asking one or two specific questions. If we used anything from these informal interviews, we give information about the interview in an endnote.

To identify people to interview, we used what often is referred to as the snow-ball technique.[43] We started by contacting and interviewing either people who we personally knew had worked on one or more of the initiatives or people whose names were given to us by Kathy Stack of OMB. During the course of those interviews, the interviewees mentioned many others who had worked on the initiative with them. When we interviewed the people suggested by our first round of interviewees, the second-round interviewees in turn gave us the names of people with whom they had worked. After several rounds of interviews, we heard fewer and fewer names that we had not already heard. In this way, we were confident that we had located most of the people who had worked on the initiatives or played an important role as an administration official, a congressional staffer, or an advocate.

The interviews lasted from about 45 minutes to over an hour. We used a standard questionnaire (see appendix B) in all the interviews, but we often departed from the questionnaire if the person that we were interviewing raised issues that we wanted to pursue. At the outset of each interview, we read a statement about the purpose of our study and outlined what we intended to do with the information that we obtained. We also assured interviewees that we would not quote them or identify them as an interview subject in any publication unless they gave us permission to do so. The interviews were recorded and then transcribed.[44]

In addition to the interviews, we also read congressional and administration documents. We checked the written records of committee hearings involving any of the six initiatives. Because many of the initiatives were inserted into large and highly controversial bills—including big appropriations bills, the Affordable Care Act, and the American Recovery and Reinvestment Act (the "stimulus bill" enacted in February 2009 in the midst of the Great Recession)—the relatively tiny and often obscure legislative provisions that established the six evidence-based initiatives received little attention. In fact, only one hearing was devoted exclusively to an evidence-based initiative.[45]

We also reviewed the conference reports that each committee with jurisdiction over the legislation wrote after the legislation had passed.[46] These reports contained the text of the bills introduced in both houses of Congress and a review of every provision in the bills and of how the House and Senate came to agreement on each provision. On a few occasions, we also reviewed the transcripts in the *Congressional Record* of the floor debates on the six bills. In addition to these sources, we examined the text of many bills and the legislative history of the bills in "Thomas," the online system maintained by the Library of Congress to provide information on legislation.[47]

Similarly, we used a host of standard documents from the administration to study how the agencies were translating the legislation into grant programs that targeted the social problems addressed by the initiatives and how the agencies selected the programs that would receive funding. Perhaps the most helpful document in most cases was the funding announcement, which goes by different names depending on the publishing agency (request for proposal, notice of funding availability, solicitation for grant applications, and so forth). This document, which is available on the website of the agency responsible for the initiative, tells potential applicants about the purpose of the grant and what they must do to apply for funds. All the funding announcements included detailed information on what it meant to be "evidence-based" as well as on how funded projects were to collect outcome information to evaluate their effectiveness. Most of the funding announcements also contained information about how the agency encouraged innovation by awarding points for new potentially effective proposals. In these cases, applicants were required to give their reasons for believing that an untested program held promise for producing measurable impacts. In addition to the funding announcements, the administrative agencies often made other information about grants available online, including explanations of how the administration developed the definition of evidence, the instructions and training given to the people who reviewed the grant applications, and in some cases the actual scores and comments about individual applications made by the reviewers.

Most of the information reported in this book came from reading and rereading the transcripts of our interviews and from standard documents, almost all of which are available online on the websites of the administering agencies. After studying the transcripts and documents, we constructed a timeline for each initiative that

—covered the administration's activities as senior officials formulated the initial legislative language or at least gave a narrative description of what they hoped to cover in the legislative language

—reviewed the major events in the legislative struggle to authorize the initiative in statute and enact legislation to appropriate funds for the initiative

—summarized the activities by the administering agencies to create the rules, definitions, and procedures that established the details of the initiative

—described the procedures followed by the agencies to announce the availability of grant funds and to determine which applicants would be funded.

While writing the descriptions of the initiatives for this book, we began with our timeline for each initiative and then referred frequently to the interviews and to congressional and administration documents and media accounts. After finishing the draft of the chapter describing each initiative, we asked three or four people with whom we had contact during the course of data collection to review the chapter and provide us with comments. We received a host of useful comments and suggestions, many of which were incorporated into our final text. When the first draft of the book had been completed, we asked four people who were familiar with the Obama initiatives to review the entire text and make suggestions about improvements, many of which we incorporated into the final draft.

Overview of the Evidence-Based Initiatives

Each initiative makes use of evidence of program effectiveness in two ways. The first is to give preference to grant proposals in which the sponsoring organization demonstrates that it is requesting funds to operate a program shown by rigorous evidence to produce the desired outcomes. The second is to use rigorous evaluation designs to determine whether a program, once in operation, has the desired impacts and to modify the program if the results are not acceptable.

It is not surprising that in order to deal with the problem of ineffective implementation, a major goal of the Obama initiatives is to require program operators to learn how to continuously evaluate their programs and to make good use of the results to increase the chances that they are having the desired impacts. One of the initiatives even developed an evaluation handbook for use by local programs.[48] All but one of the Obama initiatives require program operators to set aside funds to conduct evaluations, often by hiring third parties with experience in carrying out quality evaluations.[49] Table 1-2 presents an overview of the six Obama evidence-based initiatives. Each initiative is fully explored in a separate chapter, but here we note several distinctive features of the initiatives. Although two of the initiatives have some formula funds—money that is given to all states in proportion to some measure, such as the share of the U.S. population in each state—most of the money is awarded through a competitive process to states, community organizations, local governments, and other eligible entities. We calculate that nearly 90 percent of the approximately $4 billion awarded across all six initiatives through 2013 was done so competitively (see appendix C).

Competitive grants are an important feature of the initiatives because they help to ensure achievement of the administration's general goal of funding primarily programs that are backed by rigorous evidence or programs that have been approved by the administration as being evidence based (the latter was the case with the home visiting and Teen Pregnancy Prevention initiatives).

Table 1-2. *Overview of Six Evidence-Based Initiatives*

Evidence-based initiative	Initial funding source and amount	Administering agency	Evidence requirement	Date of first awards	Total amount awarded
Teen Pregnancy Prevention	$110 million; Consolidated Appropriations Act of 2010	Department of Health and Human Services	Programs must be identified by HHS as evidence based (tier 1); about 75 percent of funds are for tier 1 programs.	September 2010	$526 million; one cohort of grants; 102 total awards
Maternal, Infant, and Early Childhood Home Visiting	$1.5 billion; Patient Protection and Affordable Care Act of 2010	Department of Health and Human Services	Programs must be identified by HHS as evidence based; 75 percent of funds are for approved programs.	July 2010	$1.5 billion, to be allocated through FY 2014[a]
Investing in Innovation	$650 million; American Recovery and Reinvestment Act of 2009	Department of Education	There are three tiers of grants, reflecting the amount of evidence required.	August 2010	$1.1 billion; four rounds of grants; 117 total awards
Social Innovation Fund	$50 million; Consolidated Appropriations Act of 2010 (for first year; more money in subsequent years)	Corporation for National and Community Service	Evidence is incorporated into selection criteria; applicants must meet certain level of evidence by end of grant.	July 2010	$177.6 million; three rounds of grants; 20 intermediaries, 217 sub-grantees
Trade Adjustment Assistance Community College and Career Training	$2 billion; Health Care and Education Reconciliation Act of 2010	Department of Labor and Department of Education	Points are given for evidence in selection process.	September 2011	$2 billion for FY 2011–FY2014; three rounds of grants awarded
Workforce Innovation Fund	$125 million; the Department of Defense and Full-Year Continuing Appropriations Act, 2011	Department of Labor	There are three tiers of grants, reflecting the amount of evidence required; more money is awarded for higher levels of evidence.	June 2012	$146.9 million; one round of grants; 26 total awards

Table 1-2 (*continued*)

Sources: For additional information about the six initiatives, see Office of Adolescent Health, "Teen Pregnancy Prevention Resource Center" (www.hhs.gov/ash/oah/oah-initiatives/teen_pregnancy/); Health Resources and Service Administration, "Maternal, Infant, and Early Childhood Home Visiting" (http://mchb.hrsa.gov/programs/homevisiting/); Department of Education, "Investing in Innovation Fund (i3) (www2.ed.gov/programs/innovation/index.html); Corporation for National and Community Service, "Social Innovation Fund" (www.nationalservice.gov/programs/social-innovation-fund); Department of Labor, "Trade Adjustment Assistance Community College and Career Training (TAACCCT) Grant Program" (www.doleta.gov/taaccct/); Department of Labor, "Workforce Innovation Fund" (www.doleta.gov/workforce_innovation/).

a. The Affordable Care Act called for $1.5 billion in mandatory funds (meaning the administration would not have to seek annual appropriations) for the home visiting initiative for fiscal years 2010–14. However, due to the budget battles that embroiled Congress during 2011–13 and resulted in the cuts known as sequestration, the funding for home visiting took a hit. Congress reduced the home visiting appropriation by 5.1 percent in 2013, down to $379.6 million from $400 million, and by 7.2 percent in 2014, down to $371.2 million from $400 million.

The specific evidence requirements, however, vary greatly across the initiatives because the amount of rigorous evidence available differs so much across the areas of social policy addressed by the initiatives. One of the goals of the evidence-based initiatives is to increase the number of social interventions that have rigorous evidence of positive impacts on important outcome measures. Teen pregnancy prevention and home visiting, for example, are areas that have many high-quality studies of numerous intervention programs, but most of the other four initiatives have a smaller body of rigorous evidence about the impacts of model programs. By requiring funded projects to carefully evaluate their effects, the administration aims to increase the pipeline of tested intervention programs.

During the initiatives' first year, the funding ranged from $50 million for the Social Innovation Fund to $650 million for the Investing in Innovation Initiative (i3). The initiatives are being administered by four executive agencies: two by the Department of Health and Human Services, one by the Department of Education, one by the Department of Labor (DOL), one by the Corporation for National and Community Service, and one jointly by DOL and the Department of Education. Four of the initiatives gave out their first round of awards in the summer and fall of 2010, and many of the projects funded have been in operation for up to three years and are beginning to report the results of their evaluations.

The home visiting initiative and the Trade Adjustment Assistance Community College and Career Training (TAACCCT) initiative were the most expensive (at $1.5 billion and $2 billion respectively), and both were enacted within highly controversial legislative vehicles that overshadowed the evidence-based provisions. The lesson here is that it is often possible for the majority party to enact legislation that it favors as part of large bills in which the provision can get lost; the less positive conclusion is that none of the evidence-based initiatives was enacted because a majority of members of Congress was enthusiastic about promoting evidence-based policy. Indeed, it is doubtful that most members even knew that the provisions were in the legislation that they voted on.

Another important feature of all the initiatives is that they contained, either in their respective statute or their funding announcement, provisions on the evidence that would be required of applicants to win grant funds. In all six initiatives, the legislative language on evidence was fairly general or nonexistent (neither i3 nor TAACCCT contains a definition of evidence in the statute), giving the administration leeway to shape the evidence requirements to meet its own priorities. Thus OMB had ample opportunity to work with the administering agencies to shape their evidence requirements in thoughtful ways. The trick was to find a balance between evidence requirements that were so tight that few potential program operators could meet the requirements or so loose that weak evidence from flawed studies could meet them. How strong to make the evidence requirement is a central issue at this point in the development of policy initiatives to attack most social problems. Few fields of intervention have developed more than a small number of programs shown by rigorous evidence to reduce the target social problem. It follows that if only programs backed by rigorous evidence of impacts receive funding, that would greatly reduce the number of potential grantees. On the other hand, if the federal government is going to increase the use of rigorous evidence in an attempt to change the culture of program evaluation throughout the nation, it cannot use flabby standards. The administration's approach was to make the evidence requirement as strong as the state of knowledge, based on rigorous evaluations, permits. Over time, evidence standards in many fields of social intervention could become more rigorous. The administering agencies, not Congress, are in the best position to judge the evidence and to adjust grant requirements accordingly.[50]

As mentioned briefly above, all the initiatives distributed their funds to eligible entities primarily or exclusively on the basis of competition for grants between potential applicants. This approach is inconsistent with a broad tendency of policymaking in the nation's capital—namely, to distribute most grant funds by formulas to ensure that every state gets at least some of the funding. When federal grants are awarded on a competitive basis, even though federal agencies usually try to take the geographical distribution of grant funds into account, the distribution of funds across states is almost always highly skewed and some states might receive no funds at all. The main justification for awarding the evidence-based funds through a competitive process was that the administration wanted to take advantage of the pressure created by competition to spend the money on projects that meet strong evidence criteria. One of the most fundamental assumptions of the Obama evidence-based initiatives is that competition helps the administration ensure that the goals and methods laid out in its grant announcements are followed by grant applicants and that only the highest-quality applications win funding.

Plan of the Volume

Each of the six evidence-based initiatives is covered in a separate chapter. Each chapter examines the background of the initiative in question, the legislative struggle to get each initiative enacted into law and funded, the negotiations between OMB and the administrative agency responsible for the implementation and oversight of the initiative, the definition of evidence used in the initiative, the extensive work that went into the preparation and release of funding announcements, the content of the funding announcements, the process of selecting the best applicants (and a brief overview of the projects selected for funding), and the evaluation plans put in place for the initiative. After describing each initiative, we bring together in the final chapter a set of issues and conclusions about the evidence-based initiatives and their possible future role in federal policymaking, including their possible impact on the nation's social problems.

The Maternal, Infant, and Early Childhood Home Visiting Initiative

A large research literature going back more than six decades shows that parents' child-rearing practices have an impact on their children's development.[1] In fact, parents are the major influence on their children's development.[2] Parents who talk frequently to their children beginning in infancy and engage their children in back-and-forth discussions have children who perform better on tests of intelligence and school readiness. Similarly, parents who avoid physical punishment, facilitate exploration of the environment, take their children to interesting places, and select quality child care settings have children who do better in school and in life. Two respected researchers in this field have argued that interventions to improve the parenting skills of low-income mothers have a greater positive impact on children's development than quality preschool programs.[3]

An important finding of the literature on parenting is that low-income parents tend to use parenting behaviors associated with promoting positive child development less frequently than other parents.[4] In addition, low-income parents, especially single mothers, are more likely to abuse or neglect their children.[5] Given the connection between parenting and child outcomes and the finding that low-income parents engage in fewer of the practices and behaviors that boost child development and more of those that impede development, it was inevitable that researchers and educators would try to design programs to help low-income parents adopt behaviors that promote child development. Numerous programs, sponsored by both private organizations and the government, have now been designed to improve parenting.[6]

One of the best known of these programs is the Nurse-Family Partnership (NFP), developed by David Olds.[7] NFP, which started in Elmira, New York, in the 1970s with a sample of primarily poor, semi-rural, white young mothers, has been repeatedly tested for more than four decades.[8] Olds's view, shared by all home visiting programs, is that children's development can be boosted by helping parents adopt better child-rearing practices and make improvements in their personal lives. With support from the Robert Wood Johnson Foundation and many other sources, including funds from federal, state, and local governments, NFP now has well over 330 teams of nurses working with parents throughout the United States. In addition, Olds is implementing the NFP in six foreign nations (the Netherlands, Australia, England, Canada, Northern Ireland, and Scotland) as well as in several American Indian and Alaska Native communities.[9] The NFP model has now been tested by randomized controlled trials (RCTs) in Elmira, New York; Memphis; and Denver. In all three trials, the NFP produced significant positive impacts on the behavior and life course of the mothers and children, although the impacts and the length of follow-up were not the same across the trials. The Elmira trial, which has had the longest follow-up phase, produced impacts on children that could be detected well into their teenage years.[10] Olds has invested as much or more in the implementation of his model as in its development and research trials. The national NFP home office provides extensive information about the model program, its implementation, and studies of the program.[11]

The Bush Home Visiting Initiative

Over the years, Olds has met frequently with policymakers and their staffs at the state, federal, and international levels. In the summer of 2006, he arranged a meeting with a senior political appointee at the Office of Management and Budget (OMB) but wound up meeting with Kathy Stack, an influential career official there who subsequently played a major role in developing Obama's evidence-based initiatives. Olds wanted to be sure that federal authorities were aware of the extensive, high-quality evidence that supported his program, evidence that Olds believed made NFP the most evidence-based of the many types of home visiting models.[12] What was scheduled as a brief courtesy meeting between Stack, Olds, and a few additional OMB staffers turned into a two-hour session in which Stack quizzed Olds about the various random assignment studies by which his model had been tested and about his activities to replicate the model.

Impressed by both his program and the evidence supporting it, Stack saw the possibility of using the Olds program as a vehicle to increase the focus on evidence-based social programs and the use of RCTs at OMB, a goal that Stack had been pursuing for several years. As early as 2004, under Robert Shea, a senior official at OMB appointed by President Bush, OMB had issued "What Constitutes Strong Evidence of a Program's Effectiveness?," an 18-page document seemingly designed to convince federal agencies to evaluate their programs using RCTs. In the fall of 2006, as OMB was preparing the administration budget for fiscal year

2008, Stack talked with Shea about the Olds program and suggested that he recommend that the Bush administration sponsor a small grant program to help states implement the Olds program. Shea had met Olds in July 2007 at a meeting at the White House Conference Center cosponsored by the Justice Department and the Coalition for Evidence-Based Policy, an organization headed by Jon Baron, an influential Washington figure who played an important role in the development of the Obama initiatives. Like Olds, Shea was greatly interested in improving social programs by extensive use of rigorous evaluations, as shown by his aggressive implementation of the Program Assessment Rating Tool (PART), a complex system for evaluating government programs that Shea and OMB were requiring federal agencies to use on an annual basis. In addition, Shea had invited Baron to conduct a seminar with OMB officials on defining and using rigorous evidence in evaluating government programs. Given Shea's already great interest in using evidence in decisionmaking, it is little surprise that he agreed to recommend a $10 million pilot program for evidence-based home visiting to Jim Nussle, President Bush's last director of OMB.

Due in part to both lobbying by the Washington, D.C.–based Home Visiting Coalition (discussed in more detail below) and Shea's discussion with Nussle stemming from Stack's meeting with Olds, the Bush administration included a request for $10 million for home visiting programs in its fiscal year 2008 budget, which was released on February 5, 2007. The budget document noted that over 35 states conducted home visiting programs but that the programs were poorly coordinated and, more important, that states did not always use programs that were supported by evidence of success. The administration therefore recommended that its funds be used to encourage states to coordinate their use of existing funding streams and "successfully implement and sustain evidence-based home visitation programs."

Action on the Bush home visiting recommendation by both the Senate and House Appropriations Committees in the spring of 2007 foreshadowed the debate that would occur in 2009 on Obama's evidence-based home visiting initiative. The Bush administration's first goal was to get its language, preferably including the requirement that states spend the funds on nurse home visiting programs, in the House and Senate appropriations bills. Shea and Stack were working with Baron, a close ally of theirs, in building the OMB emphasis on evidence. Baron had an idea about how to get the Democratic-controlled Senate to support the Shea-Bush proposal. Baron asked Jerry Lee, a wealthy and politically adept businessman who donated to organizations that advanced evidence-based policy, to talk with Senator Mary Landrieu (D-La.), who was on the Senate Appropriations Committee, and suggest that she insert the $10 million in the appropriations bill for the Departments of Labor, Health and Human Services, and Education. Lee, a financial supporter of Landrieu's election campaign, agreed. After some discussion, Landrieu told Lee and Baron that if they could get a letter from OMB stating that the administration wanted the $10 million, she would get it in the bill. Baron called Shea, who had the letter written by Clay Johnson, a deputy director of OMB, and hand-delivered to Landrieu immediately. True to her word, Landrieu got the provision in the Senate appropriations bill.

But there was still lively dispute behind the scenes about whether states should be required to spend the money exclusively on "nurse home visitation" programs, meaning the Olds program, or whether they could spend funds on a broader array of home visiting programs. The language that Landrieu got into the Senate appropriations bill confined the money to "nurse home visitation," as requested by the administration. But the House favored spending the funds on a broader array of programs without reference to rigorous evidence. The Home Visiting Coalition as well as the National Child Abuse Coalition lobbied the Senate Appropriations Committee to adopt the House language and allow the money to be spent on any of several home visiting programs. Typical was written testimony from Tom Birch, who represented the National Child Abuse Coalition. He urged that the money be spent "to promote an array of research- and evidence-based home visitation models that enable communities to provide the most appropriate services suited to the families needing them." He went on to review rigorous evaluation studies of the Healthy Families New York program and the Parents as Teachers program that showed that these programs produced significant impacts on both mothers and children. He even stated explicitly that the results of those studies were similar to the results "found in randomized trials of NFP." Thus—two years before the Obama home visiting evidence-based initiative—conflicts over funding of home visitation programs were already referring to evaluation research to argue that programs were evidence based.

In the end, due in large part to good staff work, the House and Senate agreed to compromise during the House-Senate conference on the 2008 appropriations bill. Specifically, the House agreed to insert language requiring states to use home visiting programs supported by rigorous evidence and the Senate agreed to drop its language requiring states to use nurse home visiting programs. Both sides got part of what they wanted, and the $10 million was appropriated. This episode constitutes an early round in the ongoing fight in Washington to channel federal spending to evidence-based programs. Similar fights over the types of program that should receive support, which had begun during the Bush administration, were to occur during the Obama administration as it enacted the six evidence-based initiatives described in this book.

2008 Presidential Campaign and Transition

Besides Stack, Shea, and Baron, another Washington figure who took notice of the evidence-based NFP was Barack Obama. On June 5, 2007, Obama, then a mere U.S. Senator (and nascent candidate for president), gave a speech at Hampton University in the swing state of Virginia in which he praised the NFP and indicated a desire to scale up the program if elected president:

> There is a pioneering Nurse-Family Partnership program right now that offers home visits by trained registered nurses to low-income mothers and mothers-to-be. . . . This program saves money. It raises healthy babies and creates better parents. . . . This works, and I will expand the Nurse-Family Partnership to provide home nurse visits for up to 570,000 first-time mothers each year.[13]

Obama followed through, creating a campaign plank for an Olds-like program. According to "Blueprint for Change: Obama and Biden's Plan for America," if elected, Obama and Biden would "expand the highly-successful Nurse-Family Partnership to . . . 570,000 low-income, first-time mothers each year."[14]

Home visiting programs in general and NFP in particular were a natural choice to become part of the new administration's unfolding agenda on evidence-based initiatives. Home visiting was popular in the states, many successful model programs had evidence of positive impacts, and the well-organized Home Visiting Coalition was active in the nation's capital. Both because of evidence of the NFP's impacts from three RCTs published in refereed journals, and because NFP had well-established program replication and staff training procedures, it is easy to understand why the administration was attracted to expanding the Olds program.[15] But an important part of our story is tracing the interaction between the world of program evaluation and evidence on one hand and the world of politics on the other.

As the administration developed its home visiting initiative, the world of politics repeatedly intruded, forcing the administration to adjust its plans. One of the first intrusions was over the administration's focus on the Olds program. As early as February 2009, in a "budget blueprint" (the official budget was not yet ready), the administration promised to fund a new "nurse home visitation" program. No doubt part of the reason that the administration wanted to confine its initiative to the Olds program was because of the evidence supporting the program. However, other home visiting programs also had both good evidence of success and political influence. Those programs and their coalition were not about to accept legislation that confined funding to the Olds program.

One reason that the political system rebelled against an exclusive focus on NFP was the very success and appeal of the basic concept of home visiting. Most states, having already come to believe that home visiting had positive impacts on parents, conducted their own home visiting programs, which they paid for with both state funds and funds from any of several federal sources, including Medicaid, the Temporary Assistance for Needy Families (TANF) Block Grant, the Social Services Block Grant, and others. The fact that states already had home visiting programs, only some of which were based on the NFP, meant that if the administration attempted to restrict funding to the NFP, states were bound to object. Equally important, in previous years several members of Congress had introduced legislation to support a particular home visiting model or any of several model programs in addition to NFP. For example, in 2004, Senator Kit Bond (R-Mo.) introduced the Education Begins at Home Act (S. 2412), which he wrote in cooperation with the Home Visiting Coalition, to provide states with funds to expand home visiting programs.[16] The bill—which, interestingly, was cosponsored by Senator Obama—would have provided $400 million over three years for states to expand home visiting programs using any home visiting model program that met some modest quality standards.

Bond, twice the governor of Missouri and a U.S. senator from 1987 until 2011, played an important role in the unfolding political fate of the Obama home visiting initiative. When the senator and his wife had a baby in the early 1980s, they were visited in their home by a trained home visitor from the Parents as Teachers (PAT) program during its pilot phase.[17] Impressed by the visit, the future governor and senator became an ardent supporter of home visiting programs. When he became governor of Missouri, the state was already operating PAT at a few sites, but Bond expanded the program; in the Senate, he pushed for legislation, such as the Education Begins at Home Act, to expand PAT and other home visiting programs. When Bond retired from the Senate in 2011, he joined the board of directors of PAT, which by that time was operating throughout Missouri and at 3,000 other sites across the country.[18] PAT had modest evidence from rigorous evaluations that it produced positive impacts on both mothers and children.[19] As the Obama administration was launching its home visiting initiative, originally designed to provide funding exclusively for programs modeled on Olds's NFP, Senator Bond, now a senior and influential member of the Senate, could be expected to oppose any home visiting initiative that failed to include PAT.

As our interviews consistently showed, there were additional reasons that an NFP-only initiative was destined to have trouble in Congress. Senator Bond was not the only influential member of Congress who favored home visiting programs other than NFP. Danny Davis of Chicago (D-Ill.), a new member of the House Ways and Means Committee in 2009, had worked with Bond and the home visiting coalition on legislation. Davis had a HIPPY (Home Instruction for Parents of Preschool Youngsters) home visiting program in his district and had a personal interest in seeing home visiting expanded.[20] His staff told us that Davis also was familiar with the research—he knew that programs besides NFP had strong evidence of success and that there were limitations and drawbacks to funding only programs that had evidence from RCTs. As a result, there was little chance that Davis would support a home visiting initiative that funded only NFP.

Equally important, nearly all the groups that lobbied for children's programs in the nation's capital strongly opposed an exclusive focus on NFP. These groups had formed the Home Visiting Coalition referred to above. Since the early 2000s, long before the Obama administration came to power, the coalition had been lobbying Congress to enact legislation that would fund various home visiting programs. Members of the coalition included representatives from several model programs, including NFP, Parents as Teachers,[21] HIPPY,[22] and Healthy Families,[23] as well as from major child advocacy organizations, including the Center on Law and Social Policy (CLASP), the Child Welfare League of America, the Children's Defense Fund, Voices for America's Children, and Fight Crime: Invest in Kids. Coalitions of Washington-based groups like this are a regular feature of policymaking in the nation's capital, and they often have major impacts on congressional actions. In the case at hand, the coalition had already helped draft the Bond-Davis Education Begins at Home Act, which had been introduced in Congress as early as 2004.[24]

Each of the model home visiting programs that were represented in the coalition had its own focus, outcomes, and evidence. This diversity led to intense discussions about what legislative language the coalition could support. Despite internal differences, the coalition attempted to present a more or less unified front on Capitol Hill, and it had worked for years to build support for home visiting in general and eventually the Bond-Davis legislation in particular. The classic problem for coalitions is that although their members may be united on broad principles, they often have trouble pulling in the same direction when it comes time to adopt specific legislative language. Jane Callahan, a representative of PAT and its liaison to the coalition, put it this way:

> We worked for this Coalition for . . . years and years, and [accomplished] a lot of grassroots work, a lot of work with members on the Hill and laying the ground work with the people that ultimately ended up in the White House [under Obama]. And I also think that it helped—it wasn't easy— but it helped that the home visiting groups came together and could be on one page.[25]

Perhaps. But NFP appeared to be a wildcard member of the coalition. The other groups sometimes viewed NFP with suspicion—and NFP sometimes gave them cause. NFP tried both to be part of the coalition and to promote its own agenda on the Hill. For example, the NFP lobbyists convinced two Colorado members of the House and Senate (NFP's home office was in Denver) to introduce an NFP-tailored bill that would allow the NFP program to be funded by Medicaid and the State Children's Health Insurance Program (SCHIP). Those efforts culminated in the introduction in 2007 of legislation by Senator Ken Salazar (D-Colo.) (S. 1052) and by Representative Diana DeGette (D-Colo.) (H.R. 3024) that would have provided an option in both SCHIP and Medicaid for states to receive a federal subsidy to conduct home visiting programs. The influence of NFP's emphasis on evidence is reflected in several places in the bills, especially in the provision that the only programs that could be supported were those that

> are provided in accordance with outcome standards that have been replicated in multiple, rigorous, randomized controlled trails in multiple sites, with outcomes that improve prenatal health of children, pregnancy outcome, child health, child development, academic achievement, and mental health, reduce child abuse, neglect, and injury, reduce maternal and child involvement in the criminal justice system, increase birth intervals between pregnancies, and improve maternal employment.[26]

The only home visiting program that could meet those requirements was NFP. This is a common trick used in legislative drafting. The sponsors of legislation may not want it to seem as if they are drafting a piece of legislation for a particular group for fear of offending other groups and causing them to rally against it, so they use legislative language to describe characteristics that any organization getting money from the bill must meet. The authors of the legislation can put in so many conditions that only one organization (or a very small set of organizations) can meet all the requirements, thereby achieving the same end as they would by actually naming the eligible organization. It is notable that this legislative language, especially the requirement for "randomized controlled trials in multiple sites," again shows how much rigorous evidence was part of the legislative debate on home visiting, even before the Obama initiative began. A version of the Salazar and DeGette bills was destined to be included in a House-passed—but doomed—bill that was produced during the legislative process that eventually resulted in the legislation establishing Obamacare. Not surprisingly, NFP's solo advocacy frustrated the other members of the coalition.

The Obama Budget

Given the forces aligned against an exclusive focus on NFP, it was all but inevitable that the administration would be forced to support a broader set of home visiting programs. To understand how the administration reacted to the clouds that were gathering around its home visiting initiative, we need to examine how the administration developed its proposal.

As the Obama team began to prepare the president's proposal at the beginning of the new administration, OMB considered possible budget language. Kathy Stack, with clearance from Robert Gordon and other senior OMB officials, asked a research-savvy staffer named Farrah Freis to prepare a memo on how the campaign proposal on home visiting could be implemented, with special attention to the cost of scaling up a major initiative. In addition, both career officials and political appointees at OMB and the Department of Health and Human Services (HHS) began to thoroughly examine the evidence on home visiting programs in order to flesh out the proposal for the new president. Freis, who had previously worked on children's issues, including the Bush home visiting initiative, wrote a memo describing design options and a recommended approach for a home visiting initiative paid for by mandatory funds. She based the memo in part on the short description of Obama's plans for home visiting found in the campaign document "Blueprint for Change: Obama and Biden's Plan for America." Despite the minimal guidance provided by the document, the recommendations in the Freis memo were endorsed by both Gordon and Peter Orszag, the influential head of OMB during the first 18 months of the Obama administration.

The memo is instructive because, based on Freis's description,[27] it shows the nuances that a careful review of evidence on social programs can bring to program design and policy. Freis told us that, in accord with her expectations, a thorough review of the evidence on NFP and other home-based programs led to the conclusion that while NFP did have strong evidence of impacts, so did other home visiting programs. The science in social science is not physics.[28] It is a rare case when an abundance of social science evidence is entirely persuasive in showing that a given program works—and that it works better than all other programs of its type. In the political world there are always competing programs, each with its own advocates, and in general the federal policymaking process abhors legislation that shuts out important groups. Even if the social science were more definitive about the single best program in any given area of intervention, the political process would still be likely to oppose directing funds to a single program. "Spread the money around" is a mantra of politicians. Moreover, as was the case with all the evidence-based initiatives, there was a tension between using proven model home visiting programs and testing innovative programs. The administration eventually came to the view that all the initiatives had to find a compromise between funding model programs with rigorous evidence of success and funding innovative, promising programs that had only modest, even merely anecdotal, evidence of success.

By February 2009 the administration was under pressure to produce a budget for 2010 and thereby give federal policymakers and the rest of the nation a better understanding of the new president's priorities. In most years, the president releases his budget for the next fiscal year in February of the current fiscal year (the current fiscal year begins on October 1 of the previous calendar year; for example, fiscal year 2010 began on October 1, 2009). However, at the beginning of an administration, it often takes a little longer for the new president and his team to get their budget ready for the public. So as an interim measure, on February 26 the Obama administration released an abbreviated budget document, a 140-page summary of what would be in the new president's first budget.[29] And just as President Obama had promised during the campaign, his abbreviated budget did provide for a new home visiting initiative, which the document referred to as a "nurse-home visitation" program. Specifically, the budget called for the Department of Health and Human Services to "begin a major effort to ramp up a new Nurse-Home Visitation program."[30] The seriousness of Obama's new proposal was signaled by the fact that the budget provided $8.5 billion in entitlement funds over ten years for the program.[31] The commitment of such a large amount, the fact that the money was an entitlement and not an annual appropriation, and the fact that the authorization would be good for ten years were strong signals that home visiting would be a major initiative for the Obama administration. However, now there could be no doubt that the administration intended to put all its money in the NFP basket.

The Home Visiting Coalition was deeply conflicted by the president's proposal. The coalition loved the money, the fact that the funds were mandatory spending, and the ten-year commitment, but it realized that the administration's proposal was directly tied to NFP rather than to the array of programs eligible for funding in the Bond-Davis bill. Given their strong opposition to tying the money to NFP, coalition members began lobbying the administration to broaden the number of programs that could receive funding. Jane Callahan of Parents as Teachers summed up the coalition's goals: "We really wanted it to be the kind of bill or initiative that could provide support for a range of models, realizing from our long experience that there's no one silver bullet [for] home visiting."

In contrast, NFP's goal was to support the president's proposal and its emphasis on funding both evidence-based programs and programs that used nurses to deliver services. Tamar Bauer, an NFP lobbyist, summarized these points in an interview: "I think our number one priority was that it [the Obama initiative] remain evidence-based. The dramatic language in the President's budget proposal about the rigorous evidence—that was what we wanted number one."[32] NFP was upset because, in its view, all the other members of the coalition were attempting to weaken the language on evidence, which they saw as a provision that favored the NFP model. Tom Birch, one of the leaders of the coalition, said that he interpreted NFP's actions as their leadership saying to the other members of the coalition: "We [meaning NFP] have this whole thing to ourselves and now I guess we have to share. Do we really want to share? I don't think they really wanted to for quite a while."[33] Sensing the growing tension between the groups lobbying on the home visiting initiative, Gordon and Freis of OMB and Martha Coven and Roberto Rodriguez of the Domestic Policy Council (DPC) invited a group of advocates to a meeting at the White House on March 26, 2009. At the meeting, in an important development that was to have broad application to several of the administration's evidence-based initiatives, Gordon discussed a new idea: namely, using tiers of funding, meaning that the majority of funding would be dedicated to programs with the strongest evidence but that some funding would be available to implement and test promising and innovative programs that had only modest evidence of success. Although the administration, in consultation with the Coalition for Evidence-Based Policy and others, had been discussing tiers of evidence since at least January 26, 2009, the March meeting with advocates appears to be the first time that the tiers concept had been publicly discussed by the administration.[34]

As everyone in the meeting must have realized immediately, if there were to be tiers of funding, it followed that programs with modest evidence—programs other than NFP—would be eligible for funding. According to notes kept by Birch, during the meeting Gordon said that the administration was not "wedded" to funding exclusively for programs that used nurses. After Gordon made that statement, Roberto Rodriguez said that the major goal was to "invest in models that help support the development of children."[35] In short, the administration's position was evolving. The advocates were now assured that to qualify for funding, model programs would not have to enroll only first-born children and use nurses as the service providers, as required by the NFP program. Further, advocates were assured that programs with moderate evidence could quality for at least some funding.

During an interview, Kathy Stack of OMB made an important point about dropping the focus on nurses and NFP: If funding were focused on NFP, money would be going to a model home visiting program that had very strong evidence of success, and spending federal dollars on such programs was the sine qua non of the Obama evidence-based initiatives. Now, Stack told us, the administration would have to find a different way of ensuring that the home visiting money would be spent on successful programs.[36]

Despite the White House meeting and the administration's offer to adopt tiers of evidence, the coalition was still not completely unified. They were squabbling—Coven of the DPC called it a "cacophony" of conflicting opinions—about several provisions in the emerging legislation and budget resolution language. As the squabbling went on, another force against the administration's approach to NFP arose. As if the virtually guaranteed opposition of influential members of the House and Senate and the opposition of almost the entire children's lobby were not enough, stars from the scholarly world with extensive knowledge of and experience in the policy world weighed in against the administration's exclusive focus on NFP. On April 21, 2009, a quartet of renowned scholars—Ed Zigler of Yale, Heather Weiss of Harvard, Deborah Daro of the University of Chicago, and Ken Dodge of Duke, whose combined IQ is approximately equal to the national debt—released a public letter to the president citing several reasons that the Obama administration should broaden the funding criteria to allow model programs besides NFP to qualify. Like Obama, they supported an early childhood initiative that focused on helping parents improve themselves and their parenting, but they had three objections to a focus on NFP and programs supported by evidence from RCTs that excluded other model programs and other evaluation methods:

—Reliance solely on RCTs did not provide much information about implementing programs in communities with different characteristics.

—The NFP model restricted access to first-time parents only, leaving out over 60 percent of newborns, many born to poor families.

—A universal program providing home visiting to all parents (not just low-income parents) would be more politically viable in the long run.

The scholars were prompted to write the letter because Zigler was one of the founding board members of the Parents as Teachers program. The board chair, Susan Stepleton, had talked with Zigler about writing such a letter, and Zigler, plus staff from one or two congressional offices, called Deborah Daro, who called Dodge. Weiss and Zigler were close associates, and when Weiss contacted Zigler about the letter, she wound up signing it as well.[37]

Of the arguments made by the scholars, the most central to our concern is that random assignment studies with small samples typically do not provide much information about implementation. We examine this issue in more detail elsewhere, but this is a powerful and accurate judgment about random assignment studies as they are usually carried out. RCTs are the best way to determine whether a program produces impacts on participants, but as pointed out by Bob Granger, the former president of the William T. Grant Foundation,[38] the foundation that has done the most to support evidence-based policy, large random assignment studies typically have not focused on implementation. Without such a focus, these studies do not tell us much "about the conditions under which a program is effective, the policies that help it produce results, the capacities that affect an organization's ability to implement an innovation, or the staff practices that directly improve youth outcomes."[39]

With criticisms of their home visiting initiative piling up, senior administration officials concluded that their March 26 White House meeting with advocates had not stopped the squabbling. A fractured coalition could not effectively support the administration's initiative in Congress. That realization prompted the administration to meet again with the advocates about two months after the initial White House meeting. Chaired by Coven, the meeting was held on May 8, a few days before the administration was to release its updated and expanded budget for fiscal year 2010. Almost every advocate for home visiting programs that we interviewed mentioned the importance of this meeting. All saw it as a pivotal moment in which the groups achieved a greater degree of cooperation than before, although they were not, as we will see, completely unified. In our interview, Coven amplified her views on the importance of this meeting:

> The home visiting advocates were like the city of Babel for a while, but eventually became a single voice with a focused message. The first thing that happened after we released our proposal was that everyone wanted to make it into their particular flavor of home visiting. So we said to them, "we need to be working together, not at cross-purposes." To their credit, they went from going door to door criticizing each other's models to having a shared letterhead and consistent communications about what needed to happen.[40]

NFP also got behind the initiative, at least enough to placate somewhat the other members of the coalition. Even so, there was still tension over negotiating the legislative language on evidence. Bauer of NFP told us that after the May White House meeting, NFP recognized that all the groups "had to work as a Coalition. The discussion became more broad-based and a more all-encompassing view of what strong evidence is. And we all worked together."[41]

Nonetheless, another source of tension within the coalition was the Medicaid option that had been introduced by Salazar and DeGette in the previous Congress and that was still very much alive. NFP had engaged in discussions with staff of the House Energy and Commerce Committee on a version of the Salazar-DeGette bill that would have made it easier for states to use Medicaid funds for a home visiting program with characteristics that only NFP could meet. Again, some members of the coalition saw this as an end run around the coalition by NFP—a lobbying tactic that upset many of the advocates. Coalition member Tom Birch spoke for most members of the coalition when he told us: "Come on. We're all working together here, and now you've carved out a fail-safe [position that] we didn't work on . . . collectively."[42]

When the administration released its full budget on May 11, it publicly and officially revealed what it had been telling advocates in private meetings: namely, that it had revised its approach to evidence-based home visiting.[43] The budget, as discussed in the Office of the President's *Analytical Perspectives*, called for $124 million in 2010 and $2.2 billion over five years for home visiting. The administration wanted the funding "primarily" for programs "that have been rigorously evaluated and shown to have positive effects on critical outcomes for children and families."[44] However, the administration would allow a "smaller portion of funds" to be available for "promising models that will be rigorously tested to assess their impact."[45] With this language, the administration solved two issues: it placated the child advocates who were lobbying to allow states to use the funds to expand any home visiting program that had good evidence of impacts, and it allowed some funds to be spent on "promising" programs, thereby opening the way for innovative programs with little or no evidence to receive funding.

Congress Takes Action

While the administration was dealing with the squabbling among the advocates and the pressure from the scholarly world to broaden its initiative beyond NFP, action was proceeding on Capitol Hill. By April, both the House and the Senate Budget Committees were hard at work on their respective budget resolutions. Budget resolutions are an important part of the policy process in Washington in part because they show how much money will be available to the committees of jurisdiction for their programs in a given year. In addition, a budget resolution can make room for new funds, called "reserve funds," for specific programs that meet the conditions spelled out in the reserve fund language.[46]

The House

With both the Senate and House in the hands of Democrats, the budget committees were willing to establish reserve funds for the president's home visiting initiative, but there was lobbying over what the reserve language should say. Morna Miller of the House Budget Committee was responsible for drafting the House language. Miller talked with OMB's Robert Gordon—who as luck would have it was her neighbor—because she intended to begin by basing her draft on the language that the administration had used in the abbreviated budget. Among other questions, Miller asked Gordon which committee he thought should have jurisdiction over the home visiting program. While the administration had not considered committee jurisdiction in any detail, fighting over jurisdiction is nonetheless another example of how the policymaking process in Washington intrudes on the best-laid plans. Many a bill has met a dismal fate because committees were too busy fighting over jurisdiction to actually pass the bill. There were three contenders for jurisdiction in the House:

—The Ways and Means Committee, because of the connection between home visiting and child protection. The biggest and most expensive child protection programs—found in Title IV-B and Title IV-E of the Social Security Act—are under this committee's jurisdiction.

—The Education and Labor Committee, because many early childhood programs are under its jurisdiction.

—The Energy and Commerce Committee, because of its jurisdiction over Medicaid, which some states already used to pay for home visiting programs.

Not surprisingly, the administration tried to stay out of the struggle between committees. Because of the way that the administration was organized, responsibility for health reform went to Nancy-Ann DeParle and Keith Fontenot, from the White House and OMB, respectively, and responsibility for human services, including the evidence-based initiatives, went to Gordon, along with Melody Barnes and Martha Coven of the DPC. According to Gordon, the human services team had little "leverage" with the health team, so they simply stayed out of health issues—including whether the Energy and Commerce Committee had jurisdiction over at least part of the home visiting initiative (the NFP part).[47] If pressed, the members of the human services team might have voiced a preference for a provision that was under the jurisdiction of the Ways and Means Committee in the House and under the Finance Committee in the Senate because these committees could ensure that the money to finance the bill would fall under mandatory spending and thereby avoid the annual appropriations process. Nonetheless, the administration generally avoided involvement in the sticky issue of jurisdiction.

As Miller's discussions with the committees and the administration proceeded in March and April, it became increasingly clear to her that the administration was more committed to language on evidence than to reserving the money for NFP, which had been the administration's original proposal. OMB strongly encouraged Miller to retain the evidence-based focus but seemed increasingly willing to accept language that would spread the money around to include any home visiting program that had good evidence of impacts. Exactly as Gordon had told the child advocates, the administration's position on evidence was evolving. Over the next several months, as the various bills including the initiatives were developed, the administration had to be light on its feet as it tried to balance the interests of the various groups lobbying on its initiatives and the views of members of Congress, primarily as represented by their committee staffers. In the end, one of the greatest contributions of the Obama administration to using evidence from social science to improve social policy was its two-pronged strategy of reserving most of the money for programs that had strong evidence of success from rigorous studies and then requiring the entities implementing the programs to gather systematic evidence from rigorous evaluations on whether their programs were having the intended impacts. Now, in the early phases of the administration's evolving legislative strategy and understanding of how its initiatives should be formulated and implemented, it was the focus on evidence—not on NFP—that was its guiding star.

In addition to dealing with the committees that wanted jurisdiction and with the administration's evolving views on its goal of building evidence-based policy, Miller dealt directly with the attempts of NFP and its lobbyist to influence the reserve language that would be in the budget resolution. The chairman of the House Budget Committee and Miller's boss was the highly respected John Spratt (D-S.C.). Although Spratt himself never instructed Miller to favor NFP in the budget language or to meet with NFP, because Spratt had an NFP program in his district, his personal office staff did ask Miller to meet with the NFP lobbyist. By implication, the administration's focus on NFP would be fine with Spratt and his personal staff. In the end, Miller had to balance the Budget Committee's language on who would qualify for funds, the evidence-based focus, and committee jurisdiction, using language that would not get Spratt in an argument over jurisdiction with the chairs of the Ways and Means, Education and Labor, and Energy and Commerce Committees. Wisely, Miller's language, approved by Spratt and his staff, did not mention NFP or any other specific program model; instead, it simply referred to "a program of home visits to low-income mothers-to-be and low-income families." Miller's language on evidence required funding for programs "which will produce sizeable, sustained improvements in the health, well-being, or school readiness of children or their parents."[48] In explaining the reserve fund for home visiting, the Budget Committee report mentions that "the Committee anticipates that the legislation will fund evidence-based programs that have been tested in well-designed randomized controlled trials."[49]

The Senate, however, had a different approach to the home visiting reserve fund language. As the budget resolution was being prepared for introduction in late March 2009, Senator Patty Murray (D-Wash.), who favored making more home visiting programs eligible for funding, worked with Senator Bond to make sure that her reserve fund legislation authorized programs that did not use nurses exclusively and that accepted evidence from quasi-experimental designs (QEDs) to meet the evidence test. The Murray language was intended to offset House budget report language that favored NFP by mentioning randomized control trials (and excluding QEDs) and nurse home visitors.[50] Murray's language was made part of the Senate budget resolution, but when the two bodies met in conference on their budget resolutions, the Senate agreed to adopt the House resolution's language on home visiting.[51] However, the language in the original Murray budget resolution did in fact have a longer lifespan. Much of it is very similar to the legislative language later used to create the home visiting initiative in the Patient Protection and Affordable Care Act (ACA), enacted by Congress and signed into law by the president in March 2010. This is no coincidence because, as we will see, the ACA ended up including the Senate's—and only the Senate's—language.

While the administration avoided the jurisdictional and budget language struggles in the House, Coven, from the Domestic Policy Council, did meet with staffers of the three competing committees, encouraging them to avoid conflicts and work together to produce a good home visiting provision. Although the administration seemed to avoid taking a position on whether its funds for home visiting should be placed in the Medicaid program, there might have been advantages in doing so. NFP's strong evidence on the effects of home visiting—reduced child abuse, preterm births, emergency room use, and subsequent births (all of which save money)—allowed OMB to determine that if passed into law and implemented, the NFP would produce savings in the federal budget (score savings). "Saving money" meant that although money would be spent to run the program, the evidence indicated that the spending would generate savings through reduced emergency room visits, fewer cases of child abuse and neglect, and other positive outcomes. The administration's initial estimate was that expanding the NFP home visiting program would save Medicaid $664 million over ten years.[52] Whether the evidence on other model programs would lead to savings of that magnitude was an open question, but the administration realized that if cost savings had to be traded off in order to open up its initiative to programs besides NFP, the trade-off was necessary to keep the advocacy community united behind the initiative. As it turned out, the Congressional Budget Office (CBO), the official scorekeeper on the costs and savings of all federal legislation, did not officially score savings from the NFP or any other home visiting program. Jonathan Morancy, the CBO analyst who was given responsibility for scoring the home visiting provision, told us in an interview that after legislative action on health care and home visiting had been completed, he and his supervisors at CBO had decided that only NFP had evidence of cost savings that was strong enough to allow CBO to score savings. Therefore, once the legislative language allowed home visiting funds to be used for programs in addition to NFP, CBO would not (and did not) score any savings from any of the legislative versions of home visiting programs.

But CBO scoring does not come into play until legislative action on a bill seems likely. Most legislation follows a well-worn path of bill introduction, hearings, committee markup (in which amendments to the bill are considered and voted on), and action on the floor of the House and Senate. This series of steps is followed in both the House and Senate, and if both pass a bill, a House-Senate conference committee meets to iron out differences in the bills; thereafter, the bill must pass through the House and Senate again for a final vote. The final step is to have the president sign the bill. All the lobbying, letter writing, op-eds, news coverage, and so forth amount to nothing unless a bill is introduced and enacted.

After about six months of jockeying, Jim McDermott, chairman of the House Ways and Means Subcommittee on Income Security and Family Support, took an important step on the legislative path by introducing a home visiting bill on June 2 and holding a hearing on the bill on June 9.[53] McDermott's bill was written by a group of staffers that included representatives from his personal office, staff of the Ways and Means Committee, and staff from the office of Danny Davis, who had a long-term interest in home visiting programs and who had just landed a coveted seat on the Ways and Means Committee. According to our interview with Nick Gwyn, a senior staffer with the Ways and Means Committee, Gwyn told the administration that the committee would allow more than just the NFP program to qualify for funding.[54] By the time the McDermott bill was introduced in June, the administration's position on NFP had evolved and the McDermott provision allowing any home visiting program with good evidence to receive funding was consistent with what the administration wanted. Specifically, the McDermott language required a program to

> adhere to clear evidence-based models of home visitation that have demonstrated significant positive effects on important program determined outcomes, such as reducing abuse and neglect and improving child health and development.[55]

In addition, the language provided for priority funding for model programs with the strongest evidence.[56]

McDermott introduced and held a hearing on his home visiting bill at the same time that several House committees were working on health care reform legislation.[57] The House leadership prevailed on the committees to agree on one health reform bill that would then be marked up by each committee with some jurisdiction over parts of the bill. On July 17, the full Ways and Means Committee passed the health care bill developed by consensus among the committees with some jurisdiction. Because the committee included the McDermott home visiting provision in its health care bill, the fate of home visiting in the House was tied to action on the president's health care legislation. In addition to the Ways and Means Committee provisions, the Energy and Commerce Committee had its own provisions in the unified House health care bill. According to our interview with the Energy and Commerce Committee's chief staffer, Andy

Schneider, chairman Henry Waxman (D-Calif.) wanted to include a provision in his bill that clarified the coverage of home visiting as a service that would be paid for by Medicaid.[58] As we have seen, a provision that took this approach had originally been introduced in the House by Diana DeGette and in the Senate by Ken Salazar with considerable input from David Olds and NFP.[59]

Once Waxman agreed to have a version of the DeGette-Salazar bill in his section of the Obama health care legislation, DeGette, who was a member of the Energy and Commerce Committee, and her staff worked with Waxman's committee staff to write the Medicaid provision that was included in the House health care bill. Our interviews indicated that everyone involved in the writing of the Energy and Commerce Committee's provision agreed with the administration on the importance of evidence.[60] The language allowed funds to be spent only on programs that used "trained nurses" and that were determined by the secretary of the Department of Health and Human Services "based upon evidence" to improve maternal or child health, pregnancy outcomes, economic self-sufficiency, school readiness, family stability, or a list of other worthy outcomes. This language gave the secretary the authority to define what it meant for a program to be evidence based. It should be noted that because the McDermott provision also was in the House health care bill, the Waxman focus on "trained nurses" was only a modest problem for the child advocates and the administration because there would also be money for other home visiting programs that did not use nurses. Not surprisingly, advocates still felt some resentment toward the Waxman provision because NFP had negotiated the provision separately, which the advocates saw as NFP getting two bites of the apple.

The wide discretion given to the secretary by the legislative language in the home visiting bills under consideration in the spring and summer of 2009 was crucial to the administration's strategy for creating evidence-based initiatives. Writing good legislation calls for an equal mix of art and precise use of language. In the case at hand, the administration wanted the flexibility to work with the administering agencies (in this case HHS) to define in detail what "evidence-based" meant and to control the specific ways in which the legislation would be implemented. This requirement gave it the authority to be certain that one of its major goals—spending federal dollars on programs known to produce good outcomes—could be achieved. In all its evidence-based initiatives, the administration was trying to draw a fine line between the requirement for rigorous evidence and the flexibility to define evidence in the way that the administration thought most productive without having to worry about pesky details in the statutory language.

As the example of home visiting illustrates, the Obama evidence-based initiatives were shaped in large part after the legislation had been written and enacted.

A major purpose of our study has been to look into the inner workings not just of Congress but also of the administrative agencies that in effect define what an evidence-based initiative is and how it should be administered—always, of course, under the watchful eye of OMB. Administration control of its evidence-based initiatives rested as much on what happened after as on what happened before congressional enactment—and in the case of the home visiting initiative, no matter whether the House or Senate bills became law, the administration was assured of plenty of flexibility in implementing its program.

Following action by the Ways and Means and the Energy and Commerce Committees, the Obama home visiting initiative was joined at the hip with the controversial health care legislation, which had created such a contentious debate in the House that virtually no Republicans supported the bill. With the provisions from both committees as part of its legislation, the House passed the Affordable Health Care for America Act (not the ACA) on November 7, 2009. In this case as in so many others, the House resolved a conflict about committee jurisdiction over a new program by giving both the Ways and Means Committee and the Energy and Commerce Committee its own home visiting program. What taxpayer could mind this approach? The spotlight then switched to the Senate, which had not yet passed its health care legislation.

The Senate

During House action on home visiting, the Senate had been working on its own bill. Jurisdiction in the Senate differed from that in the House because the Senate Finance Committee had jurisdiction over both the Medicaid program and many programs aimed at helping children and families, a fact that provided a good argument for giving the Finance Committee jurisdiction over home visiting programs. In contrast, in the House the Energy and Commerce Committee had jurisdiction over Medicaid while the Ways and Means Committee had jurisdiction over most child welfare programs, an arrangement that all but ensured conflict over jurisdiction. The issue in the House was resolved by allowing both committees to put their own home visiting provisions in the health care reform legislation. A senior staffer from the Energy and Commerce Committee told us that there was never a fight over jurisdiction; it was just assumed from the beginning that each committee would have its own provision.

When the bill writing began in the Senate, roughly in the spring of 2009, the Finance Committee instituted an open process in which the Republican and Democratic committee staffers worked closely together and consulted with the offices of several committee members.[61] Thus, the Finance Committee's language on home visiting was created through the traditional route of bipartisan bill writing. However, eventually the Senate followed the House path, fell into a highly partisan fight over health care, and produced a health reform bill that no Republican senators supported when it passed the Senate. But up until the partisan split occurred—roughly in the late fall of 2009, after several months of growing opposition by Republicans—Diedra Henry-Spires and Becky Shipp, Democratic and Republican Finance Committee staffers, respectively, worked together on the legislative language. Our interviews with 25 staffers, administration officials, and advocates that specifically addressed development of the Senate Finance Committee bill showed that Henry-Spires and Shipp, undoubtedly reflecting the wishes of their bosses—Democratic chairman Max Baucus (D-Mont.) and Republican ranking member Charles Grassley (R-Iowa)—consulted widely with the staff of other Finance Committee members, with the advocacy community, and with the administration as they wrote the Senate bill on home visiting.

As in the House, one of the issues that Shipp and Henry-Spires dealt with was the language on evidence—more specifically, on whether the NFP would be favored.[62] As one of the staffers told us, most of the groups lobbying for a home visiting provision worked together to support language that would allow many programs to qualify for funding, not just NFP. The exception was that the NFP's lobbyist had a tendency, as Shipp put it, "to go rogue," by which she meant that NFP continued to try to direct all or most of the money to programs with strong evidence from evaluations that featured random assignment and programs that used nurses to deliver services.

Another issue that the Finance Committee staffers faced was that the debate over the role of evidence from RCTs had a history among child advocates that added to the contentiousness of the negotiations over the legislation. Our interviews with members of the Home Visiting Coalition showed that they had been discussing for years whether only programs with RCT evidence should be considered evidence based. Given that some members of the coalition were sponsoring programs that had not been evaluated by RCTs, it is unsurprising that the coalition was against making random assignment evidence a requirement for funding. Therefore, when the administration started its initiative with the apparent intent of focusing the money entirely or primarily on NFP, the coalition rebelled and began lobbying against the exclusion of other home visiting programs. When the committees began writing the initiative into law, they had to be very careful about how they handled the evidence requirement. Although it was somewhat unusual for legislative language to specify that the only model programs that could qualify for funding were those that had evidence from "randomized controlled research designs" or from "quasi-experimental designs," that language reflected the long-standing debate within the coalition on what counts as good evidence. The staff writing the legislation had to make it clear in the statutory language that model programs with evidence from quasi-experimental designs also could qualify for funding.

Committee chairman Max Baucus decided to put his home visiting provision in his committee's version of the health care legislation, called the America's Healthy Future Act (S. 1796). Baucus's bill passed the committee by a vote of 14-9 on October 13, 2009. Baucus had put his personal stamp on the home visiting bill by orienting the bill to maternal and child health so that it could fit easily into the health care legislation, which Baucus (and many others) regarded as a sure way to pass his home visiting provisions. Subsequently, after extensive behind-the-scenes negotiations, the Senate settled on a new comprehensive health care bill. Known as the Affordable Care Act, it included the committee home visiting program. The ACA passed the Senate on Christmas Eve, 2009. Given the huge partisan fight over the 906-page ACA, the home visiting provision received no mention on the Senate floor; as a result, the Senate adopted the provision exactly as it came out of the Finance Committee. Part of the reason that the Republicans did not cause a fight over the home visiting provision on the Senate floor may have been that Senator Bond, while opposing the overall bill, was nonetheless working behind the scenes to quell Republican opposition to the home visiting provision, which Bond strongly supported.[63] As often happens when the Senate and House have different versions of bills, the House was not completely happy with the Senate product. As one House staffer said to us: "[We] really underestimated the Senate and their ability to screw the whole thing up."

Home Visiting Enacted

Final action on the health care legislation, which still included home visiting, took a surprising turn. On January 19, 2010, in a special election held in Massachusetts, the Republican candidate for Senate, Scott Brown, won the seat that had been held by liberal icon Edward Kennedy for nearly half a century before his death in August 2009. Of the many consequences of this election, the most immediate was that the Democrats lost their filibuster-proof majority of 60 votes in the Senate. Given the unanimous Republican opposition to the ACA, it was this 60-vote, filibuster-proof margin that had allowed Senate Democrats to pass the legislation (along with its obscure home visiting provision) in the first place. The Democrats had been planning to follow the regular legislative order, which entailed sending the ACA to a House-Senate conference committee to resolve the differences between the bills. That plan would require the bill produced by the conference committee to be passed by both the House and the Senate. As a result, the plan was reduced to ashes by the loss of the 60-vote margin because every Senate Republican would support a filibuster of the conference report and now the Democrats could not stop the filibuster. It followed that the Democrats' only choice was to ship the Senate bill over to the House and have the House accept every provision in the bill by passing it exactly as it had passed the Senate the day before Christmas. This strategy would kill both the Energy and Commerce and Ways and Means Committees' versions of home visiting while the Senate Finance Committee's version would become law. As bitter a pill as it was for the House to live with the indignity of accepting a Senate bill on such an important issue without making a single change, House Democrats faced the Hobson's choice of either accepting the Senate bill and using the reconciliation process to try to pass a separate bill that contained some amendments to the ACA that the House wanted or giving up on the most important legislative issue in a generation. Thus, on March 21, 2010, the House accepted the Senate bill, including the home visiting initiative, by a vote of 219 to 212, with 34 Democrats voting against and no Republicans voting for the bill. With a giddy group of Democrats looking on, the president put his signature on the ACA on March 23, 2010.[64]

Below the radar, the administration got the essence of what it wanted on home visiting—a law that gave it $1.5 billion over five years to mount an evidence-based initiative. The law required not more than 25 percent of the funds to be spent on programs that were "promising and new," thereby leaving 75 percent of the funds for evidence-based programs that had been shown by "well-designed and rigorous randomized controlled research designs" or "quasi-experimental research designs" to produce significant impacts.[65] The money would flow for five years (2010 through 2014) unless Congress passed legislation to stop it.

In a provision that undoubtedly gained the full support of the Obama administration, the legislation trumped its own evidence-based definition by inserting language granting the secretary of HHS the authority to "establish criteria for evidence of effectiveness of the service delivery models," which in effect put the final definition of evidence-based programs in the hands of the secretary—exactly where the administration wanted it.[66]

All in all, given the unpredictable nature of the federal legislative process, passage of the home visiting provision as part of the ACA was a triumph for the administration. Primarily because of the work of senior political officials at OMB and on the White House Domestic Policy Council, the administration managed to make changes in its approach to home visiting to win the support of the child advocacy community and Congress. In the end, the legislative language gave the administration the money that it needed to pursue the initiative and statutory language that established the priority of programs supported by strong evidence from well-designed and rigorous random assignment or quasi-experimental evaluations. In addition, the legislative language gave the secretary of HHS the flexibility needed to implement the home visiting initiative in accord with the administration's vision of what it meant for a program to be evidence based. Although the administration had leaped over the legislative hurdle to advancing its evidence-based agenda on home visiting, more high hurdles lay directly ahead.

The Administration Takes Over

If the Obama administration was going to engineer a change in the way that the federal government funds social programs, legislation that gave it the authority to design and implement initiatives and the money to fund them was only the first step. A major part of what the administration was attempting to do was to change the way that the giant administrative agencies—primarily the Departments of Health and Human Services, Education, and Labor—distribute their grant funds. In essence, the administration wanted to spend most grant funds on programs that already had strong evidence of success and then subject most of the programs—both those supported by rigorous evidence and innovative or promising programs—to continuous evaluation. What follows is an explanation of how the administration shaped the home visiting initiative to ensure that grant money went to states and agencies that would spend it on high-quality, evidence-based programs and that the implementation of the programs would be continuously evaluated.

Conducting an Evidence Review

The home visiting initiative and the Teen Pregnancy Prevention (TPP) initiative (see chapter 3) differ sharply from the other four evidence-based initiatives discussed in this volume. Whereas the other initiatives require applicants for funding to identify the evidence-based program that they plan to use, both the TPP and home visiting initiatives allocate most of their funds for model programs that HHS had already identified as evidence based. In this section, we examine how HHS determined that a home visiting model program was based on evidence.[67]

By the time that the home visiting legislation passed in March 2010, HHS was already working on a thorough review of the evidence on home visiting programs. Under the leadership of career official Naomi Goldstein, the Administration for Children and Families (ACF)—and within ACF, the Office of Planning, Research, and Evaluation (OPRE), which was headed by Goldstein—had convened a work group that had been meeting regularly for several months to design a systematic review of home visiting programs. In addition, HHS hired Mathematica both to provide advice on the evidence review process and to conduct the evidence review using procedures approved by HHS. OPRE was involved in early discussions of the home visiting initiative because at first it was assumed that the initiative would be housed at ACF. As the legislative process unfolded, however, the Health Resources and Services Administration (HRSA) within HHS was increasingly involved because Congress prohibited ACF from heading the initiative. The initiative ended up being jointly overseen by HRSA and ACF, echoing the involvement of multiple congressional committees in developing the legislative text. HRSA was given the lead for implementing the state home visiting grants, ACF administered the tribal home visiting grants, and OPRE retained the lead on evaluation activities.

OPRE was well suited for the evaluation role because of its long history of rigorous evaluation, including work on welfare reform, early childhood education, and child welfare.[68] The working group included staff from the Children's Bureau in the ACF, the Office of the Assistant Secretary for Planning and Evaluation (ASPE), HRSA, and the Centers for Disease Control and Prevention. The Domestic Policy Council, OMB, and HHS leadership also followed the HHS work group's progress and weighed in on decisions. Other experienced researchers in the Executive Office of the President—such as Alexandre Mas at OMB, Cecilia Rouse at the Council of Economic Advisers, and Dan Rosenbaum at OMB—also began to carefully review the evidence and provide advice to the HHS group as it decided which model programs would meet the test for being evidence based.

The HHS work group focused on the technical aspects of how to define an evidence-based program, as it was required to do by the home visiting law. The group took up two main issues: which types of studies were rigorous enough for their results to count as evidence; and what the results had to show for a model to be considered evidence based. The group's discussions included consideration of whether quasi-experimental designs and RCTs should be weighted differently, how many separate evaluations should be required for a program to be considered evidence based, what particular outcome measures would be counted, whether the magnitude of impacts should be considered, how "sustained" impacts should be defined, how many outcomes had to be impacted by the program, and how to regard findings that were neutral or negative.

The group studied other federal evidence reviews, such as the ones in the "What Works Clearinghouse" of the Institute of Education Sciences and those in the National Registry of Evidence-Based Programs and Practices, operated by the Substance Abuse and Mental Health Services Administration. The group also engaged in extensive discussion and debate within HHS and with OMB and the Domestic Policy Council and considered public comments received in response to a *Federal Register* notice issued on July 23, 2010. Ultimately, HHS decided to follow seven steps to conduct a thorough and transparent review of evaluation research on home visiting programs. These seven steps, similar but not identical to those followed for the Teen Pregnancy Prevention evidence review (chapter 3), were conducted by Mathematica using procedures approved by HHS. Here is a brief overview of the steps in the home visiting evidence review:

Conduct a Broad Literature Review. The first step in almost any research enterprise that claims to be based on social science is to discover and summarize what is already known on a particular issue. Because it begins with what is known and then tries to build on that, social science is cumulative. In the case of the HHS home visiting team, the goal was to review all studies of home visiting model programs, which were defined as programs that reported empirical data from a set of activities, conducted all or mostly in the participants' homes, designed to improve mother or child outcomes in at least one of the eight domains specified in the legislation:
—child development and school readiness
—child health
—family economic self-sufficiency
—linkages and referrals to other services
—maternal health
—positive parenting practices
—reduction in child maltreatment
—reductions in juvenile delinquency, family violence, or crime.
    The review located more than 8,000 citations to studies of more than 250 home visiting model programs.[69]

Screen Studies for Relevance. To be considered relevant, each of the 8,000 citations had to be in English, had to meet the definition of an early childhood home visiting model, and had to have been published after 1989. In addition, the study had to use either an RCT or a quasi-experimental design or to be an implementation study. Of the original 8,000 citations, 55 percent were screened out at this stage either for not having one of these design features or for not being about home visiting programs.[70]

Rank Model Programs. This stage of the review was another sorting procedure to give priority to model programs likely to have the strongest research support. Each home visiting model was ranked on the number and quality of studies on that model and on the studies' sample sizes. Each model received 3 points for each RCT study and 2 points for each quasi-experimental study. Models also received 1 point for each study with a sample size greater than 50. The cutoff score for passing this stage of the sorting procedure was 5 points. In

addition, to be selected, the model had to have some information about implementation. This procedure resulted in the selection for the first round of funding of 11 model programs that might qualify as evidence based.[71]

RATE QUALITY OF IMPACT STUDIES. Using a standard protocol, trained
reviewers at Mathematica examined the research design and methodology of
every study of the eleven model programs selected for review and rated the
quality of each study as *high* (for example, for RCTs, having low attrition and
no reassignment of sample members; for quasi-experimental studies, meeting
What Works Clearinghouse standards on baseline equivalence of comparison
groups and other study characteristics);[72] *moderate* (studies like those rated as
high but with modest flaws); or *low* (all other studies).

ASSESS EVIDENCE OF EFFECTIVENESS OF EACH MODEL. Next, reviewers
examined the impacts on families found by each study that was rated as being
of moderate or high quality. An outcome effect was determined to be favorable
if it was statistically significant in a direction that was beneficial to parents or
children; to be unfavorable or ambiguous if the direction of a statistically significant effect "may indicate potential harm to children and/or parents"; or to have
no effect if there were no statistically significant effects. The major requirement
for a model program to qualify as evidence based was for the program to have
either 1 high- or moderate-quality impact study that found positive impacts
in 2 or more of the 8 outcome domains listed above (child development and
school readiness; child health; family economic self-sufficiency, and so forth) or
2 or more high- or moderate-quality impact studies that found impacts in the
same outcome domain. Seven of the model programs met these criteria in the
initial study review, conducted in 2010. Seven additional model programs were
found in subsequent years to meet the evidence-based criteria, bringing the current total (as of 2014) to 14 home visiting programs with the evidence-based
designation. All but 1 of the 14 programs qualified on the basis of evidence
from RCTs, not QEDs. The only program judged to be evidence based that was
evaluated solely by a QED is Oklahoma's Community-Based Family Resource
and Support Program.[73]

REVIEW IMPLEMENTATION INFORMATION. A major goal of the home visiting
initiative was to scale up, at the state level, home visiting programs determined
to be evidence based. After the original 2010 evidence review identified seven
evidence-based model programs, the next step was for states to use one or more
of those models to provide home visiting services to needy families. To facilitate
the scaling-up process, the HHS review team provided extensive information

about implementation of each evidence-based model program on its website for states to use in scaling up the model program or programs that they selected for widespread implementation. The information provided by HHS focused on cost, staffing, and training that would help states more effectively implement the model programs.[74]

ELIMINATE CONFLICTS OF INTEREST. As always, HHS was concerned about potential or actual conflicts of interest among its staff and the Mathematica team. The final step in the evidence review was to require all those involved in the review process to agree to abide by strict conflict-of-interest rules. They had to declare all financial or personal connections to the model developers or studies being reviewed. Anyone with a conflict of interest was excluded from the review process for that particular model program.

Awarding Funds

The method of funding home visiting programs was quite complex and differed greatly from that of the other evidence-based initiatives (except Teen Pregnancy Prevention; see chapter 3). The statute authorizing the home visiting program did not specify whether the funding should be formula based or competitive. After discussion, the administration decided to provide both types of funding. A major reason that the administration was willing to use formula funds was that, as stipulated by the legislation, 75 percent of every state's allocation had to be spent on model programs approved by the evidence review.[75] In order to obtain formula funding, states would first have to write a needs assessment and state plan that described, among other issues, the at-risk geographical areas of the state that could benefit from an expansion of home visiting and also identified the model programs that the state intended to use. After approving the state plans, HHS would continue to award formula funding on an annual basis. For the competitive component, HHS decided to hold yearly competitions among states that sought to undertake more expansive and comprehensive scale-ups of their home visiting programs. HHS ultimately awarded two types of competitive grants: expansion grants for states that could show that they were conducting strong programs and that submitted high-quality plans for scaling up; and development grants for states that were running good programs that were less well developed than the programs run by states that received expansion grants.

To begin the process of administering the state funding, HHS provided each state with a base amount of $500,000. Each state would then receive an amount based on the proportion of the nation's poor children under age five residing in that state and an amount equal to what that state received as part of the Bush home visiting pilot program, known as Supporting Evidence-Based Home Visiting (EBHV). Recall that nearly every state was already operating a home visiting program or programs when the Obama team started to work on its home visiting initiative in 2008.[76] To pay for their ongoing programs, states were using their own money as well as funds from the $10 million Bush home visiting initiative and one or more of several other federal sources, such as the Temporary Assistance for Needy Families Block Grant or the Social Services Block Grant. Because states varied widely in their use of funds for home visiting, the particular model program or programs that they used, and other characteristics of their home visiting programs, HHS required states to devise a plan to consolidate and coordinate the home visiting programs within their state.

Once the states had presented HHS with this preliminary plan, they were given the remaining portion of their allotted formula funds to take the next steps in planning their home visiting initiative. HHS announced a total allocation of $88 million (plus $3 million for the tribal program) in July 2010. In its needs assessment, a state had to describe those communities with high concentrations of low-income families, high rates of premature or low-birth-weight babies, or high rates of other risk factors, such as poverty, crime, drug addiction, and unemployment; assess the quality and capacity of existing home visiting programs; and assess the state's capacity for providing substance abuse treatment and counseling.

In 2011, HHS began providing both formula and competitive funds to states to begin implementing their state plans and expand home visiting. In September, HHS awarded a total of $124 million in formula grants. The individual awards ranged from $1 million (for 8 states, several territories, and the District of Columbia) up to $11.5 million (for California). In addition, $100 million was awarded in competitive grants. This part of the home visiting initiative was similar to the other evidence-based initiatives because applicants (in this case states and, later on, in several states, a nonprofit agency)[77] that submitted the best proposals got the money. A total of 9 states received expansion grants worth $66.3 million, ranging from $2.7 for Illinois to $9.4 million for both California and Oklahoma. Development grants totaling $33.7 million were given to 13 states, ranging from $1.3 million for Alabama to $3.3 million for several other states.

In 2012, HHS awarded $125 million in formula funds and $83.9 million in competitive grants. Expansion grants worth $71.9 million were awarded to ten states and an additional $12 million in smaller development grants was awarded to six states. In 2013, HHS awarded $109.5 million in formula funds to 52 states and territories, and in September of that year, HHS announced the results of its latest competition for home visiting funds, in which a total of $69.7 million was awarded to expand home visiting services in states that "have implemented a high-quality, evidence-based home visiting program as part of a comprehensive, early childhood system of care." Eligibility was restricted to states and territories that either received a competitive development grant in 2011 or had yet to win a competitive grant at all. Thirteen states received a share of the total award. In a further demonstration of the exceedingly complex nature of the grant process for home visiting, HHS also continued to provide follow-up funding to the various competitive grant winners of previous years.

Because home visiting passed as part of the Affordable Care Act, funding the initiative was not without controversy in several states that had a political objection to the health care law. Four states rejected some or all of the formula funds that HHS offered for home visiting. North Dakota was the first state to object, declining to participate in the home visiting program from the beginning. Florida and Wyoming initially accepted formula funds to begin writing the state needs assessment and plan, but by 2012 both states had backed out of the program. The following year, Oklahoma also rejected funding. Perhaps anticipating this type of backlash, Congress included a provision in the legislation stating that HHS could award funds to an eligible nonprofit within a state if the state declined to participate in the home visiting program. Prevent Child Abuse North Dakota became the first nonprofit to receive an award, from the fiscal year 2012 funds.[78] Then, during the fiscal year 2013 funding cycle, nonprofits in both Florida and Wyoming were awarded grants. Table 2-1 provides four examples of state home visiting programs, including how much funding the states received, which home visiting model programs they selected, and how states distributed their funds within the state.

Conducting Evaluations

The home visiting statute required an ambitious evaluation of programs that receive funding.[79] The statutory requirement has two parts: first, the state needs assessment referred to above and an evaluation of how the state responded to the results of the needs assessment; and second, a study, based on random assignment "to the maximum extent feasible," of the impacts of the state home visiting programs on a set of six benchmarks specified in the statute:[80]
—improvement in maternal and newborn health
—prevention of child injuries and abuse and neglect
—improvement in school readiness and achievement
—reduction in crime or domestic violence
—increase in family economic self-sufficiency
—coordination with and referral of families to other community services.
States must show progress on four of these six benchmarks in their evaluations. In addition to these measures, the statute identifies several specific

Table 2-1. *Examples of Home Visiting Grants to States*

State	Most recent funding	Models selected	State selection process
Arizona	$9.4 million competitive expansion grant in 2011; $2.7 million in formula funds for 2013	Nurse Family Partnership (NFP) and Healthy Families America (HFA)	After identifying 31 high-risk areas, the state selected the 3 highest and then decided on NFP and HFA and the promising tribal program "Family Spirit"; the state issued a request for proposals in three of the geographical areas for providers to apply for funds.
North Carolina	$3.5 million in formula funding for 2013	HFA, NFP	The state issued a request for proposals to all counties, with local health and welfare agencies participating. The 30 highest-need counties and high-risk, sub-county areas in the other 70 counties were asked to apply. State reviewers selected 8 applications to consider, then picked 5 winners. For example, the Buncombe County Department of Health was awarded $109,018 to implement NFP.
New Hampshire	$1.5 million from a competitive development grant in 2013; $1 million in formula funds for 2013	HFA	The state-appointed home visiting task force selected five high-need areas, which included four counties and a city. The task force solicited input from local agencies in these areas and convened meetings to discuss need and fit of model programs; all agreed on selecting HFA, which is now being implemented in all five areas.
Tennessee	$6.6 million from a competitive grant in 2012; $2.6 million in formula funds for 2013	HFA, NFP, and Parents as Teachers (PAT)	All counties were ranked on specific risk indicators; the state then issued a request for proposals for the 15 highest-risk counties. A review panel scored the applications, and 6 counties were selected. Three models were chosen for the 6 counties.

Source: Various state plans submitted to the Department of Health and Human Services: Arizona (www.azdhs.gov/phs/owch/pdf/homevisiting/AZ_HomeVisitingProgramStatePlan.pdf); North Carolina (www.ncdhhs.gov/dph/wch/doc/aboutus/NC-MIECHV-FY-2011-FormulaGrantFinalNarrative.pdf); New Hampshire (http://www.dhhs.nh.gov/dphs/bchs/mch/home.htm); Tennessee (http://health.state.tn.us/MCH/PDFs/MIECHV%20State%20Plan.pdf). Funding levels are from "Active Grants for HRSA Program(s): Affordable Care Act—Maternal, Infant and Early Childhood Home Visiting Program (D89)" (http://ersrs.hrsa.gov/ReportServer/Pages/ReportViewer.aspx?/HGDW_Reports/FindGrants/GRANT_FIND&ACTIVITY=D89&rs:Format=HTML4.0).

participant outcomes that the evaluations must measure, including improvement in maternal and child health and development, improved parenting skills, reduction in domestic violence, and increased economic self-sufficiency. It is not clear why the statute identified both benchmarks and participant outcomes, which in some instances overlap.

In addition, the statute also requires a national evaluation to examine how impacts vary across programs and populations and also requires a cost study. OPRE conducted a competition to choose a firm to conduct the national evaluation called for by the statute. The research and evaluation firm MDRC won the contract and is now in the process of designing and implementing the evaluation in cooperation with several other research firms and universities. The MDRC study will include an analysis of the needs assessment conducted by every state, including descriptive information on the communities targeted by the state home visiting programs; an implementation study that will provide information on both the home visiting program itself and the local factors that shape the program; an RCT impact analysis of how mothers and children are affected by the program (across the outcome domains spelled out in the statute); and an economic analysis that provides information about the cost of the home visiting programs and the savings, if any, produced by the programs. Around 5,100 families from 85 local home visiting programs in 12 states are participating in the evaluation.[81]

In addition to the features listed above, the MDRC evaluation will test the effectiveness of four of the most widely used home visiting model programs (Early Head Start, Healthy Families America, Nurse-Family Partnership, and Parents as Teachers). Each of these four programs is being implemented in at least ten states. In addition, the evaluation is designed to allow rigorous examination of how specific features of the programs are related to impacts, which could provide program operators with information that will facilitate program revision if impacts are small or not significant. The diversity of methods of data collection being employed by MDRC is impressive. They include interviews with parents; direct observations of mothers and babies in their home; tests of children's development; observations by the home visitors from the home visiting model program or programs selected by the state; and administrative data on child abuse, birth outcomes, health care use, and employment and earnings. If previous large-scale, complex evaluations conducted by MDRC, Mathematica, Abt, Westat, RAND, and other firms are any precedent, there is no question that we will learn a great deal about the home visiting programs in general and the four model programs selected for scrutiny in particular. Most important, we will learn if the programs actually produced impacts on the six benchmark outcomes specified in the statute.

The Centers for Medicare and Medicaid Services (CMS) is collaborating with HRSA and ACF to expand this evaluation in order to measure impacts on birth outcomes, infant health, and associated costs. This supplemental evaluation, which is meant to inform Medicaid reimbursement policy for home visiting services, will expand the samples of women enrolled prenatally in the two evidence-based programs with prior evidence of effects on birth outcomes (Nurse-Family Partnership and Healthy Families America).

The statute also calls for ongoing research and evaluation, using random assignment designs to the extent possible. Accordingly, in addition to the national evaluations being conducted by MDRC and CMS, there is a rich set of additional federal research and evaluation activities related to home visiting. Moreover, each of the states that received a competitive grant is required to conduct a rigorous evaluation of the activities supported by that grant. Finally, HRSA and ACF paired the benchmark data collection requirement with a requirement that grantees develop continuous quality improvement plans based on the data collected.

Conclusion

The establishment of the Obama home visiting initiative illustrates that the federal legislative process does not make special provision for evidence-based initiatives. Compromise is in the DNA of successful legislative campaigns. There always are competing interests, and sponsors of legislation have to roll with the punches. In the end, the power players—especially the president, congressional leaders, and committee chairs—are going to play a major role in determining the fate of most legislation. But while there was no special dispensation for evidence-based home visiting, there was certainly no serious opposition to the evidence-based aspects of the legislation. From the beginning, the administration established that the home visiting initiative would be evidence based, and that standard, reinforced by frequent communication between the administration and members of Congress and their staffs, shaped the developing legislation. In fact, the most serious threat to the legislation was the administration's original intent to confine most or all spending to the NFP program, a position that was opposed by child advocates, members of the academic community, and some important members of Congress. Like the claims for NFP, the claims for other model programs were based in part on reference to good studies showing that they too were "evidence based." The advocates for other programs fought fire with fire and won, in part because they convinced others that their evidence was good too.

In recent testimony before the House Ways and Means Committee, Jon Baron of the Coalition for Evidence-Based Policy argued that the HHS home visiting program's current evidence standard contains a loophole that has allowed a number of unproven or ineffective program models to qualify as evidence based. Specifically, he points out that the current standard focuses on whether rigorous evaluations have found that the model produced statistically significant effects but not on whether those effects have policy or practical importance. According to Baron, this flaw in the evidence standard has allowed some model programs to qualify as evidence based solely on the basis of statistically significant effects, even if those effects were on trivial "process" measures (such as referrals to community services) or were likely to be false-positive findings (for example, because the studies measured a large number of outcomes).[82] Baron therefore proposes an alternative and more demanding standard for a program to qualify as evidence based as well as the creation of a second tier of grants to fund and rigorously evaluate promising but not yet proven models, an approach similar to the approach used in the Department of Education's Investing in Innovation Fund (see chapter 4).

Our interviews showed that neither congressional staffers nor the child advocacy community was intimidated by the scientific nature of the evidence debate. Many congressional staffers and nearly all of the OMB and HHS officials had some familiarity with research design and statistics and were at least somewhat familiar with the research behind one or more of the home visiting model programs. HHS's implementation of the evidence provisions of the law benefited from the presence of a cadre of staffers with experience in the department's long-standing practice of rigorous evaluation. In addition, many of the Hill staffers had attended briefings or read policy briefs about the issues in the home visiting debate, especially the issues that hinged on evidence. Nearly all involved in the debate understood the logic of the Obama approach to funding programs with strong evidence of impacts and the importance of rigorous evidence and evaluation. In this regard, it is notable that both the House and Senate bills contained a separate section requiring evaluation of the home visiting programs, an important development in view of the fact that evaluation is something that Congress often overlooks.

Another important feature of the legislative process was the treatment of NFP impacts by the Congressional Budget Office. The CBO analyst scoring an early version of the Obama proposal told us that he and his colleagues decided that they would score some savings because of the evidence from random assignment studies that NFP reduced emergency room visits and had other impacts that could save the government money. Similarly, OMB scored savings of $664 million over ten years for an NFP program like the one that the administration originally proposed in its abbreviated budget. Once the home visiting initiative was broadened to include home visiting model programs other than

NFP, CBO would no longer score any savings, presumably because it thought that only the evidence from NFP—not that from other programs—was strong enough to score savings. This brief history has important implications for the future of evidence-based policy. It is possible to imagine that RCTs of social intervention programs could produce evidence of savings that would be scored by CBO, the official scorekeeper of all congressional legislation, when it estimates the costs of specific bills. Indeed, a major goal of the Obama administration's emphasis on spending federal grant funds on programs that have strong evidence of impacts is to increase the likelihood that the programs will reduce social problems such as delinquency, dropping out of school, child abuse, unemployment and low wages, and so forth. Any such reductions have the potential to reduce government spending or increase economic productivity and tax revenue, thereby producing savings that under CBO rules could be used for spending on other programs (or for reducing the deficit). It is at least possible that if the various Obama evidence-based initiatives described in this book produce positive impacts on social problems and are shown by good studies to save money, a virtuous cycle could be established in which savings from mature evidence-based programs proven to work by RCTs could be used to help finance at least some of the costs of expansion or implementation of other social programs. If this virtuous cycle can be achieved, it will constitute a major development in the nation's social policy and open the way for more effective social programs to reduce the nation's social problems at greatly reduced cost. Of course, as we emphasize later, this virtuous circle depends on widespread impacts on social problems at the local level. Even the Obama initiatives are a long way from demonstrating that they can consistently achieve those impacts.[83]

Another issue concerns the criteria by which a model program is judged to be evidence based. Perhaps only random assignment evidence would count; perhaps there would have to be two separate random assignment studies before a program could be judged to be evidence based; perhaps the criterion would be impacts from two random assignment studies or three quasi-experimental studies. How should breadth of impacts across outcome domains be weighed against duration or magnitude of impacts? How should unfavorable effects or contradictory evidence from different studies be considered? When evidence standards are updated to reflect advances in research methods, should prior studies be grandfathered in? These and other questions show how difficult these issues can become in a legislative context. When legislation is used to advance the use of evidence-based policy, decisions about legislative provisions reflect goals and values, not necessarily scientific criteria. In short, these issues will never be completely closed and can be expected to be a difficult and even contentious part of all legislation on evidence-based programs. The divisiveness and nuances of these issues, well illustrated by the home visiting debate, might be interpreted as reason to leave the technical issues to the federal agencies to the extent possible and not to the statutes.

Although it is not always obvious, skepticism is an important part of the social science enterprise. For the many social scientists who have long held the view that RCTs can play a central role in improving the quality of social programs over time, it is difficult not to be enthusiastic about the home visiting initiative. But none of the Obama initiatives—not even home visiting—have yet shown that they can produce significant impacts at scale, let alone actually contribute to reducing the nation's social problems. So stay in your seats, but hold the applause.

3

The Teen Pregnancy Prevention Initiative

Reducing teen pregnancy is an important goal of public policy because teen pregnancy imposes significant costs on young parents, their babies, and society in general. The scholarly research literature on teen pregnancy, which has been growing since at least the 1970s, now includes empirical studies showing that many programs designed to reduce teen pregnancy can actually do so.[1] As knowledge about teen pregnancy grew over the past several decades, more and more organizations developed, implemented, and sometimes conducted rigorous evaluations of programs designed to reduce teen sexual activity, increase use of birth control, and reduce teen pregnancy. In addition, state and local organizations that sponsored or conducted these programs—along with many national organizations, such as the National Campaign to Prevent Teen and Unplanned Pregnancy (National Campaign), Heritage Keepers, and Planned Parenthood—communicated a host of messages to the nation, often using social media in clever ways, about the risks of teen pregnancy for adolescents, their babies, and society as a whole.

Background

Whether all that activity actually had an impact on teen birth rates is difficult to determine.[2] What is clear, however, is that births to teenagers have declined every year except two since 1991. According to the most recent report from the Centers for Disease Control and Prevention (CDC), from 2011 to 2012 the teen birth rate fell 6 percent, reaching a historic low of 29.4 births per 1,000 young women aged 15 to 19. From the 1991 rate of 61.8 births per 1,000 young women, teen births had fallen by more than 50 percent.[3] If the teen birth rate had remained at its 1991 level, 3.4 million additional babies would have been born to teen parents between 1992 and 2010.[4] There are few social problems that afflict the nation that have declined as much and as consistently as teen pregnancy.

Even so, there are still far too many teen births in the United States, where, in 2010, nearly 370,000 babies were born to teenagers.[5] While the U.S. teen birth rate is slightly over 29 per 1,000, the rates in France, Germany, Italy, and Sweden—all nations with cultures that are at least as sexualized as U.S. culture—are below 8 per 1,000.[6] Several studies show that teen births impose large costs on the United States; a study from the National Campaign, for example, estimates the cost at nearly $10 billion a year.[7] It makes sense that the Obama administration—realizing that the U.S. rate could be lowered even more and that there was money to be saved—would decide to design and implement an initiative to reduce teen pregnancy. Equally important, it decided to develop new, more effective teen pregnancy programs and to find ways to successfully expand programs that have been shown to be effective.

Both Republican and Democratic presidents have focused attention and resources on reducing teen pregnancy. Unfortunately, the two political parties are at war with one another about the best way to do that. Most Democrats favor a comprehensive approach in which teens are taught to practice abstinence but are also instructed in the use of and assured of the availability of contraception to prevent pregnancy and sexually transmitted infections (STIs) should they decide to have sex. By contrast, many Republicans favor an abstinence-only approach that stresses the immorality of sex outside marriage and the inconsistency, even hypocrisy, of programs that preach abstinence while simultaneously teaching about birth control. Many Democrats believe that their position encompasses the Republican position because they agree that abstinence is central to preventing teen pregnancy and should be one part—but only one part—of teen pregnancy prevention programs. Nonetheless, Republicans want only abstinence to be taught. These conflicting Republican and Democratic policy perspectives percolated below the surface in Washington for many years, but in 1996 the fight broke into the open when Republicans managed to enact their abstinence-only approach as part of that year's welfare reform legislation. The Republican provision, placed in Title V of the Social Security Act, established an annual $50 million grant fund to be divided among the states to design and implement abstinence-only programs. Republicans included in the statute a strikingly clear definition of "abstinence-only" that came to be called the "A through H" definition, in reference to the designation of the sections of the Social Security Act in which it appears. More specifically, the statute states that abstinence-only education means that a program

A. has as its exclusive purpose, teaching the social, psychological, and health gains to be realized by abstaining from sexual activity;

B. teaches abstinence from sexual activity outside marriage as the expected standard for all school-age children;

C. teaches that abstinence from sexual activity is the only certain way to avoid out-of-wedlock pregnancy, sexually transmitted diseases, and other associated health problems;

D. teaches that a mutually faithful monogamous relationship in the context of marriage is the expected standard of human sexual activity;

E. teaches that sexual activity outside of the context of marriage is likely to have harmful psychological and physical effects;

F. teaches that bearing children out-of-wedlock is likely to have harmful consequences for the child, the child's parents, and society;

G. teaches young people how to reject sexual advances and how alcohol and drug use increases vulnerability to sexual advances; and

H. teaches the importance of attaining self-sufficiency before engaging in sexual activity.[8]

Given that nearly half of high school students have had sex, Democrats strongly objected to the abstinence-only program, arguing that adolescents needed instruction in and access to birth control in order to protect themselves from both pregnancy and STIs.[9] Democrats held that because of the highly sexualized nature of American culture in general and youth culture in particular, even if abstinence-only education convinced some adolescents to remain abstinent, it was inevitable that a significant fraction of teens would still engage in sexual activity and that those sexually active teens needed help protecting themselves against both pregnancy and STIs.[10] Although many Democrats agreed that abstinence should be the primary message, they opposed funding programs that provided only abstinence education and no instruction in the use of birth control.[11] Republicans countered that parents wanted their children to remain abstinent and that abstinence was the only certain way to avoid both pregnancy and STIs. A 2012 survey showed that almost 90 percent of teens themselves and over 90 percent of parents said that teens should receive a "strong message that they not have sex until they are at least out of high school."[12] Besides, Republicans argued, many federal and state programs pay for comprehensive sex education and birth control. The Medicaid program, for example, provided about $140 million for family planning services to adolescents in 2008, although it provided no funds for sex education. There are at least ten sources of federal funding for family planning, although most of them are not designed specifically for teenagers and some of them have primary goals other than teen pregnancy prevention.[13] Further, most of them provide direct medical services rather than educational or prevention services.

Taking advantage of their majority in both houses of Congress, in 2000 Republicans created another program that provided funds exclusively for abstinence-only education. The new program used the same A through H definition of "abstinence-only" as the Title V program. Given the name Community-Based Abstinence Education (CBAE),[14] the new competitive grant program provided $20 million for abstinence-only education in 2001. That sum, which was gradually increased, reached $108.9 million in 2008, making it more than twice as large as the original $50 million state formula Title V program, which continued to be funded.[15]

Democrats were implacable in their opposition to abstinence-only programs and greatly resented the use of public dollars to fund programs that they believed were inadequate because they failed to protect young people against pregnancy and STIs. By 2008, according to the Associated Press, nearly half of the states had stopped taking the Title V abstinence-only education funds and at least two more states said that they would leave the program soon.[16] Their opposition was supported by a rigorous evaluation of abstinence-only programs conducted by Mathematica Policy Research and published in 2007. Ironically, Republicans had initiated and passed legislation in 1997 providing the Department of Health and Human Services (HHS) with funds for the scientific study of the abstinence-only programs funded by the welfare reform legislation enacted the previous year.[17] The Clinton administration's Department of Health and Human Services then worked with conservatives—including Robert Rector of the Heritage Foundation, Dr. Joe McIlhaney of the Medical Institute for Sexual Health, Shepherd Smith of the Institute for Youth Development, and Peter Brandt of Focus on the Family—to recommend the best abstinence-only programs to evaluate. In addition, HHS staff visited 28 programs and attended abstinence-only education conferences to gather information about potentially high-quality programs.[18] In the end, HHS selected four highly recommended programs for the randomized controlled trial (RCT) portion of the evaluation.[19] The evaluation, based on data collected four to six years after enrollment, concluded that none of the abstinence-only programs had an impact on sexual activity or pregnancy. This study has been a mainstay of the Democrats' argument that abstinence programs do not work.

Another claim made by Democrats was that the curriculums used in abstinence-only programs contained errors. Henry Waxman (D-Calif.), widely considered one of the top experts on health programs in Congress and a senior member of the House Committee on Oversight and Government Reform, asked the committee's Democratic staff to investigate the abstinence-only curriculums and report on their accuracy. The report, issued in December 2004, claimed that "over 80% of the abstinence-only curricula, used by over two-thirds of [abstinence-only] grantees in 2003, contain false, misleading, or distorted information about reproductive health." That information, according to the report, included claims about the failure rate of condoms, the risks of abortion, the point at which life begins, the proper role of men and women in American society, and human biology and reproduction.[20]

Several years later, the Republican staff of the House Energy and Commerce Committee wrote a report explaining and defending the abstinence-only education movement.[21] The report argued that what the committee called "sexual risk avoidance" was far preferable to the comprehensive sex education programs supported by Democrats and claimed that those programs were based on the assumption that teens are going to have sex no matter what adults say: "The underlying message [of comprehensive sex education] is that abstinence may be an effective choice, but that teens cannot or will not abstain from sex."[22] By contrast, the sexual risk avoidance programs favored by Republicans make no such assumption, teaching instead that abstinence is the best approach because it avoids rather than merely reduces risk. The report holds that programs should be designed so that the "central message of the program is that abstinence is the best choice for teens."[23]

The Waxman report and the Energy and Commerce Committee report show the intense disagreement between Republicans and Democrats over abstinence-only programs. In general, Democrats claim that the conservatives who plan and conduct abstinence-only programs either are poorly informed about the science of reproduction or deliberately provide adolescents with incorrect information related to sex and reproduction. Conservatives deny those accusations, arguing that Democrats are willing to tolerate and even encourage sexual experimentation by young people. This strong, often loud, and sometimes bitter disagreement over whether programs should focus on abstinence-only or on comprehensive sex education that includes instruction about birth control perfectly illustrates one of the most serious obstacles to basing policy on evidence. Many politicians ground their position on this issue in political philosophy and even religious views, using evidence only as a means to support their previously held beliefs. In the real world of politics, strongly held personal views often are impervious to contradictory evidence. This limit on the efficacy of the evidence argument often is seen with issues such as taxes, the government's responsibility for the poor, waging war, and other important issues. Fortunately, there appears to be little disagreement between the parties that teen pregnancy is a national problem and that its reduction is an appropriate goal for government programs. However, as on so many other issues, the parties are sharply divided about the type of programs that are both most appropriate and most effective in reducing teen sexual activity and pregnancy.[24]

Another solution to the conflict between advocates of abstinence-only education and advocates of comprehensive programs is to stick with the data on effective programs, a position that the National Campaign has taken for a decade or more.[25] Moreover, Congress has been at least somewhat receptive to using evidence as a factor in drafting legislation and in making other decisions. That can be seen in the home visiting legislation discussed in chapter 2 and in the introduction of legislation in previous Congresses to fund evidence-based programs to reduce teen pregnancy (although those bills were not enacted).[26]

For our purposes, the main message from this brief review of federal policy on reducing teen pregnancy is that the Obama administration's venture into formulating new policy to improve the effectiveness of teen pregnancy prevention programs was bound to be controversial. In fact, a good reason for emphasizing evidence is that it could at least partially deflect attention from the abstinence-only debate and give members and advocates a scientific and non-ideological reason for supporting the president's initiative, especially after the administration emphasized that abstinence-only programs would be eligible for funding if the programs could show that they were effective. Indeed, the administration did approve a notable abstinence-only program called Heritage Keepers because its evaluation showed that the program, based on a quasi-experimental design, met the test for being evidence based.[27]

We draw attention to these examples of evidence-based policy because they were precursors to the Obama teen pregnancy initiative. The lawmakers in the nation's capital are not hostile to evidence. In fact, arguing that a program is evidence based is widely seen, as any number of our interviews indicated, as a reason to support a policy. Thus, at least to some degree, the Obama administration's evidence-based initiatives were planted in fertile soil. Apart from the general argument that evidence-based programs lead to better outcomes, there is the advantage in the case of teen pregnancy prevention that focusing on evidence can reduce the volume of the unproductive ideological shouting match over abstinence-only versus comprehensive programs. Regardless of program type, any program that provides rigorous evidence of a positive impact on some aspect of teen pregnancy might be eligible for funding.

The Obama Initiative on Teen Pregnancy

During the presidential campaign of 2008, Senator Obama occasionally discussed sex education in the context of reducing the need for abortion, and Senator McCain at one point criticized Obama for allegedly supporting sex education for kindergartners. Obama responded that he supported only "age-appropriate" sex education, and the topic faded into the background; it did not become a central campaign issue.[28]

Despite the modest attention given to teen pregnancy during the campaign, it was clear from our interviews of officials at the Office of Management and Budget (OMB), HHS, and the Domestic Policy Council in the White House that the administration planned from its earliest days to undertake an initiative to reduce teen births. One consideration that might have influenced the administration's thinking was the decline in teen pregnancy rates discussed above, which suggested that effective programs had already been developed, at least for teenagers, and that more progress in reducing unplanned pregnancy was possible if use of evidence-based programs could be expanded.

As the administration set about developing its policy, Melody Barnes, the head of the Domestic Policy Council, and Tina Tchen, director of the White House Council on Women and Girls, in conjunction with the revamped Office of Faith-Based and Neighborhood Partnerships in the White House, led work on what became known as the "common ground" initiative.[29] The idea was to have a broad initiative that would center on reducing the need for abortion by emphasizing family planning, sex education, and other measures, an approach that Republicans might be able to support. On World AIDS Day, December 1, 2008, less than a month after his election and a little less than two months before his inauguration, President Obama gave remarks in which he pledged to "work with Congress to enact an extensive program of prevention" (especially of HIV/AIDS) that would include "comprehensive age-appropriate sex education for all school children."[30] Members of liberal groups interested in reproduction issues—such as the Advocates for Youth, Sexuality Information and Education Council of the United States (SIECUS), Planned Parenthood, and others—lobbied for an Obama initiative on what they often referred to as "comprehensive sex education," by which they meant programs that offered instruction on teen sexual behavior, condom use, and avoiding sexually transmitted infections (including HIV/AIDS) and provided assistance to lesbian, gay, bisexual, and transgender (LGBT) youth.

In addition, many of these groups insisted on abolition of funding for abstinence-only programs, which they regarded as dangerous. Given the Bush administration's emphasis on abstinence-only education and its avoidance of programs for teens that involved instruction in condom use or that made condoms available, the liberal advocacy groups and many Democrats in Congress were intensely focused on ending abstinence-only programs and greatly broadening the federal approach in order to fund comprehensive programs that provided information about birth control and family planning. The administration did not want to pick a fight with these groups, all of which supported the Democratic Party in general and the new Obama administration in particular, but it gradually became clear that the administration wanted to focus attention on preventing teen pregnancy and funding programs that had good evidence of positive impacts on teen sexual behavior, pregnancy rates, or sexually transmitted infection (STI) rates rather than on supporting a broader comprehensive initiative. Laurie Rubiner, who was vice president of public policy at Planned Parenthood at the time and who attended several of the meetings on the common ground initiative during the transition period and the early days of the administration, thought that the initiative was too broad and unwieldy—one reason, she believed, that the administration eventually stopped pursuing it. Perhaps, she told us, "they [the administration] just decided that [the common ground initiative] was too much to bite off." Despite abandoning the larger initiative, the administration did continue to pursue one piece of it: teen pregnancy prevention.

During any presidential transition period scores of policy balloons are floated and many of them get popped by lack of agreement within the new administration, the need to focus attention and resources on a limited set of initiatives, anticipated excessive costs, or political difficulties. This is far from a scientific process. But in the case at hand, the Obama administration gradually narrowed its focus to an initiative to reduce teen pregnancy rather than trying to encompass the much broader issue of unplanned pregnancies and abortion dealt with under the common ground framework. The administration even avoided "sex education" as a framework for its initiative because sex education would invoke past political and ideological battles. An initiative to reduce teen pregnancy would be more difficult to oppose than an initiative on sex education. In the nation's capital, how an issue is framed can be the difference between success and failure. Like staff in other parts of the new administration, both during the transition period and in the early days after the inauguration on January 20, 2009, analysts at OMB were working to develop a potential teen pregnancy prevention initiative. An OMB staffer named Katie Hamm, who had joined OMB at the end of the Bush administration and who had been working on teen pregnancy issues, was assigned to focus on teen pregnancy prevention programs that had been shown by research to have good evidence of positive impacts on some aspect of teen sexual behavior. Hamm quickly discovered that teen pregnancy prevention programs had evolved over the years and by 2009 were placing much greater emphasis on teen engagement in constructive activities. Many programs, for example, included sports, tutoring, and community service activities. Hamm started by reading empirical studies of teen pregnancy prevention programs and talking with experts outside OMB; she also visited a well-known community-based program with a record of preventing teen pregnancy in New York City. Hamm and others at OMB were under time pressure because the administration wanted to insert at least a placeholder in the budget blueprint that it planned to release while they completed work on the president's full budget proposal, which was to be released later that spring.

Anticipating at least the mention of a teen pregnancy initiative in the budget blueprint, a wide-ranging group of advocates—including representatives from SIECUS, Advocates for Youth, and America's Promise—managed to get a meeting with several senior White House officials, including Valerie Jarrett, one of the president's closest advisers, and Tina Tchen. The prestige of the White House attendees showed advocates and anyone else who knew about the meeting that whatever teen pregnancy initiative was adopted by the administration would enjoy the support of the most senior officials at the White House. James Wagoner, an attendee from Advocates for Youth, told us that there was wide-ranging discussion of administration policy on sex education, STI prevention, AIDS, and similar issues. Wagoner left the meeting thinking that the major focus of the administration was on preventing teen pregnancy and not necessarily on the comprehensive agenda that Advocates for Youth favored. He and others also were concerned that the White House Office of Faith-Based and Neighborhood Partnerships, headed by Joshua Dubois, might play an important role and might want to push the initiative in the direction of abstinence-only education, a direction that Wagoner and his colleagues aggressively opposed. Wagoner told us:

> It became apparent to us at that meeting that they were all about teen pregnancy prevention initiatives—not sex-ed per se. That was their cut. That's where they were headed. . . . And so we knew from that point forward, as we were developing our strategic goals for the administration, we knew early on we weren't going to get them all.[31]

When the budget blueprint was released on February 26, 2009, the administration simply stated that its budget supported community-based and faith-based efforts "to reduce teen pregnancy using evidence-based models." On the question of abstinence-only versus comprehensive programs, the administration said that it would fund programs that "stress the importance of abstinence" but also programs that provided "medically accurate and age-appropriate information to youth who have already become sexually active."[32]

By this point, in late February or early March 2009, OMB officials realized that the tiered structure that the administration was in the process of adopting for the home visiting initiative (see chapter 2) could also be applied to teen pregnancy prevention. Although a substantial body of intervention studies showed that teen sexual activity, pregnancy, and STIs could be reduced by intervention programs, those programs were only modestly effective.[33] Few doubted that the programs could be improved, and no one, least of all at OMB, wanted to bar the door to new ideas for programs that could help persuade teens to avoid sexual activity or to use condoms and other forms of birth control if they decided to become sexually active. Most of the successful programs had been evaluated only once by rigorous methods, leaving open the question of whether they could be successfully replicated. The tiered structure, as with the home visiting initiative, was a way to direct most of the funding to programs that had strong evidence of impacts while allowing some of the money to be directed to promising and innovative programs. As it turned out, both the legislation on and the implementation of the administration's initiative, which came to be called Teen Pregnancy Prevention (TPP), was based on a two-tiered structure, with tier 1 reserved for replication of programs identified by HHS as evidence based (see below for details) and tier 2 for research and demonstration programs intended primarily to allow for development of additional model programs and innovative strategies to prevent teen pregnancy.

In early March, John Monahan, an experienced Democratic administrator who had agreed to provide senior leadership at HHS until more political appointees survived the confirmation gauntlet, was invited to a meeting with senior OMB and Domestic Policy Council officials to discuss the administration's teen pregnancy initiative.[34] Monahan already knew, by word of mouth and from the language on teen pregnancy reduction in the budget blueprint, that the White House was planning a teen pregnancy initiative. In fact, he had discussed the initiative with Naomi Goldstein and Barbara Broman, two influential and experienced senior career officials at HHS. The department had been ground zero in the fights over abstinence-only education because its staffers were responsible for implementing the abstinence-only programs and for overseeing the Mathematica abstinence-only evaluation discussed above. The CDC, the Administration for Children and Families (ACF), and other administrative units at HHS had a great deal of experience administering pregnancy prevention programs, although not all of them targeted teenagers. Thus, not surprisingly, a number of career officials at HHS were familiar with pregnancy prevention research, including research specifically on teen pregnancy prevention, and many of them were well informed about the politics of the issue in Washington. As soon as these career HHS officials had heard, on an informal basis, that the administration was thinking of sponsoring a teen pregnancy initiative, they, like the career staffers at OMB, began reviewing the literature on teen pregnancy with an eye to identifying successful prevention programs.

Monahan took Broman with him to the March meeting with OMB officials, where they discussed the initiative and the tiered funding approach. Within two months of the president's inauguration, several major characteristics of the teen pregnancy initiative were falling into place: the initiative would be evidence based, grants would be awarded on a competitive basis, and funding would be based on a tiered structure, with most of the money going to programs with strong evidence of positive impacts on some aspect of teen reproductive health but some money going to innovative programs based on a good idea or modest evidence.

On May 11, 2009, the administration released its official budget for fiscal year 2010, which revealed that the teen pregnancy initiative would consist of $110 million for "community-based and faith-based organizations to implement evidence-based and promising models to prevent teen pregnancy" and for program support, including technical assistance.[35] The HHS budget spelled out that $75 million would be reserved for tier 1 programs to "replicate curriculum-based models that have been shown through strong evaluation . . . to be effective in reducing teen pregnancy, delaying sexual activity, or improving contraception use"[36] and that $25 million would go to tier 2 programs to "develop, replicate, refine, and test" promising model programs. Wisely, the administration tried to minimize its differences with supporters of abstinence-only education by including language stating that many of the successful programs had "a strong emphasis on abstinence," even though they also provided information on contraception.

Although the administration was placing a clear emphasis on funding evidence-based programs, it was not doing so in response to pressure from members of Congress or from child advocates; it was doing so because it wanted better results from federal money spent on social programs and firmly believed that funding evidence-based programs was a good way to get those results. Adopting the tone and a few of the specifics set by the president, the administration, through a huge and sophisticated effort led by OMB and the Domestic Policy Council, was inventing its evidence-based initiatives out of whole cloth for reasons that had little to do with winning political points. Not surprisingly, it quickly became clear that advocates on both sides of the teen pregnancy debate placed their long-standing agendas well ahead of any interest in basing policy on evidence. Advocates for sex education and comprehensive programs were less concerned with evidence-based policy than with making sure that comprehensive programs were funded and abstinence-only programs were not. In the end, most of them appeared to be willing to go along with the administration if the result was more funding for projects consistent with their goals—even if they didn't completely agree with the policy framework for preventing teen pregnancy because it allowed abstinence-only programs that met the evidence criteria to be funded.

Given the administration's emphasis on evidence, advocates for comprehensive programs frequently cited the finding of the Mathematica evaluation showing that the best federally funded abstinence-only programs had no impact on teen sexual activity or pregnancy.[37] Advocates for comprehensive programs and some Democrats in Congress were concerned that the administration was not sufficiently committed to trying to dump the abstinence-only programs. They were especially concerned when Melody Barnes, the head of the Domestic

Policy Council, was quoted in a *USA Today* article in May 2009 as saying that the administration was willing to fund abstinence-only programs if they could meet the evidence standards.[38] Our interviews indicated that some of the advocates were concerned that the $25 million pot for promising teen pregnancy prevention programs would become a primary source of funding for abstinence-only programs. They were worried that tier 1 would become the "comprehensive" pot of funding, while tier 2 would become the "abstinence-only" pot.

Catching wind of the dissatisfaction among the comprehensive sex education advocates, the administration called another White House meeting for June 2, 2009. With the budget out and senior officials at both HHS and OMB beginning to settle on the specifics of a teen pregnancy prevention initiative, the administration wanted to quell as much dissent as possible as the action moved to Capitol Hill, where the bill would be drafted. Robert Gordon (arguably the main architect of the administration's evidence-based initiatives), Jenny Yeager Kaplan, Jeff Crowley, and Tina Tchen from OMB and the White House were in attendance, as were Dora Hughes and John Monahan from HHS. After Tchen and Crowley laid out the administration's plans for the initiative, James Wagoner, the lobbyist from Advocates for Youth, argued that the framing was too narrow, pointing out that any focus on AIDS prevention and LGBT youth was completely missing; moreover, he said, it was a travesty to allow abstinence-only programs to be eligible for funding. Gordon countered that the framing of the initiative was very broad and asked the advocates to name a type of program that could not be funded under the administration's "evidence-based" banner.[39] Clearly, the administration was not changing its position, although it did agree to tweak the legislative language that it was developing so that projects addressing STIs and HIV/AIDS prevention could be more easily accommodated.

It is worth noting that the advocates' concern about the focus on teen pregnancy prevention rather than on a broader initiative to fund sex education programs was shared by some members of Congress. Jennifer Drake of the National Campaign told us that Barbara Lee (D–Calif.) and some other members of Congress agreed with the advocates. Some of them appeared to want to fund only comprehensive programs, which in their view had already been shown to have impacts, rather than focus on evidence—as if everyone didn't already know that comprehensive programs worked and abstinence-only programs did not. Even so, Drake told us, there was a strong feeling among Democratic members of Congress that they should stand behind their new president and his focus on teen pregnancy prevention.

On the other end of the political spectrum, supporters of abstinence-only programs rejected the administration's approach. Valerie Huber, the head of the National Abstinence Education Association, told us that she and her group were suspicious of the administration's focus on evidence, which they thought was a smokescreen to deny funding to abstinence-only programs. Huber's position, no less than that of the comprehensive sex education groups like Advocates for Youth, illustrates that evidence alone will not trump ideology. It was widely agreed among scholars that while a few abstinence-only programs showed modest evidence of success, the evidence for comprehensive programs was stronger.[40] Nevertheless, Robert Rector, a scholar and conservative advocate at the Heritage Foundation, had written several literature reviews on abstinence-only education programs that he believed proved that such programs worked. Only three of the studies were based on a random assignment design, raising some question about the validity of most of the studies.[41] Even so, these studies—combined with a dose of political philosophy plus Rector's and Heritage's prestige among conservatives—were enough to convince Republicans that there was good evidence of the success of abstinence-only programs. In fact, the 2012 report from the Energy and Commerce Committee claims that the comprehensive approach had "failed to lower rates of teenage pregnancy" while research suggested that the "sexual risk avoidance approach" (the new term for "abstinence-only education") would lead to a "greater success than the [comprehensive] model has been able to achieve."[42] Although Republican claims that comprehensive programs had been shown by research to be ineffective while abstinence-only programs had been shown to succeed might have been questionable, Republicans were certainly correct when they claimed, as President Bush often said, that the only completely foolproof way for teens to avoid pregnancy and STIs was to remain abstinent.

Congressional Action

By June 2009, the action had shifted to Capitol Hill. An administration's legislative plans are one thing; congressional action often is another. With a majority in both houses to back them up, some Democrats in Congress had their own ideas about sex education initiatives, many of which differed, at least in emphasis, from the administration's thinking. Three efforts headed by Democrats were vying for attention on the sex education agenda in the House. One effort was headed by Representative Tim Ryan (D–Ohio) and Representative Rosa DeLauro (D–Conn.), who was one of the most influential members of the liberal wing of the Democratic Party in Congress. Ryan, who was pro-life, and DeLauro, who was pro-choice, introduced legislation designed to reduce the need for abortion by increasing funds for birth control in the context of a comprehensive program; the legislation also had strong provisions on funding evidence-based programs.[43] A second effort was the REAL (Responsible

Education about Life) Act, a countermeasure to the abstinence-only provision that Republicans had enacted in the 1996 welfare reform law. Championed by Representative Barbara Lee (D–Calif.), a member of the House Appropriations Committee, it included a definition of comprehensive sex education that was similar in structure to the abstinence-only A through H definition quoted in full earlier in the chapter.[44] A third effort, sponsored by the Energy and Commerce Committee, was a provision that made it into the ill-fated House bill during the health care debate. This provision, which would have provided $50 million a year for grants to states to create evidence-based comprehensive sex education programs, required the secretary of HHS to establish a registry of programs that met the criteria for being evidence based and that provided information to teens that was medically and scientifically accurate. An interesting aspect of the Energy and Commerce Committee legislation is that, like the Obama evidence-based initiatives, it required states to use programs that had good evidence of impacts and required the secretary to develop a registry of programs deemed "evidence-based."[45] We take this feature of the Energy and Commerce Committee bill as a sign that the focus on evidence-based social programs was spreading.

Despite the various Democratic sex education efforts, it appeared from the beginning of legislative action that both House and Senate Democrats were willing to go along with the president on his TPP initiative. Of course, consistent with traditional congressional practice, if allies cannot agree on a single program, then they can enact more than one program so that all involved can get their way. This somewhat wasteful solution would become an important part of the legislative journey that led to approval of Obama's TPP initiative.

The House and Senate Appropriations Committees, which would handle the TPP initiative,[46] had been deeply involved in teen pregnancy prevention because the Republicans had created the CBAE program in those committees in the early 2000s. The lead Democratic appropriator in the House was the powerful David Obey (D–Wis.), who was the committee's chairman. Obey, who was Catholic, nonetheless had no objection to pregnancy prevention programs because he saw pregnancy prevention as a way to reduce the need for abortion. Under his leadership, funds for pregnancy prevention in his committee report came under the heading "Reducing the Need for Abortion." Nearly all Democrats in Congress, including those who were pro-life, strongly supported programs that taught young people how to use birth control and provided them with access to birth control. According to Andrea Kane of the National Campaign, Obey "supported abstinence programs but was not opposed to contraception, so I think the fact that he played such a leadership role here is really quite an important story."[47] Kane also thought that Obey went along with the president because Obey liked the emphasis on evidence and was convinced that it showed that effective programs could reduce pregnancy and therefore the need for abortion. Obey is an example of the kind of Democrat that the administration could appeal to by focusing its initiative on teen pregnancy reduction rather than on the less precise and more ideological goal of comprehensive sex education.

Therefore it was not surprising that the bill that Chairman Obey brought to the House Appropriations Committee's markup session on July 17, 2009, contained language that was similar to the president's May budget proposal for HHS, which called for $75 million a year for grants that had strong evidence of success in reducing teen pregnancy, delaying sexual activity, or improving contraception use and $25 million a year for demonstration grants that would "develop, replicate, refine, and test additional models and innovative strategies." Obey's provision included both the $75 million a year to expand programs with rigorous evidence of success and the $25 million for promising, though unproven, innovative strategies. Moreover, it also included an additional $10 million for program support and allowed about $4.5 million, which amounted to a continuation of past funding, for evaluation of teen pregnancy prevention programs.[48]

Republicans were not thrilled about the new TPP initiative or the fact that the appropriations bill also de-funded the CBAE program. On July 17, 2009, during the markup of the fiscal year 2010 appropriations bill, Robert Aderholt (R-Ala.) and Zach Wamp (R-Tenn.) offered an amendment to restore funding for the program. During discussion of their amendment, Wamp said: "Guys, I don't want to be a bomb thrower, but [abstinence education] works; it works."[49] However, the only evidence that Wamp offered to support the claim that abstinence education works was that "parents prefer it 2 to 1." The amendment failed on a partisan vote. Consistent with Obey's long-standing support for abstinence programs, the language in the report that accompanied the appropriations bill was careful to point out that although the CBAE program had been terminated, abstinence-only programs could qualify for funding under either the $75 million provision or the $25 million provision in the TPP program if they met the criteria for either of the two provisions. The appropriations bill containing the TPP passed the House on July 24, 2009.[50]

Meanwhile, the Senate also was willing to go along with the administration on teen pregnancy prevention. The most important change that the Senate made in the House appropriations language, again reflecting the Democrats' hostility to abstinence-only programs, concerned which agency would implement the administration's evidence-based TPP initiative. Because HHS's Administration for Children and Families had administered the abstinence-only programs, Democratic senators and Senate staff apparently viewed the career staff at ACF as contaminated by the abstinence-only virus. They therefore included a provision in the Senate bill requiring the new TPP program to be administered by the Office of the Secretary and not by ACF. Senate Appropriations Committee staffers told us that they were very pleased, as was Senator Tom Harkin (D–Iowa), chairman of the Senate Appropriations Committee, to zero out the funding for the abstinence-only education programs in favor of the evidence-based TPP program.

It then took the House and Senate four months to reach a compromise agreement on the other provisions in the appropriations bill that included the TPP provision. The House passed the compromise bill on December 10 and the Senate followed suit on December 13. The president signed the bill on December 16 and, along with a zillion other provisions, the TPP program became law and was funded for its first year of operation. The competitive grants funded by the bill were designed as five-year projects contingent on future years' funding by the appropriations committees. Funding has been approved each year through 2014.

Surprisingly, the legislative story of the Obama teen pregnancy prevention initiative does not end with passage of the Obama provision in the 2010 appropriations law. Conservatives were not about to give up on preserving at least one of their favored programs, either the Title V entitlement provision that provided states with $50 million to run abstinence-only programs or the $99 million in appropriated funds for the CBAE program. Conservatives had an opening to save one of the programs during Senate Finance Committee negotiations on health care reform because Democrats on the Senate Finance Committee, especially Chairman Max Baucus (D-Mont.), wanted to replace the Title V abstinence-only program with a new program to fund projects that were supported by evidence (a move that reflected Baucus's long-standing commitment to evidence-based programs as well as the administration's emphasis on evidence) and that included education about both abstinence and contraception. The chairman's new program, called the Personal Responsibility Education Program (PREP), would provide $75 million a year for five years, about $55 million of which would go for formula grants to states for evidence-based programs and the remaining $20 million for competitive grants, grants to tribes, funds for evaluation, and funds for program support.[51] This effort to pass teen pregnancy prevention legislation in the Senate Finance Committee was completely separate from the legislation establishing the Obama TPP program by the Appropriations Committees in the House and Senate.

Our interviews of Senate staffers revealed that there had been a great deal of staff-level discussion as well as some discussion between Baucus and Senator Orrin Hatch (R-Utah), a senior Republican on the Finance Committee, about their goals in writing a teen pregnancy provision to include in Obama's Affordable Care Act (ACA). Baucus's staff had been working on the text of the PREP legislation and had shared drafts with the Republican staff. Baucus, a moderate

Democrat, included provisions in PREP to ensure that programs would be required to emphasize both abstinence and contraception, a balanced approach that he and his staff assumed would appeal to Republicans. The Republican staff, in turn, informed the committee that Senator Hatch intended to introduce an amendment that would, in effect, reauthorize the $50 million Title V abstinence-only education money because the authorization had lapsed on October 1, 2009, the beginning of the 2010 fiscal year. If both the Baucus and Hatch amendments were accepted by the committee, both sides would get at least part of what they wanted.

Baucus offered PREP as an amendment during the Finance Committee markup of his own health care bill, America's Affordable Health Choices Act, which began on September 22 and ended on October 13, 2009. To no one's surprise, the Baucus amendment passed. Senator Hatch also offered his amendment to reauthorize the Title V abstinence-only education provision, which almost everyone assumed would fail given the antipathy that Democrats had toward abstinence-only programs. Nonetheless, Democrats Blanche Lincoln (D-Ark.) and Kent Conrad (D-N.D.), from the red states of Arkansas and North Dakota respectively, and all the Republicans on the committee supported the Hatch amendment, so it also passed. Now the Senate health care bill contained the Hatch provision reauthorizing Title V abstinence-only education as well as the Baucus provision authorizing PREP. Andrea Kane, the analyst with the National Campaign, told us that the Finance Committee markup was completed quickly and late at night, that most people found out about the markup only by watching C-SPAN, and that many analysts, staffers, and advocates were shocked that the Title V abstinence education program was approved by the committee.

The House almost certainly would not have accepted the Senate's abstinence-only provision if the House and Senate had held a conference committee to iron out the differences between their respective versions of the ACA. But the surprising election of Republican Scott Brown to fill the Senate seat vacated when Edward Kennedy died brought a sudden end to the Democrats' filibuster-proof supermajority of 60 votes in the Senate. There was no doubt that Senate Republicans would kill the Obama health care legislation if they had the opportunity, in all likelihood thereby killing both PREP and the Title V abstinence-only program contained in the Senate's version of the ACA. Because Brown's election left the Senate unable to survive a filibuster of any House-Senate compromise health care bill, the only way that Democrats could pass their health care legislation would be for the House to accept every word of the initial Senate bill, thereby avoiding a new House-Senate compromise bill. So on March 21, 2010, the House swallowed its pride and enacted the Senate bill exactly as written. However, before the House would agree to pass the Senate bill, the

House Democratic leadership insisted on simultaneous passage of a reconciliation bill that included some provisions from the dead House bill. The Senate agreed to that approach, and both bills were passed exclusively with Democratic votes. Now both Baucus's PREP and the extension of the Title V program were approved. In addition, the administration's TPP program had already been enacted as part of the Consolidated Appropriations Act of 2010. One way to achieve a "compromise" is to give both sides what they want—in this case, compromise was achieved among Democrats themselves by passing both the TPP and PREP programs and between Democrats and Republicans by passing both the PREP and Title V programs. Taxpayers are not closely consulted when deals like this are cut.

HHS Shapes the Initiative

By the time that the appropriations bill containing the TPP program passed in December 2009, HHS was already well along in its plans for writing the Funding Opportunity Announcement (FOA), which would herald the competition to potential applicants, and it was working on the procedures for the systematic evidence review, which would determine which programs qualified as evidence based. HHS staffers also were planning several evaluations of the various teen pregnancy programs passed by Congress, especially TPP. Two points should be emphasized about this stage of the Obama plan for bringing evidence to bear on policy formulation and implementation. The first is that the heart of the Obama approach in all six of the evidence-based initiatives is to spend most federal dollars on programs that have been shown by rigorous evaluation to produce statistically significant positive impacts on important behaviors, in this case some aspect of sexual activity, pregnancy, or STIs among teens. However, it is no modest thing to figure out how to define significant impacts, especially because evaluation research is often messy, contradictory, and inconclusive. Evaluations of the same program often show different results. Some evaluations find significant impacts while others find none; some show impacts on certain behaviors while others show impacts on different behaviors. Moreover, the types of people participating in the program, the characteristics of the neighborhood from which the program draws its participants, the participants' ethnicity, the preparation of teachers and others conducting the program, and a host of other factors can shape the results of an evaluation. Weighing those factors in dozens or even hundreds of studies to determine which programs produce reliable impacts requires a powerful and carefully defined methodology.

The second important point about this stage of the Obama evidence-based process is that in order for an initiative to succeed, federal dollars have to go to competent program operators. Even if the administration succeeds in identifying effective model programs, unless the process adopted for distributing federal dollars puts the money in the hands of people and organizations that will use it effectively, any evidence-based approach will fail, regardless of whether it has been shown by rigorous evaluation to produce significant impacts.

We turn now to reviewing how the Obama administration operated within these constraints to get the teen pregnancy prevention initiative off the ground, beginning with the vital process of determining what exactly the administration meant by "evidence-based."

Conducting the Evidence Review

The first step in deciding who would receive the teen pregnancy prevention money was to determine which model programs would qualify as being based on evidence—and exactly how to define the term "evidence-based."[52]

That meant devising a systematic procedure for defining which model programs had rigorous evaluations showing that they had had significant impacts on the aspects of teen sexual behavior described in the legislation. The administration seemed well aware that having an effective and transparent set of procedures for identifying effective programs was a minimum requirement if people in the field were to accept its funding decisions. In Washington, there is always controversy over who gets money and who does not.

In teen pregnancy prevention, as in home visiting, many program models have been evaluated, sometimes using gold standard designs. The administration therefore set about conducting a thorough review of the evidence from these studies. To conduct the review, officials at HHS called on Mathematica Policy Research, a private research and program evaluation firm, and on Child Trends, a Washington-based nonprofit organization that analyzes research and survey data to gain insights about child and family well-being. Staff from Child Trends and Mathematica worked together to review and rate the quality of the home visiting studies.

In addition to the evidence review, even before the legislation passed,[53] senior officials at HHS had appointed a group of experts on teen pregnancy and on research design from the Office of Planning, Research, and Evaluation (OPRE), the Office of the Assistant Secretary for Planning and Evaluation (ASPE), the Office of Adolescent Health (OAH), the CDC, and other HHS offices to perform two tasks. The first was to develop a procedure to define in specific terms what it means for a program to be evidence based and then to use that procedure to identify the teen pregnancy prevention model programs that met those criteria. The second was to write the FOA explaining the grant program and announcing the availability of funds. A subgroup of the overall work group, headed by an OPRE career analyst named Seth Chamberlain, guided the evidence review, working in conjunction with Mathematica and officials in the OAH, who were responsible for writing the FOA. Naomi Goldstein, the career HHS official who headed OPRE, was the leader of the overall effort. She spent considerable time coordinating the activities of the group conducting the teen pregnancy evidence review with those of the group conducting the home visiting evidence review (see chapter 2).

In another parallel with the home visiting work group, HHS officials decided to ask Mathematica to be responsible for determining which model programs met the evidence guidelines developed by the HHS work group.[54] The result of Mathematica's work, under guidance from HHS, would be a list of programs that had been rigorously evaluated and found to produce some positive impact; those programs would be eligible for tier 1 funding. Numerous teen pregnancy prevention and sex education curriculums and programs have been developed by researchers, program operators, and commercial companies to be used by schools, after-school centers, community centers, and other local organizations that want to reduce the rate of teen pregnancy or related behaviors. Some of those programs had been evaluated; the job of the teen pregnancy working group was to identify the evaluations that met rigorous standards.

The working group faced the difficult task of translating "evidence-based" from concept into practice. "Evidence of what?" might well have been the biggest question. The working group first had to determine which outcomes were important enough to evaluate for evidence of impact in determining whether a program would be approved. Similar to home visiting programs, teen pregnancy prevention programs collect measures on many outcomes, including contraceptive use, STIs, behavioral attitudes and expectations, age of initial intercourse, number of partners, pregnancy, and others. And while the initiative was called "teen pregnancy prevention," pregnancy as an outcome for a program model is not always simple to measure. Programs that target eighth graders, for example, might not see an outcome like impact on pregnancy rates for a few years. In addition, many pregnancy prevention programs do not even measure the pregnancy rate as an outcome of their program. Another issue is that because pregnancy is a relatively infrequent outcome, detecting a difference between program and comparison groups of teens using just the pregnancy measure is often difficult. These complications led the working group to think about different ways to determine which outcomes would count as important measures of evidence of impact. As Chris Trenholm—the lead researcher on the 2007 Mathematica study that found that abstinence-only programs did not work, who was also working with HHS on the TPP initiative—told us during his interview, there are other ways to measure pregnancy by proxy: "You'll measure different behavioral risk indicators, like timing of sexual initiation, reports of youth remaining sexually abstinent; among kids who were not sexually abstinent, were they consistently using long-term contraception—outcomes like that."[55]

Another issue that the group faced was nonbehavioral outcomes. Some programs focus on "expectations" about sex and abstinence. They track whether students profess to expect to refrain from sex or use contraception. They might also measure how students characterize their attitudes toward sex. Because these nonbehavioral outcomes measure attitudes, values, or expectations, they contrast with behaviors like contraceptive use, sexual activity, and pregnancy, which measure actual behavior. Of course, as many teen pregnancy researchers point out, most studies rely on the verbal responses of the teens themselves to questions about their sexual practices, thus raising a question about the reliability of most program outcome measures—including the behavioral measures—in the teen pregnancy literature. Some researchers, however, are more skeptical of findings based on teenagers' responses to interviewers about their attitudes and feelings than of findings based on responses about their actual behavior. The working group had to ask itself whether those nonbehavioral measures could be used as reliable indicators of program success or failure. The groups supporting abstinence education, such as the National Abstinence Education Association, wanted to include attitudinal measures because studies of abstinence-only programs rely heavily on such measures.[56] Trenholm explained that the question then becomes "Where do you draw the line in terms of saying, 'This is a measure that's sufficient to be evidence of an effect or a potential effect on pregnancy.'"[57] The working group ultimately decided that only behavioral outcomes would be counted. Having made that decision, the working group still had to determine which research designs would have to be used for evidence to be considered of high-enough quality to meet the evidence-based standard. Many issues are involved here, and there are many ways to characterize a program's evidence. Trenholm explained the difficulty:

> If you took eight very basic indicators of evidence . . . [For example,] was the effect short or long term? . . . Was there an effect on multiple outcomes or one outcome? Was there replication? Was it a high or medium quality study? . . . and you consider using those to create categories, that . . . becomes two to the eighth categories, which becomes completely uncountable . . . And so that becomes a challenge . . . how do you take all of this information and condense it down to a set of categories that a policymaker can actually work with?[58]

The group tried several different categorizations of the evidence, attempting to settle on a solution that would be practical for program operators. They ultimately decided to report on replication, duration, and outcomes for each of the program models but then determine whether the program was evidence based solely on the quality of the study and statistically significant outcomes on each of the four measures that they selected as most important. The measures were

—sexual activity (including age at initiation; frequency of sex; rates of vaginal, oral, or anal sex; number of partners)

—contraceptive use (consistent use or single use of condoms or other contraceptive method)

—sexually transmitted infections

—pregnancy or birth.

To be designated "evidence-based," the model program had to have evidence (from a high- or moderate-quality study; see below) of at least one positive, statistically significant impact on one or more of the these four outcomes for the full sample in a given study, for the subgroup of males or of females in the study sample, or for a subgroup defined by degree of sexual experience at the beginning of the study. Having made choices on these important issues, the work group turned to the actual evidence review by conducting the following four-step process:

—*Find potentially relevant studies.* As is standard practice in conducting literature reviews in the social sciences, the HHS team examined four types of sources to identify all teen pregnancy studies that might be relevant. The sources included research syntheses; the websites of research and policy organizations that played any role in teen pregnancy prevention policy or research; responses to a public (Internet) notice calling for nomination of relevant studies; and a keyword search of various electronic databases. The search phase of the review produced nearly 1,000 potentially relevant studies.

—*Screen studies.* A thorough review of studies on a given topic almost always uncovers a lot of material that does not deserve to see the light of day. The work group therefore established several rules for determining whether studies were too flawed to be included in the review. The most basic requirement was that to be included, the study had to report empirical evidence on the effects of an intervention as well as numerical results and statistical analyses. In addition, it had to report program impacts on sexual activity, contraception use, STIs, or pregnancy or birth rates. The study also had to report results for American youth age 19 or under and to have been conducted after 1989. These criteria reduced the number of potentially relevant studies from nearly 1,000 to 199.

—*Assess quality of studies.* The studies that survived the initial screening were then rated for quality by a team composed of 14 researchers from Mathematica, Child Trends, and Concentric Research and Evaluation, a private research and

Table 3-1. *Rating Scheme for Assessing Quality of Studies*

Quality criterion	Quality rating		
	High	*Moderate*	*Low*
Study design	Random assignment	Quasi-experimental design with comparison group or random assignment with high attrition or reassignment to groups	Does not meet criteria for high or moderate rating
Attrition	What Works Clearing-house standards	No requirement	Does not meet criteria for high or moderate rating
Baseline equivalence	Control for statistically significant baseline differences	Baseline equivalence of research groups and control for baseline outcome measures	Does not meet criteria for high or moderate rating
Reassignment	Analysis based on original assignment to research groups	No requirement	Does not meet criteria for high or moderate rating
Confounding factors	At least two subjects in each group and no systematic differences in data collection methods	At least two subjects in each group and no systematic differences in data collection methods	Does not meet criteria for high or moderate rating

Source: Mathematica Policy Research and Child Trends, "Identifying Programs That Impact Teen Pregnancy, Sexually Transmitted Infections, and Associated Sexual Risk Behaviors" (Princeton: Mathematica, 2010) (www.hhs.gov/ash/oah/oah-initiatives/teen_pregnancy/db/eb-programs-review-v1.pdf).

evaluation firm. The reviewers participated in a day-long training session and then worked in pairs, with one member of the pair performing the review following a protocol developed by HHS and Mathematica and the other checking the work. In rating the quality of each study, the team considered five criteria: study design, attrition, baseline equivalence of the program and comparison groups, whether any participants had been reassigned from the program group to the comparison group or vice versa, and whether there were confounding factors. The standards for rating the quality of studies were based on the standards developed by the Institute of Education Sciences for its What Works Clearinghouse. Table 3-1 summarizes the factors considered in assigning the ratings of high, moderate, and low quality to the studies. Only studies that used random assignment, had low attrition, and had no subjects who switched between the experimental and control groups were awarded the high rating. Moderate-quality studies were random assignment studies with flaws such as high attrition rates and studies that used a quasi-experimental design with a well-matched comparison group.[59] Studies that did not meet the criteria for high quality or moderate quality were judged to be low quality. The 106 studies rated as low quality were dropped from further review.[60]

—*Assess evidence of effectiveness.* As in all its evidence-based initiatives, the administration wanted to fund primarily projects using model programs that had been shown by at least one rigorous evaluation to produce positive impacts on key outcome measures. This phase of the review began with documentation of the evidence provided in each study of impacts on the outcome measures of interest. Some program models had more than one published study, in which case all impacts from all studies were documented. After identifying each impact, the review proceeded to identifying the measure on which the impact had been reported, identifying the sample or subgroup to which the impact applied, determining the length of the follow-up period, and identifying the magnitude of the impact and the reported level of statistical significance. For example, a random assignment study by Susan Philliber and her associates of the Carrera program of the Children's Aid Society, which focused on disadvantaged black and Hispanic youth ages 13 to 15, found that three years after the program began females in the treatment group were significantly less likely to have become pregnant and to report being sexually active than control-group females. Both impacts were statistically significant.[61] Thus, the HHS/Mathematica review group found that the Carrera program met the criteria for being a tier 1 evidence-based program.[62] The studies were then classified in a framework defined by whether the study was of high quality or moderate quality and, within those two overall categories, by whether the impacts had been replicated, whether they were sustained or only short term, and whether they were found for only a subgroup of the study sample (see table 3-2).

In consultation with Mathematica and others in the review group, HHS used the results from the evidence review to identify the programs that met the criteria for high or moderate quality and had evidence of significant impacts. In the end, 28 model programs were determined to meet the criterion of having at least one statistically significant impact on at least one of the four acceptable outcome measures.[63] Those programs were judged to be evidence based and eligible for tier 1 funding. The 28 programs, plus three additional programs approved by HHS subsequent to the initial selection in 2010, are summarized in table 3-3. It is worth noting that of the 31 programs, 13 increased contraceptive use and 21 decreased some aspect of sexual activity. But only 5 model programs decreased pregnancy rates, and only 5 decreased STI rates (some programs produced impacts on more than one outcome).

Table 3-2. *Quality Criteria for Teen Pregnancy Prevention Programs*

Evidence category	Replicated impact	Sustained impact	Short-term impact	Only subgroup impact
High-quality studies				
Portion of sample showing impact	Full sample	Full sample	Full sample	Subgroup
Duration	Year or more	Year or more	Less than one year	Any
Replicated	Yes	No	Either	Yes or no
Number of programs	0	6	10	3
Moderate-quality studies				
Portion of sample showing impact	Full sample	Full sample	Full sample	Subgroup
Duration	Year or more	Year or more	Less than one year	Any
Replicated	Yes	No	Either	Either
Number of programs	0	2	3	4

Source: Mathematica Policy Research and Child Trends, "Identifying Programs That Impact Teen Pregnancy, Sexually Transmitted Infections, and Associated Sexual Risk Behaviors" (Princeton: Mathematica, 2010) (www.hhs.gov/ash/oah/oah-initiatives/teen_pregnancy/db/eb-programs-review-v1.pdf).

In summary, the evidence review followed strict procedures to identify potentially relevant teen pregnancy reduction programs, to sort through the studies of model programs and pick the ones that met well-defined quality standards, to develop a definition of quality studies, and to determine whether the studies showed an impact on one or more of the four outcome measures of interest. So far, a total of 31 model programs have been found to produce at least one impact on one of the four selected outcome categories and therefore to be eligible for tier 1 funding. These are the model programs that applicants for tier 1 of TPP funding have to use to be eligible. As in the other Obama evidence-based initiatives, another tier of funding, which had less money than tier 1, was specifically designed to allow for innovation. In tier 2, projects could use adaptations of one of the 31 evidence-based programs or other programs that had some evidence of success or had at least shown promise in order to be eligible for funding.

Developing the Funding Opportunity Announcement

The work led by OPRE defined what it means to be "evidence-based," and to date HHS has identified 31 teen pregnancy prevention programs that meet that standard and therefore are eligible for funding. But the administration also needed to produce an FOA to let the public know that $100 million a year was available to conduct evidence-based teen pregnancy reduction programs and to explain the rules under which various entities could apply for the funds. The newly created

Table 3-3. *Overview of Teen Pregnancy Prevention Program Models Eligible for Tier 1 Funding*[a]

Program	Brief description
Aban Aya Youth Project	Afrocentric social development curriculum focused on African American children grades 5–8
Adult Identity Mentoring (Project AIM)	Program to reduce sexual risk behaviors of low-income youth ages 11–14
All4You!	Program to reduce unprotected sex among adolescents ages 14–18
Assisting in Rehabilitating Kids (ARK)	Program to increase abstinence and safer sex practices, delivered in small group setting
Be Proud! Be Responsible!	Program to encourage behavior modification and build knowledge about safe sex
Be Proud! Be Responsible! Be Protective!	Program to reduce unprotected sex among pregnant and parenting teens
Becoming a Responsible Team (BART)	HIV curriculum for African American adolescents
Children's Aid Society (CAS), Carrera Programs	Holistic approach to empower youth to make decisions for a productive future; aimed at 11- to 12-year-olds
¡Cuídate!	Program to teach Latino youth ages 13–18 skills for making better decisions and negotiating safer sex practices
Draw the Line/Respect the Line	Classroom-based program for grades 6, 7, and 8 to teach skills to prevent HIV/STIs/pregnancy
FOCUS	Curriculum-based program to educate youth on responsible behavior and relationships
Horizons	Program for African American adolescent females to improve knowledge and skills related to practicing safe sex
It's Your Game: Keep It Real	Classroom and computer-based program for grades 7 and 8 to address sex-related knowledge, skills, and attitudes
Making a Difference!	Program focused on sex education and responsible behavior
Making Proud Choices!	Program focused on safe-sex–related knowledge, attitudes, beliefs, and skills
Promoting Health among Teens! Abstinence-Only Intervention (formerly known as Promoting Health among Teens!)	Program focused on negotiation skills, behavior, and attitudes related to safe sex and presentation of correct information about STIs and pregnancy

Program	Brief description
Promoting Health among Teens! Comprehensive Abstinence and Safer Sex Intervention (formerly known as Comprehensive Abstinence and Safer Sex Intervention!)	Abstinence and safe-sex intervention to provide information about safe sex and pregnancy prevention
Raising Healthy Children (formerly known as the Seattle Social Development Project)	Youth development program in a school-based setting to help adolescents reduce sex-related risk factors
Reducing the Risk	Program to develop attitudes and skills that help prevent pregnancy and HIV/STIs
Rikers Health Advocacy Program (RHAP)	Program to teach problem-solving skills to prevent HIV/AIDS among high-risk youth
Safer Sex	Clinic-based individual intervention to reduce incidence of STIs
Sisters Informing, Healing, Living, and Empowering (SiHLE)	Peer-led, group-level social skills training for African American youth at high risk for HIV
Sexual Health and Adolescent Risk Prevention (SHARP) (formerly known as HIV Risk Reduction Among Detained Adolescents)	Single-session, group-based intervention to reduce sexual risk behaviors for adolescents in juvenile detention
Sisters Saving Sisters	Program for Latina and African American female adolescents to reduce unsafe sex practices
Teen Health Project	Community-level intervention to help teens develop skills to maintain their avoidance of HIV risk behavior
Teen Outreach Program	Youth development program focused on healthy behaviors, life skills, and sense of purpose
Teens and Adults Learning to Communicate (Project TALC)	Program to teach coping skills to parents living with HIV and their adolescent children
What Could You Do?	Interactive DVD with four vignettes on knowledge related to reproductive health and STIs

Source: Department of Health and Human Services, Office of Adolescent Health, "Evidence-Based Programs (31 Programs)" (www.hhs.gov/ash/oah/oah-initiatives/teen_pregnancy/db/programs.html).

a. HHS originally identified 28 programs as evidence based. The review was ongoing, and since the original designation, three more programs have been added to the list of tier 1 evidence-based program models: Heritage Keepers Abstinence Education (a classroom-based curriculum that teaches the benefits of abstinence); Safer Choices (a multi-component STI/HIV and pregnancy prevention program for high school youth); and Respeto/Proteger (a six-session HIV prevention program for young Latino parents with children).

OAH was responsible for writing the FOA. The office was created just as work on the FOA began, so Evelyn Kappeler, the career civil servant in charge of the new office, had mostly new staffers, although most of them had experience in other agencies. As work proceeded, there were many meetings, mostly by conference call, with the staffers at ACF and OPRE who were working on the evidence review as well as with staffers, including political appointees, at the White House and OMB. After the FOA was drafted, it was reviewed by the grants management staff and the general counsel in the Office of the Assistant Secretary for Health, where Kappeler's new OAH was located. Final approval for the FOA was given by OMB.[64] Based on our interviews, writing the FOA was a routine process, with individuals, both career staffers and political appointees, across several HHS agencies working together and in consultation with the White House and OMB.

The legislation that created the TPP program required the funds to be awarded on a competitive basis, but there were a host of additional issues that had to be resolved during the writing of the FOA. In the end, OAH decided that the grants would be for five years, with the first six months to one year used for planning and piloting the projects. The legislation authorizing TPP had required two tiers of funding, tier 1 for replication of programs that already had been well evaluated and tier 2 for adaptations of programs with some evidence of success. Applicants for tier 1 grants would be required to use one of the 31 (28 the first year) evidence-based model programs identified by the evidence review. However, in order to allow for development and testing of new models and new practices, tier 2 programs were not required to use one of the 31 programs, but they did have to "replicate, refine, and test additional model and innovative strategies for preventing teenage pregnancy." The legislation allotted $75 million for tier 1 programs, $25 million for tier 2 programs, and $10 million for program support and technical assistance.

Another important decision was that rather than give out grants under which recipient organizations would be relatively independent operators, HHS decided to use cooperative agreements, which would give the department much more control over the programs and implied a much more hands-on approach by HHS. Our interviews with HHS officials involved in the initiative indicated that the department wanted to carefully monitor and provide assistance as needed to ensure high-quality evaluations of every project.

Finally, the announcement explained that four levels of funding would be available, depending on the scope of the program being proposed. The funding ranges were as follows:

—Range A: $400,000 to $600,000
—Range B: $600,000 to $1 million
—Range C: $1 million to $1.5 million
—Range D: $1.5 million to $4 million.

The FOA stipulated that only projects implemented in multiple sites would be eligible for funding in ranges C and D and that HHS would work with grantees that won grants of this size to develop an independent, high-quality evaluation of their program. Applicants for range A and range B grants were not required to submit an individual evaluation plan but, as explained below, were part of other teen pregnancy evaluations that the department was conducting.

Awarding Grant Funds

The process of distributing federal dollars by the executive agencies is constrained by many requirements. Perhaps the most important is that the process must be fair and transparent. In addition, the process cannot violate the legislation that authorized the administration to allocate the funds in a certain way. Because of these and other restrictions, over the years federal agencies have developed procedures for selecting panels of reviewers who almost always make a sincere and competent effort to approve only applicants that most closely meet the requirements that the agency has established and that seem most likely to achieve a program's goals.

The FOA was released on April 1, 2010.[65] Applicants were required to submit a letter of intent by May 3 stating that they planned to apply for funding. The application itself was due on June 1. HHS received approximately 1,100 applications, which were reviewed in a process overseen by HHS working with LCG, a grants management firm.[66] The reviewers were trained by the contractor, although HHS developed the curriculum and material used in the training. Reviewers were assigned to one of 24 panels, each including ten reviewers. Reviewers scored all the applications assigned to their panel using a standard form developed by HHS. Points were awarded to each proposal in the five following categories:

—project approach and work plan (35 points)
—organizational capacity and experience (25 points)
—project management and staffing (15 points)
—evaluation plan and performance measurement (15 points)
—budget (10 points).

Reviewers on each panel discussed their scores during conference calls and then submitted their final forms to the contractor, where the results were tallied and submitted to HHS.

Final decisions on funding were made by the assistant secretary for health in consultation with OAH, which would have responsibility for administering the TPP program. In making the decisions, the assistant secretary considered, in addition to the quality of the proposal as scored by the reviewers, the national geographic distribution of the programs, the rural or urban location of the programs, and other factors. The awards for the TPP funds, along with the awards for the PREP funds, were announced in an HHS press release issued on September 30, 2010.[67] Wisely, OAH closely coordinated the TPP and PREP Innovative Strategies programs. The tier 2 programs in TPP used the same funding announcement as PREP, and the evaluation plans for the two programs were closely coordinated, along with the broader PREP formula component (explained in more detail below).[68] A total of 75 awards were made under tier 1 of TPP to replicate evidence-based programs, while 19 awards were made under tier 2 to test innovative programs. OAH also contributed $9.8 million from tier 2 funds to a joint initiative with the Centers for Disease Control to support several community-wide teen pregnancy prevention programs.[69] To provide more specific information about the types of TPP projects that received funding, table 3-4 presents an overview of three of the tier 1 and three of the tier 2 model programs.

Developing an Evaluation Plan

Given the administration's affinity for rigorous evidence, it is hardly surprising that HHS would develop an elaborate plan for conducting high-quality evaluations of its teen pregnancy programs.[70] The evaluation plan involved both the TPP (including the community-based teen pregnancy reduction programs led by the Centers for Disease Control and Prevention) and PREP. Three tier 1 TPP programs are being evaluated at nine different implementation sites—three sites for each of three model programs (the three programs are summarized in table 3-5). These three programs qualified for tier 1 funding because they had previously been shown to produce significant impacts by a rigorous evaluation. Thus, all of these evaluations are replications. Results from the evaluation, which is using a random assignment design, will be available beginning in 2015. Abt Associates, a research and evaluation company, was hired by HHS to work with the nine sites to conduct the evaluation.

The second set of evaluations, called Evaluation of Adolescent Pregnancy Prevention Approaches, involves three tier 2 programs from TPP and three programs from PREP Innovative Strategies as well as one innovative program— which Mathematica was evaluating for HHS before the TPP and the PREP programs were enacted by Congress—that was not federally funded. HHS decided to focus the Mathematica contract on the six TPP and PREP sites. Impact evaluations for each site will be available beginning in late 2014 through 2016.

In addition to the 2 sets of evaluations reviewed above, 16 of the largest TPP tier 1 grantees and all TPP tier 2 and PREP grantees that were not involved in the Evaluation of Adolescent Pregnancy Prevention Approaches had to conduct their own evaluation. The majority of those evaluations involve random assignment. The program operators that were awarded TPP grants had to outline the

Table 3-4. *Overview of Three Tier 1 and Three Tier 2 Teen Pregnancy Prevention Grantees*

Grantee	Award amount	Program model	Number of youths served	Location
Tier 1				
Youth Services of Tulsa	$431,543	Sexual Health and Adolescent Risk Prevention (SHARP)	1,400 a year	Tulsa
Southern Nevada Health District	$997,257	¡Cuídate!	1,200 a year	Las Vegas
Youth Catalytics	$600,000	Teen Outreach Program	200–500 a year	Charlotte, Vermont
Tier 2				
State of Alaska Division of Public Health	$599,985	Adaptation of tier 1 program Promoting Health among Teens	225 a year	Anchorage
Tulane University	$547,239	Comprehensive web-based adaptation of tier 1 program Sisters Informing, Healing, Living, and Empowering (SiHLE)	300 a year	New Orleans
University of Louisville Research Foundation	$963,330	Adaptation of Reducing the Risk (tier 1) and Love Notes	360 a year	Louisville

Source: Department of Health and Human Services, Office of Adolescent Health, "Evidence-Based Programs" (www.hhs.gov/ash/oah/oah-initiatives/teen_pregnancy/resources/db/index.html).

evaluation that they would conduct as part of the grant application process. HHS hired Mathematica to provide technical assistance to the program sites on developing their evaluation methodology and implementing their program. Results from these evaluations will be available beginning in 2015.

The fourth set of evaluations consists of evaluations of ten community-wide teen pregnancy prevention efforts that employ a quasi-experimental design. Changes in trends in teen birth rates in each of the ten intervention communities will be compared with changes in trends in matched control communities. The fifth set of evaluations focuses on the PREP state and competitive grant programs. This set, which entails random assignment evaluation of four

Table 3-5. *Brief Description of Three Evidence-Based Model Programs Being Evaluated*

Safer Sex	• Clinic-based intervention to reduce the incidence of STIs and improve condom use among females • Discussion of the consequences of unprotected sex following a seven-minute video on HIV • Customized to reflect interests and risk level of participants • Fewer than ten sessions total
¡Cuídate!	• Name means "Take care of yourself" in English • Culturally based program designed to reduce HIV sexual risk among Latino youth, ages 13 to 18 • Helps youth develop the knowledge, attitudes, and skills needed to reduce their risk for HIV • Includes small-group activities and role playing to practice negotiating abstinence and condom use • Six one-hour sessions over two or more days
Reducing the Risk	• Focuses on development of attitudes and skills to prevent pregnancy and transmission of STIs • Covers risk assessment skills, communication, decisionmaking, planning, refusal strategies, and delay tactics • Includes significant focus on abstinence: "Abstinence is presented as the best, safest and most common choice for high school students, but Reducing the Risk also recognizes that some students are sexually active" • Sixteen class sessions on the various topics

Sources: Safer Sex: John B. Jemmott III, Loretta Sweet Jemmott, and Geoffrey Fong, "Abstinence and Safer Sex HIV Risk-Reduction Interventions for African-American Adolescents: A Randomized Control Trial," *Journal of American Medical Association*, vol. 279 (1998), pp. 1529–36; ¡Cuídate!: Antonia Villarruel, John B. Jemmott III, and Loretta Sweet Jemmott, "A Randomized Controlled Trial Testing an HIV Prevention Intervention for Latino Youth," *Archives of Pediatric and Adolescent Medicine*, vol. 160 (2006), pp. 772–77; Reducing the Risk: Douglas Kirby and others, "Reducing the Risk: A New Curriculum to Prevent Sexual Risk-Taking," *Family Planning Perspectives*, vol. 23, no. 6 (1991), pp. 253–63.

PREP-funded programs, also provides a descriptive study of the design and implementation of PREP state grant programs. This effort also is carried out by Mathematica on behalf of HHS. Impact evaluation findings for these sites will be available beginning in 2016.

Taken together, these five sets of evaluations present a broad and deep measure of the effects of the various types of teen pregnancy prevention programs being operated by HHS. There has never been an interlocking set of evaluations of teen pregnancy programs like this one. It is especially impressive that most of the evaluations involve RCTs.

Conclusion: What Are We Learning?

The story of the Obama evidence-based initiative on reducing teen pregnancy provides valuable lessons for those who believe that expanding evidence-based policy is a useful strategy for improving the effectiveness of the nation's social programs. The first lesson, which applies to all of the Obama evidence-based initiatives, is that the legislative process gives no special dispensation to legislation to establish and fund programs simply because they are evidence based. The federal legislative process is a world unto itself, controlled by its own rules. Almost equally important, the social issue addressed by any particular evidence-based initiative is almost certain to have a legislative history that will have an impact on the legislative process. The ongoing conflict between Republicans and Democrats over the content of sex education programs, especially over how much to emphasize abstinence and how much to emphasize contraception, had an impact on the Obama legislation, although in the end the president's initiative emerged more or less unscathed. The adoption of the Hatch amendment to continue the Title V abstinence-only program gave Republicans a major part of what they wanted. On the other hand, Democrats did end the CBAE program, which had been established by Republicans in the appropriations process in 2000.[71] Both the administration and Finance Committee Chairman Baucus, despite the history of bad blood between Republicans supporting abstinence-only programs and Democrats supporting comprehensive programs, were willing to bury the hatchet by allowing the Title V program to continue without further resistance after the vote on the Hatch amendment in the Finance Committee. In addition, President Obama and Baucus allowed abstinence-only programs to qualify for funding by their respective pregnancy prevention programs (TPP and PREP) if they met the evidence standards required by the statues and spelled out in funding announcements. Indeed, the text of the PREP legislation specifically required that programs teach adolescents about both abstinence and birth control.

Another lesson about the legislative process that could influence future evidence-based initiatives is that legislation with a moderate price tag, such as the TPP, often can slip through the congressional gauntlet almost unnoticed if it is part of a bigger bill. Despite the long-standing debate over what types of teen pregnancy prevention programs should receive federal funding, because the TPP program was tucked away in a major appropriations bill, which contained hundreds or even thousands of provisions, it passed the House and the Senate without serious floor debate. Another major factor in TPP's favor was that Democrats on the Hill, who controlled both houses of Congress at the time, wanted to go along with their new president. If the president wants evidence, some seemed to reason, let him have it. Other Democrats, such as chairmen Obey and Waxman in the House and chairmen Harkin and Baucus in the Senate, had a history of supporting evidence-based programs and may have supported TPP (and PREP as well) in part because they advocated the idea of evidence-based policy. But appealing to evidence as a means of supporting social programs is not always effective. When Republicans took over the House in the off-term elections of 2010, they tried to kill TPP on more than one occasion, in large part because many conservatives oppose anything that is not abstinence only and because Republicans were opposed to most Obama initiatives, regardless of the merits of evidence-based programs. Fortunately, TPP was rescued from oblivion by the Senate.[72] Even initially successful presidential initiatives can be vulnerable when the political winds change.

The teen pregnancy debate brings us back to President Obama's inaugural address, in which he said that his administration would support programs that work and reform or end programs that do not. The federal government does, nonetheless, have a reputation for continuing popular programs no matter what the evidence shows, in part because program supporters inside and outside Congress lobby to continue the programs. Even so, as noted above, the administration and Democrats in Congress were able to kill the CBAE program, which was established and funded by appropriations bills, saving about $100 million a year. On the other hand, the administration failed to kill the $50 million Title V abstinence-only program, which was rescued by the politics that prevailed in the Senate Finance Committee, including support from two moderate Democrats who were expecting difficult reelection campaigns. Regardless, the TPP initiative showed that it was possible to end a program that had been shown by rigorous evidence to be ineffective and use the money saved to support new model programs supported by rigorous evidence. This is certainly a promising strategy for improving the effectiveness of the nation's social policy.

Of course, many Republicans would not agree that the evidence shows that abstinence-only programs fail to reduce teen pregnancy or births.[73] Comprehensive programs that include both abstinence education and education on birth control seem to be ascendant, showing that the abstinence-only movement has made real progress in influencing the content of the programs that now predominate. But the survival of the Title V abstinence-only program, despite its unpopularity among Democrats in Congress (who controlled both houses of Congress and the presidency during the debate over TPP) and most members of the liberal advocacy community in Washington, shows that ending programs is often more difficult than enacting them in the first place. The U.S. political system makes it very difficult both to cut ineffective programs and to expand effective programs—the two goals of the Obama evidence-based movement.

Another issue with broad implications is highlighted by the four program outcomes that HHS selected to measure impacts on teen pregnancy. As discussed, to be eligible for funding, a teen pregnancy prevention program had to produce a significant impact on contraceptive use, sexual activity, STIs, or pregnancy rates. However, the government's major goal is to reduce teen pregnancy, although reducing STIs also is an important goal because of their consequences for both public health and the long-term health of sexually active teens. Even so, the process developed by HHS to identify evidence-based programs gave the honorific title "evidence-based" to many programs that did not have evidence of impact on either pregnancy or STI rates, allowing them to qualify for funding if they showed only impacts on contraception or sexual activity. In fact, 13 of the 31 evidence-based programs had impacts on contraceptive use, and 21 had impacts on some aspect of sexual activity among teens. But only 5 reduced STIs, and only 5 reduced pregnancy rates.[74]

We are not criticizing HHS for deciding to fund programs that were judged to be successful on the basis of increasing contraceptive use or reducing sexual activity. After all, both results might be expected to have some impact on pregnancy and STI rates in the long run. As Jim Shelton, a senior political appointee in the Department of Education, pointed out to us regarding the Investing in Innovation (i3) initiative, if you set the evidence bar too high, you are not going to get many proposals. In the case at hand, there simply are not many programs that even measure teen pregnancy or STI rates.[75] In the long run, however, these programs will not achieve their most important goals unless they show that they can reduce pregnancy rates or STIs, because that is what the public is paying for and that is where the long-term payoffs will be.

Perhaps the most important outcome of the teen pregnancy initiative at this point is that the federal government has given its evidence-based imprimatur to 31 teen pregnancy prevention programs. Not only is federal funding now being directed primarily to these effective model programs, but it also is being used to expand and strengthen the evidence base. A number of proven models are being subjected to additional evaluation in new settings, and promising and innovative programs or adaptations of proven models are being evaluated—mostly by RCTs—to determine whether they produce impacts. Of the tier 1 grantees, 14 are evaluating their programs in RCTs, and 15 of the 18 tier 2 grantees are having their programs evaluated by RCTs.[76] Perhaps a little optimism is in order: the elaborate and innovative approach taken by the Obama administration may yield better program models for reducing teen pregnancy, STIs, and associated risk behaviors and simultaneously benefit the thousands of teens now participating in the programs. Even more to the point, the rigorous evaluations of these programs now taking place will provide Congress and the public with highly reliable information about whether the programs are in fact producing their intended outcomes.

4   The Investing in Innovation Initiative

Democrats traditionally have been joined at the hip with unions. But from early in his Senate career, Barack Obama dropped hints that he might not go along with the historical Democrat-union coalition on education, despite the fact that picking a fight with a trusted and rich ally is one of the most difficult—and potentially dangerous—things that a politician can do. As it turned out, the degree to which Obama was willing to oppose union views on public education showed both his willingness to take risks to achieve his goals for K–12 education and the extent to which the Democratic Party had been infiltrated by education reformers—some with lots of money to spend—who did not give unions an inch.[1]

Consider legislation that Obama wrote in 2006, early in his brief Senate career, to create what he called "innovation districts." The legislation would have provided cash rewards to states that paid teachers for improving student learning, built their reform programs on evidence of success, and stopped funding for programs that did not work.[2] Reviewing that legislation, union officials might well have been concerned about this new guy's plan to "reward" teachers for student learning. True, the legislation called for local education agencies to work with unions and other stakeholders, but the goal was to "establish a metric to determine the effectiveness of teachers, administrators, and schools." Even worse from the union perspective, that metric could "be used as the basis for systems of pay, incentives, and placement." Adopting a pay-for-performance policy for teachers and administrators is a move guaranteed to outrage teacher unions. To put it another way: pay for performance is not a favorite policy of organizations like teacher unions, which have to represent the interests of many mediocre and poor performers.

Developing the Legislative Proposal for Investing in Innovation

But Obama was just getting warmed up. Even before his inauguration, he had a team working on what grew into one of the biggest education initiatives in federal history. During that period, the president-elect met in the transition office on 6th Street, ten blocks from the White House, with Jon Schnur, one of his top advisers on education policy during both his time as a senator and the presidential transition. Also present at the meeting were future secretary of education Arne Duncan, future White House chief of staff Rahm Emanuel, future White House domestic policy chief Melody Barnes, and a future senior deputy assistant to the president, Heather Higginbottom. Their purpose was to discuss the new administration's education agenda. With the country mired in the depths of the worst economic crisis since the Great Depression, the administration, along with virtually all Capitol Hill Democrats—now in the third year of their majority in both the House and Senate—planned to follow the Keynesian course and enact a huge spending bill. The American Recovery and Reinvestment Act (ARRA) was designed to promote economic recovery by injecting what eventually amounted to more than $800 billion in federal funds into the economy. But that was not its only purpose. Emanuel set the tone for the bill with his famous declaration "You never want a serious crisis to go to waste"[3]—meaning that Congress should use the stimulus bill to enact long-standing items on the political agenda, such as education reform, health reform, reform of federal regulations, and so forth.[4]

Which brings us back to the president's meeting in the transition office. According to Schnur, Obama said that he wanted his education strategy to be driven by three goals: to develop policies and practices that would produce better educational outcomes for children, especially poor children; to feature policies and practices that had the potential to attract support from members of Congress and others; and to develop and defend the administration's proposals in a way that avoided "poking anyone in the eye."[5] Obama's principles set the tone for the legislation that Duncan, Schnur, and others at the Department of Education and the Office of Management and Budget (OMB) were to develop, although Obama's lieutenants may have poked an eye or two along the way.

The president and his advisers knew that they had to move fast to get their education provisions in the ARRA because the administration and the Democratic leadership on Capitol Hill intended to push the bill through Congress at the speed of light. In the end, after a great deal of negotiation within the administration itself, the decision was made to pursue two major innovative education initiatives, which became Race to the Top (RTT) and Investing in Innovation (i3). According to Schnur's comments during our interview, which were confirmed in several interviews with congressional staffers, the i3 initiative was to be based on a proposal that Schnur had originally developed with George Miller (D-Calif.), chairman of the House Committee on Education and Labor, and Miller's staff.

Restored to the chairmanship of the House Committee on Education and Labor after Democrats took control of the House in the 2006 elections, the powerful and widely respected Miller was determined to have a substantive bill to reauthorize No Child Left Behind (NCLB), which was on the congressional calendar for the 2007–08 session. To help develop his bill, Miller requested a meeting with Schnur and several of the nation's leading education reformers, including Wendy Kopp of Teach for America, Tim Daly of the New Teacher Project, and Mike Feinberg of KIPP. Schnur talked with several of the invited participants before the day of the breakfast meeting to work out a proposal that they could offer during the discussion with Miller. The essence of the proposal was to establish a "Grow What Works Fund," which the federal government would use to support education and nonprofit agencies that could show, through good data, that they were conducting a program that had positive impacts on student performance. Rewarding successful innovation also would give education agencies a financial incentive to develop successful programs. This proposal was a cousin of the legislation introduced in 2006 by freshman Senator Obama;[6] the two were linked through Schnur, who was an adviser to both Obama and Miller. The breakfast meeting, which also included Miller's chief of staff Alice Johnson Cain (who would play a major role in drafting what would become i3), resulted in Miller's decision to draft a legislative provision along the lines proposed and put it in his NCLB reauthorization bill. Cain was responsible for supervising the provision's drafting.

Miller then worked with Buck McKeon (R-Calif.), the senior Republican on the committee, to develop a bipartisan bill that contained many of their ideas for reauthorization, including the Grow What Works Fund, now given the official title of "School Support, Recognition of Success, and Bringing Success to Scale" in section 1117 of the Miller-McKeon draft bill.[7] The draft was released to the public on August 28, 2007, and a hearing on the bill was held on September 10, 2007. But that was as far as reauthorization of NCLB got during the 2007–08 Congress. As it turned out, the ideas behind section 1117 had a longer life span than the NCLB reauthorization, primarily because the administration of Barack Obama, who was swept into office with huge fanfare in the presidential election of 2008, was focused on promoting innovation in education and expanding programs and practices that work.

A second important meeting to plan the new president's education initiative was held in the Oval Office on January 29, a little more than a week after Obama's inauguration. Schnur, Emanuel, Duncan, and other presidential advisers, including top political strategist David Axelrod, were present. As the group discussed the education initiatives, Axelrod questioned the political wisdom of tying funding to evidence rather than following the usual practice of using formula grants to make sure that every state got at least some money.[8] Axelrod was referring primarily to the Race to the Top funds, but the same point applied to i3.[9] Funding only programs that showed evidence of success or promising, innovative programs had been a major focus of the Miller/Schnur initiative since Miller introduced his bill with McKeon in 2007. Now that President Obama was hearing questions in the Oval Office about the political viability of the administration's plan to establish a firm link between funding and evidence that programs work, an important moment had arrived. If the president had agreed to back off the evidence-funding link at the beginning of the administration, i3 might have been a very different initiative, which could in turn have had impacts on the other evidence-based initiatives examined in this book, all of which depended—at least in part—on competitive grants. But the president immediately nixed the criticism. According to Schnur, Obama was very clear that he wanted to pursue RTT and i3 while maintaining a strong link between funding and good evidence that programs produce impacts on student learning. The president told the group that funding based on performance was the central idea of both RTT and i3.

Moving the Action to Capitol Hill

In accord with the president's instructions, action on both RTT and i3 moved to Congress for legislative drafting along the lines proposed by the president. The administration was intent on completing the drafting in time to include both RTT and i3 in the stimulus bill because doing so would greatly increase the chances that both provisions would be passed by Congress. After all, generous funding would be available (the major goal of the ARRA was to spend money to prime the economy) and the provisions would be engulfed by the hundreds of other provisions in the massive ARRA. In addition, Democrats regarded the ARRA as must-pass legislation, and they could pass it in the House and the Senate without any Republican votes.

Major action on the stimulus legislation was controlled by the House and the Senate Appropriations Committees. Pushed by the economic crisis, Congress and the president were moving so fast that Congress did not have time to fool around with traditional, time-consuming congressional procedures, often referred to as "regular order." Like other Democratic leaders, David Obey (D-Wis.), chairman of the House Appropriations Committee, wanted to enact the ARRA as speedily as possible to get the money out to state and local governments where it would do the most good and perhaps contribute to an economic revival.

The entire text of the i3 provision in ARRA was less than one page.[10] According to our interview with Schnur, which was consistent with interviews with several congressional staffers, drafting the final language was a collaborative process.[11] A senior Obey staffer wrote an initial draft and passed it around for discussion and comment. There were conversations with officials at the Department of Education as well as with Senator Ted Kennedy's staff (Kennedy's Health, Education, Labor, and Pensions Committee would have jurisdiction over the RTT and i3 provisions in the Senate) and with Alice Johnson Cain of Chairman Miller's staff, who, like Schnur, was a principal architect of the earlier iteration of i3 (the Recognition of Success and Bringing Success to Scale grants in the NCLB discussion draft). Miller, who had previously endorsed the innovation fund concept after working with Schnur on the NCLB discussion draft, strongly supported the i3 provision. Both Miller and Rahm Emanuel, the president's chief of staff, urged Obey to accept the RTT and i3 provisions and their respective $4.35 billion and $650 million price tags.[12] Once Obey agreed, the bill sped through the appropriations process in the House. Several staffers—Obey's chief of staff Cheryl Smith in particular—told us that everything was so hectic in trying to enact the stimulus legislation that i3 was hardly noticed.

Under the heading "Innovation Fund" in Section 14007 of the stimulus bill, the i3 provision specified the types of education entities that could apply for funds, stipulated that they had to have a record of reducing the achievement gap between students from different backgrounds, and required eligible organizations to partner with a nonprofit organization (including foundations). Another provision clarified that the purpose of the fund was to allow local education authorities (LEAs) with evidence of closing achievement gaps to "expand their work and serve as models for best practices" and "to identify and document best practices that can be shared, and taken to scale based on demonstrated success."[13] That is broad language, and it gave the administration a great deal of flexibility in using the i3 funds, especially in establishing strong evidence standards—something the legislative language does not do. The administration welcomed the opportunity to define the evidence standards later, thereby avoiding worries about exactly how to explain the term "evidence-based" in the legislative text. Besides, it simply was not clear in January 2009, at the very beginning of the Obama administration, that even the most experienced people at OMB knew exactly what language on evidence they wanted to use. Far better to get general language in the statute, figure out the exact language later, and then put the final language in the announcement of availability of i3 funds. In the end, the language declared that most applicants had to show that they would implement programs that had been shown by rigorous evidence to produce positive impacts on teacher, administrator, or student performance.

As long as the administration did not violate the statute, it could use the flexibility in the statutory language to require applicants to use evidence-based interventions. In fact, we came to believe that a strength of the evidence-based initiatives was that the administration created teams of senior officials, competent program specialists in the various federal agencies responsible for implementing the initiatives, and other officials throughout the administration—especially at OMB—to create definitions of "evidence-based" that are solid, durable, and perhaps a model for future initiatives. As we will see, developing the i3 definition of "evidence-based" turned out to be no exception.

It is doubtful that anyone, even the research-savvy senior staffers at OMB, could have created a useful and effective definition in time to include it in the January 2009 ARRA legislation. At the very least, the definition of evidence for i3 had to be vetted with senior people at OMB and the Department of Education to ensure that everyone accepted it. Our interviews with Jim Shelton—a senior Department of Education official put in charge of the i3 initiative by Secretary Duncan—and with several other officials showed that working out the definition of evidence-based and other details of the i3 initiative involved long hours and a great deal of discussion both within the department and OMB and between them.[14]

The ARRA was highly contentious in both the House and the Senate, although in the context of such a huge bill, the i3 provision and even the RTT provision did not generate a great deal of discussion or conflict. The negotiations among Democrats drafting the RTT legislation were more important and time consuming than discussions over i3. In fact, some of the staffers that we interviewed told us that attention to i3 was swamped by the focus on RTT. After all, the RTT provision cost $4.35 billion while the i3 provision cost $650 million. Because no one paid much attention to a mere $650 million provision in the context of the $800 billion–plus ARRA and the $4 billion–plus RTT, the administration was able to secure the money for i3 using legislative text that gave it plenty of room to maneuver.

The House enacted the ARRA almost exactly as the Democratic members and their staffers had written it. Given the substantial differences in rules between the House and the Senate, if the majority party in the House can hold the votes of all of its members, victory is ensured because, unlike in the Senate, the minority party does not have the option of filibustering or using other effective procedural tactics to defeat legislation. With very rare exceptions, such as overriding a presidential veto, which requires a two-thirds vote, the majority wins in the House. The House vote, taken on January 28, 2009, was 244-188, with no Republicans supporting the bill.[15] To the extent that substance was an issue, Republicans did not like all the spending in the ARRA. They would have preferred to devote more of the resources in the bill to tax cuts, a goal that they would follow in the Senate with some success.

The path that the ARRA took in the Senate was quite different from the relatively smooth path that it enjoyed in the House. Republicans forced Democrats to adopt some of their amendments, thereby increasing the number and magnitude of tax cuts in the bill. Despite their success in modifying the bill, all but three Republicans (Olympia Snowe and Susan Collins of Maine and Arlen Specter of Pennsylvania, who would soon switch to the Democratic Party) voted against the ARRA, which passed the Senate on February 10 by a vote of 61-37. After a Conference Committee meeting in which the Democrats reached a compromise between the House and Senate bills, the ARRA passed both houses of Congress, essentially along party lines, and was signed into law by President Obama on February 17, 2009, less than a month after his inauguration. The i3 initiative and RTT had cleared their first hurdle.

Transforming the Legislation

As discussed, the text that established i3 as part of the ARRA was general enough to give the administration plenty of room to fashion a program to its liking. With the benefit of hindsight, it is now clear that the administration made full use of that flexibility in at least five distinct ways: ensuring that most of the money was used to fund projects that conducted programs supported by rigorous evidence; working in concert with career officials and political appointees in the Department of Education to fashion the evidence requirements and write a funding announcement; finding a way to use some of the money to support innovative programs; ensuring transparency in allocating funds; and creating a host of administrative procedures that the Department of Education could use to ensure that funds went to organizations that had the capacity to effectively implement evidence-based or innovative programs.

Using the Flexibility of i3

First, administration officials working on the initiative were clear from the beginning that their goal was to fund organizations that were using proven or promising, innovative programs to improve student achievement; close achievement gaps between students from poor and more affluent families as well as gaps between racial and ethnic groups; increase graduation rates; and increase postsecondary enrollment and graduation rates. In addition, the administration wanted to fund organizations that had the capacity to help develop a database of educational practices and programs that show evidence of significant positive impacts.[16]

Second, although the administration may not have recognized it at the time, i3 would become a centerpiece and model of its evidence-based initiatives, influencing several of the others. OMB played its usual leadership role, but senior officials at the Department of Education—especially Secretary Duncan, Deputy

Secretary Anthony Miller, and Assistant Deputy Secretary for Innovation and Improvement Jim Shelton[17]—were anxious to work with OMB and the White House to make i3 a hallmark of administration policy and of President Obama's and Secretary Duncan's achievements in education policy. In many administrations, serious and often disruptive tensions exist between leaders in the White House and administrators in the executive agencies. But on most of the Obama evidence-based initiatives, the White House, OMB, and the executive agencies worked well together. On the i3 initiative in particular, senior officials at the Department of Education, the Institute of Education Sciences (IES), OMB, and the White House managed to compromise with each other and eventually reach agreement on all the important issues. Especially surprising was the fact that, as shown consistently by our interviews of officials at the Department of Education, OMB, and the White House, career officials and political appointees worked closely together, seemingly without serious tension.

Third, the administration used i3 to firmly establish the importance of achieving balance between evidence and innovation by creating tiers of funding that reserved most of the money for implementing programs that already had strong evidence of success and less but some money for programs that had more modest evidence of success or that were innovative and promising but had not yet been well tested. This feature of i3 was necessary for both conceptual and political reasons. The administration, especially Robert Gordon, a senior official at OMB who was more or less the quarterback of the administration's team for planning and conducting all six of the evidence-based initiatives, quickly understood that their evidence-based initiatives could not focus only on programs supported by strong evidence. There were just too many people in the administration—not least in the Department of Education—and on Capitol Hill who believed that innovation was vital. True, the administration's long-term goal was to dramatically increase the fraction of federal grant dollars spent on programs and practices supported by strong evidence, but unless resources were also devoted to developing and testing new practices and programs, where would the innovation come from? The tiers-of-evidence approach—by using most of the available funding to scale up effective practices and programs but leaving ample resources for innovative and promising programs—was a workable solution to this dilemma.

Fourth, the i3 initiative was notable for transparency. Especially because the competitive nature of the grants would cut out many local education authorities, the administration wanted to ensure that the process of deciding who would win the funds was fair and transparent. Providing large sums of money to LEAs and nonprofits on a competitive basis rather than by formula was controversial. Most administrations would rather provide funds to states on a formula basis, often in proportion to the number of people (or poor people) that live in each state. This approach ensures that every state gets some money. In contrast, when funds are awarded on the basis of the quality of proposals, some LEAs will submit proposals that are mediocre or worse and receive no funds. Because often the poorest states and LEAs submit the lowest-quality proposals, it follows that competition in grant funds can easily increase the geographic inequity in federal funding. Administration officials, awarding funds through a process that was sure to be controversial, therefore wanted complete transparency regarding why and how decisions were made. In addition, the administration wanted to build a precedent for using evidence both to allocate funds to successful programs and, through high-quality evaluations, to determine on a routine basis whether funded programs were producing their intended outcomes. Those goals would have been undermined if the process of picking the winners had been perceived as biased.

Fifth, as part of its approach to ensuring that money was given to organizations that were capable of using it to produce impacts on important educational outcomes, the administration developed a host of routine administrative processes and procedures that the agencies could use again and again to award funds to such organizations, which would be expected to improve their performance by analyzing continuously collected evidence on student outcomes. An especially noteworthy part of the administrative procedures is the role that the Institute of Education Sciences played in rating the evidence presented by an applicant to support its proposal.

Defining "Evidence-Based"

Deciding what it means for a program to be evidence-based was a major issue in developing all six of the administration's evidence-based initiatives. Regardless of one's views on how to define the term, the administration gets quality points for wrestling with this issue, for being guided in large part by the well-developed definitions of high-quality evidence used by the IES, and for adopting a workable definition that is a good compromise between insisting on rigor and allowing room for innovation. A little reflection reveals the problems that the administration had to solve if it hoped to build its evidence-based initiatives on a solid foundation. Consider these questions:

—Is one positive evaluation of a program enough to put it in the top tier of evidence, thus making it eligible for the highest amount of funding?

—Should program evaluations conducted at multiple sites involving many subjects from different ethnic and socioeconomic backgrounds receive the same weight as smaller evaluations conducted at one site with a small and homogeneous sample?

—What should be done if some evaluations show that a given program produces significant impacts while other evaluations of the same program find no impacts or even negative impacts?

—Should a well-designed study with high levels of attrition be considered equivalent to a similar study with low attrition? If not, what level of attrition is acceptable?

The administration's task was to wade into these and other thorny questions to provide definitive answers. Social scientists can argue incessantly about questions like these, which they face on a routine basis, without developing a consensus. But the administration did not have that luxury because, in the end, the executive agencies were going to award money based in large part on whether applicants had gold standard evidence, good but not gold standard evidence, or only suggestive evidence. If you plan to give away public money on the basis of different levels of evidence, you must define those levels precisely and present a compelling rationale for adopting a particular definition.

To begin the process of making i3 into an evidence-based program, in early summer 2009 OMB called a meeting that included many of the administration officials who would create and implement i3. Robert Gordon of OMB was there, playing his usual role as the administration's quarterback in working with the agencies, along with Kathy Stack, a senior career official at OMB who also played an important role in several of the other initiatives, and Allison Cole, a career official at OMB with extensive knowledge of education programs. Joining them were Jim Shelton and others from the Department of Education. Shelton and Gordon became the most important administration officials involved in the effort to give shape to i3. Our understanding of the administration's decisions on i3 are based on interviews with nine administration officials who worked directly on the initiative, but especially Gordon, Shelton, and Cole.[18]

An important theme that received extensive attention during this initial meeting was the tiers concept. Shelton proposed that the quality and strength of evidence should play a role in determining whether a given educational program or practice would be funded and, if funded, the amount of money that the program would receive. At this point in the discussion, Cole suggested that perhaps the tiers of grants could be tied to standards for measuring the rigor of research and evidence developed by the Institute of Education Sciences for its What Works Clearinghouse. Cole had served a stint at IES, arguably the unit of the federal government with the greatest commitment to generating rigorous evidence and the best procedures for doing so.[19] The participants in the meeting—especially Shelton, who had already been thinking about how to incorporate evidence into the selection criteria for the grants—decided that the IES standards provided a good template for the i3 tiers.

After the meeting, Cole was tasked with drafting the evidence standards based on the definitions used by the IES What Works Clearinghouse. During our interview with her, she recalled many meetings with Gordon as they talked through the thorny, complicated, and nuanced issues involved and painstakingly went over the precise language for each of the tiers until both she and Gordon were satisfied with the definitions. As Cole described it, Gordon would articulate the general vision and it would be up to Cole to draft language for the standards; Gordon would then review the draft. Their conversations covered issues such as which outcome measures to select and how to deal with differences across studies in the size of the impact on outcome measures. The goal was to develop standards for three tiers of evidence roughly corresponding to strong evidence, modest evidence, and weak evidence, along with the specific definitions that would allow program applicants and reviewers to understand the differences between the three levels.

As our interview with Jim Shelton showed, some within the administration were conflicted about how strong the evidence standards should be, especially for the top tier (referred to as the "scale-up tier" by the administration), which had the highest level of funding and the strictest evidence requirements. Both Shelton and Gordon were concerned that strong evidence standards would give an advantage in the competition for i3 funding to organizations that had the resources to pay for high-quality evaluations of their programs in the past. But a more important concern for both of them was that there were many questions in education for which rigorous evidence is in short supply. Little is known, for example, about how best to prepare teachers to maintain order in the classroom; few preschool curriculums have been shown to teach math concepts effectively to preschoolers; and few remedial programs have shown that they can teach math and literacy skills successfully to students who enter college or community college with low skills. In fact, as recently as 1999, the National Academies had declared that knowledge from educational research about effective teaching and learning programs was surprisingly thin. "In no other field is the research base so inadequate," the organization wrote in an official report.[20]

Research on educational practices and programs has done some catching up since 1999, due in large part to the creation of IES by legislation enacted in 2002 and aggressively implemented by the Bush administration, in particular by Grover J. "Russ" Whitehurst, the first director of IES.[21] Under Whitehurst's leadership, from 2002 to 2008, IES funded at least 70 studies on a wide range of educational practices that used random assignment designs. As a result, knowledge about educational practices and programs that is based on reliable evidence is now growing. In a recent article about IES, Gina Kolata of the *New York Times* reported that by 2013 the Institute had sponsored 175 RCTs.[22] Even so, given the time that it takes to plan and execute most large-scale random assignment studies, knowledge of effective educational practices and programs is building at a stately pace. If the designers of i3 had insisted on spending all the money on programs that had strong evidence of success from gold standard studies, not many LEAs and nonprofits would have been able to apply for grants and those that could have would have been severely restricted in the choice of educational practices or programs for which they could seek support. The tiers allow programs with decent but not gold standard evidence to qualify for funding through the middle ("validation") tier and innovative programs or practices to qualify based on some evidence or even reasonable hypotheses through the bottom ("development") tier. As it turned out, the overwhelming majority of programs funded under i3 were in the second and third evidence tiers, clearly justifying Sheldon's and Gordon's concern about the scarcity of programs and practices supported by gold standard evidence.

Eventually almost everyone involved in i3 agreed that if the evidence requirements were too high the Department of Education would be at risk of receiving few proposals. Still, because a major goal of i3 was to build the capacity of states and LEAs to conduct RCTs to evaluate their programs, the administration would not back away from strong evidence requirements for at least the top tier of grants. Another reason to insist on high standards for top-tier grants was that i3 was designed to send a strong signal to education agencies that RCTs would be the expected evaluation standard in the future.

THREE TIERS OF EVIDENCE. Shelton, Gordon, and others came to believe that having tiers of evidence would allow organizations that had not been able to evaluate their programs with expensive and time-consuming RCTs to qualify for lower levels of funding through the validation and development tiers. Requirements for the top tier could be met only with studies that supported causal conclusions, such as a well-designed and well-implemented study of a model program conducted at several sites or more than one well-designed and well-implemented study of a model program conducted at a single site.[23] The studies could be RCTs or quasi-experimental designs. The middle tier accepted programs evaluated by random assignment or quasi-experimental designs with minor flaws. The bottom tier required only modest evidence as long as programs were innovative and program operators could show that they had promise by presenting at least a reasonable hypothesis of why the program would produce impacts (table 4-1).

In considering these tiers, it is useful to recall the administration's goal in making evidence of effectiveness a primary determinant of whether grant programs are funded and at what level. The administration believed that the impacts of

Table 4-1. *Evidence Requirement for Three Types of i3 Grants*

Research characteristic	Type of grant		
	Scale-up	*Validation*	*Development*
Strength of research	Strong	Moderate	Preliminary
Internal and external validity	High internal validity and high external validity	(1) High internal validity and moderate external validity; or (2) moderate internal validity and high external validity	Potential efficacy for some participants and settings suggested in theory and practice
Strength of evidence from research	(1) More than one well-designed and well-implemented experimental study or quasi-experimental study; or (2) one large, well-designed and well-implemented randomized controlled trial conducted at multiple sites	(1) One well-designed and well-implemented experimental or quasi-experimental study with a small sample size or other conditions that limit generalizability; (2) one well-designed and well-implemented experimental or quasi-experimental study with lack of equivalence between intervention and comparison groups but no other flaws related to internal validity; or (3) correlational research with strong statistical controls for selection bias	(1) Evidence that the proposed practice, strategy, or program has been attempted previously, albeit on a limited scale, and yielded promising results; and (2) a rationale for the proposed practice, strategy, or program based on research findings or reasonable hypotheses

Source: Based on table 3 in *Federal Register* 75, no. 48 (March 12, 2010), p. 12084.

programs supported by federal dollars could be substantially increased if program operators implemented model programs that had been rigorously evaluated and thereby proven to produce positive impacts. Gordon, Shelton, and other senior officials in the Obama administration believed that more effective programs would reduce the magnitude of the many social problems afflicting the nation and that developing programs supported by rigorous evidence was the way to achieve that goal.

MANDATORY EVALUATION PLAN. To further emphasize the importance of evidence, as in all but one of the Obama evidence-based initiatives,[24] i3 applicants were required to submit an evaluation plan. The "evidence" in "evidence-based" has two distinct meanings for the Obama administration. Not only is the quality of supporting evidence a major criterion for getting programs funded, but once they are funded, the administration also insists on evaluating most programs as they are being implemented to see whether they are having their intended impacts.[25] Therefore, i3 applicants had to include a detailed plan for an independent, third-party evaluation of their program, and the administration encouraged high-quality designs that were at least as rigorous as the level of evidence presented in the grantee's application. In addition, after the initial round of funding, the administration awarded a five-year grant to Abt Associates, a research firm skilled in program evaluation and rigorous design, to help i3 evaluators plan and conduct their evaluations. A total of 117 evaluations of i3 programs are currently being conducted, 50 of which are RCTs; 13 of the remaining evaluations are employing quasi-experimental designs.[26] If this is a sign of how i3 will influence the evaluation of major education programs in the future, it seems reasonable to think that evaluation will play a more important role in LEAs' decisionmaking and perhaps even become a standard part of the way that some LEAs conduct business.

ABSOLUTE AND COMPETITIVE PRIORITIES. In addition to the rules of evidence, the administration decided to inform applicants of the education issues that they considered "absolute priorities," meaning that only proposals that addressed at least one of the priorities would be considered for funding. The administration identified four areas of importance for promoting educational achievement—similar to those for Race to the Top—in which they would award grants:

    —*Innovations that support effective teachers and principals.* That the first absolute priority was promoting teacher and principal effectiveness suggests that the administration viewed quality teaching and leadership as the most important way to improve educational outcomes. Applicants could propose to identify, recruit, develop, assign, retain, or reward effective teachers or "remove" ineffective teachers. It is especially notable that the announcement specifically mentioned that the method of evaluating teacher and principal effectiveness should be determined through a measurement system that, among other criteria, was based on evidence from rigorous designs and included assessment of student performance. Again, the Obama administration did not shy away from empha- sizing an approach to teacher assessment that directly challenged teacher unions.

—*Innovations that improve the use of data.* Yet again, the administration emphasized the importance of using data to evaluate programs and specifi- cally mentioned using program data to measure "student achievement or stu- dent growth" in assessing "teacher, principal, school, or LEA performance and productivity."

—*Innovations that complement the implementation of high standards and high-quality assessments.* The priority here was to show how applicants can tran- sition to more frequent and sophisticated use of standards that promote and assessments that measure student progress toward college and career readiness.

—*Innovations that turn around persistently low-performance schools.* Under this priority, funds are to be used to either turn around schools that are "per- sistently lowest-achieving" or are subject to corrective action or restructuring under the No Child Left Behind Act.

In addition to these four absolute priorities, the administration recognized four "competitive preference priorities." In order to be considered for funding, a proposal had to address one or more of the absolute priorities. By contrast, the competitive preference priorities were not mandatory; rather, they consti- tuted a mechanism by which a proposal could receive extra points. In what was expected to be a tight competition, many applicants undoubtedly would realize that every point counted and thus would try to address the competitive prefer- ence priorities if they could. The competitive preference priorities were innova- tions that improved

—early learning (birth through third grade) outcomes

—college access and success

—the education of students with disabilities or limited English proficiency

—student learning in rural schools.

Deciding Who Gets the Money

On October 9, 2009, the administration placed its preliminary funding announcement for i3 in the *Federal Register* and invited comments from the public.[27] After receiving nearly 350 comments, the administration prepared the final version of the i3 rule, called the "Notice Inviting Applications," which was announced publicly on March 12, 2010, in the *Federal Register*.[28] To qualify, applicants had to submit proposals for programs that would have an impact on students, with the highest level of evidence of impact required for the scale-up tier, the next highest for the validation tier, and the lowest for the development tier. Although it could be argued that the distinctions between the three tiers of evidence are somewhat arbitrary, they are nonetheless about as clear as the current status of social science research permits (see table 4-1).

Applicants for the scale-up tier could receive up to $50 million, applicants for the validation tier up to $30 million, and applicants for the development tier up to $5 million. In the end, the administration was so serious about funding programs that met the evidence requirements for their respective tier that it conducted a separate review by IES researchers and reviewers at the Department of Education trained in the What Works Clearinghouse standards to make sure that the evidence provided by the applicants met the standard. An important procedural point that differentiates i3 from the other initiatives is that evidence was an eligibility criterion in i3, not just another part of an application that reviewers scored. Therefore, if the evidence cited by applicants did not meet the level of evidence required by the tier for which they were applying, the application was dropped from further consideration, no matter how good the proposal was.

A Special Role for Foundations

The administration was intent on involving the nonprofit sector in education reform. Many new administration officials, including two of the top officials in the Department of Education (Anthony Miller and Jim Shelton), had private sector backgrounds that included, in Shelton's case, extensive experience with foundations. They, along with Secretary Duncan, also considered the nonprofit sector—especially foundations—a vital ally in the fight to reform public school programs on the basis of rigorous evidence of effectiveness. In the spring of 2009, several presidents of major foundations requested a meeting with Secretary Duncan to discuss the new administration's emerging education priorities and goals. They also wanted to discuss the 20 percent matching requirement for i3 grantees, which would most likely have to come from foundations and which some of the foundation presidents thought was a little steep. Secretary Duncan used the occasion to fully explain the administration's goals for the i3 initiative and to urge the foundation leaders to play an important role in the initiative. According to our interviews with Shelton and Miller, the secretary hoped that foundations would become infected by the evidence-based virus and would begin to demand high-quality evaluations of the intervention programs that they funded with their own money. The secretary and his team believed that inducing foundations to follow the administration in basing their funding decisions in large part on evidence would result in foundations spending their billions of dollars on social programs of proven effectiveness. In that way, foundations could play a decisive role in promoting evidence-based policy and in changing the culture of the many organizations that they supported by persuading them to emphasize the importance of obtaining rigorous evidence of program impacts.

An important idea to facilitate foundation involvement in i3 emerged from the meeting. As mentioned, the administration planned to require projects that won the i3 competition to secure matching funds equal to 20 percent of their grant amount. Most of that money would have to come from foundations. The foundations decided on an efficient way to get information about the nature of the programs that the organizations that planned to apply for i3 funds were proposing: namely, to have them post the information at a central online location. The foundations, which would control the website, could review specific proposals, get information about the sponsoring organizations, and use that information to decide whether they wanted to explore the possibility of providing matching funds for a project. The foundations subsequently created a website (FoundationRegistryi3.org), which eventually received nearly 700 proposals for the foundations to review, of a total of nearly 1,700 proposals submitted to the department for i3 funds.[29] The CEO of the Bill and Melinda Gates Foundation said that the registry "pave[d] the way for a new approach to leverage technology for philanthropic collaboration—increasing access, efficiency, and effectiveness to drive greater impact in the field." In the end, 12 of the nation's biggest foundations committed $500 million to match the initial $650 million in i3 funds made available by the Department of Education.[30] The foundations included the Gates, Annie E. Casey, Carnegie, Ford, Mott, MacArthur, Lumina, Walton Family, and Kellogg foundations, among others.

Conducting Grant Reviews

The administration made a strong effort to help potential applicants understand and successfully complete the application process, which was bound to be a difficult and complex undertaking for LEAs and nonprofits. Because the amount of money at stake—around $650 million—was enormous, there would be many applications to process. As it turned out, there were 1,698 applications: 19 for scale-up grants; 355 for validation grants; and 1,324 for development grants. In addition, it was a challenge to explain to applicants the guidelines on the types of evidence (see table 4-1) so that they understood the grant tiers for which they were eligible to apply. The grant reviewers from the Department of Education also had to be able to distinguish among the types of evidence needed for each tier and to make sure that the applicants met the requirements.[31] Developing the best evidence guidelines in the world would be futile unless the reviewers understood them and applied them accurately in awarding grants.

In the face of these challenges, the administration designed a grant application process that had five phases. In the first phase, the administration selected

Table 4-2. *Point System for Scoring i3 Applications, 2010*

Selection criterion	Points, by type of grant		
	Development	Validation	Scale-up
A. Need for project and quality of project design	25	20	15
B. Strength of research; significance and magnitude of effects	10	15	20
C. Applicant experience	25	20	15
D. Quality of evaluation	15	15	15
E. Strategy and capacity to bring to scale	5	10	15
F. Sustainability	10	10	10
G. Quality of management plan and personnel	10	10	10
Total	100	100	100

Source: Department of Education, "Investing in Innovation Fund (i3): Overview of the i3 Review Process, July 26, 2010" (www.google.com/?gws_rd=ssl#q=Department+of+Education%2C+%E2%80%9CInvesting+in+Innovation+Fund+(i3)%3A+Overview+of+the+i3+Review+Process%2C+July+2 6%2C+2010.%E2%80%9D).

more than 330 "highly qualified" official peer reviewers, mostly from outside the government, and provided them with training on how the reviews were to be conducted. The Department of Education then began the review process by classifying the nearly 1,700 applications according to the type of grant requested and the absolute priority pursued by the proposal and then assigning the applications to reviewers. In the second phase, the peer reviewers assessed the proposals assigned to them in accordance with department guidelines. Table 4-2 summarizes the seven criteria by which reviewers judged the proposals and the points that could be awarded for each of the three types of grants for each of the seven criteria. Five of the criteria (A, C, E, F, and G) were considered by reviewers who were subject matter experts; the remaining two criteria (B and D) were reviewed by evaluation and evidence experts.[32] Reviewers entered their scores and comments into the department's computer system. The computer adjusted for effects of any reviewer or panel bias as indicated by scores that were consistently higher or lower than those of other reviewers or panels.

In the third phase, Department of Education staffers confirmed several aspects of the applications of the highest-scoring proposals before they were made public. Among other items, staffers affirmed that the winning applicants were LEAs or partnerships between LEAs and nonprofits; that the practices, strategies, or programs proposed by the applicant would benefit high-need students; and that the evidence met the requirements for the funding tier for which the applicant had applied. The staff review, performed by Department of Education staffers who had been trained in What Works Clearinghouse standards, was an important step to be sure that all the winning applicants did in fact meet the evidence requirements. Insisting that LEAs and their private sector partners use evidence to obtain federal dollars is what the administration hoped would begin to change the nature of federal grant making in education—and equally important, would make LEAs and their partners realize that the federal government was now making more decisions about who gets grant funds by examining the evidence that the program had impacts on important outcomes. If you want fundamental changes in the way that organizations do business, you have to use strong incentives—and few incentives are stronger than $650 million in payoffs for good evidence. The road to federal funding in i3—and, to a great extent, in the five other Obama evidence-based initiatives—was paved with rigorous evidence.

The fourth phase of the review process was to announce the applicants with the highest scores, which was done on August 5, 2010. Those applicants were assured of getting grants if they could obtain the required 20 percent match from the private sector. The administration awarded 4 scale-up grants (21 percent of the proposals that were in this evidence tier), 15 validation grants (4 percent of proposals), and 30 development grants (2 percent of proposals). All 49 programs selected for funding in all three evidence tiers attracted the matching funds that they needed to qualify for federal dollars. The fifth and final phase was for the Department of Education to announce the final grantees and then, subsequently, to monitor implementation of their proposals.

To provide a concrete idea of the types of proposals that were funded, table 4-3 gives a summary of two winning proposals from each of the three tiers of grants. Grants were awarded to address all the absolute priorities, although the four scale-up grants addressed just two of the priority areas—teacher and principal effectiveness (Teach for America and the KIPP Foundation) and school turnaround (Success for All and the Reading Recovery program). Winners were located in 23 states and Washington, D.C.[33] As can be expected when grants are awarded on a competitive basis, many states and many more LEAs were left out of the funding.

Reactions to the 2010 i3 Grant Selections

As would be expected when nearly $650 million is awarded in a competition that involves around 1,700 applications, responses to the announcement of winners were mixed. One of the major criticisms was of the review process that the Department of Education used to pick the winners—in particular, that the department had relied on more than 330 reviewers to score the proposals. Although all received training from the Department of Education, critics believed that some of the reviewers showed poor judgment. In a blog entitled

Table 4-3. *Overview of Selected i3 Awards*

Project	Grantees/partners	Grant amount (length)	Intervention
Scale-up			
Reading Recovery	Ohio State University and consortium of 18 other university partners in various states	$45.6 million (5 years)	Short-term literacy intervention focused on one-on-one tutoring for lowest-achieving first graders; includes network of university training centers to target low-performing schools; the goal is to train 750 teachers a year to serve a total of around 500,000 students.
Success for All	Twelve public school districts across the country; Colorado Department of Education; Johns Hopkins University; Pennsylvania Department of Education	$49.3 million (5 years)	Whole-school turnaround program for Title I elementary schools; provides training materials for staff providing cooperative learning, reading, tutoring, and support services; the goal is to add 1,100 schools to the national network, expand training capacity, and operate more effectively.
Validation			
Model Classroom Innovation	Children's Literacy Initiative, Camden City Public Schools; Newark Public Schools; Philadelphia school district; Chicago Public Schools	$21.7 million (5 years)	Program for raising teacher quality to improve student literacy achievement; train K–3 teachers in high-impact, evidence-based literacy instruction practices; the goal is to train 456 teachers in 38 selected public schools, reaching 45,600 students a year.
Virginia Initiative for Science Teaching and Achievement (VISTA)	George Mason University; 47 school districts; 6 universities; Virginia Department of Education	$28.5 million (5 years)	Comprehensive professional development program to improve instruction and student performance by training more than 800 K–12 science teachers in elementary and secondary schools, reaching more than 80,000 students.

(continued)

Table 4-3 (*continued*)

Project	Grantees/partners	Grant amount (length)	Intervention
Development			
CollegeYES	Alliance for College-Ready Public Schools; International Society for Technology in Education; Kijana Voices	$4.99 million (5 years)	College access and success program delivered through the Alliance for College-Ready Public School network of charter schools in the Los Angeles area; aligns curriculum with Common Core College/Career standards; uses technology to help students develop science, technology, engineering, and math (STEM) skills; provides professional development courses for teachers to advise students on college readiness and preparation; integrates technology projects into courses.
Every Child Ready	Apple Tree Institute for Education Innovation; Apple Tree Early Learning Public Charter School; DC Prep Academy; Early Childhood Academy; FOCUS; other university, private school, and public school district partners	$5 million (5 years)	Preschool intervention model that integrates special education students into general education classrooms; includes full-day instructional program; monitors students and uses data to ensure progress; level of instruction depends on progress, with additional individual support provided as needed; the goal is to help children arrive at kindergarten with skills that they need to succeed.

Source: Abstracts of these projects can be accessed at Department of Education, "i3 2010 Highest-Rated Applications" (www2.ed.gov/programs/innovation/2010/i3hra-list.pdf).

"How Did Parents as Teachers Win an i3 Grant?" well-known education authority Sara Mead noted what seemed to be several flaws in the grant process.[34] For openers, the department made it clear that grants would be given only for proposals that addressed K–12 education. As Mead argued in her blog, although the birth-to-third-grade category was a competitive priority, the "i3 guidance and briefings for applicants" made it clear that applicants addressing this priority "also had to address grades K–12." But Parent as Teachers (PAT), which received a grant, was a home visiting program that had no necessary relationship with the schools and involved primarily parents of children from birth to three years of age. To all appearances, PAT's proposal was not even eligible for the competition, which apparently both the reviewers and the department failed to detect. On the selection criterion "Strength of Research, Significance of Effect, and Magnitude of Effect," reviewers awarded highly discrepant scores. One reviewer awarded the maximum number of points and noted "no weaknesses" in PAT's evidence. While PAT has been evaluated by both quasi-experimental and RCT evaluations, most of them showed only modest impacts, and one of the RCTs found no significant differences between the program and control groups. On balance the evidence may have been strong enough to win an award, but PAT should not have been give the maximum score for strength of research; moreover, according to Mead, someone familiar with the evaluation studies of PAT would not have noted that the supporting evidence had "no weaknesses." It is little wonder that, as reported by Kim Smith and Julie Petersen of Bellwether Education Partners, a survey showed that about 65 percent of those familiar with the i3 grant award process judged the scoring to be "too random," in large part because of "insufficient protocols and controls for reviewers."[35]

Another frequent criticism was that i3 did not live up to its name, Investing in Innovation. According to the respected education researcher Rick Hess, of the American Enterprise Institute, the 49 awards were made mostly to programs that showed little innovation and were, as he called them, "been there, done that" programs.[36] Hess was especially critical of the Department of Education for virtually prohibiting participation by the private sector, in which a great deal of education innovation was taking place, especially in the development and use of education technology. Further, all the scale-up awards, which together amounted to nearly $200 million—around 30 percent of the total funds awarded—were to well-known programs that had been around for many years and could hardly be considered innovative.[37] In defense of the administration's scale-up selections, however, it is reasonable to point out that as suggested by the term "scale-up," programs in the top tier were selected precisely because they had been shown to produce significant impacts and were given money to determine whether they would continue to deliver excellent results when they were implemented in new locations ("scaled up"). Indeed, a rational approach to expanding the list of effective social programs is to develop innovative programs, test them in limited samples and locations, and, if they are successful, scale them up to scores or hundreds of locations while continuing to test them for effectiveness. That defines the i3 strategy precisely. In fact, it defines the strategy for all the Obama evidence-based initiatives.

This approach not only represents a potentially effective way to strike a balance between innovation and replication but also clarifies the role of innovation. The term "innovative" should be applied to ideas that have not yet been carefully tested by using rigorous research designs. Innovative programs are new, exciting, and hopeful. But before we can be confident that they can deliver on their promise, they must be tested. Once they have been tested, it seems misleading to call them innovative. In the Obama strategy, the scale-up stage is not designed to identify innovative programs but to expand programs that have already been found to be effective on a limited basis to see whether they will continue to work at scale.

Subsequent Rounds

Partly in response to these and other criticisms, the Department of Education made a number of changes to i3 in the second year of competition (2011). Award amounts and matching requirements were changed, along with absolute and competitive priorities. The department also revised the selection process, directly affecting the way that evidence was considered. The major changes were made in the following areas:

—*Amount of awards.* Due to reduced funding for i3 in the second year (only $150 million was available for new grants, a major drop from the $650 million available in the first year),[38] the department decided to lower the amount of new awards. For 2011, the scale-up grants were worth, at most, $25 million (down from $50 million); the validation grants, up to $15 million (down from $30 million); and the development grants, $3 million (down from $5 million).

—*Priorities.* The Department of Education also changed the absolute priorities that applicants were required to address. They eliminated one priority (improved use of data systems) and added two more: science, technology, engineering, and math (STEM) education and improving achievement in rural schools. The carry-over priorities from 2010 pertained to effective teachers and principals, standards and assessments, and low-performing schools.

—*Competitive preference priorities.* The department also changed the secondary (optional) competitive preferences. Early learning, college access and success, and students with disabilities and limited English proficiency were retained. Improving productivity and technology were added, bringing the total number of competitive preference priorities to five. In addition, applicants were limited to two competitive preference priorities to be included in the scoring of the application. Applicants could still target more competitive preference priorities, but no more than two would be reviewed and scored.

—*Matching requirements.* The department also changed matching requirements from 20 percent to 5, 10, and 15 percent for scale-up, validation, and development grants respectively.[39] The change was made because it was proving difficult for projects to raise the very substantial matching funds required in the first round of funding. As always, setting the level of matching funds is more art than science. The department and advocates favor higher matches because higher matches bring more total dollars into a project, allowing quality to be improved or more children to be served. However, if the match is very high, good projects may not be able to raise the required amount; if they cannot, they do not receive federal funding through i3. Because the department received many complaints about the high matching requirements in the first round from applicants, potential applicants, and the foundations that were putting up the money, it reduced the matching requirements for all three tiers of grants.

—*Evidence and review process.* The biggest changes in the second year were in the application review process. Because of the complexity and difficulty of selecting the 2010 grantees, which nearly overwhelmed the Department of Education and its reviewers, the department simplified the 2011 review process. The changes had a direct effect on how evidence was considered, but the eligibility requirements remained unchanged.

Recall that in 2010 there were seven selection criteria, labeled A-G (see table 4-2). Scale-up and validation proposals (but not development proposals) were first reviewed by five peer reviewers—three subject matter experts who scored selection criteria A, C, E, F, and G and two evaluation experts (not from IES) who scored the evaluation and evidence criteria (B and D). After this first round of reviews, the highest-rated applicants were reviewed again by Department of Education evaluation experts (including staffers from IES) to determine whether the evidence that they cited in support of their proposed project met the level of evidence required by the tier for which they were applying. In 2010, development grant applications were reviewed somewhat differently. First, those applications were scored by three subject matter experts on selection criteria A, C, E, F, and G; then, only the 100 highest-scoring development grant applications were reviewed by the evaluation experts on criteria B and D.

In 2011, the review process was streamlined to avoid overwhelming the department and its reviewers. First, all three levels of grant applications were reviewed by Department of Education reviewers to make sure that the evidence presented met the level required by their respective tiers and that they met all the other eligibility criteria. This review resulted in many applications being rejected. Next, the full application was reviewed in accordance with four selection criteria (down from seven in 2010) to arrive at a total score (see table 4-4). In this second round of competition, the Department awarded 23 grants (1 scale-up; 5 validations; and 17 development) worth about $150 million.

For the third round of competition in 2012, the department again adjusted the selection criteria and the scoring process. Applicants were required to address in criterion B whether they were using the best evidence to support their program

Table 4-4. *Point System for Scoring i3 Applications, 2011*

Points, by type of grant

Selection criterion	Development	Validation	Scale-up
Need for project	35	25	30
Quality of project design	25	25	30
Quality of evaluation	20	25	20
Quality of management plan and personnel	20	25	20
Total	100	100	100

Source: Department of Education, "Investing in Innovation Fund (i3) Program; Guidance and Frequently Asked Questions; FY 2011 Competition" (www2.ed.gov/programs/innovation/2011/applicant.html).

or practices, including the question of "the extent to which the services to be provided by the proposed project reflect up-to-date knowledge from research and effective practice." Applicants also were required to demonstrate "the importance and magnitude of the effect expected to be obtained" and show how the project "will substantially and measurably improve" outcomes; compliance with all of those criteria was to be demonstrated by "research-based evidence." In the third round, the department awarded 20 grants, including 8 validation and 12 development grants, totaling more than $140 million. In the fourth round, in 2013, the department selected 25 grant applications from a total of 618, awarding 18 development grants and 7 validation grants worth around $134 million. After four rounds of i3 grants, the department has awarded around $1.1 billion in grants, including 5 scale-up grants, 35 validation grants, and 77 development grants.

Early Results

Although it is far too early to determine whether i3 will succeed in achieving its goals, the first large-scale evaluations of some of the six Obama evidence-based initiatives were published as we were working on the final draft of this book. Three separate random assignment evaluations of three of the four scale-up grants from the first round of awards (in 2010) were reported in the summer and fall of 2013. It is useful to consider the importance of these evaluations. As we have stated repeatedly, no matter how impressive the Obama evidence-based initiatives have been in design and execution, the acid test is whether the various model programs produce impacts on important outcomes on a large scale or operators improve their programs if initial evaluations show poor impacts. Until results of this type are reported, interested observers must reserve judgment about what might be expected from the Obama initiatives or from similar initiatives that might be undertaken in the future.

Now we have the first preliminary indications that three of the most highly touted programs from one of the Obama evidence-based initiatives are producing significant impacts.[40] A rigorous evaluation involving 1,253 children found that after one semester, children participating in the Reading Recovery program scored in the 39th percentile while controls scored in the 19th percentile on a widely used test of reading comprehension.[41] Similarly, an evaluation of the Success for All (SFA) program involving 2,956 students from 37 elementary schools found that after one year, students in the SFA schools had word attack skills (such as the ability to break a word down into its component sounds to make sense of it when reading) that were 7 percentile points higher than those of children in the control schools.[42] Both of the evaluations were of scale-up programs funded by i3 dollars. A third recently published large-scale study was conducted by Mathematica Policy Research to examine the impacts in eight states of the Teach for America (TFA) program, a third model program now being implemented with scale-up funds from i3. Neither those eight TFA programs nor the Mathematica evaluation were supported by i3 funds, but because the Mathematica study, which was supported by IES, met the highest standards for RCTs and examined the same types of TFA programs that are now being evaluated as part of i3, the results seem pertinent to assessment of i3.[43] The Mathematica evaluation showed that after one year the high school math students of TFA teachers scored higher on state math tests than the students of regular math teachers from the same school and the students of math teachers trained by a non-TFA program, by an amount that was equivalent to around 2.6 months of learning.

Although not yet definitive—we would like to see whether student performance continues to be positively affected for several years following the end of the intervention before getting too excited—these three evaluations suggest at least that the i3 initiative picked effective model programs for scale-up funding. It seems reasonable to conclude that i3 is off to a decent start.

A Few Generalizations

Several points about the i3 initiative are worth emphasizing. The first is that i3 illustrates the essential components of the Obama administration's definition of an evidence-based initiative. Although we discuss these components in greater detail in our concluding chapter, where we view them from the perspective of all six Obama initiatives rather than just i3, the components include a clear statement of the goals that grant applicants must pursue; a requirement to distribute funds on a competitive basis so that only projects meeting the administration's definition of "evidence-based" and other criteria can receive funding; a requirement that applicants detail the evaluation evidence showing that their intervention program produces impacts on the measures they are targeting; funding tiers, with stronger evidence requirements and more money for the top tier; the use of professional review panels to determine which applicants should receive grants; a special review of the evidence supporting a program's claims of effi- cacy by professionals versed in research and evidence; and the requirement that applicants provide details of the research designs that they will use to evaluate their programs.

Another issue that we explore in more detail in the final chapter is our expec- tation that many of the i3 evaluations, especially of programs in the validation and development tiers, will show modest or no impacts.[44] The administration hired Abt Associates, a highly reputable research firm, to help the 117 operators of i3 programs and their evaluation partners design and conduct their evalua- tions, a decision that will almost certainly improve evaluation quality. But the better the evaluations, the more likely they are to show that some programs do not produce significant impacts. As Jon Baron of the Coalition for Evidence- Based Policy has pointed out, of 90 interventions evaluated by randomized con- trolled trials funded by IES since 2002, 88 percent were found to have weak or no positive effects. Similar results are produced by RCTs of clinical interven- tions in medicine.[45] Even in business studies, Jim Manzi reports that between 80 percent and 90 percent of studies of new products or strategies commis- sioned by Google and Microsoft found no significant effects.[46]

Our interviews with administration officials, including those working on the i3 initiative, suggest that local programs are going along with the Obama emphasis on evaluation, in many cases enthusiastically. Our discussions with Abt officials working on the i3 evaluation team and with MDRC officials work- ing on both the home visiting evaluation team and the Social Investment Fund team (see chapter 5) also suggest that local programs are cooperating with the evaluations and playing an active role in their implementation.[47] But how will program directors, their staffs, their boards, and their funders respond if and when the evaluations show that their programs are not producing significant impacts? In our view, this is a crucial issue that will play an important role in the success and staying power of all the Obama evidence-based initiatives. If evaluations are to help programs improve, they must provide continuous infor- mation so that program staff can adjust the programs in response to any find- ings that show modest or no impacts. This issue is now playing out in hundreds of local programs supported by the Obama initiatives, 117 of which are part of i3. Abt will release a major report that includes some impacts in late 2015, although some individual projects may release reports even earlier (in addition to the preliminary i3 results for the scale-up grants published in late 2013 and described above). At that point, one hopes that both the administration and the various evaluation experts that the administration has hired to work with local programs will help program operators accept an evaluation if it finds that they need to improve their programs and let them know that the administration will help them do so. The evidence-based culture that the administration is attempting to build should include a commitment by federal agencies to work with programs and continue their funding as long as the programs are using evidence to improve their outcomes and are showing progress.

We also want to draw attention to the depth of the Department of Education's commitment to evaluating the results of the i3 programs. First, the department set aside funds specifically for a national technical assistance effort, which the Abt research firm was selected to head up, to help projects plan and conduct their evaluations. Second, the department required every project funded at any of the three tiers of grants to include a detailed plan for an independent, third-party evaluation. That requirement is essential if the administration is to advance the importance of evaluation in the eyes of local program directors and encourage them to use evaluation in their attempts to improve their programs. Third, all five of the scale-up programs (four from 2010 and a fifth from the 2011 competition) have contracted with research-savvy organizations, using funds from their own budgets, to conduct RCTs of their programs' impacts, and sometimes the Department of Education has supplemented those funds. There are few other federal programs that have shown, in both their actions and their budgets, a level of commitment to evaluation equal to that shown by the department on its i3 initiative.

Another lesson from the i3 initiative also concerns evidence. We talked to program operators who submitted grant proposals and were thoroughly confused about the role that evidence played in the review process. In truth, the role of evidence was a little confusing because in the first round the administration decided to use evidence as both an eligibility criterion and a selection criterion. The administration knew that IES and the Department of Education did not have the internal personnel to review all 1,698 proposals on the evidence requirements, so they decided to conduct the review by outside experts first and have the proposals rated on all seven selection criteria (table 4-2). During the selection criteria review, evaluation experts scored the proposals on the two criteria dealing with evidence (strength of research supporting the effects of the proposed program and the quality of the evaluation proposal in their application) while substantive reviewers scored the proposals on the other five selection criteria. After this stage, the highest-rated proposals—those with scores of 80 points or more of a possible 100—passed to the next stage, in which IES and Department of Education staff reviewed the greatly reduced number of proposals remaining to see whether they met the evidence standards for the tier for which they were applying. Thus, high-ranking proposals, which had already been evaluated once on the quality of their evidence, were then examined again to determine whether they met the all-or-nothing standards that the administration had established for each funding tier.

There are two issues with this approach to scoring proposals. First, scoring a proposal before determining whether it is eligible to be part of the competition seems politically unwise. A good example of why that is so is provided by an application for a scale-up award by the National Math and Science Initiative's Partnership to Increase Student Achievement and College Readiness. Their proposal received a total score of 90 in the first round of reviewing, the third-highest score of the five scale-up applications. But the subsequent IES review determined that their evidence did not meet the standards for the scale-up tier and their application was rejected. Critics of the i3 reviewing process blame the department's overly regimented and inflexible system of scoring proposals for such results.

Second, reviewing the evidence separately from the rest of the proposal seems to have been an effective way to determine whether there was good evidence to support the claim that the overall program had impacts on children. But evidence provided by the sponsoring LEA or nonprofit organization that the overall program had impacts did not necessarily demonstrate that there was evidence for the specific proposal that the LEA or nonprofit organization submitted for funding. A good example is the application from the widely respected KIPP education program. Its proposal cited good evidence of the impact of its comprehensive school reform model on student achievement in middle schools, but as one of the program reviewers noted, its i3 proposal was to expand and test a specific part of that program: namely, the project to train effective principals. The way that the KIPP program trained principals may have been an underlying cause of the positive impacts of its comprehensive school reform model, but there was no way to know until the training program had been tested separately. Therefore, in the case of the KIPP proposal, the evidence did not specifically address the project for which the program was requesting i3 funds.

In our view, these issues are modest and should not detract from the judgment that the overall review process meets high standards for thoroughness, transparency, and effectiveness. Nor should they detract from the conclusion that thus far the i3 initiative is showing promise. We point out above that in 1999 the National Academies concluded that there was no other field of social science in which the "research base [is] so inadequate" as it is in education. With the establishment of the IES by Congress in 2002 and the implementation of i3 beginning in 2010, research on and evaluation of principles, practices, and programs in the field of education are making a leap forward. There is little doubt that IES has revolutionized educational research and evaluation and that, especially through its What Works Clearinghouse, it has begun to steadily accumulate a trove of educational practices that have been shown by rigorous evaluation to be effective. If i3 has its intended impacts on the field of education and especially on LEAs, not only will the list of effective education practices and programs be expanded, but tools for further development and implementation of effective practices also will be established in many LEAs around the country. Similarly, the ties between LEAs and evaluation experts outside LEAs will be strengthened, opening the possibility of still more gold standard evaluations and further program development. Even so, there are more than 13,500 public school districts in the nation and fewer than 120 are participating in i3.[48] Public education in the United States still has a long way to go if it is to increase its use of evidence to test and refine educational programs on a routine basis. Nonetheless, the field of education seems to be moving in the right direction, and the i3 initiative is playing an important role in that endeavor.

5

The Social Innovation Fund Initiative

The United States is blessed with thousands of small nonprofit organizations that aim to improve life in their communities. According to the *Nonprofit Almanac,* nearly 1.6 million tax-exempt organizations operate in the country, of which about 950,000 are public charities and nearly 100,000 are private foundations.[1] The Urban Institute estimated that in 2010 nonprofits that provide human services received about $100 billion through contracts and grant agreements with government agencies.[2] Many of these organizations focus on social problems, especially ones that afflict children, such as poor performance in school, dropping out of school, delinquency, neglectful or abusive parenting, and family violence. Such local nonprofit organizations have always been a major building block of American society. As early as the nineteenth century, the American flair for creating local organizations to attack almost every problem imaginable amazed Alexis de Tocqueville, who regarded the art of forming associations as a fundamental factor in America's progress and a central feature of American genius.[3]

Like a number of American businesses, many of those community-based nonprofits grew and became statewide, regional, or even national in scope. In recent years, a pattern of dramatic expansion seems to have appeared among organizations designed to improve education. Teach for America and KIPP are two examples, but there are others.[4] Such programs follow a path that would not have surprised Tocqueville: somebody has an idea; that person works out the details with others, often by forming a small organization and raising money at the local level; and word spreads that the organization is having a positive impact on some social problem. At that point, the organization often tries to kick into a higher gear by looking for money to finance additional staff, open additional sites, improve administration, produce more sophisticated communications, and so forth—all in order to serve more people in need. However, expanding a small nonprofit social organization is usually quite difficult and often the attempt does not succeed, leaving many small organizations starved for resources and incapable of expanding—or sometimes even surviving.

The Social Entrepreneurs Movement

During the boom in American business in the 1990s, when hundreds or even thousands of small businesses, many of them newly founded, expanded dramatically, a number of people involved with small nonprofit organizations began to think of themselves as a social version of business entrepreneurs. A central feature of capitalist economies is that they encourage good ideas that show promise of making money to attract investment capital and expand. Indeed, the nation has legions of investors combing the country looking for good investment opportunities—the next Apple, perhaps, or Dell. Although many small business enterprises do not succeed in attracting investment capital and those that do succeed may nonetheless fail for other reasons, this model of attracting expansion capital—starting small with a good idea, producing a product or service for which people are willing to pay, and demonstrating growth potential—is hugely successful. If Joseph Schumpeter's characterization of capitalism as "creative destruction" is apt, this model is the creative part.

But a question arises: why isn't there a similar model for social investments? Why is it that a new widget can often attract expansion capital but new ideas for attacking social problems have great difficulty—even ideas that have been implemented and have demonstrated some success? Part of the answer is certainly that although America has thousands or even millions of people looking for an opportunity to make money by investing in enterprises that produce a profit (if you include the people who invest in the stock market), investing in social programs almost never produces a direct financial return to the investor.[5] Still, over the last two or three decades, leaders in the nonprofit sector and their patrons, both foundations and wealthy philanthropists, increasingly sought to attract investment capital to successful social programs so that the programs could expand and serve more people in need. Their efforts led to a host of new ways to expand such programs.

Many people in the field credit Bill Drayton, a lawyer and management consultant who in 2005 was named by *U.S. News and World Report* as one of the nation's best leaders, with being the first social entrepreneur. Drayton has spent decades identifying and supporting leaders who had both a vision for social innovation and the experience, knowledge, and drive to develop and expand organizations that could successfully attack social problems.[6] Drayton scoured the world to find such individuals, and when he found them, he helped them develop their business and leadership skills and attract the capital that they needed to launch or expand their organizations. In 1980, Drayton established Ashoka, which grew into the largest network of social entrepreneurs in the world; today the organization has nearly 3,000 fellows in 70 countries. Ashoka provides startup organizations initiated by its fellows with "financing, professional support services, and connections to a global network across the business and social sectors."[7]

Despite being a rich nation that spends almost $1 trillion on government programs for poor and low-income families,[8] the United States has made surprisingly little progress since the 1970s in combating major social problems such as poverty, nonmarital births, delinquency, lack of economic mobility, violent and dangerous neighborhoods in almost every major city in the nation, and lack of educational achievement among children from disadvantaged families. Recognizing the unmet need for more effective social programs and the existence of many small local programs that seemed to be successfully fighting poverty and many other social problems, in 1995 Vanessa Kirsch—a leading social entrepreneur who founded the Women's Information Network in 1989 and Public Allies in 1992—spent a year on an information-gathering expedition to 22 nations. During that time she met with other social entrepreneurs, community leaders, and political figures to discuss, among other issues, the financing and sustainability of community-based organizations.[9] Her trip convinced her that the lack of capital to expand successful social programs was a universal problem, one that inevitably meant that many successful but small-scale social programs could not grow, no matter how good their results.

To address the problem, in 1998 she founded New Profit, an organization committed to raising capital to support promising nonprofit programs in education, workforce development, public health, and poverty reduction. A primary goal of Kirsch's new organization was to serve as a kind of intermediary by raising funds from "highly engaged investors who [are] passionate about doing more with their philanthropy."[10] In addition to raising money, another key goal was to discover local organizations that could demonstrate that they provided successful social services and that they were able to expand—or in the language of social entrepreneurs, to "scale up." Of course, showing that local programs work is a large and complex undertaking, but more about that later.

Both Drayton of Ashoka and Kirsch of New Profit are leaders in what is now widely seen as a new kind of philanthropy, sometimes referred to as "venture philanthropy." Although definitions of the term differ, the concept has three primary tenets: first, that there are many successful but unheralded social programs at the community level, often based on a unique approach to fighting a social problem; second, that there is evidence supporting claims that these programs produce a measurable social good (for example, higher test scores, less delin-quency, reduced school dropout rates, increased college enrollment, or better health or mental health); and third, that with increased investment capital, these model programs could expand, in both the sense of serving more people at the local level and the sense of replicating themselves in new sites throughout a state, region, or nation. The difficulty of attracting capital to finance scaling up is seen as the major barrier to expansion.

In the long run, the promise of venture philanthropy is that, as in business, investors will discover high-quality products and services and invest in them and that as a result, effective and growing programs will reduce many of the nation's social problems. Or, as those devoted to fighting social problems often say, such programs would "move the needle" on the national incidence of the problems that the programs attack. The trick is to find investors who are look-ing not for a financial return but payback in the form of a reduction in social problems. An important part of the strategy to convince investors that there are opportunities for productive investment is evidence that the programs in which they might invest actually produce social benefits. This aspect of the venture philanthropy movement brings the movement alongside the evidence-based movement, in which the key goal is to produce rigorous evidence of program impacts. An important part of the discussion in this chapter is how the ven-ture philanthropy and evidence-based movements worked together to expand the use of rigorous evaluations to discover which community-based social pro-grams were truly successful and ready for scaling up.

Kirsch's New Profit began implementing the new venture philanthropy con-cept by raising funds—with assistance from the business consulting firm Moni-tor Group[11]—and by selecting a portfolio of small nonprofits that were, in the view of New Profit, successfully attacking social problems. In 1999 New Profit opened its initial portfolio of community-based organizations to receive finan-cial support and advice, including Jumpstart, Citizen Schools, and Working Today, all of which have reputations for effectively addressing social problems.

In February 2005, New Profit, with funds from the Knight Foundation, spon-sored a national conference of like-minded people who believed in the promise of community-based organizations and the theory that, with adequate capital, they could expand into new settings, thereby "moving the needle" on national social problems. The 2005 conference, held at the Mohonk Mountain House in New Paltz, New York, was restricted to around 65 or 70 people, but most of them were influential leaders in the foundation world, many had extensive experience raising funds for their own social ventures, and many had direct experience in founding and expanding social programs, such as Teach for America[12] and City Year.[13] Our interviews with people who attended the conference indicated that the highlight was a speech by Washington insider and media favorite David Gergen. As one of the participants put it, Gergen told the group that they needed to develop a national agenda in order to effect real change:

> If you social entrepreneurs are running around sticking your fingers in the dike without dealing with the forces that pushed the water over the top, you're basically condemning yourselves to irrelevance because the size of your impact will just never amount to much.[14]

Going Political

The Gergen talk fired up the conference. Kim Syman of New Profit, the main conference organizer, summarized its effect on the group: "So that was provocative, and it caused us to think. . . . What could we actually do to create more opportunity for the innovations that are really delivering results to grow more effectively?"[15] A big part of the answer was to continue creating intermediary organizations that could identify quality local programs, teach those programs to evaluate their outcomes, and help finance their expansion, a process that New Profit had initiated in 1999. Syman also told us that Gergen's challenge caused the social entrepreneurs to "transcend their individual organizations" and come together to create a "shared policy platform" that could lead to political advocacy.[16] As a result, conference participants made two important decisions that eventually became a major factor in the Obama administration's decision to spend considerable political capital to create the federal investment program that came to be called the Social Innovation Fund (SIF).[17] First, they decided to form a coalition of intermediary organizations like New Profit that could attract and use investment funds to identify successful small-scale social programs in order to help them expand. Second, they decided to go political.

While still maintaining its focus on raising private capital from foundations and wealthy individuals, the coalition began to lobby the government in the hope of attracting another source of investment capital. To augment that effort, in 2007 several participants in the 2005 New Profit conference established America Forward, a nonpartisan organization of about 40 "results-oriented, entrepreneurial nonprofit organizations" that included some of the nation's most successful social intervention programs, such as America's Promise Alliance, the Children's Aid Society, Apple Tree, KIPP, Jumpstart, Teach for America, and YouthBuild USA.[18] As is typical for groups trying to influence federal policy, America Forward hired a prominent Washington lobbying firm, the Sheridan Group, headed by Tom Sheridan, a top-tier lobbyist in the nation's capital.[19] The goal of the venture philanthropy movement now was to get federal legislation enacted that would, among other things, provide venture capital—but to intermediaries that would invest those funds in social programs that had shown that they had positive impacts on social problems. As the intermediaries themselves and as Tom Sheridan understood when we interviewed him in 2012,[20] the intermediaries, not the federal government, would identify and award funds to successful social programs. According to the America Forward vision, the nation would have many intermediaries that would keep their finger on the pulse of local programs so that they knew which were having the biggest impact on reducing social problems. All that the intermediaries needed was money. Then, as the local programs began to be implemented, the intermediaries would help operators evaluate their programs to determine whether they were having the desired impacts and to improve the programs.

At the suggestion of the Sheridan Group, in 2007 America Forward created a book of policy proposals to support venture philanthropy[21] and began marketing the proposals to the 2008 presidential campaigns of both Republican and Democratic candidates.[22] As Tom Sheridan told us in our interview, the McCain and Romney campaigns met with the America Forward representatives, but ultimately they were wary of signing on to a policy that sounded like big government. Even the Hillary Clinton campaign declined to support the SIF approach.[23] Carlos Monje, a representative from the Obama campaign who later joined the Obama administration and played an important role in developing the SIF legislation, organized a group of ten or so senior campaign staffers to meet with the Sheridan Group. In part as a result of that meeting, the Obama campaign showed interest in the concept of venture philanthropy and agreed that if elected, Obama would consider legislation that embodied support for social entrepreneurs. The Obama campaign already had a strong community service orientation, which the social entrepreneurs solidified and expanded through the concept of intermediaries and the emphasis on evaluation, both of which were consistent with the direction that the transition team and then the new administration wanted to take anyway. As Tom Sheridan told us, the campaign—and probably Obama himself—liked the major ideas supported by the venture philanthropy groups.

The campaign's enthusiasm for the SIF approach is not surprising in view of the many connections between the Obama circle and the ideas that America Forward was selling. Michelle Obama was on the board of Public Allies in Chicago and had worked with Vanessa Kirsch, the head of New Profit and one of the prime movers of the America Forward coalition. There also were connections between the Obamas and former Pennsylvania senator Harris Wofford, who was a senior adviser to the Sheridan Group.

By 2008, social entrepreneurs were conducting a kind of pincers movement to get the SIF provision in legislation. One group worked outside the Obama campaign and another inside the campaign and eventually within the Obama administration itself. Many of those inside the new administration were influential thinkers with formidable backgrounds in social innovation and a lot of political connections. One of the most experienced and influential was Michele Jolin, whose career included a stint with Senator Barbara Boxer (D-Calif.) on the Banking, Housing, and Urban Affairs Committee and service as the chief of staff on President Clinton's Council of Economic Advisers. She also spent five years (1999–2004) as a senior vice president at Ashoka, where she worked with hundreds of social entrepreneurs in the United States and around the world, launching a series of global projects to help them scale up their programs and directing the replication of many successful social programs—experiences that led her to give serious thought to the role of social entrepreneurs.[24] She also spent several years at one of Washington's most politically influential left-of-center think tanks, the Center for American Progress (CAP), where she headed the presidential transition project, which provided ideas and specific policy proposals for the incoming Obama administration. In her role at CAP, she co-edited *Change for America: A Progressive Blueprint for the 44th President*.[25]

While at CAP she also wrote a seminal document of the venture philanthropy movement, "Innovating the White House," published in 2008.[26] As suggested by the article's title, Jolin lays out the particulars of the role that the federal government in general and the White House in particular should play in the venture philanthropy movement. A major challenge in defining a role for government in providing support for private organizations is how to support the organizations without entangling their programs in a morass of government rules and regulations. One solution, of course, is just to give the money to organizations that the government believes to be effective and let them continue on their way without encumbrance. However, that approach violates the principle, accepted by both the left and the right and above all by taxpayers, that government must be accountable for how it spends taxpayer dollars. There is a delicate balance between government assistance and government interference or control; a major goal of the venture philanthropy movement now became figuring out how to achieve that balance. Like many others, the movement wanted federal dollars but not federal control. In this regard, Jolin proposed four goals for federal policy when investing in social programs:

—Improve access to growth capital.

—Provide seed capital to create a pipeline of innovation.

—Invest in tools to determine what works (roughly, evaluation measures and methods).

—Remove outdated tax and regulatory barriers to innovation.

Achieving the fourth goal would in all likelihood reduce government interference in social programs run by nonprofits, but the other three could open the door to serious government interference in private sector programs. Exactly how the federal government can support innovative programs without subjecting them to excessive federal interference is an important issue. How the legislation—and even more, the regulations and funding announcements—that established the Obama SIF initiative dealt with those tensions is discussed later, but at least on paper, the SIF does seem to involve only minimum federal interference, with one exception. The federal government insists on evidence of outcomes for the programs conducted by all the organizations that receive funding from the SIF. Demanding evidence of success—especially if the evidence must meet rigorous standards like those imposed by the Obama administration—does place a serious burden on the time, personnel, and financial resources of local organizations and their sponsors. Requiring evidence of past success as well as continued use of rigorous evaluations to qualify for federal funding could be a source of ongoing tension in all the evidence-based initiatives covered in this book.

Jolin also argued that the White House should establish an Office of Social Innovation and Impact. Although she proposed numerous specific functions for the office, in our judgment the three most important are elevating the importance of social entrepreneurship by having a White House office, with its obvious publicity benefits; figuring out how to help nonprofits evaluate themselves (she recommends a special fund to finance rigorous evaluations of innovative programs); and giving social entrepreneurs a bigger voice in the administration's public policy debates. The Obama administration did in fact establish the office recommended by Jolin (called the Office of Social Innovation and Civic Participation) and selected Sonal Shah, a close associate of Jolin's, to head it. Jolin was unable to accept the top position because she had complex family responsibilities, not least a newly adopted child. Even so, she agreed to work with Shah on a part-time basis.

Another person who played a leading role in the social entrepreneurs movement and helped smooth the way for social innovation in the Obama administration was Shirley Sagawa, a Harvard-trained lawyer with a distinguished career as a congressional staffer, social entrepreneur, and author who was now at the Center for American Progress. She was a presidential appointee in the administrations of both George Bush the elder and Bill Clinton. In the Clinton administration, where she served as a special assistant to the president for domestic policy, she played a central role in the legislation creating the Corporation for National and Community Service (CNCS)—the eventual home of the SIF program—and served as the first managing director of CNCS. She also was a senior staffer for the Senate Labor Committee, where she led the drafting of the National and Community Service Act of 1990. According to some of her colleagues who participated in our interviews, she is the "founding mother of the modern service movement." She is important to the SIF initiative because she was on the Obama transition team, where she helped draft the legislative language on the SIF.

Social Entrepreneurs and Evidence

Before going further into the SIF story, a few words about social entrepreneurs and evidence are in order. This book deals with the role of social science evidence in the formulation, enactment, and implementation of the Obama evidence-based initiatives. A problematic aspect of the selection of the Social Innovation Fund as an initiative is that most community-based organizations of the type that are the heart of the SIF initiative do not have a strong history of using rigorous evidence. Many community-based organizations, like many members of Congress, specialize in relating impressive anecdotes about a favored social program to convince people that they are having major impacts on social problems. Fortunately, the social entrepreneurs movement asked for investment capital not only to help community-based programs finance their work but also to help them improve their ability to measure results and use the results to improve their programs. As Jolin put it, nonprofits "lack adequate tools or methods to capture their impact."[27] This concern with evidence begs the question of whether community-based programs actually have an impact, which is the most important question. By the time of the SIF initiative, however, a major goal of the social entrepreneurs movement was to help local programs determine what, if any, impact they were having. In 2004 David Bornstein published *How to Change the World*—according to Nicholas Kristof of the *New York Times*, the "bible" of the field of community-based organizations.[28] Bornstein held that as the social entrepreneurs movement expanded, programs were subjected to "heightened attention to performance" in order to "demonstrate their efficacy."[29]

All of the Obama evidence-based initiatives face the questions of what kind of evidence shows whether programs work and, if they don't work, how they can be improved. The initiatives also need to determine how local programs can learn to collect and analyze evidence to answer those questions. The administration, especially the Office of Management and Budget (OMB), has done a lot to emphasize and defend its view that rigorous evidence of positive program outcomes should be a central criterion in federal grant making and program implementation. A crucial issue here is the definition of "rigorous evidence." The Institute of Education Sciences, which has served as a guide for much of the Obama administration's thinking on evidence-based initiatives, is explicit in stating that only program evaluations that feature random assignment can be considered for top-tier grants.[30] But OMB had to compromise in developing its evidence standards for the SIF and other initiatives, in large part because many programs that may be producing good results have not been evaluated by rigorous studies. As discussed previously, several participants in the Investing in Innovation (i3) initiative from the Department of Education, including Jim Shelton and Tony Miller,[31] told us that they were concerned that if the administration set the bar too high for what it would accept as good evidence, very few potential grantees would be able to meet it and the administration's evidence-based initiatives would collapse. The tier structure for evidence in the i3 and other evidence-based initiatives is a creative way to maintain the emphasis on evidence from random assignment experiments while nonetheless allowing funding of programs with lower-quality evidence. The fact that none of the evidence-based initiatives explored in this volume require evidence from RCTs to qualify for the top tier of funding shows the administration's willingness to compromise with reality. Necessity can force compromises in formulating good policy.

For methodological purists, we would draw attention to what in all likelihood will be an important outcome of the administration's compromise approach to evidence. The administration is a cheerleader of sorts for rigorous evidence. Senior officials at OMB, in the White House, and in several of the cabinet-level departments are trying to lead thousands of community-based, education, university, foundation, and contract organizations that compete for federal dollars to understand the new rules of the game: namely, that the federal government gives money primarily to organizations that test their programs by use of rigorous designs. We would not be surprised—and could cite a lot of anecdotal evidence to support our view—if something like a cultural change is occurring across the country as a result of the Obama evidence-based initiatives. We detected pretty clearly in our interviews with many of the movers and shakers in the social entrepreneurs community that nonprofit organizations often lack good evidence of program effects and that one of their central goals is to help them develop the ability to evaluate their programs by collecting rigorous evidence of impacts, often by working with evaluation experts.

At the very least, talking about the importance of evidence of results has become de rigueur among social entrepreneurs. Only time will tell whether that talk signals an underlying commitment by the leadership of the social entrepreneurs movement, intermediary organizations, foundations, and individual donors to insist on high-quality evaluations of community-based programs with the best designs affordable. Over the long run, any improvement in the regard for, definition of, and use of rigorous evidence would be an important indication of what the Obama evidence-based initiatives had achieved. If the evidence-based movement is to become a permanent force in the nation's efforts to attack social problems, it will have to survive what is almost surely coming if evidence-based evaluation becomes the norm—a wave of local programs shown by good evaluations to be producing tepid results or worse. We will return to this point many times, particularly in the concluding chapter.

The major point here is that the social entrepreneurs movement was beginning to emphasize evidence. Everyone wants to know whether programs work and, if they are not working, how they can be improved. In politics it has always been popular for policymakers to tell their constituents and taxpayers that they can show that they are spending taxpayer dollars wisely. What is new is the public definition of "good evidence," brought to federal policymaking by the Bush administration's OMB and Institute for Education Sciences and expanded greatly by the Obama OMB team, which has raised the bar on the quality of evidence. The leaders of the social entrepreneurs movement and their major spokespersons—Kirsch, Sagawa, Jolin, Sheridan, and Drayton—certainly talk as if they are committed to conducting high-quality evaluations and letting the chips fall where they may.

An anecdote here is telling. As the administration's SIF initiative was being shaped, Jeff Bradach, the head of Bridgespan, a highly respected consulting group that helps nonprofit and philanthropic organizations achieve effectiveness and efficiency, attended a meeting of intermediaries and philanthropists in Washington in the spring of 2009. At the meeting, Jolin laid out criteria that the White House was considering for the SIF regulations, including one requirement that addressed rigorous evaluation, and then asked the potential intermediaries whether they could meet those criteria. They all raised their hands, claiming that they could. Bradach's reaction: "Whoa! That feels like an overly optimistic perspective given how few funders subscribe to anything like the standards the SIF is proposing."

The point is that meeting rigorous evidence standards is often difficult, even for experienced organizations with access to evaluation experts. Whether the inchoate field of intermediary organizations and the foundations and venture philanthropists who support them can develop and use evaluation expertise—and whether they are motivated to provide the resources necessary to do so—remains an open question that will play a major role in determining whether the SIF program succeeds in bringing its emphasis on high-quality evidence to the venture philanthropy movement. If evidence does become a routine part of the movement, experience shows that many programs with good reputations will be found not to produce major impacts.[32] Although the reasons that programs do not produce impacts vary greatly, among the most prominent are inconsistent or flawed implementation of model programs, difficult participants or participants that are more disadvantaged than the population that participated in the original program, or major differences in the setting in which the program is implemented. Regardless of the reason, when programs produce tepid or nonsignificant impacts, a very important and largely unexplored question arises—Now what do we do? We return to this issue in our concluding chapter.

Precursors to Obama's SIF Legislation

In addition to lobbying the 2008 presidential campaigns, America Forward's members were lobbying on Capitol Hill to have funds approved for federal investments in community-based programs and to get support for authorizing intermediaries to identify and select local programs worthy of federal funding. The idea of providing venture capital for social programs had reached the Senate Health, Education, Labor, and Pensions Committee (HELP), where the powerful chairman, Edward Kennedy (D-Mass.), was working with Orrin Hatch (R-Utah), a senior Republican on the committee, to reauthorize the CNCS. Created by legislation in 1993, the $1 billion CNCS is an important part of our story because Kennedy and Hatch's reauthorization bill—introduced in the Senate on September 12, 2008 (before Obama was elected president) as the Serve America Act—contained a new program, of the kind that America Forward was lobbying to create, to be housed at CNCS.[33] Called the Community Solutions Fund, the Kennedy-Hatch program was a forerunner of the SIF legislation that was enacted later during the first year of the Obama administration.

Our interviews with HELP Committee staffers showed that Senator Hatch's office was intensively involved in drafting the Community Solutions Fund, which made Senate reauthorization of CNCS bipartisan from its inception. The fund authorized $50 million in 2009, which was to rise to $100 million by 2013, for CNCS to fund competitive grants to entities that were either grant-making institutions or partnerships between grant-making institutions and a local government agency. The grant-making entities would then award competitive subgrants to community organizations to replicate or expand proven initiatives in low-income areas. This intermediary funding structure captures a major feature of the federal support for community-based programs that the social entrepreneurs movement was trying to attract—and that would later be a major feature of Obama's SIF program. Further, the Kennedy-Hatch legislation directed CNCS to contract with an independent entity to evaluate the intermediaries and their subgrantees to determine whether they were producing results, to provide technical assistance to the intermediaries and the subgrantees, and to maintain a clearinghouse for best practices resulting from the Community Solutions Fund, another central feature of Obama's SIF.

As is their custom in election years, both the House and Senate adjourned early to give their members time to campaign before the 2008 elections. The October 2, 2008, adjournment did not leave time for action on the Kennedy-Hatch

Serve America Act, which had not been introduced until September, less than a month before Congress adjourned. Action on the bill would have to await the new Congress and, as it turned out, a Democratic president who would have plans to revise the Kennedy-Hatch Community Solutions Fund to create the Social Innovation Fund.

The Obama Presidential Transition

The period of transition between presidents—roughly from the time that the presidential election ends, in early November, until the inauguration of the newly elected president at noon on January 20—is characterized by intense excitement and formidable amounts of work. The work is conducted mostly by people who have been party loyalists throughout their careers and who worked for the president-elect's campaign. They usually are experienced, competent professionals, but they must work in hectic circumstances to complete a staggering amount of work within a limited period of time using partial and often inadequate information. Nonetheless, they are determined to get the new administration moving.[34] The two major reasons for the excitement and hard work are, first, that jobs, some of them very important, are being filled with the most highly qualified people that can be found and persuaded to serve and, second, that the new administration's agenda is being created and put in place.[35] Broad campaign promises are being converted to detailed proposals, sometimes in legislative language. In part because many of the most important staff appointments, which usually involve playing a direct role in the formulation of administration policy in either the White House or an executive agency, require Senate confirmation—which often takes months—every new administration has an elaborate transition team. In the Obama case, the transition effort included seven teams (policy working groups), each focused on a particular priority area, such as the economy, education, health care, and so forth.[36] The team responsible for the SIF initiative was called Technology, Innovation, and Government Reform. Both Michele Jolin and Sonal Shah, her colleague at the Center for American Progress, were members of that team. Another close colleague of Jolin's, Marta Urquilla, who had a background in innovative social programs, also was a member of the team and subsequently became a senior staffer at CNCS.

Three factors that shaped the SIF now came into play. First, while she was still at CAP, Jolin had written a brief paper on her long-standing recommendation that the While House establish an office of social innovation. That paper appeared in a 700-page, 2.2-pound volume called *Change for America*, edited by Jolin and Mark Green—a widely known author, former public official, public interest lawyer, and Democratic Party operative. The book, to which many of the Democratic Party's leading thinkers had contributed, might not have been a blueprint for the Obama administration, but comparing its recommendations to the new administration's policies in a variety of areas would suggest that some of those policies came from the same computer as the recommendations.[37] Second, the White House Office of Social Innovation and Civic Participation[38] was formed, and Shah, a person with a diverse background in global finance, environmental issues, disaster relief, and community-based organizations, was selected to head the office. Shah's resume included senior positions with the Department of the Treasury, the Center for Global Development, the Center for American Progress, and Goldman Sachs, where she was a vice president focused on green initiatives. The fact that Jolin and Shah, two influential Democratic insiders who were now members of the Obama transition team, wanted to establish the SIF program sent a clear message that the new administration would support legislation like the Kennedy-Hatch Community Solutions Fund. It didn't hurt that Melody Barnes, Obama's choice to head his Domestic Policy Council, an extremely important position in most presidential administrations, was a strong supporter of both the SIF and the Office of Social Innovation. The administration would join Kennedy and Hatch, modify their bill, and help get the bill through Congress.

As the goal of quickly writing legislation on social innovation policy became clear, OMB joined the fun. Unsurprisingly, OMB had a highly competent staffer who could be the lead expert on the SIF. One of the vital characteristics of OMB can be summarized in one word: skepticism. I long ago concluded, after many years in Washington, that the three places where you can get the least biased, most honest, and most evidence-based answer to any question are the Congressional Research Service, the Congressional Budget Office, and OMB. Kelly Kinneen, the main analyst for the SIF, had an undergraduate degree in English and American literature from Harvard, where she had been a fine basketball player. The *Harvard Crimson,* the student newspaper, said of her basketball prowess: "Kelly Kinneen is a powerful argument for including heart as a statistical category."[39] She went on to get a master's degree in public administration at Columbia.

As befits an OMB analyst, she was skeptical of what exactly the SIF was all about and skeptical that the impacts of most community-based organizations were supported by good evidence. However, another important characteristic of OMB analysts is that they are keen observers of politics. Given the influence within the administration of Jolin, Shah, and others and the fact that the White House Office of Social Innovation and Civic Participation had been established by the spring of 2009, Kinneen and her colleagues at OMB, including or even especially Robert Gordon and Kathy Stack, realized that action on the SIF was inevitable. As Gordon and others at OMB saw it, their role was to make the evidence standards as high as possible—just as they were doing with all the evidence-based initiatives.

The Action Moves to Capitol Hill

Although the Kennedy-Hatch Serve America Act had failed to pass before the 110th Congress ended in 2008, when the new Congress began in 2009, there was renewed action on a bill to reauthorize CNCS and establish a host of new service programs. Both the House and Senate advanced their own versions, which included the provisions for the Community Solutions Fund (now called the Social Innovation Fund) from the earlier Kennedy-Hatch Serve America Act.[40] By February, Jolin had started at the White House and had briefed Michelle Obama on the prospects for passage of the Serve America Act, assuring her that the White House would continue working with Hill staffers, especially staffers for senators Kennedy and Hatch, to get the legislation enacted.[41] Jolin herself as well as other White House staff fulfilled that promise, in part by holding dozens of briefings with senators and their staffs. In addition, our interviews showed that Melody Barnes and Rahm Emanuel repeatedly lobbied both inside the White House and on the Hill to get the Serve America Act and its SIF provision through Congress. Meanwhile, the America Forward coalition continued its lobbying to pass the act. Several of those that we interviewed told us that few members of Congress or their staffs expected the Serve America Act to pass, but lobbying by the administration and the American Forward coalition convinced the House and Senate to act. The bill passed the Senate on March 26 and the House on March 31. Obama signed it into law on April 21, 2009.

It is instructive to compare the version that Kennedy and Hatch first introduced in 2008 with the final bill.[42] The basic structure remained intact: CNCS would award grants to intermediary organizations, which would in turn identify successful or promising nonprofits to receive subgrants. The most important difference between the bills, at least for our purposes, is new language in the SIF that requires applicants to meet certain standards of evidence.[43] The senators and staff members who wrote the original Serve America Act subsequently worked with the Obama administration and America Forward to add the evidence provisions to their bill, which, until the new language was added, consisted mainly of provisions on services.

Because community-based organizations do not have a tradition of conducting strong evaluations through the use of rigorous designs, the language on evidence and evaluation in the SIF law is quite extensive. The section on purposes states that a major goal of the law is to "assess the effectiveness" of the SIF programs and to fund "experimental initiatives focused on improving outcomes." Intermediaries are required to explain in their application their "evidence-based decision making strategy" for selecting subgrants and to "partner with a research organization to carry out rigorous evaluations to assess effectiveness." In selecting subgrantees, intermediaries must select organizations that are trying to produce "measurable outcomes" and that "are committed to the use of data collection and evaluation for improvement of the initiatives." In addition, subgrantees must either describe how they have used evidence produced by "rigorous evaluations on program effectiveness including, where available, well-implemented randomized controlled trials" to assess program effectiveness or declare that they have "a well-articulated plan to conduct, or partner with a research organization to conduct, rigorous evaluations to assess effectiveness." The language on evidence is in part a result of the entrepreneurs movement's success in convincing organizations that provide social services to focus serious attention and resources on evidence and accountability. At least as important, the evidence provisions demonstrate the relentless pressure from OMB to make the evidence requirements of all the administration's evidence-based initiatives as rigorous as possible.

While getting the SIF authorized was a solid accomplishment by the administration, it was only a first step. Unless an authorization is for an entitlement, for which money is automatically appropriated, authorizing legislation must be accompanied by legislation that actually appropriates the funds required. While the Serve America Act legislation authorized $50 million for the SIF in 2010, to rise by $10 million each year until 2014, the administration would still have to convince the House and Senate Appropriations Committees to fund the SIF at that level. Like the new SIF program, about one-third of federal government programs are funded by appropriations that must be voted on by Congress and signed by the president every year. So now the administration was back on the Hill to get the money.

It often takes six months or more to write appropriations bills and get them through Congress. In Congress, a lot can happen in six months. Under regular order, the president submits his budget by the first Monday in February. The House and Senate Budget Committees and the other committees of Congress that have jurisdiction over spending programs then hold hearings. The hearings often focus on issues that senior members of the committee select or issues that have been thrust onto the agenda by current events. Within six weeks of receiving the president's budget, the committees of each house must submit to their respective Budget Committee a legislative plan (their "views and estimates") that addresses the issues under their committee's jurisdiction and recommends specific budget levels, stating the receipts and expenditures that they expect for the next fiscal year.

The chairs of the House and Senate Budget Committees use the views and estimates to prepare the first draft of the official House and Senate budget resolutions. The budget is treated like a regular piece of legislation in each house. Thus, a chairman's or chairwoman's bill is introduced in the Budget Committee and marked up and passed by the committee, giving the minority party and all individual members of the committee an opportunity to amend the draft bill, referred to as the "chairman's mark," if they have the votes. The budget resolution then proceeds to the floor of each house and is voted on. If there are differences between the House and Senate bills, which there almost always are, a House-Senate Conference Committee is held to resolve the differences; when that is done, the final resolution must again pass both houses. The president does not sign the resolution. Once adopted by the House and Senate, it becomes the official budget plan of Congress for that year.

The initial budget resolution is supposed to be reported by April 1 and should be officially adopted by April 15. As both the House and Senate have shown in recent years, the leadership of both parties and the Budget Committees of both houses are willing to violate their own rules with impunity.[44] Nonetheless, Congress enacted the budget resolution in 2009 and then followed regular order to write the twelve appropriations bills that contained the funding for every federal program and activity in domestic and foreign policy for fiscal year 2011.

The majority party always introduces the initial bill in each of the subcommittees of the Appropriations Committee. Democrats therefore had control over whether the money for the administration's SIF provision would be in the bill introduced by the committee chairs in the House and Senate. Democratic staffers of the House and Senate Appropriations Committees were somewhat skeptical of the SIF. They knew that it was a presidential priority, and for that reason they knew that their members would be likely to approve the appropriation. But some staffers said the SIF sounded like programs that already existed (such as the various set-asides within block grants for "programs of regional and national significance"); some even referred to the SIF legislation as a "bailout for nonprofits." On the other hand, some staffers were pleased with the 3:1 match, which required projects to raise $3 from private sources (mostly foundations) for every $1 that they received from the federal government. Appropriations staffers were happy too with the emphasis on evaluation because appropriators look for evidence of effectiveness when allocating taxpayer funds.

The SIF emphasis on innovation also was an issue for appropriators. Funds for the SIF were first appropriated in 2009, 10 months after passage of the American Recovery and Reinvestment Act and 14 months after the bailout of AIG.

At the time, the country was in a deep economic downturn and government investments were being focused on immediate relief efforts. Appropriators considering the SIF had to choose between investing their scarce dollars in known programs or investing them in brand-new, "innovative" programs. Inevitably, some innovative programs will succeed and some will fail. If a program fails, taxpayers demand to know why the federal government is experimenting with their money. Of course, if a program succeeds, taxpayers have no complaints, but innovation requires a level of risk that taxpayers may not be prepared to take and appropriators may easily be blamed for taking. For example, one of the appropriations staffers mentioned the outcry when Solyndra, a green energy company, went bankrupt after having received federal loan guarantees based on its innovative technology. Presidential candidate Mitt Romney went so far as to call the energy initiative "gambling away taxpayer dollars." In such an environment, choosing to fund a new innovative program often is difficult.

One of the appropriations staffers on the Senate side urged the administration to define the goals of the SIF more fully and clearly and, despite the administration's desire to fund innovative programs, to ensure that funded programs had at least some level of evidence of success so that there would be accountability for the federal dollars spent on them.[45] The staffers also asked the administration why it did not just put the money in existing programs that showed some evidence of success.

The administration, especially Kelley Kinneen at OMB and Marta Urquilla at CNCS, lobbied appropriations staffers on both sides of the Hill. Kinneen had originally had some of the same questions about the SIF that were now being raised by appropriations staffers, but it was nonetheless her job to answer the staffers' questions and present a solid case for funding the SIF. In large part because of the intense lobbying by OMB and the White House—and also because of the deference that Democratic appropriators felt that they should extend to their new president—the administration did succeed in convincing appropriators in both the House and Senate that the SIF deserved $50 million.

True to form, the overall appropriations process during 2009 was difficult even with Democrats in control of both houses of Congress and the presidency. It took until the middle of September for both houses to pass something called the Consolidated Appropriations Act of 2010, which included the appropriations passed by the Labor, Health and Human Services, Education, and Related Agencies Subcommittees of the Appropriations Committee in the House and Senate. It then took another three months for the House-Senate Conference Committee to meet, for both houses to pass the conference report, and for the president to sign the law. On December 16, 2009, after the president signed the bill into law, the administration had its $50 million for the SIF.[46]

The First Lady and the President Commit
the Administration to the SIF

After the president signed the Serve America Act, which contained the SIF provision, but before the funds for the SIF initiative had been appropriated, the
administration demonstrated its confidence that it would eventually get the
money from Congress. The administration had Michelle Obama, in one of her
first overtly political acts as first lady, announce in a major speech on May 5 that
the administration would create a $50 million fund to provide financial sup-
port for nonprofit, community-based groups that conduct programs focused
on education, health care, and economic mobility. In characterizing the administration's intent, she said that "by focusing on high-impact, result-oriented
nonprofits, we will ensure that government dollars are spent in a way that is
effective, accountable and worthy of the public trust."[47]

Then, on June 30, as the White House, OMB, and CNCS were starting work
on the all-important grant solicitation document—the Notice of Federal Funds
Availability (NOFA)—the White House Office of Social Innovation convinced
the president's staff that it would be useful to hold a public event in the White
House on social innovation programs in general and the SIF in particular. The
event featured a speech by the president, in which he highlighted the SIF, especially the idea of finding innovative, successful community-based programs and
scaling them up.[48] He also talked about how his administration was focusing on
evidence-based initiatives, including not only the SIF but i3 and home visiting
as well. The president's talk provided a concise overview of the SIF program and
how the administration was planning to implement the initiative, illustrated
here in an extended passage from the speech:

> And that's precisely the idea behind the $50 million innovation fund
> included in the Edward M. Kennedy Serve America Act—an initiative
> designed to assist community solutions like these that we're asking Con-
> gress to fund this year.
>
> We're going to use this fund to find the most promising non-profits in
> America. We'll examine their data and rigorously evaluate their outcomes.
> We'll invest in those with the best results that are most likely to provide a
> good return on our taxpayer dollars. And we'll require that they get match-
> ing investments from the private sector—from businesses and foundations
> and philanthropists—to make those taxpayer dollars go even further.
>
> And today, I'm announcing that I'll be asking Melody Barnes, who is
> our director of the Domestic Policy Council, and our innovation team to
> lead this process, traveling across the country to discover and evaluate the
> very best programs in our communities.

And we won't just be looking at the usual suspects in the usual places. We won't just be seeking the programs that everybody already knows about, but we also want to find those hidden gems that haven't yet gotten the attention they deserve. And we'll be looking in all sorts of communities—rural, urban, and suburban—in every region of this country, because we know that great ideas and outstanding programs are everywhere—and it's up to us to find them.

This passage touches on most of the important features of the SIF: finding successful local programs; investing taxpayer dollars to scale up those programs; rigorously evaluating the results; and requiring programs to match federal funding with private dollars. An issue that could be raised is that the president seems to imply that his staff—and Melody Barnes in particular—would be picking the best local programs (the "hidden gems"). But a central part of the social entrepreneurs movement is that determining which local programs should be funded is done not by federal officials but by intermediary organizations, such as New Profit, the Edna McConnell Clark Foundation (see below), and the Mayor's Fund to Advance New York City.[49] That is the major point of having intermediary organizations—to identify and support the best programs. People who worked on the speech told us that the president was not referring to the SIF when he made the statement about the administration finding the local gems; rather, he was talking about something called the Community Solutions Tour, which was in fact conducted later by Melody Barnes.[50] The purpose of the tour was to bring attention to small, community-based organizations. Even so, some of the major figures in the social entrepreneurs movement thought that the president was referring to the SIF. Here is how Kim Syman reacted during our interview to the president's "hidden gems" comment:

> The idea was not to find tiny, little, hidden gems and scale them up. And we really were concerned when the President actually articulated it that way the first time he talked about it publicly. It sounds really good but that wasn't really the intent. The intent was to say: "There are a set of things [programs] out there that we think are actually having a significant impact and could make a lot more progress in our communities against these problems if we [social entrepreneurs] could grow those things."

The social entrepreneurs wanted the intermediaries to develop relationships with foundations and other funders so that they could increase the capital going to developing and expanding their programs. In short, they wanted the federal dollars and the leverage that those dollars would provide with potential funders, but they did not want federal control. Above all, they did not want the federal government picking the winners. Among the other reasons that they wished to avoid federal control was their hope of presenting the SIF primarily as a private sector effort and not a big government initiative. Yes, the federal government was putting up some of the money, but private organizations would pick the best local projects; in addition, nearly all the projects would be from the private sector and would be funded primarily by private dollars.

In the bigger picture, however, the "hidden gems" comment in the president's June 30 speech was little more than a blip. Rather, the president showed how deeply his administration was committed to basing its funding decisions on evidence and to producing new evidence of the impact of social programs:

> We're going to take this new approach, this new way of doing business, government-wide. So we've already set up a What Works Fund [referring to the Investing in Innovation initiative] at the Department of Education—$650 million in the Recovery Act that we'll be investing in the most successful, highest-impact initiatives in our school districts and communities. . . . At the Department of Health and Human Services, we're working on a new home-visiting initiative connecting nurses and other trained professionals with at-risk families to ensure that children get a healthy, safe, and smart start to life. We'll be seeking out the very best programs to achieve these goals—ones with the strongest record of success—and we'll test promising approaches to see what works and what doesn't. . . . Our government can rigorously evaluate these solutions and invest limited taxpayer dollars in ones that work.

The clear implication of the president's June 30 speech was that the administration intended to make decisions on which social programs to spend its money on based on rigorous evaluation of those programs. The June 30 speech, linking the SIF with i3 and home visiting, was the most expansive description of the administration's burgeoning evidence-based agenda.

Writing the NOFA

The most important task that the administration had to tackle to implement the SIF was writing the Notice of Federal Funds Availability. As with all the Obama evidence-based initiatives, if federal dollars did not go to organizations that could select and then implement programs that had rigorous evidence of success, the funds would be much less likely to produce positive impacts on social problems—and producing positive impacts was the bottom line of the entire enterprise. We would argue that administration of the SIF was trickier than that of the other initiatives because in this case the federal government would pick the intermediary organizations and they in turn would pick the local programs that would get the money. This extra step in the funds distribution process weakened the administration's control of where the funds wound up. Picking the right intermediaries, then, was vital to the success of the SIF initiative.

A team of officials from CNCS, the White House Office of Social Innovation, and OMB undertook the writing of the NOFA. One issue from the beginning was that CNCS did not have a lot of experience in relying on evidence to design and implement programs. As a result, OMB focused on helping CNCS manage the SIF as an evidence-based program. Officials at CNCS did not resist the evidence-based emphasis of the SIF, but they worried that if the evidence standards were too high, relatively few entities could qualify to serve as intermediaries and probably even fewer community-based programs could meet the standards. Susannah Washburn, a long-time employee at CNCS who had worked in both the Clinton and Bush administrations, told us that the involvement of OMB reached the point of "micromanagement."[51] But Washburn also told us: "I understand why [OMB micromanaged the SIF] because we just really don't have a lot of evidence to prove that our programs [at CNCS] really make a difference at all. . . . And so I think OMB was well aware of that and want[ed] to push us to get stronger evidence."

The administration struggled to balance its desire for high evidence standards with the realization that there were few, if any, community-based programs that could meet them. Kent Mitchell, then a strategic adviser at CNCS, told us, "The evidence just isn't there yet to support the growth of a full-fledged marketplace that's governed by what works."[52]

Lance Potter, who headed the evaluation team at New Profit, felt that many community-based social programs lacked the capacity to conduct rigorous evaluations. All of these views on evidence are reminiscent of comments by Jim Shelton and Tony Miller at the Department of Education about the evidence base for i3; namely, that it was thin. The practical consequence in both cases was a compromise on the most basic goal of the Obama evidence-based movement: to ensure that the evidence requirements were not so strong that most programs operating in the field could not meet them. In our view, this compromise in writing the evidence standards was less a lowering of the standards than it was an accommodation of reality. Moreover, the administration's thinking, as discussed, was that it had no choice but to accept at the outset the existing evidence, however modest, in both the education initiative (i3) and the community-based programs initiative (SIF) and then build evidence over time by requiring rigorous evaluation of all funded projects. It would not have advanced the administration's cause—increasing the use of evidence—to put the intermediaries selecting the community-based programs in the position of pretending that there were a lot of potential grantees that had gold standard evidence of their program's effects.

The solution to the dilemma of shortage of evidence-based programs was developed by Robert Gordon, Jim Shelton, and the team working on i3: namely, to establish tiers of evidence in which the top tier included programs with rigorous evidence from high-quality random assignment or quasi-experimental evaluations, a middle tier that included programs with moderate evidence of success, and a bottom tier that included programs with only preliminary evidence based on a reasonable hypothesis and perhaps some evidence from research to support the hypothesis.

The results of the months of work by CNCS, OMB, and the White House on converting the broad legislative language of the SIF into a viable social program were embodied in the NOFA. The final version of the notice, which was released on February 16, 2010,[53] can be summarized by discussing the purpose of the initiative, the issue areas addressed, the entities eligible to receive funds, and the uses of evidence.[54]

PURPOSE. According to the NOFA, the SIF has three purposes: to promote investment in effective nonprofit community organizations to "strengthen their evidence base" and to expand programs in order to serve more low-income communities; to identify innovative and effective approaches to solving social problems and to share information about those approaches; and to develop a new infrastructure for grant making at the community level through the use of intermediaries.

PRIORITY ISSUE AREAS. The administration wanted to be able to explain the types of social problems that the SIF initiative aimed to solve and also to take steps to minimize the overlap between the goals of its various evidence-based initiatives. Rather than allow initiatives to address any of the huge range of social problems that afflict most of the nation's communities, the NOFA planners, with encouragement from OMB, decided to concentrate on three issue areas that on their face are important to both local communities and the nation: improving economic opportunity for disadvantaged young people; establishing youth development and school support programs to prepare children for academic success or productive work; and promoting healthy futures by helping youth avoid risky behaviors and reducing the risk factors that lead to mental or physical illness. The NOFA noted that the goals pursued in each of the three priority areas had to be measurable and that all the programs had to evaluate their impacts on the specific outcomes targeted by the local programs.

Structure of the SIF Initiative. The most innovative feature of the SIF, and one supported strongly by the social entrepreneurs movement, was the role of intermediary organizations. One of the basic concepts of the movement, going back to Bill Drayton's Ashoka and Vanessa Kirsch's New Profit, was that intermediary organizations would both raise capital to fund successful programs and keep their ear to the ground for word of innovative and successful community-based programs. Kirsch's view, which enjoyed widespread support among social entrepreneurs, was that intermediaries could do a much better job than the federal government of identifying successful community-based programs. As a result, the NOFA made it clear that in the competition for SIF dollars, the successful applicants would be those that were capable of serving several functions, the most important of which was picking effective community-based programs and helping fund them.

The intermediaries would conduct their own competitions among community-based programs, which would apply to the intermediaries for federal SIF funds. A somewhat tricky part of the competition was that nearly all the potential intermediary organizations had preexisting relationships with a variety of community-based organizations. To avoid having intermediaries fund projects with which they were already working and ignore other projects, the NOFA required that intermediaries widely publicize the availability of funds and conduct an open competition to identify which community-based organizations would win. But to accommodate the possibility that intermediaries had preexisting relationships with effective community programs—which CNCS did not want to eliminate from the competition—the NOFA also allowed applicants for intermediary grants to include preselected community-based organizations provided that the organizations had previously been selected as a result of a competitive application process.

The Role of Evidence. The NOFA says that CNCS will fund the SIF programs capable of producing "transformative change." The way to identify such programs is to select those that have demonstrated, using experimental or quasi-experimental designs, that they have "sizeable impact."[55] The NOFA goes on to identify four ways in which use of evidence will be promoted. First, in the competition for funding, intermediaries must emphasize their experience in using rigorous evidence to select their subgrantees. Second, CNCS "encourages" intermediaries to use evaluation tools and the data that they generate to monitor the replication and expansion of subgrantee programs. Third, intermediaries are required to have a plan for evaluating subgrantees' programs on the basis of measurable outcomes. Fourth, CNCS's broad goal is to encourage government, foundations, and the entire nonprofit and philanthropic communities to "use evidence and evaluation in systematic ways."[56]

Selecting Intermediaries and Subgrantees

The NOFA was especially clear in spelling out how the intermediaries and subgrantees would be selected. The obvious intent of the detailed explanation was to ensure that the best possible intermediaries—and in turn, the best possible subgrantees—would receive federal funds.

Intermediaries

In the SIF initiative, as in all the Obama evidence-based initiatives, selecting the highest-quality grantees possible is crucial to success, but selecting intermediaries of the highest possible quality in the SIF is even more important than selecting high-quality grantees in the other Obama initiatives. In the other initiatives, if a poor-quality grantee is selected, funds are wasted on only one program. However, if a poor-quality intermediary is selected in the SIF initiative, the intermediary may be less likely to select high-quality subgrantees—and even if it does, it may not be able to provide adequate guidance to them, especially in the all-important area of program evaluation. To be eligible to be a SIF intermediary, an organization has to meet six criteria:

—be an existing grant-making organization

—declare itself as either a geography-based SIF or an issue-based SIF, focused on one of the three broad outcome categories[57]

—have a strong track record of using rigorous evidence in grant competitions

—have a plan to expand proven initiatives "that have been shown to produce sizable, sustained benefits"

—have an appropriate conflict-of-interest policy

—demonstrate the ability to meet the matching requirement for the amount of grant funds requested.

The NOFA clarified that the most important part of the intermediary's application is the design of the program, which is worth 45 percent of the applicant's total score. This part includes the goals and objectives of the program, the applicant's use of evidence in its past operations, the community resources that it can call on, and the specific activities in which it proposes to engage. Another 35 percent of the score depends on the applicant's organizational capacity, including its ability to exercise oversight of and provide assistance to subgrantees. The applicant must be able to show that it has a history of effectively using its resources to provide timely help to other organizations, especially with regard to evaluating performance and demonstrating impact. Intermediaries also are required to have the organizational capacity to maintain sound fiscal oversight of subgrantees. Finally, 20 percent of the applicant's score depends on its cost effectiveness and the adequacy of its budget.

In addition to referring to the importance of evidence throughout the NOFA, CNCS included a section devoted to explaining the agency's definition of evidence tiers and the ways in which it expected intermediaries to use evidence. The NOFA labels the tiers "strong evidence," "moderate evidence," and "preliminary evidence" and defines them, respectively, as including studies with strong internal validity (usually meaning random assignment studies implemented in multiple sites under real-world conditions); studies with high interval validity but limited generalizability or with high external validity but moderate internal validity; and studies that present a reasonable hypothesis with some support from research. The NOFA is admirably frank about the administration's belief that many potential intermediaries (not to mention subgrantees) might not have a history of using strong evidence under CNCS's definition but nonetheless makes it clear that applicants should demonstrate as much history of using evidence as they can and show how they intend to use evidence in selecting subgrantees and helping them evaluate their programs.

CNCS followed a thorough process for selecting reviewers of applications from potential intermediaries.[58] They developed an internal "reviewer profile" to identify the characteristics that they were seeking and then compared the profile with a CNCS database that contained the names of hundreds of possible reviewers. Once the potential reviewers had been selected, they were sent a letter of invitation to participate in selecting the intermediary organizations. Those who accepted were required to fill out a history of their employment and the organizations with which they had been affiliated for extended periods. CNCS then reviewed their histories and identified actual or potential conflicts of interest. If conflicts were identified, the potential reviewers were given a chance to mitigate the conflict. Many potential reviewers were rejected at this point. The 48 outside experts who survived the initial screening were placed on review panels and assigned applications that did not create a conflict of interest for the reviewer. Before reading any proposals, reviewers were given an orientation and training session. There were 16 panels, each with 3 reviewers. Panel decisions were made by consensus, a procedure that minimized the chances that a single reviewer could drive the selection process.

Eleven intermediaries were selected from the 54 applications that complied with the terms of the NOFA, and awards were made on July 22, 2010.[59] Table 5-1 describes the intermediaries and gives the amount of money that they were awarded for 2010–14. Four of the intermediaries focus on economic opportunity, three on healthy futures, three on youth development, and one on more than one of the priority issue areas.

For a better understanding of the type of organization that was selected to be an intermediary, we turn to a more detailed review of the Edna McConnell

Table 5-1. *Overview of the Eleven Intermediary Organizations Selected in the 2010 SIF Competition*[a]

Intermediary	Funding	Number of subgrantees	Project issue area	Purpose of intervention
Jobs for the Future	2010–11: $7.7 million 2012: $2 million 2013: $ 3 million	21	Economic Opportunity	Provide job training
Local Initiatives Support Corporation	2010: $4.2 million 2011: $4.2 million 2012–13: $8.4 million	47	Economic Opportunity	Provide workforce development and asset building instruction to boost earnings, reduce expenses, and coach low-income families on how to make better financial decisions
Mayor's Fund to Advance New York City	2010: $5.7 million 2011: $5.7 million 2012: $5.7 million 2013–14: $11.4 million	18	Economic Opportunity	Reduce poverty by advancing the education, employment, and financial savings of low-income adults and families
REDF (Roberts Enterprise Development Fund)	2010–11: $3 million 2012–13: $3 million	9	Economic Opportunity	Increase opportunities for employment for those facing barriers to employment
Foundation for a Healthy Kentucky	2010–11: $2 million 2012: $1 million	9	Healthy Futures	Improve access to health services and reduce health risks and disparities in health care and outcomes
Missouri Foundation for Health	2010–11: $2 million 2012: $894,636	7	Healthy Futures	Reduce risk factors for and prevalence of tobacco use and obesity
AIDS United	2010: $3.6 million 2011: $600,000 2012: $1.9 million 2013: $2.16 million	13	Healthy Futures	Increase access to care and improve health outcomes for low-income individuals with HIV
New Profit	2010: $5 million 2011: $5 million 2012: $5 million 2013–2014: $10 million	6	Youth Development	Provide assistance along path from high school to college to career

Intermediary	Funding	Number of subgrantees	Project issue area	Purpose of intervention
Edna McConnell Clark	2010: $10 million 2011: $10 million 2012: $10 million	12	Youth Development	Improve educational skills and workforce readiness
Venture Philanthropy Partners	2010–11: $4 million 2012: $2 million	6	Youth Development	Help to meet education and employment needs of low-income youth
United Way of Greater Cincinnati	2010–11: $2 million 2012: $1 million	8	Multi-issue	Focus on "cradle to career" development of low-income children and youth

Source: See Corporation for National and Community Service, "Funded Organizations," 2014 (www.nationalservice.gov/programs/social-innovation-fund/funded-organizations).

a. CNCS made both one-year and multi-year grants to these intermediary organizations. In subsequent years, CNCS provided continuation funding to intermediary organizations based on their progress and performance, according to the terms of the original grant.

Clark Foundation (EMCF), one of the organizations selected.[60] In 2012 EMCF had net assets of $864 million and made grant awards of $48.3 million, making it one of the nation's leading foundations focusing on children. More specifically, it funds projects to help 9- to 24-year-old children and youth from low-income families who have dropped out of school or are idle (out of school and out of work), involved with the juvenile or adult justice systems, transitioning out of foster care, or engaging in high-risk behaviors such as crime or unprotected sex. In short, they focus on programs that help troubled youth. As of 2012, the foundation had continuing relationships with 20 community-based grantees that served 142,500 youth in 49 states, Washington, D.C., and Puerto Rico.

EMCF's practice of philanthropy is distinctive in several respects. First, it selects promising organizations, not just promising projects, for funding with an eye to creating a long-term relationship with the organization. Its goal is to help community-based organizations grow and prosper by helping them improve their management, raise money, and use high-quality evaluations to determine whether they are having impacts and to improve their program. Second, to help build these organizations, EMCF has ongoing relationships with MDRC, a widely known and respected company that specializes in large-scale program evaluations,[61] and with Bridgespan, which consulted with CNCS in designing the SIF initiative. Third, EMCF is a perfect fit for the role of the SIF intermediary because of its roots in funding community-based projects, its emphasis on helping community-based organizations become more efficient and effective, and its long-standing commitment to rigorous evaluation.

Not surprisingly, given its role as a leading funder and program builder, EMCF saw the SIF as an opportunity to increase its investments in community-based organizations and help them expand while continuing to build evidence to measure their impacts and continually improve their outcomes. After applying for and receiving $10 million a year in SIF funds (the largest SIF grant awarded), EMCF formed an agreement with 14 investors, who eventually committed $56 million over three years in SIF matching funds. EMCF then undertook a thorough national grant solicitation and review process to select subgrantees. The foundation subjected the 225 applications that it received to several rounds of review involving its own staff, senior staff from MDRC and Bridgespan, and several other experts. The review process was guided by a scoring system based on the quality of the proposed program and its supporting evidence (40 percent), the level of disadvantage of its population and whether the applicant was located in an underserved area (20 percent), the quality of leadership and growth potential of the organization (20 percent), and the financial and operational strength of the organization (20 percent). EMCF awarded funds to nine grantees the first year and was funding a total of 12 subgrantees by the third year. The subgrantees raised $4 million in matching funds; combined with the $56 million contributed by EMCF's investors, those funds helped the organization produce the $60 million in matching funds required by the SIF statute.[62]

One of the distinguishing characteristics of EMCF is that it has a long record of commitment to rigorous evaluation and use of information from evaluations to improve the programs of the organizations that it works with. Their major strategy for helping subgrantees conduct rigorous evaluations is to work closely with MDRC. Both EMCF and MDRC took the evaluation charge of the SIF initiative seriously. MDRC sent experienced members of its team out to talk with EMCF's subgrantees in order to gauge their ability to conduct an RCT and to study their intake process in order to figure out the best way to conduct a random assignment evaluation.[63] MDRC also maintains constant contact with the subgrantees to see how their evaluations are proceeding and to answer any questions they might have.

Based on almost any set of reasonable criteria, EMCF is an ideal intermediary. The foundation has its own endowment, which produces annual revenues that it can invest in high-quality local programs. In addition, its philosophy of philanthropy is not just to select good intervention programs but also to work with them on a continuing basis to help them develop, with the help of MDRC and Bridgespan, in terms of their efficiency and their ability to conduct high-quality evaluations and use the evaluation data to improve their programs. Should our prediction that many subgrantees will have disappointing initial evaluations prove true, EMCF will be in a strong position to help them respond positively to the bad news and dig in to improve their programs and impacts. It might be hoped that all the intermediary organizations will function in similar fashion and stick with their subgrantees if they do not succeed at first. That kind of commitment can be expected to play a major role in determining whether the SIF achieves its potential.

Unfortunately, CNCS's selection of EMCF and the other ten initial intermediaries was not achieved without public controversy. An unfortunate incident was touched off by a widely respected scholar, Paul Light. Light, who is the Paulette Goddard Professor of Public Service and the founder and head of the Global Center for Public Service at New York University, was one of the reviewers in the intermediary selection process. On August 18, 2010, less than a month after the intermediaries had been announced by CNCS, he used his blog for the *Washington Post* to argue that the selection process was flawed and that some of the awards might have reflected favoritism more than merit.

Light wrote:

> SIF is also becoming a study in what doesn't work in government transparency. Contrary to the Obama administration's promise of sunshine in government, SIF has refused to provide basic information about its process for choosing the 11 winners. It has yet to release a full description of its final criteria, for example, the names of all reviewers, or even a simple list of all applicants.[64]

He went on suggest that CNCS might have been so cautious about releasing information because of "the possible disconnection between some of the ratings and the selections." He gives as an example an organization that he had reviewed that had "serious weaknesses in its capacity to manage federal dollars, and submitted meager assurances on cost-effectiveness and budget accuracy," yet still was awarded a grant.

As often happens when someone of Light's reputation publicly criticizes a federal program, on August 21 the *New York Times* published its own view of the SIF's decisionmaking process.[65] The *Times* article reported that many others in the nonprofit sector, including the respected *Nonprofit Quarterly,* had been concerned about the SIF selection process. The article also pointed out that two senior officials at CNCS had ties with organizations that won grants, raising the specter of favoritism. In the article, Marta Urquilla (one of the administration officials that we interviewed about the SIF), speaking for the administration, denied the charge of favoritism, pointing out that neither of the officials that the *Times* named had any role in the intermediary selection process and therefore could not have influenced the choice of grantees. The article also revealed that the organization that Light had mentioned as an example of a possible disconnection between ratings and selections was the well-known and greatly respected New Profit. It then revealed that New Profit had spent $67,000 in 2008 and 2009, using funds from America Forward, to lobby for the legislation that created the SIF, implying by this revelation that SIF officials might have favored New Profit out of gratitude.

On August 23, just after the *Times* piece ran, CNCS posted on its website the applications of all the winning organizations as well as the reviewers' ratings and comments.[66] In addition, New Profit, the organization that submitted the application that Light had questioned, posted its application on its own website. Subsequently, the CNCS Office of the Inspector General announced that it intended to interview some of those who had participated in the SIF review process.[67]

In our view, this episode demonstrates the value of an open grant selection process. Most of the other Obama evidence-based initiatives featured openness by making public a great many details of their grant selection processes. Whenever a federal grant-making agency seems reluctant to publish information about how it awarded grants, it opens the door to accusations of the type made by Light, which resonated with the nonprofit community and the media. But CNCS responded appropriately by releasing abundant information shortly after publication of the Light blog and the *New York Times* article and by offering reasonable responses to most of the major charges levied against them.

This episode raises another important issue about federal grant making. The underlying question is whether the secretary of the federal agency making a grant should overrule the recommendations of reviewers. In most and perhaps nearly all cases, federal legislation gives the secretary the legal right to overrule reviewers. Even if under normal circumstances secretaries attempt to follow reviewers' recommendations, we would argue that there are cases in which they should overrule reviewers. The secretary represents the president, who is popularly elected, whereas reviewers represent only their own views and values. Further, the secretary often has a broader view of the goals of the grant process than reviewers do. The secretary might, for example, want to achieve geographical balance in awarding grants or make a few awards that are of special interest to the secretary's agenda. In the case at hand, it appears that Light was not challenging the legal right of the secretary to ignore some of the recommendations of reviewers; rather, he was challenging the secretary's reasons for doing so, implying that some form of favoritism, not good policy or even political reasons, motivated the choice. A lesson here is that if the secretary has a good reason for overruling reviewers, he or she needs to make the general reason for the selection public, make the reviews and the applications public, and then be ready to take some lumps.

Subgrantees

Although each of the intermediaries had its own process for selecting subgrantees, certain common patterns were followed by all or nearly all of the intermediaries. All conducted a national search, issuing a request for proposals and widely advertising the availability of grant funds from the SIF. Most intermediaries then followed at least a two-step process in soliciting and judging applications. In the first step, potential applicants were asked to submit a letter stating that they intended to apply for funding and answering several questions about their organization, the type of programs that they hoped to conduct, the target population, and other basic information. The intermediaries then selected the most promising potential applicants, often involving their own staff and outside reviewers in the selection process. Those who were invited to apply for funds were then required to submit a formal application describing their organization, the theory of change underlying their intervention program, the projected number of participants, their staffs, the goals of their program, information about the community in which they were operating, their financial status, and their proposed budget. All the intermediaries required applicants to provide extensive information about their experience in conducting evaluations of their programs and their use of data. Applicants also were required to explain their plans for evaluating the program for which they were requesting funds. Several of the intermediaries also conducted site visits to assess the applicants that they were most interested in funding.

Some of the intermediaries departed somewhat from the basic procedures for identifying subgrantees outlined above. A few had specific plans for the type of program that they wanted to run, and some even had a particular program model in mind. They then looked for local organizations that could implement it. The Mayor's Fund to Advance New York City, a SIF intermediary, used SIF funds to replicate five successful antipoverty programs that it had been conducting in New York City. One of the programs was Jobs Plus, a work program for adults who lived in public housing that had been shown by a randomized controlled trial to increase employment and earnings of public housing residents.[68] The subgrantees that won grants from the Mayor's Fund to implement the Jobs Plus program were BronxWorks in New York City and the San Antonio Housing Authority. A similar example is provided by the Local Initiatives Support Corporation, a SIF intermediary with offices in New York City and elsewhere.

Its Financial Opportunity Center model aimed to help poor people find jobs, build assets, and improve their financial decisionmaking. Subgrantees located in Chicago, Detroit, Houston, and seven other cities won funds to replicate the Financial Opportunity Center.

First Three Rounds of Grant Competition

Like several of the other Obama evidence-based initiatives, the SIF has been refunded in the annual appropriations process multiple times since its original funding in 2010. This multiyear funding has allowed CNCS to conduct grant competitions each year except 2013 and to expand both the number of intermediaries and the number of subgrantees, bringing the totals to 20 intermediaries and 217 subgrantees by the end of 2013. (There was no SIF competition in 2013 because of a lack of funding, so the number of grantees remained the same.) Total federal funding for the SIF reached $177 million and intermediaries and subgrantees had raised matching funds of well over $400 million through the 2010, 2011, and 2012 competitions. Around 270,000 people had been or were being served by SIF projects.[69] For the second round of competition, in 2011, CNCS made several important changes that strengthened the evidence and evaluation requirements. For starters, intermediaries would not be allowed to apply with preselected grantees; instead, they were required to run competitions for subgrantees that did not have a preexisting relationship with the intermediary. CNCS also required all new subgrantees to have, at a minimum, preliminary evidence of positive impact. Moreover, intermediaries had to detail their plans for how they would help their subgrantees achieve at least a moderate level of evidence by the end of the subgrantee funding period.

CNCS also changed its point system for selecting intermediaries to include 25 points specifically for "use of evidence." In the first round, up to 45 points were available for "program design," with "use of evidence" as an undefined subfactor. But in the second competition, CNCS singled out "use of evidence" as a specific scored component, yet another indication of how seriously CNCS has been taking the SIF evidence requirement. For the 2011 competition, CNCS also changed the selection process for intermediaries.[70] The first step in the process is now a compliance review to make sure that the applicant meets requirements concerning budgeting and deadlines. CNCS then conducts an initial eligibility review in which each applicant must declare itself as either an "issue-based" or a "geographically based" applicant. If an applicant made it to the third stage, the application would be reviewed by an expert panel of outside peer reviewers. After the external review, the best applicants would move on to an internal review conducted by CNCS officials. In this final stage, CNCS officials would take into account the distribution of grantees and other considerations—such as addressing problems in underserved communities—in deciding which intermediaries would receive funding. Following these new procedures, CNCS funded five new intermediaries, which, in turn, funded 48 new subgrantees.

In round three of the competition in 2012, CNCS slightly modified its scoring criteria and selected four new intermediary organizations, which received $2 million each over two years. CNCS also provided continuation funding to the existing intermediary grantees, for a total of $33.9 million.[71] CNCS announced a new round of grants for 2014, in which up to $65.8 million was made available.[72] CNCS offered five webinars and conference calls to help potential applicants learn about the SIF program and how to apply for funding.

Evaluation

Although we do not yet have outcome data from the 87 intervention programs being conducted by the 217 SIF subgrantees, CNCS has approved evaluations for 77 of the programs.[73] Of those, 28 (36 percent) are RCTs and 36 (47 percent) are quasi-experimental. Given that many of these evaluations are being conducted by organizations that have little previous experience with evaluations, let alone RCT evaluations, one may be speculate that a new view of the importance of quality evaluation is taking hold among community-based organizations. Moreover, our interviews with people involved with the SIF as well as a meeting with CNCS personnel in August 2013 and a telephone discussion in May 2014 with Lily Zandniapour, the evaluation program manager at CNCS, made us aware of many activities that the agency has employed to promote evaluation. For example, the agency conducts an annual meeting with intermediary organizations that features panels and other activities related to evaluation. In addition, the agency prepared an extensive "how-to" manual on program evaluation for use by intermediaries and subgrantees.[74] The agency also hired the firm JBS to work with intermediaries and subgrantees on their evaluation plans and the firm ICF International to conduct a national assessment of the impacts of the SIF on intermediaries' and subgrantees' capacity to conduct evaluations and on their views of the importance of evaluation. The ICF assessment, to be published in 2015, will compare the SIF programs with those of two groups of community-based organizations to determine whether evaluation is used more extensively in the SIF network and put to better use in improving the programs. The ICF report will also examine whether and if so how the SIF funds affect an organization's activities and development.

At this point in the evolution of the SIF program, it seems reasonable to argue that CNCS is working hard to get good evaluations of outcomes produced by its network of programs and to establish evaluation as a major expectation of both the intermediaries and the subgrantees in the SIF network. Regardless of what the evaluations show about the effects of SIF community-based programs, the extensive evaluation-related activity and the conduct of so many well-designed evaluations shows that the SIF is fulfilling a major goal of the Obama evidence-based initiatives by making evaluation a central feature of more than 200 community-based programs around the nation. Perhaps other community-based programs will take the hint.

Concluding Thoughts

Enactment and implementation of the SIF initiative owed a lot to the spade work of the social entrepreneurs movement. The leaders of the movement, such as Vanessa Kirsch, Shirley Sagawa, and Michele Jolin, developed the idea of the intermediary and its functions, initiated the emphasis on evidence, fought to get CNCS reauthorized, and carried their views into the Obama transition team and then into the White House. At that point OMB, with its emphasis on evidence from rigorous evaluations, entered the picture and strengthened the SIF evidence requirements. Wisely, the administration listened to the evaluation experts at OMB and squeezed about as much data and strong evaluation requirements out of the SIF initiative as possible, given the modest state of evidence and program evaluation in the field of community-based programs. Now the fate of the SIF initiative rests in the hands of 20 intermediaries and more than 200 local programs around the nation. Whether these community-based programs can improve their effectiveness is still an open question. But one factor that differentiates the SIF from most other federal social policy initiatives is that soon we will have the evaluation data needed to determine whether the programs conducted by the subgrantees are having an impact. That is more than we know about most federal grant programs. If the subgrantees really do represent the best and most innovative of the community-based programs—and if the intermediaries and subgrantees take the charge to use evidence to improve programs seriously—there is reason to believe that many of their programs will be successful, if not initially, then in the long run.

Beyond that, a major goal of the SIF initiative is to change the culture regarding evidence use by community-based social programs throughout the nation. If 20 of the best intermediaries and more than 200 of the best community-based organizations succeed in using evidence from evaluations to improve their outcomes, it is possible to believe that the use of evidence will expand to many more community-based programs. If it does, the real payoff will be increased positive impacts on the most important social problems that afflict the nation's children and youth. Although the federal government would fund the programs, they would have been "discovered" mostly by private intermediaries and would be operated mostly by private community-based organizations. It is not inconceivable that conservatives could come to regard these local organizations as part of Edmund Burke's "little platoons of civil society" and therefore worthy of public support. This likelihood is greatly increased by the fact that more than half of their operating funds are supplied by the private sector. In this age of highly partisan politics, especially at the federal level, all involved should seek initiatives with potential for bipartisan support and strengthen them.

6

The Workforce Innovation Fund Initiative

Promoting employment is one of the most important goals of social policy, in part because employment can enable individuals and families to become financially independent and thereby reduce or even eliminate the need for public benefits. American society has a strong tradition of pursuing self-sufficiency. The social safety net, supported by federal, state, and sometimes local dollars, is premised on the idea that able-bodied individuals will do everything possible to support themselves rather than accept public benefits, almost always by finding and accepting employment. From young people hoping to become self-sufficient adults to adults trying to escape dependence on welfare, a job is the ticket to success. But in a competitive market economy, potential employees must have the skills, aptitude, and attitudes that employers are looking for. If they don't, they will be offered low wages, minimal if any work benefits, and often little job security. For a variety of reasons, millions of Americans in every generation struggle to find and hold a job that pays a decent wage.

Since at least the English Poor Laws of the sixteenth century, a fundamental dilemma of public policy has been how to use public or private funds to help the poor and their children avoid destitution without enticing them into dependence on welfare.[1] Modern research, mostly by economists, shows unequivocally that welfare does reduce work effort. Normally the effect is that employees work fewer hours, although some withdraw from employment altogether. There is little agreement about the magnitude of these effects.[2] In the United States, the welfare reform legislation of 1996 was a major attempt to address this dilemma by imposing tough work requirements and other conditions on parents (usually mothers) who participate in the nation's major cash welfare program, Temporary Assistance for Needy Families (TANF) (called the Aid to Families with Dependent Children program before 1996). Conditions include a five-year limit on cash benefits for most recipients and sanctions in the form of benefit reduction or even elimination for those who fail to meet the requirements developed by each state for work preparation or actual work.[3] Similarly, the Unemployment Compensation (UC) program has had a mandatory job search requirement since its enactment in 1935, although the requirement seems not to be enforced very aggressively. In the past, there was a sharp distinction between people who drew unemployment benefits, which was widely thought of as an insurance program (recipients' wages are taxed to pay for the benefit),[4] and welfare mothers, many of whom had a spotty work history. That distinction has been all but abandoned in the new workforce system.

The Workforce System

Given the work requirements in federal and state transfer programs as well as the strong societal ethic of self-support, federal and state programs to promote employment and training are essential. Today, rather than distinguish between different types of people who need a job, the government's approach to promoting employment is increasingly a matter of creating a system that provides assistance to all people who need jobs or want better jobs. There is widespread agreement that welfare-dependent adults, unemployed individuals (who sometimes are displaced workers who lost their jobs because of plant closings or downsizing, often during an economic downturn), disabled people who can work, youth trying to gain a foothold in the labor market, veterans, and several other groups should be able to get public services and that their needs are similar enough that they can be served by the same system.

In accordance with this view, the government has developed an elaborate workforce development system, run primarily by state governments and local agencies under federal guidelines that give state and local agencies a good deal of authority and flexibility. As in any system that focuses on customer service, the most important action is at the local level. There are at least 600 Workforce Investment Boards (WIBs), which have at least 12,000 business members.[5] Each of the WIBs, which are authorized by federal law, serves a specific geographic region. Under the federal statutes, WIBs make all decisions about the design and operation of the workforce system in their geographic area, including development of a plan for local workforce activities, selection of the operators of the most important employment and training services , development of a budget, oversight of all employment and training programs, negotiation of performance measures with the state governor, participation in developing the statewide employment statistics system, and promotion of the involvement of private sector employers in the system.[6]

A key part of the workforce system is the nation's approximately 3,000 One-Stop Centers[7] (rebranded by the Obama administration as American Job Centers),[8] which were developed over the last two decades, with at least one center located in every WIB geographic area. The One-Stops can be thought of as the nerve centers of the nation's employment system—the local sites where employment services are delivered; where access to numerous specialized programs, often run by local nongovernment agencies, is available; and where workers can examine a wide range of information on the local and national job market. They provide three levels of free services to anyone who walks through the door. These services, offered in sequence, begin with "core" services, which focus on helping people find a job that allows them to be self-sufficient; "intensive" services, offered to clients who have been unsuccessful in finding employment, which include assessing skills, developing an individual employment plan, and providing career counseling; and job training, which involves classroom and on-the-job training in preparation for employment.

Two notable features of the One-Stop Centers are the number of employment and training services that are available at or through the One-Stop site and the number of local organizations that are required to be involved in those services. The employment and training services are provided by a host of programs, including those for youth, adults, veterans, migrant farm workers, dislocated workers, and ex-offenders. The programs available at the One-Stops include the Job Corps; the Native American Program; Youth Opportunity Grants; Youthbuild; Green Jobs Innovation Fund; and several demonstration programs. The range of local organizations required by statute to be partners in the One-Stop Centers includes the organizations that conduct the programs authorized by the Workforce Investment Act (WIA); the U.S. Employment Service; the organization that runs both the Department of Education's Vocational Rehabilitation Act programs and the department's Career and Technical Education programs; the organization that runs the Department of Health and Human Services's welfare-to-work grants and its training activities under the Community Services Block Grant; and four additional programs administered by the U.S. Department of Labor and one by the Department of Housing and Urban Development.[9]

Primarily because of cuts during the initial years of the Reagan administration, federal spending on employment and training programs has declined greatly since reaching its peak of nearly $29.4 billion a year (in inflation-adjusted 2012 dollars) in the late 1970s.[10] By 2012, only $6.5 billion was spent on employment and training.[11] Few if any broad areas of social policy have sustained cuts of that magnitude. A primary argument for the cuts by Reagan officials was that the programs were ineffective. Our interviews showed that officials in the Obama administration also were concerned that the programs were ineffective. Rather than cut them, however, Obama officials at both OMB and the Department of Labor wanted to fix them—a goal that is shared by nearly every party with an interest in the U.S. employment system.

Reforming the Workforce System the Obama Way

Although there had been little discussion of the workforce system during the 2008 presidential campaign, federal labor force policy and its impact on state and local workforce policies was, from the earliest days of the administration, very much on the minds of officials at the Office of Management and Budget (OMB), the White House, and, of course, the Department of Labor (DOL). With the unemployment rate at 8.3 percent by February 2009 and headed to 10 percent in less than a year, the administration was taking office in the context of the worst economic downturn since the 1930s, when the Great Depression engulfed the nation. Under those circumstances, it was natural—especially for Democratic officials who held Keynesian views—to think about a stimulus bill to get the economy moving. It was also natural for any administration to think about what could be done to help individual workers. Therefore, to deal with unemployment, the administration and the Democrat-controlled Congress quickly enacted what became the biggest expansion of the unemployment compensation program in history. In the five years between 2008, the first full year of the recession, and 2012, the year in which some of the UC expansions began to phase out, a total of $520 billion was spent on UC benefits for unemployed workers.[12]

All that action on unemployment was fine for dealing with an emergency, but top officials at OMB, the White House, and DOL were also concerned about the long term. In our interviews with officials in all three agencies, we found a high level of dissatisfaction with the workforce system and especially the Workforce Investment Act.[13] The WIA, the major source of funding for the workforce system, funds and defines the functions of the One-Stop Centers. But many officials at OMB and the White House thought that the WIA was outmoded. As Melissa Bomberger of OMB put it during our interview:

> One of the frustrations with [the] workforce system as it stands now is [that] it's mostly formula money.[14] And the system rolls along and does what it's always done. And it's very decentralized, and in a formula program I think it's fair to say that it's hard to drive reform. It's hard to get— there's really nothing motivating states and locals to be innovative.[15]

Officials at OMB and DOL wanted to reform the workforce system through evidence-based initiatives, which would also include a substantial focus on innovation, given the relative lack of evidence on effective programs in the field. Seth Harris, the second-in-command at DOL (and later the acting secretary), was having similar thoughts.[16] Harris and OMB officials, especially—again— Robert Gordon, were in frequent touch as the administration developed its 2011 budget proposal for DOL. The idea that Harris and OMB were pushing was a competitive grant program, comparable in many respects to the Investing in Innovation (i3) initiative. Harris told us that the administration wanted to get the money for the new grant program from the current workforce system by taking a modest amount of money from the major WIA grant programs and then, as in all the administration's evidence-based initiatives, requiring the states to compete for the funds. Not everyone at DOL favored this approach, and many of the outside organizations that lobbied DOL regarding its grant programs did not like the idea of removing money from the current formula grant programs in order to increase competition. As seen with several of the other evidence-based initiatives, the political system often prefers formula grants to competitive grants because under the former every state gets at least something, whereas under the latter many states could and often do lose out in the competition. This political reaction to competitive grants is especially strong when someone proposes—as the administration was now doing—to remove money from formula grants to establish a competitive grant. To avoid this problem, one strategy that the administration considered was to increase the amount of money in the WIA grant programs and then use the new money to support the competitive grant approach that the administration favored. This idea died quickly when it became apparent that new funds designated specifically for the Obama workforce initiative under the WIA would not be forthcoming.

Harris told us that he knew during his initial discussions with Gordon and other officials at OMB and the Domestic Policy Council that they wanted to use the same tiered approach that they were planning to use with the i3 initiative (see chapter 4). As mentioned, under this approach, which we have dubbed "more money for more evidence," the largest grant awards would be put into the top tier, reserved for programs with rigorous evidence; smaller grants would be available in the second tier, for programs based on good but second-best evidence; and the least amount of money would be available in the third tier, for innovative programs based on a promising idea or a good logic model.[17] Harris, like Jim Shelton at the Department of Education in his negotiations with OMB over the i3 initiative, was concerned that there were not very many evidence-based programs in the field of employment and training. Imposing a strict requirement for rigorous evidence on applicants hoping to qualify for competitive grants would therefore result in relatively few proposals being submitted for the larger awards. However, Harris reasoned, as long as DOL could fund innovative programs as part of the third tier, his approach to reforming employment and training programs was compatible with the tier approach.

Obama released his budget for fiscal year 2011 on February 1, 2010. The budget contained the Workforce Innovation Fund (WIF), which OMB and DOL had worked out together after some consultation with the Department of

Education. The budget also contained the administration's principles for WIA reform. Two important elements of the DOL budget were two new innovation funds, the Youth Innovation Fund and the Workforce Innovation Fund. By leveraging money from formula grant programs in the WIA, the administration wanted to establish the two funds for a combined total of $261 million. The goals of the two funds were similar: namely, to test promising approaches to training, to break down the walls between the 40 or so DOL employment and training programs,[18] to build evidence about effective programs, and to invest in programs that had rigorous evidence of success. The Youth Innovation Fund, with around $154 million, was designed to encourage innovative programs to deliver summer and year-round work experiences for youth. The Workforce Innovation Fund that was intended to become one of the administration's evidence-based initiatives would be financed with around $107 million taken from the programs for adult and dislocated workers, the most expensive programs in WIA.[19] The WIF would test both evidence-based and promising strategies to expand apprenticeships, conduct on-the-job training programs, and foster regional and sectoral collaborations.[20] The administration also proposed to have the DOL and the Department of Education collaborate on the innovation grants by planning and conducting educational activities and workforce activities that were mutually reinforcing and to encourage states to coordinate their labor and education programs as well.

Unfortunately, in 2010 Congress was deadlocked on the budget for almost the entire year and had to resort to passing numerous continuing resolutions to fund the government on a short-term basis. Meanwhile, the administration was also continuing negotiations with Congress over appropriations for fiscal year 2012.

Fighting over the 2012 Budget

While Congress fought over appropriations for fiscal year 2011, the administration was using the time to revise and perfect the WIF and other proposals for its fiscal year 2012 budget. On February 14, 2011, the administration released its 2012 budget. This time, the president proposed a $379 million fund to be used by the Departments of Labor and Education to create a WIF program that would encourage states and regions to compete for funds by submitting proposals to transform their employment and training programs and their public workforce system. As in the president's 2011 budget proposal, the funding would be created by taking money from existing WIA programs. The new WIF fund would encourage all the innovative activities proposed in the 2011 DOL budget summarized above, but the activities were now expanded to include reforms to the workforce system itself. To promote those reforms, the administration also proposed allowing states to seek waivers of most requirements of the current statutes establishing the workforce system if they needed to do so in order to implement their reforms of the system. But the House refused to go along with the waiver language, probably because Republicans did not want to give Obama the authority to change the workforce statutes.

As the budget process for the fiscal year 2012 budget unfolded during the spring and summer of 2011, Congress was still enacting CRs to authorize spending for 2011 (people who think calculus is confusing should consider the federal budget process). In other words, Congress was fighting over the 2011 appropriations bills while it worked on the appropriations bills for 2012, thereby making 2011 a very busy year. The situation was even more complicated because the administration and Congress were also determined to reauthorize the WIA. Therefore, the administration, especially Robert Gordon, was working to secure the WIF initiative by writing language into both the WIA reauthorization, which required working with the education committees in both the House and Senate, and the Labor–Health and Human Services–Education appropriations bills, which required work with the House and Senate Appropriations Committees. As it turned out, the ill-fated draft of the WIA reauthorization did include an innovation title, which contained the authorizing language for WIF that the administration had worked out with the education committees. The provision, entitled "Workforce Innovation and Replication Grants" (which can be found in the June 2011 discussion draft of the bill),[21] was to be used to pay for

> innovative new strategies and activities that are designed to align programs and strengthen the workforce development system in a state or region . . . in order to substantially improve the education and employment outcomes for adults and youth served by such a system and the services provided to employers under such system.

Surprisingly, both Republicans and Democrats seemed to agree on this language. However, because the parties differed greatly on many other provisions, the WIA reauthorization had become hopelessly stalled.

Once it became clear that the WIA would not be reauthorized during the 2011 legislative session, the only game in town for the administration's WIF initiative was the appropriations process. Fortunately, the administration had anticipated that the WIA reauthorization might fall through and had made plans for just such an eventuality by working on language with the appropriators in both the House and Senate for their fiscal year 2011 appropriations bills. After much discussion with Appropriations Committee staffers in both houses, the

Senate decided that the approach that the administration proposed—putting additional money in WIA grant programs and then skimming the money off the top for the WIF—would be too controversial. They knew that the states and advocates for the current workforce system would object to at last getting more money only to have it diverted to implement some new idea that the administration had. Instead, the Senate proposed a simple line-item appropriation of $125 million for WIF, and the House accepted the proposal.

However, to finance the $125 million, the administration proposed and the appropriators accepted a reduction in a pot of money controlled by state governors. Specifically, the proposal was to reduce a governors' discretionary fund in the WIA from 15 percent of the adult and dislocated workers formula grants to 5 percent. Not surprisingly, this proposal raised stiff opposition among the governors, who complained bitterly that, in a shining example of the federal government's high-handedness, it simply overrode the state governments' preferences for spending the money. The Republican governor of Iowa, Terry Branstad, who was vice chair of the National Governors Association's Education and the Workforce Committee, later made the point succinctly: "We're saying that we as governors and our directors of workforce development are much more in tune with what the labor force in our state needs than the people in Washington, D.C."[22] Despite the objections from the states, the appropriators approved the proposed financing mechanism. Regardless of the confusion caused by all the continuing resolutions on appropriations during 2011, the work on appropriations bills for 2012, and the (wasted) work on the WIA, the WIF passed the House and the Senate on April 15, 2011, as part of the last continuing resolution providing appropriations for fiscal year 2011. The bill, called the Department of Defense and Full-Year Continuing Appropriations Act of 2011, contained funding for many federal departments, including Labor, Health and Human Services, Education, Agriculture, Commerce, and Justice. Nestled away in Title VIII, section 1801, of the bill was one paragraph that established the WIF with an appropriation of $125 million.[23]

Like the other initiatives, WIF requires the funded projects to be evidence based. In addition, the projects must be "innovative" or must "replicate effective evidence-based strategies." This language is almost an open invitation to use funding tiers. The appropriations language also allows money to be spent on "strategies that align and strengthen the workforce investment system," demonstrating the administration's desire to permit comprehensive reforms of the workforce system itself. The administration wanted to send a strong message that innovation and experimentation related to both specific training programs and the workforce system itself were highly desirable. At last, the administration had a legislative provision and $125 million to launch its workforce initiative.[24]

Developing the Solicitation for Grant Applications

DOL and OMB had been talking about the WIF initiative for more than two years by the time it was finally funded by Congress in April 2011. Everyone from OMB and DOL involved in the development and enactment of the legislation therefore had a good idea of what the administration wanted, although how to write the notice of funding availability to tell potential applicants what they had to do to get the funds still had to be determined. In the Department of Labor, the notice is called the Notice of Availability of Funds and Solicitation for Grant Applications, but it is usually, for obvious reasons, referred to just as the Solicitation for Grant Applications (SGA). Developing the SGA would inevitably involve many meetings and discussions within DOL and between DOL and OMB. An internal DOL working group headed by Jane Oates, the assistant secretary of the employment and training division, was formed to develop the SGA. The major goals of the WIF, everyone now agreed, were to develop and scale up innovative and effective programs, to raise the possibility of state reforms of the workforce system itself, and to require evaluations of as many funded programs as possible.

DOL sponsored webinars and conference calls with various stakeholders to explain its goals for the WIF and to solicit ideas. DOL was a fan of giving flexibility to local workforce agencies and programs. As Gina Wells, a career official at DOL, put it during our interview, DOL wanted to "let this innovation bubble up from the local level, particularly because the workforce system is so nuanced in terms of local labor markets."[25] On the other hand, OMB wanted to identify a few strong reform models supported by at least some good evidence and then encourage states to follow those models. The Career Pathways[26] and Washington State I-BEST programs[27] are examples of the workforce approaches that OMB wanted to feature. The final grant solicitation identified several examples of approaches that local workforce agencies could take to win the competition but left a good deal of room at the local level for choice and innovation.

OMB and DOL agreed that one of the initiative's major goals was to have an impact on the entire field of workforce preparation so that rigorous evidence would become a standard part of program operating procedures. Although OMB and DOL agreed on that primary goal, there was nonetheless a problem, one shared to some degree by the Social Innovation Fund (chapter 5) and the Investing in Innovation Fund (chapter 4): a weak tradition of rigorous evaluation in DOL programs. DOL had hired evaluation companies to conduct national evaluations of the Job Corps[28] and the Job Training Partnership Act,[29] and there were organizations—like the Upjohn Institute in Kalamazoo, Michigan—that had a tradition of high-quality research and evaluation of labor force programs.[30] However, local workforce agencies would need procedural changes and a lot of assistance if they were to become experts in conducting evaluations and using the evaluations to improve their programs. Gina Wells told us in our interview that state and local workforce agencies did not "have a culture of evidence like education does" and that as a result, in discussions about how the workforce agencies should function, participants do not "[base] those arguments on evidence."[31] Despite Wells's view that education had a more robust evidence culture than labor, it may be recalled from the i3 chapter (chapter 4) that Jim Shelton of the Department of Education was equally worried that education institutions did not have a culture of evidence. But considerations such as this did not deter OMB or the White House. They were firmly behind trying to change the culture of the federal government, state governments, and local agencies, both public and private, to encourage, cajole, or force all those who operate social programs to generate and use evidence on a routine basis. Efforts to engineer change of this magnitude can be expected to encounter some resistance. Not surprisingly, many DOL officials besides Gina Wells were worried about making the role of evidence too prominent. Here's what Grace A. Kilbane, a senior career official at DOL, had to say about placing too great an emphasis on evidence and evaluation:

> The overarching premise coming into this [the WIF initiative] was that evidence would drive every new idea and if you didn't have rigorous evidence it really wasn't evidence. That bothered me, I can tell you. It's not that I think it's a bad idea. It's just that we don't have it. We don't have that level of rigorous evidence for most of the things that we do. . . . We have the most long-term unemployed workers that this system has ever had to deal with. We've got all these people falling out of the middle class. And we're saying we're not going to fund anything innovative unless it's got rigorous evidence behind it? . . . You've got to be able to respond to new problems when they come up.[32]

Kilbane neatly employs one of the classic arguments against insisting on spending federal dollars only on programs that are backed by rigorous evidence: namely, that innovation to meet new problems must be accommodated. The response that OMB had developed to address this issue was to use tiers of funding to achieve a balance between programs supported by rigorous evidence and innovative programs. The bottom tier in the WIF and i3 initiatives required at most suggestive evidence, and projects that had no more than a good logic model also could receive funding. Gordon and others at OMB were powerful and persuasive enough to deal with this and other problems raised by experienced career officials and then push the initiatives ahead.

An issue closely related to DOL's concern about lack of evidence in the field was emphasized by Mary Alice McCarthy, another career official who was working with the group writing the SGA. McCarthy agreed that many programs had interesting ideas for systems reform but not much evidence; therefore, she strongly favored the requirement that, at a minimum, a program present a clear logic model for its proposal in order to receive funding at the lowest tier. She worked on the language in the SGA that would describe the logic model requirement.[33] Roughly, the logic model would need to explain what the project wanted to achieve, what actions it would take to get the desired outcome, why the project designers had reason to believe that their intervention would produce impacts, and how they would measure its success or lack thereof. Requiring a logic model forced projects to focus on the evidence that they would need to determine whether they were making progress. The system put in place by DOL to score proposals awarded up to 25 of 105 possible points for the strength of the project's logic model, thereby demonstrating how serious DOL was in requiring potential projects to focus on outcomes even when they did not have much evidence.

Yet another issue that concerned career and political officials at DOL was the administration's focus on system reform. Not only is system reform complex and difficult, but there is little evidence on the effects of reforming systems. McCarthy told us that system reform is "much more difficult than showing the impact at the program delivery level, where you have employment outcomes or educational outcomes. Systemic reform, where you're changing policies or you're reorganizing government agencies—how do you do that? So that was actually one of our biggest challenges."[34]

The 42-page, single-spaced SGA was released on December 23, 2011, about eight months after passage of the WIF authorizing legislation and nearly three years into the Obama administration.[35] The SGA makes it clear that the essence of the WIF initiative is tiered funding and the requirement that applicants present a program evaluation plan along with their proposal. The SGA begins by laying out the background of the workforce issues that the administration intended to address, including a very high rate of long-term unemployment, the lack of skills and credentials that characterizes far too many workers,[36] and a huge job-seeker-to-job-vacancy ratio. To combat these problems, the SGA argues, the workforce investment system "must deliver services that are cost-effective, demand-driven and high-impact."[37] The SGA then explains what the administration proposes to do through the WIF, pointing out that the WIF is one of several administration initiatives, including Investing in Innovation and the Social Innovation Fund in particular, that "seek to use evidence to design program strategies." The SGA states that WIF funds are intended first to help states, local workforce agencies, and their partners "retool" their service delivery strategies and their policymaking and administrative systems in order to improve outcomes and, second, to evaluate the effectiveness of their reforms. As discussed, the administration encourages reform of both workforce services and the structure of the local workforce system because

> innovation at the systems level, where policies, organizational structures, planning processes, performance measurement, procurement, investment priorities, and information management systems reside, is necessary to support service delivery strategies that result in better outcomes and lower costs.

The SGA then provides a list of the types of reform that the WIF supports, including those that aim to

—deliver services more efficiently and achieve better outcomes

—support both system reforms and innovations that facilitate cooperation across programs

—ensure that education, employment, and training services are developed in partnership with specific employers

—emphasize building knowledge about effective practices through rigorous evaluation.

Not surprisingly, the SGA also emphasizes evaluation. In addition to informing grantees that DOL would have a national evaluation coordinator to help them design and conduct their evaluations, the SGA contains an entire section entitled "Integrating Evaluation into Grant Activities." Potential grantees are informed that every grant application must have a detailed plan for a third-party evaluation (provided for in the budget), for which applicants can spend up to 20 percent of their funds. Applicants must specify the outcome measures that they are using to evaluate the success of their project and how data on outcomes will be collected. The SGA identifies seven criteria by which the applicants' data collection plan will be scored, such as how the applicants' information management computer system will capture and analyze the outcome data and how applicants will measure the costs and efficiency of their project.

Jean Grossman, a distinguished researcher and program evaluator at Princeton who was also a senior vice president for research at Public/Private Ventures, was hired by DOL as the department's first chief evaluation officer, charged with helping with the WIF and one or two other projects, including the TAACCCT initiative (see chapter 7). Grossman played an important role in designing the scoring system for the evaluation proposals. She and members of the team working on the SGA decided on a two-stage process in which only evaluation proposals that received the highest scores would be reviewed by the evaluation experts. The evaluation experts could rate the applicants' proposed evaluations as strong, moderate, or weak. DOL would fund only those proposals with strong or moderate evaluation plans—and only moderate evaluation plans that listed clear steps that the applicants could take to improve the evaluation plans would be approved. ETA would work with the applicant to see whether the evaluation plan could be improved. Another part of the evaluation requirement was that the level of rigor (strong, moderate, or weak) for the evaluation plan should at least meet—if not exceed—the level of evidence that the applicant cited for the proposed grant project. Wells told us: "We wanted to allow for the possibility that someone had a really good technical proposal and just didn't have the resources to bring the right folks to the table to design a really good evaluation. We wanted to have a little bit of flexibility to play with that and help them strengthen it." But as Wells and others told us, because DOL was trying to build evidence of workforce programs that would improve outcomes, such as by increasing employment or wages, "we don't want to be funding projects, no matter how promising they sound, without a good plan to evaluate them at an appropriate level of rigor."[38]

It is doubtful that any previous SGA from the Labor Department included such expansive and detailed requirements for program evaluation, which sent a clear signal to the field of employment services that learning to evaluate programs had become an important factor in winning grants from DOL. As in the other Obama evidence-based initiatives, the insistence on rigorous evaluation is a central part of the administration's goal in trying to change the culture of federal grant making.

The SGA also laid out what the DOL called the "continuum of innovation strategies." As in all the evidence-based initiatives, the continuum referred to is the relative strength of evidence supporting the strategy that a grantee might propose. The SGA goes on to define the continuum of evidence with reference to the tiers concept and informs potential grantees that DOL recognizes three tiers of evidence-based strategies along the evidence continuum:

—The lowest tier, including new and untested ideas for which there is little or no evidence. In this case the applicant must present a strong logic model. The size of the grants for this tier is $1 million to $3 million.[39]

—The middle tier, including promising ideas that "have been implemented and tested previously" and for which more rigorous evidence is needed. Applicants can cite evidence from "a variety of studies ranging from a simple pre-post data analysis or return on investment analysis to a study that includes an impact evaluation that employs a comparison group design." The proposed evaluation must be explained in detail in the application and the results must be at least as rigorous as the existing evidence that supports the project. The size of grants for this tier range from $3 to $6 million.

—The highest tier, including proven ideas already supported by rigorous evidence that can be adapted and expanded. Again, the application must detail the evidence. The application must then "provide compelling arguments for the need and potential for success in expanding the scale of the proposed service, product and/or system change." The SGA seems to strongly recommend a randomized controlled trial (RCT) for evaluating service delivery innovations and quasi-experimental designs for evaluating structural innovations. Proposals in this tier can receive from $6 to $12 million.

Another important part of the SGA is a ten-page section with details on how the proposals are to be scored, using a 105-point system. The factors that DOL considers in the scoring are the description of the problem that the proposal addresses (10 points); the description of the project, including the evidence review (45 points); work plan and project management (20 points); project leadership and leadership of the organizations involved (10 points); evaluation plan and data reporting (15 points); and a bonus of 5 points if the application involves a consortium of workforce organizations.

Selecting the Best Applicants

The review process for the WIF initiative is similar in many respects to the process for the other initiatives. It is organized in two steps. In the first step, panels of reviewers score all the proposals; in the second step, evaluation experts score the highest-rated proposed evaluation plans. An interesting twist on the review process was that panel members could talk directly with the authors of good proposals if they had questions or thought that a proposal was good overall but could be strengthened in some way. In fact, applicants submitting proposals that were rated "strong" in the first step and "moderate" in the second step were given the chance to revise and resubmit their proposals. Revisions of the evaluation plan were especially likely. Awards were made to WIBs, state workforce agencies, certain other workforce entities, and consortia of WIBs or state workforce entities. If the awards were given to counties or state departments of labor, they had to partner with a WIB and local businesses.

On June 14, 2012, the department announced the first round of WIF grantees. DOL awarded a total of $146.9 million to 26 applicants. For the lowest tier of funding (programs with new and untested ideas), DOL awarded $32.6 million to 12 projects; for the middle tier of funding (Promising Ideas), DOL gave $46.1 million to 8 projects; and for the highest tier of funding (Adapting Proven Ideas), DOL gave $68.1 million to 6 projects.

Table 6-1 provides basic information about nine of the selected projects, including the five highest-rated grants, in the tier of proven ideas (tier C), and two examples each of grants in the lower two tiers (B and A). The awards range

Table 6-1. *Subgrantee Awards from the Workforce Innovation Fund Evidence-Based Initiative*[a]

Project	Lead grantee	Award amount/ project category (type)	Description of project (evaluation)
LA Reconnec-tions Career Academy (LARCA)	City of Los Angeles Workforce Investment Board	$12 million/ Adapting Proven Ideas (C)	Focuses on youth dropout and unemployment by addressing barriers to employment and basic skills gaps and providing education, career guidance, and other services. The goal is to serve 1,200 out-of-school youth ages 16–24 (random assignment evaluation and implementation study).
Electronic Ohio Means Jobs (e-OMJ)	Ohio Department of Job and Family Services	$12 million/ Adapting Proven Ideas (C)	Attempts to transform Ohio's public workforce system to improve service delivery by introducing an online platform for job seekers. The goal is to deliver services more effectively and efficiently, streamlining 77 programs and 13 agencies (random assignment evaluation with existing One-Stop approach as the control group).
Illinois Path-ways Initiative: Moving Regional Sector Partnerships to Scale in Manufacturing	Illinois Depart-ment of Commerce and Economic Opportunity	$11.99 million/ Adapting Proven Ideas (C)	Focuses on skilled workforce shortages in manufacturing. Project will include career pathways and bridge programs and other support services to help both employers and the most vulnerable populations, including low-income and long-term unemployed adults, through six to eight regional manufacturing partnerships (evaluation by quasi-experimental design).
Startup Quest	Alachua Bradford Regional Work-force Board, FloridaWorks, local WIBs as part of the Busi-ness Advocacy and Self-Employment Consortium (BASEC)	$11.95 million/ Adapting Proven Ideas (C)	Focuses on entrepreneurial training, business incubation, and intensive mentoring targeting the long-term unemployed, especially military veterans. The model provides training and technical assistance in promoting entrepreneurship and attempts to connect jobseekers with employers while presenting self-employment as a viable option (random assignment evaluation).

Project	Lead grantee	Award amount/ project category (type)	Description of project (evaluation)
The Accelerating Connections to Employ- ment Initiative (ACE)	Baltimore County Department of Economic Development, Division of Workforce Development	$11.87 million/ Adapting Proven Ideas (C)	Seeks to improve skills, employment, and earnings by implementing an accelerated, integrated instruc- tional/occupational training model targeting 1,200 to 1,600 low-skilled job seekers. The program is modeled on Washing- ton State's I-BEST program at community colleges; it also includes a systems reform component (propensity score matching evaluation).
Linking Innova- tion, Knowl- edge, and Employment (@LIKE)	Riverside County Economic Development Agency	$6 million/ Promising Ideas (B)	The program, which serves disconnected young adults ages 18–24, has three goals: provide a better package of services to participants, create a replicable model of service, and enhance collaboration between the three Workforce Investment Boards (Riverside, San Bernardino, and Imperial Counties in California) that submitted the proposal (evaluation by comparison group study; comparison group randomly selected).
Oh-Penn Inter- state Region Pathways to Competitive- ness	West Central Job Partnership	$6 million/ Promising Ideas (B)	The project seeks to enhance cooperation across state lines (Ohio and Pennsylvania) and improve the sector strategy to align employment and training with the needs of manufacturers in the area—which is located near oil and shale deposits—by building career pathways (evaluation to include implemen- tation, outcomes, and return on investment analysis).

(continued)

Table 6-1 (*continued*)

Project	Lead grantee	Award amount/ project category (type)	Description of project (evaluation)
Silicon Valley Alliance for Language Learners' Integration, Education, and Success (ALLIES) Innovation Initiative	County of San Mateo and the local WIB	$2.6 million/ New and Untested Ideas (A)	Initiative aims to expand the network of support for adult immigrants to help them succeed in the workforce system by connecting them to high-need regional career pathways (evaluation is a mix of process, output, and outcome and cost-benefit analysis).
Steps up to STEM: Addressing the STEM Skills Shortage in New York's Greater Capital Region	Fulton, Montgomery, and Schoharie Counties Workforce Development Boards	$2.99 million/ New and Untested Ideas (A)	Goal is to address the STEM skills shortage in the region, targeting in particular disadvantaged youth, low-income adults, and dislocated workers. Program runs a STEM awareness campaign and provides job seeker recruitment and preparation, employment recruitment, and professional development services (evaluation for implementation and outcomes).

Source: U.S. Department of Labor, "Workforce Innovation Fund Grantee Awards" (www.doleta. gov/workforce_innovation/grant_awards.cfm).

from $2.6 million to $12 million. Projects target youths who have dropped out of school, unemployed workers, workers who want to upgrade their skills, and recent immigrants. In accordance with the Department of Labor's emphasis on system reform, the Ohio project, for example, proposes to retool a major part of the state workforce system by introducing an online platform for job seekers that will be easier and more efficient for customers to use than the current system. The Ohio project will also streamline the number of programs and agencies, again making it easier for customers to know what is available and to select their best option for training and other services. Four of the projects summarized above propose to evaluate their program by the use of random assignment.

Can the Nation's Workforce System Be Improved?

In the context of our larger story about evidence-based initiatives, four points about the WIF initiative deserve emphasis. First, as with all the other evidence-based initiatives, working with Congress to enact legislation to authorize and pay for WIF turned out to be difficult, complex, and time consuming. In this case, because several of the administration's plans were foiled by Congress, the White House and OMB had to have a legislative plan B. In fact, the plan for authorizing the program through the normal authorization process fell through because the vehicle in which the WIF was riding—the reauthorization of the Workforce Investment Act—stalled in Congress, leaving the administration temporarily in the lurch. But the administration had anticipated that the WIA reauthorization might die an untimely death and was planning a second option to secure WIF funding through the annual appropriations process. That strategy turned out to be successful. As the legislative history of WIF demonstrates yet again, efforts to enact and fund future evidence-based initiatives will require careful planning and creative legislative strategizing on the part of any administration or congressional committee that hopes to expand them. In addition, legislative sponsors must be prepared to invest some political capital in the effort.

The administration's experience with WIF illustrates a second useful point: the key to using evidence to inform policy in fields of intervention that do not have a strong evidence base is to use the tiers as a template and then adjust the level of evidence required for each tier according to what the field can handle. For every area of social policy, there is a continuum of evidence, ranging from numerous rigorous studies to few rigorous studies. The goal of evidence-based initiatives should be to adjust the levels on each tier in a thoughtful way that encourages the field to keep striving to produce more rigorous evidence and more successful intervention programs.

A third point highlighted by WIF raises interesting challenges for program evaluation. DOL was interested not just in helping state and local workforce agencies use programs that had good evidence of success but also in pursuing reforms of the workforce system itself at the state or local level. The state of Ohio, for example, received money to make substantial changes in its workforce system by developing an online platform that could be used efficiently by all job seekers and by streamlining the state's 77 workforce programs, which were administered by 13 different state agencies. Those seem like worthy and potentially effective reforms of the state's workforce system, but how will Ohio know whether the reforms are in fact effective? The state is now answering this question by randomly assigning people who apply for services and agree to participate in a study to either the state's traditional One-Stop service system or to its new streamlined electronic system in order to collect information on a set of outcome measures, including the number of applicants in each group who get jobs and their satisfaction with the services.[40] A potential issue with this evaluation design is that many applicants may elect not to participate in the study, thereby raising questions about generalizability of the results. Another issue is that it would be better to randomly assign many local agencies to the new system or to the traditional One-Stop system and then compare the average performance of the two groups of agencies. Under the current design, only one agency has adopted the new system and only one agency is continuing to operate the One-Stop system, which reduces the generalizability of the outcomes. The goal of an experiment in systems reform is to determine whether the results would generalize to many more locations. If the new program is tried in only one location, there could well be something about that location that played a major role in the results. Despite these drawbacks, if the current design is carried out as described, it would provide results with good internal validity. The Ohio example demonstrates that even complex changes in workforce systems can sometimes be subjected to evaluation by random assignment designs.

The relative paucity of random assignment studies conducted by workforce agencies throughout the country raises a fourth and final important issue. Until more is known about how the 26 WIF grants are being implemented, it appears to us from our interviews that both DOL and the state and local workforce agencies are now taking baby steps on a very long road. True, as we have noted repeatedly, all six of the evidence-based initiatives are fundamentally about culture change, but the degree of change that the nation's labor force agencies must undergo seems to be more dramatic than that of the agencies implementing most of the other initiatives—with the possible exception of the Corporation for National and Community Service and the intermediaries and community-based subgrantees implementing the Social Innovation Fund. Efforts to convince agencies that are busy operating programs on constrained budgets and perhaps conducting a somewhat haphazard evaluation here and there to suddenly conduct gold standard evaluations—and to restrict their programs as much as possible to model programs that have good evidence of success—are bound to encounter resistance, especially from people who do not think random assignment studies are as essential for program improvement as many scholars and members of the Obama administration do.

It was not always so. According to some of our interviews, for many years DOL had a tradition of engaging in high-quality research to support its mission of developing and evaluating high-quality employment and training programs. But some people believe that the huge budget cuts during the Reagan era fell heavily on the department's research capacity. In addition, the Office of the Assistant Secretary for Policy Evaluation and Research, which was led by a series of prominent labor economists and researchers, was terminated early in the Reagan administration. For almost three decades, according to this view, research and evaluation at DOL had a much lower priority than in the pre-Reagan years.[41] A few people that we interviewed seemed optimistic that the creation by the Obama administration of the new post of chief evaluation officer and the appointment of two distinguished researchers, Jean Grossman and Demetra Nightingale, as the first two chief evaluation officers shows a new respect at DOL for the need to return to the tradition of high-quality evidence and program evaluation. Changing the culture of evidence at DOL and hundreds of state and local workforce agencies throughout the nation promises to be an arduous and drawn-out process. The Obama administration's WIF initiative is a step in the right direction, but unless the next administration continues the Obama reforms, WIF will be in danger of having only a modest and perhaps fleeting impact on the nation's workforce development system.

7 | The Trade Adjustment Assistance Community College and Career Training Initiative

The story behind the development of the Trade Adjustment Assistance Community College and Career Training (TAACCCT) Grant Program is as long and complicated as its name. The program, according to one OMB official, has "a fascinating history . . . and a horrible acronym." From the earliest days of the Obama administration, officials, especially those at the Office of Management and Budget (OMB) and the White House, were interested in creating a major initiative on community colleges. In light of the struggling economy, the administration saw higher education and workforce development as important priorities. President Obama announced a focus on both in his first address to a joint session of Congress, delivered on February 24, 2009.[1] The president called on every American to "commit to at least one year or more of higher education or career training," and he mentioned community colleges as an appropriate place to fulfill that commitment. The president also announced what came to be known as the "2020 goal." By the year 2020, Obama said, "America will once again have the highest proportion of college graduates in the world."[2]

The 2020 goal spurred work by the administration on a number of fronts, including plans for a massive infusion of funds into the community college system that came to be known as the American Graduation Initiative (AGI). Officials at the Department of Education (ED) were already at work on a comprehensive student loan reform proposal when the office of White House chief of staff Rahm Emanuel called Martha Kanter, the deputy undersecretary of education, to say that the president was interested in a substantial investment in community colleges—somewhere on the order of $10 to $15 billion. Kanter, who had recently joined the administration in the summer of 2009 and who would end up playing a major role in the development of the initiative, was not surprised at the request. There was tremendous political support for community colleges throughout the administration and at the ED. Summing up the general attitude at the department, she noted that "there was a commitment to raise the national profile and understanding about the significant role of community colleges in American higher education. There was tremendous support for moving ahead with this particular program."[3]

Administration officials saw the community college system as a valuable, underused resource in the overall push to expand higher education and workforce training, especially for students from disadvantaged backgrounds. Given the dire economic situation at the time and the increasingly globalized economy, community colleges were a more affordable and accessible option for getting a postsecondary education, which could lead to a better job than a person could get with just a high school degree. They could provide workforce training, skills development, and vocational certificates as well as remedial education for students who were not prepared for college because of deficient reading and math skills. Those offerings are well designed for Americans who would soon be looking for their first job, who were out of work, or who were looking to upgrade their skills. In pursuing an initiative on community colleges, the administration wanted to shift the focus from access to completion—to helping students not only attend college but also obtain credentials and ultimately get a job or a better job.

The sprawling system of community colleges in the United States provides open access, affordable education, and vocational training to more than 12 million Americans annually. The nearly 1,200, mostly public, institutions across the United States enroll more than 40 percent of the nation's undergraduates. During the Great Recession, from 2007 to 2009, community colleges saw their enrollment increase by 17 percent as many unemployed workers tried to upgrade their skills in hopes of getting a job. Tuition, averaging $3,260 a year, remains cheap compared with tuition at a public four-year institution, which averages nearly $9,000 a year.[4] Students tend to be "nontraditional"—older, part-time, or from underrepresented populations, including minorities and immigrants. Forty-eight percent of all black and 56 percent of all Hispanic undergraduates in the United States attend a community college, and nearly 40 percent of all community college students represent the first generation in their family to attend college. Perhaps the biggest challenge that community colleges face is that nearly 60 percent of incoming students require some type of remedial education—which, in addition to being a black mark against the nation's K–12 education system, makes completion of a certificate or degree that much more difficult. Research shows that not only do remedial courses fail to help students make up for literacy and numeracy skills that they missed in the K–12 system but they also are associated with increased dropout rates.[5] In short, remedial courses generally do not work.

Developing the American Graduation Initiative

During the spring of 2009, the ED took the lead in developing the AGI, but OMB sought to include the Department of Labor (DOL) in the discussions as well in order to maintain the focus on employment outcomes. Career officials and political appointees at both departments, along with officials at OMB and the Domestic Policy Council (DPC), began laying out the priorities for the initiative. Administration officials also worked with staffers for Representative George Miller (D-Calif.), the leading Democrat in the U.S. House of Representatives on education issues and the chairman of the Committee on Education and Labor. Even in the early discussions, outcomes and evidence played an important role in shaping the direction of the initiative. Julie Peller, an education policy adviser to the Education and Labor Committee, described the goal of the initiative as "trying to find ways to incentivize and encourage community colleges to get successful outcomes for their students" and then scale up the effective programs.[6]

The administration developed the proposal during the spring and summer of 2009, eventually marrying it with the president's proposed student loan overhaul and college financing initiative. The administration wanted to eliminate giving federal subsidies to private lenders for student loans in favor of making federal loans directly to students; the savings from direct lending would then be used to fund the community college initiative. On July 15, Congress released the Student Aid and Fiscal Responsibility Act (SAFRA), combining student loan provisions and a community college initiative (the AGI). In a July 24 report, the Congressional Budget Office (CBO) estimated that the administration's plan for reforming the student loan system would save $86.8 billion over ten years (2009–19).[7]

On July 14, 2009, the president unveiled his AGI proposal at an event at Macomb Community College in Michigan.[8] Reiterating the 2020 goal from his State of the Union address, the president called for 5 million more Americans to obtain a higher-education degree or certificate in the ensuing decade. The president said that the AGI was a way to "reform and strengthen community colleges like this one from coast to coast so they get the resources that students and schools need—and the results workers and businesses demand." The rhetoric that he used for the AGI was similar to his rhetoric for the other evidence-based initiatives. He talked about the investment in community colleges much the way that he talked about the Investing in Innovation (i3) initiative or the Social Innovation Fund (SIF), which were in development around the same time.[9] The goal of the AGI would be to "propose new funding for innovative strategies" and "offer competitive grants, challenging community colleges to pursue innovative, results-oriented strategies in exchange for federal funding."[10]

The following day, SAFRA was introduced in the House of Representatives. Along with provisions expanding Pell Grants and reforming the federal student loan program, the legislation included $7 billion over ten years for community college programs and reform, plus an additional $2.5 billion for construction and renovation.[11] The community college reform legislation had two main components. First, from 2010 through 2013, $630 million would be available each year for grants to community colleges for "innovative programs" or "programs of demonstrated effectiveness, based on the evaluations of similar programs funded by the ED or DOL or other research on similar programs."[12] The grants to community colleges would be for four years, and each would be for at least $1,000,000. Applicants were required to detail how the grant would help students reach graduation benchmarks set by the school. The grants could be used for creating or implementing programs that would increase graduation rates and help students obtain credentials or employment. Grantees were required to set benchmarks for closing the gaps between underrepresented groups and the mainstream student population in enrollment and college completion rates; addressing local workforce needs; and improving employment outcomes for students. Second, the legislation would appropriate a total of $630 million a year for six-year grants (from 2014 through 2019) to states "to implement the systematic reform of junior and community colleges . . . by carrying out programs, services, and policies that demonstrated effectiveness under the evaluation" of the grants from 2010–13. In plain English, there would be two stages of funding. From 2010 through 2013, grants would be available each year to community colleges for "innovative programs" or "programs of demonstrated effectiveness." Then, from 2014 through 2019, grants would go to states to be used to scale up the reforms and interventions that proved successful during the first stage. The legislation also called for the creation of a research hub (to be called the Learning and Earning Research Center) to help community colleges manage and use student data to improve employment and education outcomes. With $50 million a year for the 2010–13 period, the administration would set up state longitudinal databases and the Learning and Earning Research Center, which would develop ways to measure the progress of the community college reforms and help collect and disseminate data and research on effective community college programs. In addition, the initiative included $50 million annually from 2010 through 2019 for competitive grants to colleges and universities, philanthropies, or other entities "to develop, evaluate, and disseminate free high-quality online training, high school courses, and postsecondary education courses." Together the proposals added up to $7 billion over ten years, from 2010 through 2019.[13]

The Political Reality

If the administration's legislation passed, the scope of the investment in community colleges would be immense, and it would reflect the administration's preference for competitive grants and evidence of effectiveness in designing its grant programs. But the community college proposals soon became entangled in the chaotic, heated, and messy negotiations over health care reform. Nothing in Congress—especially not something worth multiple billions of dollars—happens in a vacuum, and nothing is unaffected by the prevailing political winds. And therein lies the rub for the community college initiative. Only a complicated mix of politics, legislative maneuvering, and sheer luck can explain how a $12 billion investment in community colleges under the AGI, which appeared on several occasion to be dead, had become a $2 billion investment under TAACCCT by the time that the dust settled in the spring of 2010.

After the American Recovery and Reinvestment Act (ARRA) was passed, within a month of President Obama's inauguration, health care reform became Obama's top domestic policy priority. By July 2009 the three House committees responsible for drafting parts of the health care legislation had released their bills. After the House Democratic leadership convinced the committees of jurisdiction to combine their three plans into a single legislative proposal, the politics of health reform began to heat up and many members of Congress, especially Democrats, began to hear from their constituents. During the August 2009 congressional recess, many lawmakers returned to their districts to face a fierce constituent backlash over health care reform. A common factor in the opposition was the Tea Party, which had gained strength and spearheaded protests against the health care reform proposals that had been forged by Democrats in both houses of Congress.[14] As the summer dragged on, the prospects for any bipartisan cooperation on health care reform became increasingly bleak, causing some Democrats to raise (quietly) the possibility of using a special legislative maneuver known as reconciliation to pass a health reform bill. Reconciliation was originally designed to enable Congress to make changes more easily to a mandatory spending program such as Medicare or to make other budget cuts, both of which might be difficult to do under regular order, which requires that bills go through committees of jurisdiction and be open to amendment. In recent years, reconciliation has been used to reduce spending, reduce revenues, and increase the debt limit. No filibusters are permitted and debate on a reconciliation bill is limited, the idea being that such restrictions would make the legislation easier to pass. There also are strict rules in the Senate, codified by the late Robert Byrd (D-W.V.), about what can be included in a reconciliation bill. Namely, the provisions must deal only with spending or revenue and must not increase the budget deficit within a given budget window (usually five years), and the bill cannot amend Social Security. A reconciliation bill is subject to challenges under the Byrd rule, with the Senate Parliamentarian serving as the rule keeper, and senators are allowed to raise an objection to any part of the legislation that they consider "extraneous" and therefore impermissible.[15]

As negotiations on health care reform got under way in the spring of 2009, the Democrats, seeing many potential hurdles to passage of a bill, wanted to keep all their options on the table. Democratic Budget Committee leaders, at the urging of Rahm Emanuel, instructed the committees with major jurisdiction over health care reform[16] to leave open the possibility of doing a reconciliation bill. Republicans sharply criticized the reconciliation idea and the president's support for it, arguing that the proposal was, according to Senator Judd Gregg (R-N.H.): "the Chicago approach to governing: Strong-arm it through. . . . You're talking about the exact opposite of bipartisan. You're talking about running over the minority, putting them in cement and throwing them in the Chicago River." Even some Democrats were less than thrilled about the plan. Among them was Senator Blanche Lincoln (D-Ark.), who said that reconciliation would create "kind of a divisive atmosphere" that "would just be sticking [Republicans] in the eye."[17] Perhaps the major reason for the criticism was that reconciliation removed the option of a filibuster, the most potent weapon by which the minority party in the Senate can force the majority party to choose between bipartisan amendments or, often, the death of its bill.

As negotiations continued, Democrats abandoned the idea of attempting to pass the entire health care reform bill as a reconciliation measure, but the Budget Committee retained language in the budget resolution that left open the possibility of using reconciliation at a later date. That decision would end up having implications not just for health care reform, but also for the administration's proposed initiative on community colleges. Despite being consumed by the health care debate, the House managed to continue its work on SAFRA, the bill that contained the student loan reforms and the community college initiative. On September 17, the House passed SAFRA by a vote of 253–171. The road ahead in the Senate—where the bill faced strong opposition from Republicans, who threatened a filibuster, and even from some Democrats—was more difficult.

Although the House was able to pass the AGI as part of SAFRA, its ultimate fate would be tied to health care reform. On November 7, after rancorous debate, the House passed its health care reform legislation. The Senate followed suit and passed its own bill, the Patient Protection and Affordable Care Act, on Christmas Eve 2009. The next step would have been to appoint a House-Senate Conference Committee to reconcile the differences between the House and Senate bills and reach final agreement on a bill that would then be passed by both houses and signed into law by the president. On January 19, 2010, however, the voters of Massachusetts threw a bomb into the Democrats' plans. In a political stunner, Republican Scott Brown won a special election to fill the Senate seat that had belonged to liberal icon Edward Kennedy for nearly half a century. Brown's election stripped the Democrats of their filibuster-proof majority in the Senate and threw the entire future of the health care legislation into doubt. The administration and congressional Democrats spent the first few months of 2010 scrambling to determine how the health care reform legislation could proceed, given the political reality that a House-Senate conference report would not pass in the Senate because of the Republican right to filibuster. On March 4, Obama endorsed the idea of using reconciliation so that Congress could, in his words, "finish its work" on health care reform by passing the Affordable Care Act (ACA) and the companion reconciliation bill.[18] Under a plan developed by Democratic leaders, the House would pass the Senate bill (the ACA) and would then pass a reconciliation bill that contained some changes to the Senate version of health care reform requested by House Democrats. The reconciliation bill, as noted, would not be subject to a Senate filibuster—and the ACA, if passed exactly as it had passed the Senate, would not need to be voted on by the Senate again because there would be no need for a House-Senate conference report. Despite strong Republican objections that this approach amounted to an attempt to "jam the bill through Congress,"[19] Democrats formalized a plan to use reconciliation to avoid insurmountable problems in the Senate under regular order. Of course, Republicans themselves had used reconciliation when they were in the majority to enact controversial pieces of legislation, including the 1996 welfare reform law.

Meanwhile, SAFRA, the bill containing the president's student loan overhaul and the community college initiative, seemed increasingly in jeopardy. Facing opposition, Democrats had previously discussed using reconciliation to pass SAFRA in the Senate, giving the president a major legislative victory. Now, however, Democrats would have to use reconciliation primarily to enact changes to the Senate-passed Patient Protection and Affordable Care Act because only one reconciliation bill a year is permitted. Even so, Democrats saw an opportunity to score a double victory: they could include the student loan overhaul in the reconciliation bill and use the budgetary savings to offset some of the costs associated with health care, ensuring that the bill met the Byrd rule requirement that a reconciliation bill not increase the deficit and ensuring that it met the spending targets specified in the budget resolution. There was one potential problem that might not be solved by this strategy—there might not be any money left for the community college initiative.

On March 17, the House introduced the Health Care and Education Reconciliation Act of 2010, which, in accordance with the compromise worked out between House and Senate Democrats and the White House, contained several amendments to the Senate health care bill. The student loan savings tabulated for SAFRA would be used to help offset the costs associated with the health care amendments, allowing the reconciliation bill to continue achieving its budget targets. In the March 17 draft of the reconciliation bill, enough money was available to ensure that, remarkably, the AGI remained in the legislation, including the $7 billion for community college reform that had been earmarked in the SAFRA legislation and the original proposal. But that provision soon changed. Over the next four days, the House scrambled to finalize the legislation, protecting the health care changes, which were the Democrats' top priority. Members and staffers worked furiously through draft after draft, responding to updated budgetary scoring and the rulings of the parliamentarian, the official arbiter of what was allowed in reconciliation bills. The AGI soon ran into trouble: a report from CBO, the official scorekeeper of costs and savings in all legislation, revised downward the cost savings associated with some of the student loan provisions. Whereas a July 2009 CBO estimate put the savings from the student loan reform package at $86.8 billion, the new report from March 2010 scored only $67 billion in savings.[20] That reduction, along with concerns about a likely Byrd rule challenge on their AGI provision, led House Democrats to strip out the AGI—much to the administration's dismay.

The prospects for resurrection looked grim, but a few administration officials, particularly Robert Gordon at OMB, remained undaunted. He and others spent a few hectic days attempting to concoct a way to save at least part of the community college initiative. A potential way to secure money for a community college initiative would be to find an existing authorized program and use reconciliation to fund the program. OMB was being exceptionally cautious regarding what was allowed in the reconciliation bill because the administration needed to pass the bill as part of its ACA strategy. If something controversial or something that violated the Byrd rule was put in the bill, it might be subject to a point of order or the entire package might lose votes, which the Democrats could not afford. So OMB needed to find a program that had already been authorized but had not been implemented. It was a good plan, but there was still a problem. Normally the AGI would have been included in the health and education title of the reconciliation bill (Title II). Unfortunately, all of the funds in that title of the bill had to be used to pay for the health care amendments and no money was left. But some money was still available in Title I (Coverage, Medicare, Medicaid, and Revenues).[21] On Saturday, March 20, just hours before the final vote in the House, Mark Zuckerman, a top staffer for Chairman Miller, discovered an obscure authorizing provision for the Trade Adjustment Assistance (TAA) program, which had been created by ARRA and, miraculously for the administration, was related to community colleges. Zuckerman alerted Gordon, who worked with a career official at OMB, Melissa Bomberger, to produce legislative language that would tie $2 billion to the TAA authorization in the ARRA.

The provision that Zuckerman uncovered was the Community College and Career Training Grant Program, in section 278 of the ARRA. In classic Washington fashion, the provision had been passed without fanfare and then was seemingly forgotten. A new government program—an amendment to the Trade Act of 1974—had been authorized and had entered the vast bureaucratic abyss, unfunded and poised for oblivion. The program, which called for competitive grants to community colleges to assist workers who had been displaced or affected by foreign trade, was to be housed at the DOL. Because the health care reconciliation bill was on the verge of passage, Gordon and others were convinced that they could secure funding for this provision to create their community college initiative. The provision affected the TAA program, which meant that it fell under the jurisdiction of the Ways and Means Committee. That was essential to the administration's plan because it meant that funding for the grant program could come from Title I of the reconciliation bill, which included revenue that was under jurisdiction of the Ways and Means Committee. Gordon and Bomberger realized that they could secure $2 billion over four years under this title of the bill for the TAA and community college provision authorized by ARRA and then use all the flexibility that they could find in the TAA authorizing language to implement their community college initiative.

The following day, March 21, the House passed its reconciliation bill, which included both SAFRA and, in section 1501, the provision that funded the ARRA program on TAA and community colleges. Through the TAA and community college provision, the administration secured $500 million a year for fiscal years 2011–14, with a guarantee that not less than 0.5 percent of the funds would go to each state. Four days later, the Senate passed the reconciliation bill with minor amendments, which the House in turn approved the same day. On March 30, at Northern Virginia Community College, President Obama signed the Health Care Education and Reconciliation Act of 2010 into law. Known by its elegant title of Trade Adjustment Assistance Community College and Career Training Grant Program, the administration had secured $2 billion for the president's community college initiative, thereby achieving what the president and his administration saw as a major step toward his "2020 goal" of boosting the number of Americans graduating from college.[22]

Development of TAACCCT

In a matter of days, the president's American Graduation Initiative went from dead to reincarnated in another form. Now the administration faced the difficult task of designing the initiative—and the especially challenging problem of broadening the types of students who would be eligible for services. Administration officials wanted to achieve the goals of the original AGI legislation if possible, but they were legally obligated to observe the original TAA legislative requirements. Doing so required achieving a delicate balance of bureaucratic, legal, and political considerations. For starters, because of the quirks of the legislative process, the AGI was created at DOL, although the administration had wanted the ED to play the lead role. Now, DOL would be in charge—although OMB pushed Labor to accept input from Education. Needless to say, that created potential for conflict. Martha Kanter of the ED remarked, "Well, I think it's [fair] to say that both agencies had a wealth of ideas about how the dollars should be allocated, but Labor had the final say."[23]

Each federal agency has its own culture, operating procedures, and approach to policy. At least part of the reason that OMB had initially pushed for housing a community college initiative at the ED was that Gordon and others perceived more of a focus on reform and evidence there than at Labor. Officials from both agencies who worked on TAACCCT recognized the potential for disagreement.

To begin the process of designing the initiative, career officials and political appointees at the Departments of Labor and Education, along with officials from OMB, set up a working group. From the beginning, OMB pushed both departments to consider how they could incorporate evidence into the design of the initiative. While the AGI made explicit reference to funding programs that had evidence of success, the authorizing language for the new TAACCCT initiative lacked any language about evidence. There was no mention of funding successful programs or of making evidence of program effectiveness and evaluation an important component of the program. As a first step in that direction, OMB and DOL decided to create the position of chief evaluation officer. After an intensive search, DOL hired Jean Grossman, a veteran researcher and expert in program evaluation. Among other important positions, she had served as vice president of research at Public/Private Ventures, a respected research firm, and she had led many rigorous impact evaluations of social programs covering issues from teen pregnancy to job training. In her new capacity at DOL, Grossman, who started in April 2010, was charged with helping the agency make program evaluation a greater priority than in the past. One of her first tasks was to get a strong evidence requirement into the TAACCCT.

The working group had to first figure out what the major priorities would be and who would be eligible to apply for grant funds. While OMB and the ED continued to refer to the AGI, with its focus on community college completion rates and broad institutional reform, as a model, the TAACCCT, by law, had to target workers displaced by changing patterns of trade. Still, OMB saw the new funds from TAACCCT as a way to begin funding more innovation and capacity building—to help community colleges develop and test new curriculums and program models that could improve workforce outcomes for students. By the summer of 2010, the administration had already applied the competitive, tiered evidence model to i3, which they held up as a potential template for TAACCCT.

While competitive grants were not necessarily new to DOL, the department had less experience and expertise in building capacity and improving program models than in funding direct worker training or existing model programs. In our interview, a senior Labor Department official laid out the challenges in pursuing the direction preferred by the OMB. She pointed out that the TAACCCT was not the kind of education and training program that the department was used to funding; it usually allowed states and local workforce agencies a lot of flexibility in providing services. Those programs, in which clients receive services for a period of time through well-established administrative procedures, are very different from what the administration wanted to do with the TAACCCT initiative. In the new initiative, DOL and workforce agencies were charged with working with community colleges, developing new training curriculums, ensuring that the new programs led to skills or certificates for jobs that were available in the local economy, and consulting with local employers to keep up with the skills in demand at a given time.[24]

In setting the priorities for the grants, Grossman worked with her colleagues to conduct a literature review of the research on community colleges in order to discover and assess what educational strategies were successful and decide where they might focus the grant funds. Were there program models or curriculums that did in fact help students (especially the disadvantaged) obtain certificates and, ultimately, employment? What challenges and impediments did students face in completing course requirements at community colleges? Were there particular features of successful courses or curriculums that could be applied in other settings and possibly scaled up? Answers to those questions would help shape the TAACCCT grant program.

Evidence

The word "evidence" does not appear in the authorizing legislation for the TAACCCT program. The secretary of labor is directed to award grants based on "the merits of the grant proposal submitted by the eligible institution."

But, as with the other Obama evidence-based initiatives, the administration, particularly OMB, was determined to make evidence play a prominent role in TAACCCT. Despite the lack of language on evidence in both the authorizing and the appropriation laws, the administration followed its familiar pattern of writing standards of evidence into the grant notice (in this case called the Notice of Availability of Funds and Solicitation for Grant Applications, or simply SGA). But because there was so little evidence on the effects of community college programs, TAACCCT, perhaps more than any of the other evidence-based initiatives, confronted the intense challenges, complexities, and compromises inherent in translating an abstract notion of "evidence-based" into a practical reality.

By the time that the administration started work on TAACCCT, the ED was in the process of conducting the first round of the i3 grant competition, including its three tiers of evidence and the different standards required for each tier. Senior administration officials saw i3 as an important model for future grant competitions at the ED and beyond. OMB in particular argued for setting a high bar for evidence, using the top tier as a way to push the education field to think more about program outcomes and evaluation. The long-term goal would then be to fund primarily programs that had evidence of success based on rigorous evaluations. However, recognizing that there often is a dearth of evidence on successful programs, the administration developed the two lower tiers as a way to fund programs that had promising evidence, were "innovative," and might one day have enough evidence to scale up. As the TAACCCT was being developed, OMB pushed DOL to consider the i3 tiered model for the community college grants. OMB officials thought that at the very least, the initiative should force applicants to focus on outcomes—especially on whether community college students who participated in particular programs or curriculums obtained credentials and employment.

As in the case of i3, some officials working on the initiative were concerned about setting the evidence bar too high, arguing that there was not enough rigorous evidence of impacts of community college programs and that most of the evidence that was available came from programs that focused on education, not on trade-displaced workers. If the TAACCCT grants were tiered, with the most money reserved for the most evidence, very few—if any—programs targeting trade-displaced workers would qualify.[25] On the other hand, if the majority of funding was reserved for nonexistent trade-displaced programs, the initiative would not succeed. As one official put it:

> There was definitely some back and forth . . . we can't go 100 percent best evidence because it's going to leave way too many colleges out and way too

many types of programs out. And I think that's also the case [for] TAA workers in particular or dislocated workers . . . there's much more evidence on the education side than there is on the workforce development side. And so it's DOL and . . . a workforce-focused program at the end of the day that's funding education capacity; there [was] a little tension on that.[26]

Another major challenge to incorporating evidence into the initiative was capacity. The program offered $500 million a year for community college programs and curriculum development. Because there was plenty of financial incentive for every community college to apply, officials were expecting several hundred applicants—but that would mean scoring several hundred applications. DOL simply did not have the internal capacity to evaluate and score the evidence standards, particularly because the timing of passage of the legislation left them with a tight schedule for making the first round of awards in 2011. Unlike the ED, which has researchers at the Institute of Education Sciences trained in applying the What Works Clearinghouse evidence standards, DOL does not have the same internal expertise to draw on. Grossman was sympathetic to those concerns. While she favored an increased focus on evidence, she also recognized that the DOL was right to be cautious:

> The weak link in all of these evidence-based initiatives is how the panels are formed. . . . So you can write a great RFP [request for proposals], but if someone doesn't know the difference between a randomized comparison group and a nonrandomized comparison group and they get equal points—well, you're stuck.[27]

Grossman described some of the many questions raised about how to structure the review panels, particularly in regard to evidence: Would there be an evaluation specialist on each review panel? Would there instead be two rounds of review for each grant: one for content and one for the quality of evidence? Would only the proposals deemed strong with respect to content and operations have their evaluation evidence judged? Grossman emphasized during her interview that a major constraint in implementing evidence-based initiatives is the difficulty of finding enough experts in the evaluation of workforce development programs who are willing and able to serve on review panels.

The decision to use tiers of evidence, as OMB wanted the DOL to do, required a decision on how much money to put into each tier. OMB wanted the most money to go into the highest tier of grants—to the applicants with the most evidence—to send a signal to the workforce development field that the administration was serious about the importance of evidence. DOL resisted, arguing for putting the most money in the middle tier. In general, the department resisted applying the tiered concept to the grants at all, arguing that nothing would get funded in the highest evidence category and that it simply did not have the capacity to review the evidence. Ultimately OMB acquiesced: there would not be three levels of funding for TAACCCT. Instead, DOL agreed to create three levels of evidence (strong, moderate, and preliminary) using the i3 definitions. Applicants would have to specify which level of evidence they were citing in their application and they would receive points for describing it, but funding amounts would not be directly tied to evidence in the way that they are for i3.

In short, the TAACCCT was not a case of more money for more evidence—with one exception. Although there were no discrete tiers of funding, the working group developed another option to encourage applicants to focus on evidence: it decided to offer more funding to applicants who demonstrated an especially high level of evidence. If an applicant could do so, the project might qualify for a "break the cap award," worth more than the highest regular award. High-evidence applicants would be subject to a separate review by evaluation and evidence experts. Such applicants could qualify for the larger award by demonstrating that the proposed project included replicating at multiple sites strategies that "have been shown by prior research to have strong or moderate evidence of positive impacts on education and/or employment outcomes."[28]

Evaluation

Another major goal of the Obama administration's evidence-based initiatives is to get grantees to evaluate their programs by using rigorous designs when possible, often by drawing on technical assistance from evaluation experts. The working group discussed how to incorporate this priority into the new TAACCCT program. Requiring good evaluations in the TAACCCT initiative was especially important because of the general lack of evidence on community college programs. Given that many of the eventual grantees would be implementing programs with no more than preliminary evidence, evaluation would be an essential part of beginning to build an evidence base for such programs as well as expertise in the field of community college program evaluation.

However, there were concerns about how to design the evaluation requirements that all applicants would be required to meet. Members of the working group worried about the real-world constraints in attempting to get all the applicants to design and submit evaluation plans. As with the evidence component, DOL's capacity was one constraint. In order to be valid, evaluations must be well designed and well implemented. Some officials in the working group worried that the department could not assess the individual evaluation plans of all of the applicants because of the number of experts that would be required to score all the potential applications. Grossman described the situation:

> I felt myself sort of waffling. . . . I was . . . backing what the career folks [at the Department of Labor] said because they knew [the department] didn't have enough staff to do it [assess the evidence and the evaluation plans of all the applicants] and they didn't want to . . . put us out there and make us fall on our face because we didn't have enough staff. . . . On the other hand, I said we really do need to figure out a way to evaluate if we're trying to incorporate evidence, but there is this real-world constraint. . . . wanting the right evaluation goals but dealing with the real world.

Ultimately, the working group could not reach agreement on doing individual evaluations of grantees. TAACCCT therefore reflects a compromise on the evaluation front. Applicants are not required to submit a plan for an individual evaluation as part of their proposal for funding, as they are in i3. In lieu of evaluation plans, Grossman and others pushed for a sophisticated set of outcome measures that every project would have to collect and report to DOL, along with comparable measures for some type of reasonable comparison group. She helped develop the idea of having the grantees select a cohort comparison group against which they could measure the outcomes of the TAACCCT program participants. The grantees would have to set benchmarks for program outcomes, including goals for attainment of credentials and employment. The working group eventually developed seven outcome measures that all grantees must track for both TAACCCT program participants and the comparison group:
—entered employment rate
—employment retention rate[29]
—average earnings
—attainment of credits toward degrees
—attainment of industry-recognized certificates of less than one year
—attainment of industry-recognized certificates of more than one year
—graduation rate for degree programs.
    Grantees are required to report on these outcome and benchmark figures annually. The evaluation requirements in the first round of TAACCCT program grants are the weakest evaluation requirements of all the evidence-based initiatives.

The Solicitation for Grant Awards

The Department of Labor released the SGA for the first round of TAACCCT grants on January 20, 2011. The final document represented months of discussion of the priorities and goals of the initiative and numerous compromises between the various competing interests at DOL and OMB. The SGA laid out four funding priorities for grantees:

—accelerate progress for low-skilled and other workers

—improve retention and achievement rates to reduce time taken to complete certificate or degree requirements

—build programs that meet industry needs, including by developing career pathways

—strengthen online and technology-enabled learning.

The SGA presented relevant research on how to achieve each priority, hoping to steer applicants toward strategies that had some evidence of producing positive impacts. For example, under the first priority, to accelerate progress for low-skilled and other workers, the SGA described the Integrated Basic Education and Skills Training Program developed by Washington State.[30] Known as I-BEST, this program uses a classroom intervention involving two teachers who simultaneously instruct students in basic educational concepts and career-specific skills. The idea is to tie basic education skills and more career-specific skills together in a way that makes the former more relevant to the latter. Evidence from a quasi-experimental study shows promising results, as measured by credits earned toward a college credential, points gained on tests of basic skills, and occupational certificates earned.[31]

In addressing the balance between the narrower focus on workforce development for TAA workers and broader system reform, the SGA noted that "while the solicitation supports education and training programs suited to this target population [displaced workers], the Department of Labor expects that once the programs are implemented, they would also benefit a wide range of individuals."

With respect to evidence, the SGA reflected another compromise. The SGA recognized the three levels of evidence that i3 promulgated as a way to categorize evidence for particular programs, but unlike in the i3 initiative, applicants with the lowest level of evidence could still qualify for the largest awards. Evidence-based design would be worth 15 points (out of 100) in the selection criteria. As the SGA says, "The applicant must clearly describe the evidence on which the proposed education and training services are based, and how the evidence indicates that the proposed strategies will lead to improved education and employment outcomes." However, "all applicants, regardless of whether they present strong, moderate, or preliminary evidence, may get the maximum points for this section."

In the SGA, the evaluation compromise is worth 25 points. This section asks grantees to set performance targets for their programs and to indicate how they will track students' progress toward reaching those targets. It requires the grantees to identify a comparison group of students against whose outcomes they can measure TAACCCT students' outcomes. The SGA reflects the compromise that the working group reached—abandoning the idea of grantee evaluations but accepting the need for some type of information about program outcomes. Grantees also are required to agree to participate in a national evaluation should the department decide to undertake one. The SGA notes that "these grantees may be required to use a random-assignment lottery in enrolling project participants."

The Grant-Making Process

Grant applications were reviewed by selection panels consisting of one federal reviewer (usually from DOL) and two outside reviewers. DOL is responsible for hiring the outside reviewers, who usually are retired federal workers. The panels assessed the applications using the rubric laid out in the SGA:

—statement of need (30 points)

—workplan and project management (45 points, including 15 points for evidence)

—measurement and evaluation of progress and outcomes (25 points).

Awards

The first round of awards was announced on September 26, 2011. After receiving 257 applications, the department made 32 awards, totaling $422 million, to states or consortia of states. Specifically, they made 9 awards ranging from $2.5 million to $5 million for individual applicants and 23 awards ranging from $5 million to $20 million for single and multistate consortia. The statute required that all states receive no less than 0.5 percent of the funding. After the first round of competitive awards, 15 states (plus Puerto Rico and the District of Columbia) had received no funding. Either they did not submit a qualifying application, or no community college within the state was included in any of the consortia awards. As a result, DOL worked with these states to develop a passable proposal for obtaining TAACCCT funds. In the end, the department made awards totaling $54.8 million to the remaining 15 states plus D.C. and Puerto Rico.

Examples of First-Round Grant Winners

Although the first round of TAACCCT grants made for fiscal year 2011 did not feature specific tiers of grants, the grants examined below approximate the types of grants that would be awarded in a tiered structure like that of the i3.[32] It is interesting to note the range of reform proposals approved and the lack of evaluation evidence available for many of the specific elements of what the grantees proposed. This is in contrast to a field such as education, where there are many well-known and widely implemented model programs, curriculums, and whole-school reforms. For TAACCCT, the modest research base is more descriptive and theoretical than rigorous and causal. There is a lack of rigorous evaluation research that would allow the field to draw causal conclusions about specific program models for reform. The first round of TAACCCT winners were, as with i3, on a continuum in terms of the size and scope of projects and the strength of evidence supporting them; however, the evidence bar, even for the largest awards, was necessarily set a lot lower than in i3. Below we present three examples of funded projects to illustrate these points.

TIDEWATER COMMUNITY COLLEGE. The single largest winner in round one was Tidewater Community College, the lead grantee on a project that includes all 23 community colleges in Virginia. The applicants received a $24.1 million award. This award can be roughly compared with awards in the i3 "scale-up" category. The application notes that a task force in Virginia previously devised the "Achieve 2015" reform plan, which focuses on "evidence-based recommendations" to help the state's community college system better serve the state.[33] The Tidewater TAACCCT project proposes to focus specifically on health sciences occupations and goes on to lay out seven strategies for reform that address the competition priority issue of "Improving Retention and Achievement Rates and/or Reducing Time to Completion."

One strategy that the Tidewater group is proposing is to have each community college hire a full- or part-time adult career coach or experiential learning/job placement coordinator. The application cites "moderate" evidence for this strategy, noting that the Virginia Community College System has a "fully developed, successful, research-based, high-school-based career coach model," which Tidewater plans to adapt as necessary to apply the lessons learned in high school to the community college setting. The evidence cited in the proposal is from a study of high school career coaches that included mostly survey data about student and principal satisfaction with the program and data about enrollment in community colleges (no control group was included).[34] Tidewater also proposes to adapt a program originally implemented by the City University of New York (CUNY) system, called Accelerated Study in Associate Programs (ASAP). A major component of the ASAP program is individual career advising, with an emphasis on trade-impacted workers in health sciences. Tidewater cites the "moderate" evidence from a study of ASAP that used a matched cohort at multiple sites to measure effectiveness.[35]

Another strategy for which Tidewater cites specific evidence is the E-WISe system (Automated Early Warning and Intervention System), which involves aggressive outreach to students who are at risk of dropping out or not succeeding.[36] The tool uses data systems to identify and track such students in hope of providing guidance to help them succeed. The Tidewater application notes that there is "not a plethora of evidence supporting the automation of [aggressive] advising" but goes on to mention a 2004 policy report from the organization ACT that recommended, following a meta-analysis of 109 studies, aggressive advising (often referred to as "intrusive" advising in the literature) as a strategy that could increase retention.[37]

Tidewater also proposes to create a new career studies certificate in health sciences that combines a health sciences degree with workforce training so that students are ready to work upon graduating and have access to priority job placements. This approach is linked to the career pathways strategy. The application explains that a team will "review together the research" to design the new certificate program and offers some initial ideas based mainly on a "preliminary case study" from Tennessee Tech Centers, which states explicitly that

> this is not an evaluation or formal outcomes assessment of the system or any of the individual Technology Centers. Instead, this report describes how the Centers are organized, how they operate, and how they are able to achieve completion rates far higher than their counterparts among community colleges in Tennessee and around the nation."[38]

That this type of preliminary—or at best moderate—evidence is cited as support for a course for reform is a good illustration of the state of the evidence in the community college field and the challenges inherent in implementing an evidence-based initiative for community colleges. Further, offering reform proposals, including plans for systemwide reform, of such a diffuse nature—instead of proposals for specific, well-evaluated model programs or interventions—shows how broadly defined the TAACCCT evidence-based undertaking is.

George C. Wallace State Community College–Hanceville. A project that might be considered similar to one that would receive a "validation award" under i3 (a project supported by moderate evidence) is the Partnership for Accelerated Learning through Visualization, Engagement, and Simulation (PAVES), a collaborative effort of the George C. Wallace State Community College–Hanceville, other community colleges in the area, and the University of Alabama–Birmingham. The applicants received a grant of $9.5 million. The goal of PAVES is to improve existing degree and certification programs for trade-displaced workers in four high-demand industries. The proposal aims to implement four "evidence-based" strategies, one of which expands the use of new simulation and visualization programs to help students learn new skills by, for example, learning to operate complex machinery under real-world conditions. Officials will work with researchers to design, implement, and expand the use of these simulations at the participating community colleges. For evidence, the proposal draws from a study of interactive, web-based teaching programs in which participants were randomly assigned to various learning groups—including groups that received visual-only, audio-only, or audio-video instruction and groups that were given no instruction—in order "to learn and free recall a list of 14 items associated with construction of a wood-frame house." In the study, the audio-video and video groups did the best; the authors noted that "findings provided constructive feedback on the efficacy and usability of three-dimensional (3D) dynamic visualizations in web-based distance education."[39]

The second strategy, which the applicants call "another strong evidence-based strategy," is expanding the use of prior learning assessments (PLAs) to evaluate the college-level knowledge and skills that students might have gained outside the classroom and that might count toward college credit. By offering credit for such skills, schools could help students reach upper-level courses faster and obtain credentials more quickly. The proposal cites a Council for Adult and Experiential Learning correlational study that included more than 60,000 students at 48 colleges and universities and found that students with PLAs did better and were more likely to graduate than students without them.[40]

The third strategy is student coaching. According to the application, student coaches provide a "critical non-academic support service" that increases retention and graduation rates, and the applicants propose to expand that service. As evidence, the application cites a study featuring a randomized controlled trial (RCT) that found that after six months, coached students were 5.2 percentage points more likely to still be enrolled than their non-coached peers, a statistically significant difference, with effects persisting at 12, 18, and 24 months.[41]

The fourth strategy is to make extensive use of online learning. Many courses that will be part of the TAACCCT program will combine classroom lectures and discussion with online learning. The community colleges participating in PAVES already offer more than 300 online courses, and the grantees plan to provide online courses to an additional 1,400 trade-impacted students. One course offered is a course in welding. The welding course originally included a total of 14 weekly sessions; however, the course was reduced to 7 classroom sessions by adapting several of the lectures and some of the instructional materials for online presentation. The colleges promise to use TAACCCT resources to develop 130 new units (roughly, one-hour learning sessions) of instruction that will be used by 2,655 new students over the 3 years of the grant.

NORTH GEORGIA TECHNICAL COLLEGE. This $2.55 million grant to North Georgia Technical College ($2.5 million is the minimum that a state can legally receive under the legislation that funds TAACCCT) is akin in size and scope to a "development" award under i3. Because the health care industry is growing rapidly, the college proposes attracting potential health care workers through a TAA career pathway project that aims to help participants earn a range of credentials necessary for existing health care jobs, including as EMTs, medical assistants, paramedics, and pharmacy technicians. The college's proposal offers strategies to address all four of TAACCCT's priority areas.

Evidence for the particular changes proposed is thin, as can be expected for a project considered for the lowest tier of grants. Among the strategies proposed for which specific evidence is cited is adapting existing dual-enrollment GED programs—which encourage students to quickly begin specific occupational courses at community colleges while still pursuing their GED—to implement the health care program. The proposal notes that the dual-enrollment GED adaptation was selected "because evidence-based articles indicate 'underprepared students have the best shot at success when they can move into college-level courses as soon as possible.'" The source referenced is a research brief on remediation from the nonprofit Complete College America.[42]

All three proposals illustrate both the promise and the challenge of TAACCCT and evidence-based policy as applied to community colleges. TAACCCT asked applicants to think specifically and systematically about strategies for reform and the evidence behind them. Getting applicants to lay out in detail their proposed reforms, the evidence supporting them, and the expected outcomes at least provides a framework for improving the quality of decisionmaking by community colleges in developing programs and curriculums to help students obtain credentials and employment. While it is unreasonable to expect applicants to cite exclusively causal research for specific model programs, they should nonetheless be expected to describe specific reform ideas and any evidence indicating that the strategy might accomplish the desired outcomes. The reality is that there is a shortage of rigorous causal research about specific model programs for community college reforms. TAACCCT, with the more robust evaluation components added in the second and third years (see below), has the opportunity to begin accumulating evidence on outcomes produced by specific reform programs that can be used for worker training by community colleges.

Round Two

The administration made several changes to the TAACCCT program for the second round of awards in 2012. First, DOL revised the program's core elements and top priorities, making evidence-based design the top priority. The other priorities were

—stacked and latticed credentials (which includes eliminating duplication across programs that help workers obtain employment and working with industry to develop industry-wide standardized credentials)

—online and technology-enabled learning

—transferability (which includes improving the career pathways for workers so that, for example, their credits transfer across institutions to streamline the degree attainment process)

—strategic alignment (making sure that programs are well coordinated with at least employers and industry, the public workforce system, and other educational institutions).

Responding to concerns from members of Congress that the first round of TAACCCT grants had strayed too far from the intent of the authorizing statute, the administration also attempted to strengthen the focus on trade-displaced workers during the second round. Applicants would be required to provide evidence that they were serving such workers through, for example, partnership agreements with employers or outreach with community organizations.

In an important change, grant applicants for the second round of funding were required to submit a plan for a third-party evaluation, and the SGA stated specifically that a "rigorous, quantitative evaluation of impact on participants using a random-assignment experimental design is strongly encouraged." Three major factors led to the change. First, OMB kept insisting that evaluation was vital to the success of the TAACCCT program, especially in light of the fact that many funded programs did not have strong evidence of effectiveness. Second, first-round grantees expressed a lot of confusion about the comparison cohort reporting requirements; many did not know exactly how to design the comparison group and collect the required data. That uncertainty helped underscore the need to clarify and strengthen the evaluation requirement for the second round of TAACCCT grants. Third—and perhaps most important—DOL explicitly authorized the winners to use a portion of their grant award to fund an evaluation, something that was prohibited during the first round.

The administration also modified the way that the formula component of the TAACCCT works. In accordance with the legislation, each state must receive no less than 0.5 percent of the funding. As a way to encourage more states to apply for the second round, the administration decided to fund state applications separately from consortium applications. All states would be eligible for an award of $2.5 million (0.5 percent) to $3 million, and the awards would be considered separately from the $5 to $15 million awards made to the larger consortia applicants. The administration's goal was to ensure that all states were represented in an initial competition so that officials did not have to work with them separately to develop a qualifying proposal later. The administration's hope was that creating this semi-separate competition would encourage more community colleges to submit applications because they would not have to compete with the more comprehensive consortium applications; instead, there would be a dedicated funding stream to ensure that each state had a community college represented. Unfortunately for the administration, this change did not produce the desired results.

The administration received only 177 applications in the second round. After reviewing the state applications first, it found that 22 states still did not have a fundable application, including 3 states that had failed to submit an application or have an institution within the state do so. On September 19, 2012, the administration made 27 awards ranging from $2.5 million to $3 million for single-institution applicants along with 27 awards ranging from $5 million to $15 million for single-state and multistate consortia applicants.

Round Three

For round three, the administration added another core priority: alignment with previously funded TAACCCT Projects. Applicants were required to reference all funded projects from rounds one and two and make sure that their proposals aligned with, rather than duplicated, those projects. Furthermore, applicants could choose to expand on a previously funded program by offering more credentials or an online-based learning component to complement that program. Round three also included the three tiers of evidence (although still without tying specific grant amounts to particular levels of evidence), and applicants were directed to describe the level of evidence appropriate to their proposed program.

On September 18, 2013, the administration made 20 awards to community colleges or consortia and 23 awards to individual institutions, for a total of $474.5 million. Fourteen states were still left without a fundable application in the third competition because no community colleges in those states submitted an application or joined a consortium of community colleges that received funding.

Conclusion

Unemployment, especially of the long-term variety, is among the greatest problems facing the nation. Unemployment was rising when the administration took office in January 2008, and although it has declined from its high of 10 percent in October 2009, it is still high by historical standards (6.2 percent in July 2014)[43] and has been declining at the slowest pace following a recession since World War II.[44] In addition, there is great concern among economists that regardless of the current state of unemployment, the American workforce is not equipped with the skills needed to fill the technological jobs that characterize the nation's economy, which is shaped in large part by technological change and international competition. A recent study by the Organization for Economic Cooperation and Development found that the United States was ranked

16th of 23 nations on a survey of the literacy skills of adult workers and near the bottom of the list on numeracy.[45] It can be no surprise, then, that the new administration wanted not only to boost employment, but also to address the underlying issue of improving the job skills of workers. Its approach had three basic characteristics: to use community colleges to improve employment skills through short-term education and training that leads to some type of certification; to make the initiative evidence based, much like the other Obama initiatives explored in this book; and to carefully evaluate the results of the programs, improve them as necessary, and thereby to build up a stable of tested workforce interventions led by community colleges.

But as happened with several of the other evidence-based initiatives, adventures on the path to enacting the TAACCCT initiative disrupted the administration's plans (the fact that it ended up with its never-ending acronym being a testament to the treachery of that path), illustrating yet again that Congress gives no special consideration to legislation that deals with evidence-based programs. Nonetheless, the administration managed to jam its community college initiative into the 2010 health care reconciliation bill and obtain $2 billion in funding for the initiative. Because of the requirements of the legislation, the administration had to change two central features of its plan. First, the program had to be administered by DOL instead of the ED; second, it had to provide training to workers displaced by trade. The administration used various stratagems to serve other groups, but doing so was difficult. The lesson here for future efforts to establish evidence-based programs is that legislative strategies must be carefully conceived and that often the weight of the White House and OMB must be fully, even aggressively, behind the legislation, especially when unexpected bumps in the road appear, as they often do.

Arguably, another limitation of the initiative was the formula component. The minimum state funding requirement undermined the power of the competitive portion of the grant program and led to an extra level of complexity in implementing the program. States that did not submit (or were not party to) a quality proposal were nonetheless guaranteed funding, provided that they worked with DOL to develop an eligible proposal. This constraint further illustrates just how important competitive funding is to the success (and transformative potential) of evidence-based initiatives.

Any training and employment initiative had to take into consideration the fact that the field of employment and training is not noted for its commitment to high-quality evaluations. If evidence is to play a major role in the development and improvement of social policy, it is important to begin promoting the use of evidence in fields that lack an evidence tradition. Fortunately, in the past decade or so, a literature that deals with evaluation of community college programs by the use of RCTs has started to develop, in large part because of funding by a series of foundations (especially the Lumina Foundation for Education) and the ED and the capacity of research firms like MDRC to conduct large-scale RCTs.[46] The money that DOL threw into employment and training programs at community colleges through the TAACCCT initiative gave a much-needed boost to evaluation of community college programs.

The TAACCCT initiative's plan for using evidence and generating more evidence from rigorous evaluations has two major components. The first is a modification of the i3 tiers of evidence approach whereby the TAACCCT recognizes three tiers of evidence but does not make the level of evidence a criterion for funding eligibility. Thus, even preliminary evidence could receive the top score for evidence and qualify for the highest grant amounts. The second major component, one shared by all six of the Obama initiatives, is the emphasis on helping program operators develop expertise in designing program evaluations and using the results to improve their programs. In this case, DOL specified in the SGA that all projects awarded funding would be required to submit outcome data on seven measures that the department (with advice from OMB) determined to be important. Applicants also were directed to state how they would identify a comparison group that would allow them to make at least some guesses about whether their program was having the intended effects on the outcome measures.

Under the rules of evidence followed by the administration (reviewed in our introductory chapter), any comparison group not created by random assignment is flawed and the internal validity of the evaluation is compromised. Even so, developing methods to collect good outcome data is a major step in the right direction for DOL; perhaps a flawed comparison group is better than no comparison group, despite the fact that little confidence can be placed in the findings.

The TAACCCT initiative shows how flexible the administration, as represented primarily by OMB, is being to advance its evidence-based mission. DOL does not appear to be well prepared by tradition and experience to conduct an evidence-based initiative. Yet DOL met OMB partway by greatly increasing the use of evidence in selecting its grantees and in evaluating the outcomes of funded programs. Further, the department hired a knowledgeable and widely respected researcher, Demetra Nightingale, as its chief evaluation officer after the equally respected Jean Grossman returned to academia. Using a football analogy to describe the DOL's progress, we would say that the department has the evidence-based-policy ball at about the 50-yard line. It is moving toward the goal line, but we need to study its next several plays to determine whether evidence-based policy will allow the nation's community colleges and state employment agencies to forge effective partnerships and deliver on the promise of evidence-based employment and training programs.

8 | *So Far, So Good*

The Obama administration is trying to combat the nation's major social problems through a well-conceived plan for using rigorous evidence of success as a basis for developing, testing, and expanding effective domestic social programs. To promote the development and use of such programs, the administration is undertaking six evidence-based initiatives that cover the waterfront of the nation's social issues, including infant and child health and development, preschool education, K–12 education, pregnancy and sexually transmitted diseases among teens, student performance, and community college education and job training. The general strategy followed by the administration in carrying out the initiatives is to encourage state and local organizations to use model programs that have been shown to be effective through rigorous evaluation by offering them the opportunity to qualify for competitive grants. The organizations that win grants must also carefully evaluate the impacts of their model programs in order to improve them if the programs are not having the intended impacts.

About 700 social intervention programs and only slightly fewer evaluations are now being conducted around the country to test the administration's evidence-based strategy. In that respect, the Obama initiatives are unlike many other social policy initiatives, which do not require evaluation of results. In addition to funding programs that have proven positive impacts, all six initiatives fund programs that, although they are not supported by rigorous evidence, are promising. In this way, the initiatives allow room for organizations to develop and test new interventions that, if successful on a small scale, can be further tested and scaled up to determine whether they will produce the same impacts in other sites. The scope of this systematic attempt to use rigorous evidence to develop new programs and scale up effective programs is unprecedented. If successful, it could have far-reaching effects on the nation's social policy and could lead to a reduction in many of the nation's leading social problems. But we want to make clear, as we have throughout this volume, that the impacts of the Obama evidence-based initiatives on the social problems that they address— the most fundamental measure of their success—will not be known for several more years, when evidence from a substantial fraction of the ongoing program evaluations will become available.

Major Elements of the Evidence-Based Initiatives

One of the top goals of our work has been to describe the six Obama evidence-based initiatives in detail so that future political figures or parties could learn from the Obama experience and mount their own initiatives even more effectively and efficiently. After all our interviews and many discussions of our findings with the people that we interviewed, the scholars and policy analysts who reviewed our book, and the advocates, staffers, and scholars who attended the numerous meetings at which we presented and discussed our findings, we have concluded that there are five central features of the process by which the Obama administration created its evidence-based agenda and policies:

—stellar leadership by senior officials in the White House, OMB, and the executive agencies

—a relentless focus on using evidence both to select successful programs and to suggest ways to improve programs

—development of clever and persistent legislative strategies to enact the six initiatives and senior officials' commitment of the time and effort needed to do so

— use of competitive grants rather than formula grants to distribute federal funds

—use of review panels to assess grant applications.

Leadership

The first and arguably most important feature of the Obama evidence-based strategy is the leadership that the administration received from senior officials in the White House, OMB, and the administrative agencies. For those who know something about how things work in the nation's capital, it will be no surprise that the most important and visionary leadership came from OMB in general and Robert Gordon in particular. OMB officials were stringent about including strong evidence requirements in every initiative, although as befits keen political operatives in Washington, they also were flexible. The tiers concept developed by the administration—roughly speaking, it offers grant applicants more money for more evidence—provides strong incentives for applicants to develop and use evidence-based intervention programs while it also allows funds to be used to test new programs. OMB guided the federal agencies through the grant-making process, offering ideas and assistance and using persuasion and the firmness that Washington insiders expect from OMB to try to achieve the administration's goals.

Having talked with an array of administration officials in the White House and at OMB, we were not able to identify exactly who first thought of mounting a series of evidence-based initiatives. It seems likely that various senior officials wanted to conduct evidence-based initiatives, looked for opportunities to do so, and wound up with a total of six. Both our interviews and the documentary record make it plain that the team at OMB, especially Peter Orszag, Jeff Liebman, Gordon, and Kathy Stack, were thinking about bringing evidence to bear on grant making from the very first days of the administration. All four were students of rigorous evaluation, and Orszag and Liebman had conducted randomized controlled trials (RCTs), including a widely noted study of how to use tax returns to expand savings.[1]

But the leadership did not stop at the walls of OMB. President Obama himself said in his first inaugural address that his administration would expand programs that worked and end programs that did not. In a meeting in the Oval Office during the first days of the administration, the president chose to stick with competitive grants for his Race to the Top program rather than follow his staff's political advice to use formula grants so that every state would get some money. He wanted to use competitive grants, as Jon Schnur and Education Secretary Arne Duncan had recommended for both Race to the Top and Investing in Innovation (i3), so that his administration could select the proposals that best advanced its goals—one of which was to stress the importance of using evidence in evaluating and funding social programs. Similarly, in his White House speech about the Social Innovation Fund initiative in June 2009, the president declared his administration's emphasis on using evidence to guide policy choices and mentioned three of the initiatives by name.

It is little surprise, then, that senior officials on the White House staff—especially Melody Barnes, who was the first head of the Domestic Policy Council (DPC), and Martha Coven, another important member of the DPC who later took a senior position at OMB—spent a great deal of time working on the various initiatives. In particular, they met with advocacy groups and talked with members of Congress and their staffers at critical moments during the legislative battles, ensuring that the initiatives were enacted and funded. They also carefully monitored the work between OMB and the executive agencies as the details of the initiatives were being created. Even the president's first chief of staff, Rahm Emanuel, devoted personal time to lobbying Congress on behalf of the initiatives.

The leadership provided by the executive agencies also was critical. We would single out Jim Shelton at the Department of Education, Seth Harris and Jean

Grossman at the Department of Labor, and Naomi Goldstein at the Department of Health and Human Services (HHS), who played a supervisory role in two of the six initiatives (home visiting and teen pregnancy prevention). An important factor in the development of the evidence-based initiatives was the close and largely harmonious relationship between the policy brokers at OMB and the White House who were implementing the president's agenda and the senior officials at the four executive agencies that played major roles in designing and implementing the initiatives. Relations between presidential administrations and the executive agencies often can become strained and frayed; as a result, serious conflicts sometimes arise, creating a barrier to implementing a president's agenda. In our interviews with senior officials and staffers at OMB, the White House, and the four executive agencies administering the initiatives, we specifically asked whether there was tension or conflict between career officials and the political appointees responsible for carrying out the president's agenda. Hardly anyone reported any signs of tension or strong disagreement on the issues. In fact, several political appointees mentioned how much they had been helped by career officials and how much they trusted them.

As a result, all four executive agencies contributed heavily to designing and implementing the initiatives. The biggest differences between the OMB/White House team and an executive agency arose in the administration's dealings with the Department of Labor (DOL). Officials in the Employment and Training Administration were not enamored of competitive grants and were especially concerned because the field of employment and training—particularly the federal/state workforce bureaucracy—did not have a tradition of basing decisions on rigorous evidence. The Department of Labor therefore had to adjust to major changes in its standard operating procedures if it was to implement effectively the two evidence-based grant programs for which it is responsible. Yet by all accounts, the senior administrators at OMB and Labor—as well as Jean Grossman, who was hired by Seth Harris, the deputy secretary of labor, to be the first head of program evaluation for DOL—handled the differences with professionalism. In the end, DOL did a reasonably good job of carrying out the administration's agenda on evidence, in part by working out compromises with OMB to make the two Labor Department initiatives somewhat consistent with the department's traditional ways of doing business.

The cooperative working relationship between the administration's career and political officials was reinforced by good luck. As it turned out, in every corner of OMB and the White House and often the executive agencies, there were true believers in evidence who had scholarly backgrounds and often experience in conducting random assignment research. The list began with Orszag, who had conducted random assignment experiments and was devoutly committed to evidence-based policy. His vision was not only to design and implement a series of evidence-based grant programs but also to develop ways to get the executive agencies to perform rigorous evaluations of their own most important programs. At one point, the administration tried to get a pot of money from Congress to provide financial incentives for agencies to conduct evaluations, but Congress balked. Orszag left OMB in July 2010, but the office was still packed with career staffers who carried out Orzag's evidence-based agenda.

Like Orszag, Jeff Liebman and Alex Mas, senior officials at OMB, each had a doctorate in economics and played an important part in explaining the administration's policies on evidence to outsiders and occasionally to members of Congress and their staffers. The Council of Economic Advisers also was jammed with researchers who were strong backers of the evidence-based approach. One of them, Cecilia Rouse, another Ph.D. economist, played an active role in advising others at the White House, OMB, and HHS, especially on issues directly related to the quality of evidence.

It would be a serious mistake in describing the leadership that conceived and conducted the Obama evidence-based initiatives to leave out the career staffers at OMB. As we make clear throughout this volume, analysts at OMB played important roles in developing all six initiatives. But the most important career staffer was Kathy Stack, who had been at OMB for over 20 years. Near the end of the Bush administration, she brought the evidence-based Nurse-Family Partnership program to the attention of other senior officials at OMB and then expanded the use of evidence-based models under a $10 million home visiting initiative, enacted by Congress in 2008. She also brought the new home visiting program to the attention of Gordon at the beginning of the Obama administration in 2009. After important adaptations were made, the program that Stack had designed became the blueprint for the much larger home visiting program created by the Obama administration.

Stack had a long history of trying to get both OMB and the executive agencies to focus more attention on evidence and the role of rigorous evaluations, especially RCTs, in determining the effectiveness of various grant programs. In pursuing the evidence-based agenda both before and after the Obama administration assumed control of OMB, she met with senior officials at OMB, organized meetings between OMB officials and people outside the agency, and organized meetings on the role of RCT evaluations in evidence-based policy. She also brought Jon Baron and his Coalition for Evidence-Based Policy to OMB to consult and conduct seminars on how to promote RCT evaluations. Eventually Stack developed a network of senior career officials at OMB and other agencies who wanted to pursue the evidence-based agenda. Realizing the value of her activities on behalf of evidence-based policy, in 2013 OMB appointed her to be its adviser for evidence-based innovation. Stack will be instrumental in attempting to help the administration that takes over after the 2016 presidential election to maintain or even expand the Obama evidence-based agenda. Whether she can succeed in this vital endeavor is an open question; nonetheless, she is the queen of evidence-based policy at OMB and the administrative agencies.

Ironically, the central figure in the entire Obama effort on evidence-based policy was Robert Gordon, a lawyer who has never conducted an empirical study (he does, however, share a Harvard background with many of the evidence gurus in the Obama administration).[2] Gordon did have an impressive background in education, having served as a senior adviser to Joel Klein, the controversial but effective chancellor of education in New York City, one of the hot spots of education reform in the United States in the years leading up to the Obama presidency.[3] Gordon also had served a stint at the Center for American Progress, where he wrote about education and other social issues.[4] Precisely where he became a devotee of random assignment evaluations is unclear, but from his perch at OMB, he probably did the most to pull together the administration's evidence-based agenda and to implement the six initiatives. Gordon was the cajoler in charge of getting the agencies to accept the need for rigorous evidence, based on random assignment if possible. In particular, he was effective in convincing the political and career officials at the agencies to craft their respective initiatives to distribute grant funds on the basis of rigorous evidence that programs would work and on high-quality plans for evaluating the programs. His name came up more frequently that anyone else's during our interviews, not only with people from the administration but also with advocates and Hill staffers. If there were a king of evidence-based policy in the Obama administration, Gordon would win the title hands down.

Two Uses of Evidence

The central feature of the Obama evidence-based approach is its requirement that applicants produce two distinct types of evidence. The first is rigorous evidence of past program effectiveness, which increases the odds that funded programs will have positive impacts on the social problems that they address. The administration employed two approaches to achieve that goal, either or both of which should be a central part of future evidence-based efforts. One approach is to let applicants choose the program that they want to operate and require them to demonstrate in their application that the program is backed by rigorous evidence of past success. In most cases, that means that applicants use curriculums or programs that have been shown by rigorous studies to produce impacts. The grant eligibility criteria also require organizations to provide evidence that they know how to implement the program with fidelity—that is, that they have good leadership, a good record of implementing social programs, and a sustainable budget. In some cases, applicants may have direct experience running the program for which they are requesting funds or a similar program and can report their experience and results with that program in their application.

The second approach that the administration used to increase the odds of selecting programs with proven effectiveness was to conduct a literature review itself—with considerable help from a reputable research company, in this case Mathematica Policy Research—to identify such programs. Both the home visiting and teen pregnancy prevention initiatives took this approach. The administration's review, based on clearly specified evidence standards (see chapters 2 and 3), has resulted in identification of 14 home visiting programs and 31 teen pregnancy prevention programs that meet the "evidence-based" criteria. The administration then gave funding priority to and spent a majority of funds on organizations that proposed to implement one of those evidence-based programs.

The second type of evidence required under the Obama approach is evidence of the effectiveness of nearly all funded programs from ongoing evaluations of those programs. In most cases, a grant includes money to conduct the evaluation. As a result of the evaluation requirement, there are now hundreds of evaluations, many employing RCTs, in progress for nearly all projects across the six initiatives. Not only will the evaluations yield public information about whether the programs are successful, but they also will contribute to two of the underlying goals of the Obama initiatives: first, building a stable of evidence-based intervention programs designed to address a host of the nation's most important social problems and, second, teaching program operators to conduct high-quality evaluations of their programs or to find individuals (usually university-affiliated evaluation experts) or evaluation firms to help them conduct the evaluations. Both are essential to growing the evidence-based culture. It would be difficult to exaggerate the importance of evaluations in building up the evidence base on intervention programs.

Legislative Strategy

The Obama initiatives illustrate an important lesson: the Congress of the United States does not extend any special privileges to legislation designed to establish evidence-based programs. The administration and its allies in Congress employed all the tricks known to knowledgeable practitioners of the legislative arts to enact the evidence-based initiatives. Two tricks in particular were important. One was to hide legislative provisions of relatively modest cost and succinct language in a much larger bill on its journey through Congress. Most of the six initiatives were originally enacted as part of very large bills. This strategy is even more likely to work if little is done to draw attention to the provision—if it flies under the radar, so to speak. Five of the six initiatives had no hearings, most were in the bill introduced by the chairman of the committee of jurisdiction, none was amended on the floor of the House or Senate, and only one was even mentioned in floor debate.[5] The hiding-the-needle-in-a-haystack principle works especially well if the bill in which the provision is hiding is destined to be enacted by Congress. Thus, evidence-based provisions were passed in the huge American Recovery and Reinvestment Act (ARRA), the Affordable Care Act (ACA), the reconciliation bill that accompanied the ACA, the Edward M. Kennedy Serve America Act, and major appropriations bills. Granted, those bills were controversial, but Democrats had a majority in both houses and were passionately committed to passing all of them, which eventually they did.

Ideally, evidence-based initiatives would be able to pass on a strong bipartisan vote. But in a fallen world, the lesson for proponents of future initiatives is "Find a big bill that must pass and hide your favored provision in it." Even so, if the evidence-based movement is to become truly influential, it will need to convince members of Congress, their staffers, and organizations that lobby on behalf of children and social programs that evidence-based policy is effective and widely acknowledged to be the best way to make progress against the nation's social problems. The evidence-based movement will succeed in Congress when demonstrating that a program has rigorous evidence of success behind it persuades both Republicans and Democrats to vote in favor of the program.

Another key point about the bills that delivered the six evidence-based initiatives is that the administration was completely devoted to passing them. Gordon of OMB, Barnes and Coven of the Domestic Policy Council, and other senior administration officials—including Rahm Emanuel, the president's chief of staff, in one case—did whatever was necessary to get the bills through Congress. When the evidence-based provisions were having trouble on the Hill, senior administration officials were there to overcome the problems, often by talking directly with members of Congress. In the case of the teen pregnancy prevention and home visiting initiatives, the administration organized meetings with child advocates to make sure that they were working together effectively on the Hill. Without that level of commitment, it is likely that some of the initiatives would not have made it through Congress.

A final point shines light on a potentially important impact on the legislative process of programs supported by rigorous evidence. Congressional Budget Office (CBO) analysts are experts in social science research. They read studies and then determine, as they did in the case of the Nurse-Family Partnership, whether the evidence shows that a program has the intended impacts and whether those impacts, such as a reduction in child abuse and neglect or a reduction in the use of emergency rooms, saves money in other federal (and state) programs. If the program saves money in other entitlement programs,[6]

CBO can score savings and subtract the savings from the cost of the legislation to compute net costs, an important factor in whether any legislation is enacted. Budget rules specify that under most circumstances, Congress cannot pass legislation unless it is "deficit neutral," meaning that it does not increase the deficit. Supporters of evidence-based policy should realize the full implication of the deficit-neutral rule. If social science intervention programs can provide rigorous evidence that they produce measurable benefits that save money, then federal policymakers can create a virtuous cycle by funding those programs, thereby saving federal dollars, which in turn makes room, under CBO scoring rules, for enactment of new or improved social programs. Perhaps it would not be an exaggeration to claim that the Obama strategy of concentrating federal dollars on programs that produce impacts could permit expansion of certain high-impact social programs despite the relentless focus on federal spending cuts that now characterizes the federal budget process.

The recent interest in "paying for success" programs illustrates the focus on program savings.[7] The idea behind the programs is to offer private organizations such as for-profit businesses or foundations the opportunity to help fund the operation of a government social program that they think will produce the desired impacts and thereby save the government money. If the program does save money, as with any investment, the investor might earn a profit; if it doesn't, the investor loses his or her investment. The terms are spelled out in a written agreement before the social program begins, hence the term "social impact bond," which often is used to describe such agreements.

One of the first projects employing this new financing arrangement is being conducted by the research firm MDRC, with investment funds from Goldman Sachs.[8] The goal of the project is to reduce recidivism among juvenile delinquents in the Rikers Island detention center in New York City. If recidivism is reduced by the project, which teaches the juveniles the social and emotional skills that they will need to help them avoid problems when they leave jail, the city will save money. The impacts of the program are being assessed through an evaluation that uses a quasi-experimental design. As do programs that score savings under the CBO's rule, paying-for-success programs use savings to pay for themselves. Both the example of saving money under CBO scoring rules and the pay-for-success programs illustrate the powerful potential of the Obama evidence-based strategy for improving the ability of government social programs to save money.

Competition for Funds

The administration, led by OMB, developed an elaborate and mostly effective plan for deciding which organizations would get money to implement evidence-based programs and to evaluate the programs' effectiveness. Several key features of the effort to award funds to organizations that would do the administration's bidding on evidence were important, to varying degrees, in all six initiatives.

Federal grant funds usually are awarded on a formula basis or a competitive basis. With formula grants, every state gets a share of the federal dollars that are allocated to the grant program, usually in proportion to some measure of the state's population or, in some cases, the population of children in poverty. The federal political system has a preference for formula funds because every state gets at least something. Members of both the House and Senate want to serve their state, counties, or cities and are understandably upset—as are their constituents—when they come home empty handed. The disadvantage of formula grants is that as long as states meet the basic requirements of the grant program, they get the money. Such an approach was not to the administration's liking because senior officials running the evidence-based initiatives wanted states and public and private organizations to compete for the money by submitting creative and thoughtful proposals, knowing that if they did not submit a superior proposal, they might not get any money. Under competitive grant making, the administration would select only the best proposals and ignore those that were mediocre or worse, thereby increasing the chances that the winning applicants could and would run successful programs. This feature of the evidence-based initiatives seems important enough to suggest that most future evidence-based grant making should award funds primarily on a competitive basis. Let the best evidence win.

But there are two cases in which formula grants might be used to advantage in an evidence-based agenda. For example, the home visiting initiative gave each state formula funds to use to conduct a needs assessment and to plan a statewide strategy for making maximum use of the home visiting funds that they were already getting and the funds that they would soon get from the initiative. In that case, using formula funds would seem to be wise, especially because it is in the national interest for every state to have such a strategy. For another example, if the administration or Congress determines that a particular model program or set of programs has been demonstrated to produce substantial benefits on a broad scale, then it might make sense to give every state formula funds to scale up the effective program.

Another important feature of the grant-making process is the emphasis on outcome measures. There is no substitute for valid measures of outcomes in any evidence-based enterprise. At first glance, this feature of the Obama initiatives seems easy to fulfill. Simply decide what trait or behavior the administration (and often the entire field of social policy) wants to increase or decrease and then measure its incidence. There are at least two problems with this seemingly straightforward approach. First, many social programs are attempting to change behaviors that, if they occur, will occur in the future. Even if short-term behaviors are affected, the real goal is to influence long-term outcomes. In the case of teen pregnancy prevention, for example, education classes that begin in junior high school or even earlier in some states cover the mechanics of human reproduction and the value of waiting until after high school to have sex; they also teach students how to avoid situations in which sexual contact might occur, how to say "no," and so forth. By high school and sometimes earlier, students may receive instruction in the use of condoms and other forms of birth control. Yet the goal, at a minimum, is to help teens graduate from high school—often four or five years after the first "human relationships" courses—without having become pregnant or having caused a pregnancy. Evaluators therefore cannot measure the major outcome that the classes are designed to prevent for three or five years or more. Teen pregnancy and birth rates have declined every year except two since 1991, but until recently nonmarital births among those in their twenties and thirties were accelerating.[9] Perhaps the most important goal of the nation's policy on sex education and family planning is to avoid not just teen pregnancy but rather all unplanned births outside marriage, most of which now occur among women beyond their teenage years. Given that the average age of marriage is now about 29 for men and 27 for women, achievement of a major goal of these programs cannot be measured for a decade or more.[10]

Arguably the best solution to the problem of long-term outcomes is to measure intermediate outcomes. Graduating from high school without a pregnancy is a reasonable intermediate outcome and very important in itself. Programs also measure attitudes about sex, age at first sexual experience, frequency of sex, and number of sexual partners. All of these attitudes are meaningful in their own right and impacts on them may have impacts on longer-term measures of nonmarital births. Carefully selecting both intermediate measures and long-term measures is a vital part of an evidence-based strategy.

Another problem with accurately measuring outcomes is that for many important behaviors and abilities, the measures are far from perfect. Not all outcomes of evidence-based initiatives can be easily or accurately measured. Using attitudes about sex as an outcome for teen pregnancy programs, for example, leaves a lot of room for measurement issues, the most important of which is the difficulty of tying attitudes to actual behavior. Just because teenagers say that they know that they should not have (or are not having) sex does not necessarily mean that they won't (or aren't). In addition, some young people know which answers they "should" give on opinion surveys, so they have a tendency to give those answers, raising the question of whether verbal statements accurately reflect their attitudes or behavior.

Notwithstanding these and similar measurement issues, deciding what outcomes to measure is another essential part of the evidence-based initiatives. One

approach to specifying the outcome measures is to insert them in the authorizing legislation. This approach leaves little doubt about what Congress wanted
the outcome to be when it authorized or appropriated funding for the program.
The home visiting initiative statute, for example, is especially clear: it specifies
"quantifiable" outcomes that funded programs must measure and report three
years and five years after the program begins. They include

—improved maternal and newborn health

—prevention of child injuries, abuse, neglect, or maltreatment and reduction of emergency room visits

—improvement in school readiness and achievement

—reduction in crime or domestic violence

—improvement in family economic self-sufficiency

—improvement in coordination with and referrals to other community
resources and supports.[11]

This list of outcomes may seem excessive, but measures of most can be found
in records maintained by local and state organizations like hospitals, schools,
and departments of social services. Furthermore, most of these outcomes have
been reported by studies in the home visiting literature.[12] The outcomes specified by Congress make it clear that states and local organizations running the
home visiting programs must become adept at using administrative data from
reliable sources as well as at collecting data of their own.

If the desired outcomes are not in the authorizing statutes—and even if they
are but are stated in general terms (consider the breadth of the data required
to assess "maternal and newborn health")—the administration is well within
its rights to specify more detailed measures in the funding announcement. In
most of the initiatives, the administration did so. Without specific, accurately
measured outcomes, there can be no evidence-based programs.

The bottom line on measurement is that organizations that want to adopt
the evidence-based approach must become adept at selecting reliable outcome
measures and employing reliable ways to capture the necessary data through
observation, tests, ratings, interviews, data collected by other programs, administrative records, and other means. Similarly, organizations that work with the
same children year after year (such as preschools, schools, departments of social
services, and juvenile justice agencies) must focus on collecting and efficiently
storing longitudinal measures of important outcomes.

There is greater controversy over defining the types of scientific method used
to determine whether social programs are having an impact on outcomes. The
officials at OMB most responsible for the evidence-based initiatives were all true
believers in random assignment designs. As spelled out in our introduction and
in a more detailed and convincing manner in Jim Manzi's *Uncontrolled*,[13] many

social scientists believe that random assignment designs are the best way (some would say the only way) to establish causality in social science in general and in program evaluation in particular—and they are supported in that view by a recent report from the National Research Council and Institute of Medicine.[14] In many respects, the heart and soul of the Obama evidence-based movement is its strong preference for using the most rigorous evaluation designs, especially the RCT. As shown, all six of the initiatives aimed to use rigorous evidence in two ways that the evidence nerds at OMB and in many of the executive agencies believed would revolutionize federal social policy: to select programs that had been shown by rigorous evidence to produce impacts and to conduct high-quality evaluations of the impact of funded programs.

But how should rigorous evidence be defined? Many researchers, administrators, congressional staffers, and even members of Congress have come to believe that the best and most reliable evidence about program effects comes from RCTs. Some go so far as to argue that no program can be considered successful unless it has been shown by an RCT to produce positive impacts. Now imagine the position of the Obama administration. Most of the OMB officials behind the initiatives believed that the RCT is the sine qua non of quality evaluation. However, in some cases they were trying to establish the Obama initiatives with agencies that did not have a tradition of using random assignment, with agencies whose senior officials had little background in program evaluation using rigorous designs, and in fields that did not have many intervention programs supported by evidence from RCTs. Thus, regardless of what the OMB officials might have believed about the importance of RCTs, they realized that they had to accommodate reality. Jim Shelton at the Department of Education and several of the people that we interviewed at both the Department of Labor and the Corporation for National and Community Service were worried that the lack of evidence from rigorous evaluations would severely limit the number of applications that they would receive if random assignment were required for funding.

Table 8-1 summarizes the evidence requirements in all six of the Obama evidence-based initiatives by giving both the pertinent statutory language for each initiative and the pertinent language in the funding announcements issued by each of the four agencies requesting proposals. The statutory language on evidence includes words like "rigorous," "positive outcomes," "randomized controlled research designs," "rigorous evaluations," and "evidence-based strategies." Only the Trade Adjustment Assistance Community College and Career Training (TAACCCT) initiative has no statutory language on evidence because its statutory language was written independently of the TAACCCT and a provision establishing a program associated with the Trade Adjustment Assistance Act was expropriated by the administration at the last minute to authorize spending for

Table 8-1. *Type of Evidence Required in Six Obama Evidence-Based Initiatives*

Initiative	Statutory requirement	Agency evidence review or funding opportunity announcement requirement
Home Visiting	"Significant" "positive outcomes" from "randomized controlled research designs" or from "quasi-experimental research designs"	At least one high- or moderate-quality impact evaluation (by implication, an RCT or quasi-experimental evaluation that meets certain requirements).
Teen Pregnancy Prevention	"Proven effective through rigorous evaluation"	At least one high- or moderate-quality impact evaluation (by implication, an RCT or quasi-experimental evaluation that meets certain requirements).
Investing in Innovation (i3)	Language about effects that programs must have demonstrated in order to be considered eligible but no language on the type of evaluation designs that produced the evidence	Evidence from RCTs or quasi-experimental designs (strong, moderate, and preliminary tiers); preliminary tier includes reasonable hypotheses.
Social Innovation Fund (SIF)	Evidence from "rigorous evaluations of program effectiveness," including RCTs	Must have evidence of impact; definitions of evidence are consistent with those for i3.
Workforce Innovation Fund (WIF)	"Evidence-based strategies," but type of study not defined	Three tiers of grants, each tied to specific level of evidence.
Trade Adjustment Assistance Community College and Career Training (TAACCCT)	No language on evidence	Strong evidence, defined as a "study or multiple studies whose designs can support strong, causal conclusions" and show a "statistically significant, substantial, and important impact" (by implication an RCT or quasi-experimental design).

Sources: Home Visiting statute: H.R. 3590, Patient Protection and Affordable Care Act, Section 511(c)(3)(A)(i)(I); Home Visiting agency: Office of Planning, Research, and Evaluation, "Home Visiting Evidence of Effectiveness Review: Executive Summary" (OPRE Report 2013-42), September 2013, revised June 2014 (http://homvee.acf.hhs.gov/HomVEE_Executive_Summary_2013.pdf); Teen Pregnancy Prevention statute: Labor, HHS, Education, and Related Agencies Appropriations Act of 2010, Title II, Department of Health and Human Services, Office of the Secretary; Teen Pregnancy Prevention agency: Office of Adolescent Health, "Overview of the Teen Pregnancy Prevention Research Evidence Review," not available; Investing in Innovation statute: American Recovery and Reinvestment Act of 2009, Section 14007(a)(3)(c); Investing in Innovation agency: National Archives and Records Administration, *Federal Register*, March 12, 2010, table 1, p. 1205; Social Innovation Fund statute: Edward M. Kennedy Serve America Act of 2009, Section 1807(f)(4)(A); Social Innovation Fund agency: Corporation for National and Community Service, Social Innovation Fund, "Evidence and Evaluation," undated (www.nationalservice.gov/programs/social-innovation-fund/evidence-evaluation); Workforce Innovation Fund statute: H.R. 1473, Department of Defense and Full-Year Continuing Appropriations Act, 2011, Title VIII, Section 1801(3); Workforce Innovation Fund agency: U.S. Department of Labor, "Notice of Availability of Funds and Solicitation for Grant Applications for Workforce Innovation Fund Grants" (SGA/DFA PY-11-05), undated (www.doleta.gov/grants/pdf/SGA-DFA-PY-11-05.pdf); Trade Adjustment Assistance and Community College and Career Training Grant Program statute: No provision on evidence (see text for explanation); Trade Adjustment Assistance and Community College and Career Training Grant Program agency: U.S. Department of Labor, "Notice of Availability of Funds and Solicitation for Grant Applications for Trade Adjustment Assistance Community College and Career Training Grants Program" (SGA/DFA PY 10-03), undated, p. 3, footnote 1 (www.doleta.gov/grants/pdf/SGA-DFA-PY-10-03.pdf).

the TAACCCT initiative.[15] The evidence language on i3 also is minimal because the i3 provision was enacted as part of the ARRA barely a month into the new administration. At that early date, the administration had only tentative ideas about expanding evidence-based policy and had not yet decided how to define "evidence-based." Moreover, officials from OMB and the Department of Education were focused on other provisions in the ARRA, especially the $4.35 billion Race to the Top competition, which the administration—including the president—saw as a major part of its legacy. Compared with $4.35 billion and a legacy, the $650 million i3 initiative was not much more than an afterthought, except among a very small group of administration insiders.

But when it came to the funding announcements, which were written for organizations applying for funds, the evidence language was more detailed and explicit. Even i3, which had minimal statutory language, explicitly required evidence from RCTs or quasi-experimental designs for certain tiers of grants. In fact, four of the six initiatives require evidence from RCTs or quasi-experimental designs. The other two initiatives have language that at minimum requires good evidence to qualify for funding. For example, the Workforce Innovation Fund (WIF) announcement states that the Department of Labor will provide three tiers of grant funding based on the level of evidence, including "strong evidence" for the highest tier, although it does not give a detailed definition of "strong evidence." The TAACCCT initiative encourages applicants to use programs that are supported by "a study or multiple studies whose designs can support strong, causal conclusions" and references the i3 definitions of evidence. Under any reasonable principles of research design, only RCTs and quasi-experimental designs can support "strong, causal conclusions."

OMB's ultimate vision for these initiatives was that most of the grant funds would support programs backed by RCTs, but reality intervened: in some cases the evidence base was thin because there were few or no successful model programs backed by RCTs. Even so, if the lion's share of federal grant dollars were spent on programs that had been shown by either RCTs or quasi-experimental designs to produce significant impacts, the nation's social policy would be much more effective than it is now. Equally important, if the initiatives placed smart bets when selecting programs with only preliminary evidence, they would create a pipeline of social intervention programs that gradually increased the number of effective programs and enabled a greater share of funding to be spent on programs backed by RCTs or quasi-experimental designs in the future.

Review Panels

The final major element of the Obama evidence-based strategy is the provision for panels of competent professionals to carefully review the applications for evidence-based grants and make recommendations about who should get the grants. For most federal grants, the secretary of the agency involved has the power to make the final determination regarding who gets the money, but all the agencies use review panels to examine the grant proposals and make funding recommendations to the secretary. The secretaries usually follow most of the recommendations of their review panels. Thus, a major determinant of whether the initiatives will succeed is the quality of the review panels. For example, the Obama evidence-based strategy would not work if the panels awarded funds to organizations—even those using evidence-based programs—that did not have the administrative capacity to conduct the programs effectively. Realizing that fact, the administration made a serious effort to select and train good review panels. In the case of i3, IES devised a training course to make sure that reviewers understood the requirements of the grant solicitation, especially the role of evidence in selecting grantees, and the reviewers were trained in applying the What Works Clearinghouse standards. All of the evidence-based initiatives had both written instructions and at least a brief oral orientation on the requirements for being a reviewer and on how the review panels would function.

It is difficult to judge how effective the review panels were in making their selections. There were some objections to the selections, especially to the i3 selections and to the selections of the intermediary organizations in the SIF initiative. In the SIF case, part of the problem was that the administration did not release enough information about the selections. But one thing that nearly all the other agencies have done, especially after the first round of grants, is to release a great deal of information about the selections, often including the proposals that were funded and those that were not funded and even reviewers' rating sheets.

Based on the experience with the Obama initiatives, several obvious recommendations can be made about how to choose review panels: select reviewers as carefully as possible; make sure that they are well trained for the task of reviewing; include evidence experts in the process; and release as much information about the review process as possible on the day that the final selections are released or shortly thereafter.

Signs of Success

The long-term goal of the administration's evidence-based initiatives is to make progress in reducing the social problems that afflict the nation, especially those that harm children and families. But even under the best of circumstances, it will be many years before it is known whether the programs funded under the initiatives are actually leading to reductions in those problems. Nonetheless, the administration doesn't have to wait several years to decide whether the initiatives are achieving at least some of their goals. There are many signposts along the path between the current location and the ultimate destination. But what are those signposts? How will the nation—even more to the point, Congress—know whether the Obama evidence-based strategy is a success or is at least moving in the right direction? Here are four signs of success by which the initiatives can be judged.

The Initiatives Survive the 2017 Presidential Transition

The fate of the Obama evidence-based initiatives depends in large part on the next presidential administration, which will assume control of the executive branch at noon on January 20, 2017. Given the general disdain in which Republicans hold President Obama and their dislike of most items on his agenda, the chances that the initiatives will survive a Republican president seem modest at best. Even if the next president is a Democrat, the tight federal budget means that the president will not have a lot of cash lying around to fund his or her own agenda and so may terminate one or more of Obama's evidence-based initiatives to make room for others. A reasonable conclusion is that all six of the Obama initiatives are likely to be under threat when the next president takes office—and possibly under mortal threat if the next president is a Republican.

If the evidence-based initiatives are to have a long-term impact on American social policy, the mere survival of the Obama six, doubtful as that might be, is not enough. If the Obama vision of using evidence to expand programs that work and reform or terminate those that do not is to flourish, it will be necessary to expand the current approach of encouraging, cajoling, or forcing more and more federal agencies to subject their grant programs to rigorous evaluations and use the information obtained thereby to determine future funding. Expanding the evidence-based approach will require champions at OMB. There is no question that career OMB staffers like Kathy Stack and others will continue to do everything that they can to expand the use of evidence by OMB and the administrative agencies, but unless future presidents, their senior White House and OMB staffers, and their political appointees in the departments put expanding the use of evidence on the agenda, it simply will not happen. It seems highly doubtful that requiring evidence in awarding federal grants will become a campaign issue, so whether the next administration and the one after will continue and expand the Obama initiatives is difficult to predict. Almost all the important decisions regarding the evidence initiatives will take place behind the scenes at the White House, the executive agencies, and Congress. At this point, the outcome is anyone's guess.

A Culture of Evidence Is Established

A major sign of success will be a gradual change in what might be called the culture of program operation and evaluation. There are tens of thousands of programs, located in every community in the nation, that attempt to improve social well-being. They include programs in local schools, departments of social services, health clinics, and churches; juvenile justice programs; and a host of programs sponsored by community-based organizations that address every social problem imaginable. As they now operate, many of these programs have written goals, a budget, a program or curriculum of some sort that specifies a set of activities designed to achieve their goals, and staff members who administer and implement the program. If the Obama initiatives are successful, more program operators will begin to employ rigorous methods to systematically evaluate their programs. Many small community-based programs may not have the resources to conduct quality evaluations, but those that can, should. Over time, more and more operators could develop the expertise needed to mount their own rigorous evaluations or work out arrangements with local, state, or private universities or evaluation firms to continuously evaluate their programs. They will also develop and improve their ability to interpret the results of evaluation studies and use the results to improve their programs.

Another sign of culture change would be that the boards (including school boards) that oversee social programs begin to expect information on program participants' outcomes and to use that information to judge the success of programs and hold the administrative and service delivery staffs accountable for them. In addition, program administrators would become more adept at using evaluations to assess the performance of both their program and staff members who work with program participants. Because effective staffers often work in poor programs and vice versa, evaluating both is essential. As part of this process, outcome information would become an official part of the criteria used to evaluate, pay, and promote both administrators and teachers and other program personnel.

If systematic evaluation by rigorous methods and use of evaluation results to improve programs is to become standard operating procedure throughout the country, the culture of evidence must flourish not only in local organizations but also in foundations, state and federal agencies, national child advocacy organizations, and legislative bodies at all levels of government. One encouraging outcome of the Obama initiatives is that foundations have offered significant support for the initiatives, especially i3 and the Social Innovation Fund. For example, the Edna McConnell Clark Foundation is serving as an intermediary in the latter initiative and also has an ongoing relationship with the research and evaluation firm MDRC to help its own grantees evaluate their programs. These developments can be taken as signs of commitment to evidence-based policy by some of the major foundations involved in domestic social issues. An important question now is whether the same foundations will demand rigorous evaluations of their grantees and use the results to determine, at least in part, their future funding decisions. Similarly, if the evidence-based movement is to prosper, school systems, departments of social services, and state governments must also undergo the same kind of culture change. If they do not, the evidence-based movement may come to be regarded as little more than a passing fad.

Early Positive Outcomes Are Achieved

About 700 projects are now funded under the six initiatives and nearly all are being evaluated. The evaluations undoubtedly range in quality from mediocre to very good and from collecting only outcome measures to conducting quasi-experimental and random assignment studies. Each of the six initiatives funds a mix of projects—usually organized into tiers depending on the quality of the supporting evidence—that use program models with strong, moderate, or weak-to-nonexistent evidence of success from previous evaluations. It seems likely that projects using model programs with evidence of success from random assignment studies will produce some significant impacts while projects using innovative programs with much less evidence—or no evidence—will be more likely to fail. Both Jim Manzi[16] and Jon Baron[17] have estimated that around 80 to 90 percent of innovative programs tested by RCTs produce no impacts or small impacts. Nonetheless, that leaves 10 percent of innovative projects that might be expected to produce significant impacts.

The projects on the top and the second tier of evidence in several of the initiatives might be expected to have higher rates of success because they are operating programs that have been shown by RCTs or quasi-experimental evaluations to produce impacts. Recent rigorous evaluations of three of the four top-tier i3 model programs from the 2010 round of funding have reported significant impacts (see chapter 4).[18] If these early successes can be replicated by, say, 20 or 30 percent of the projects reporting results in 2014 and 2015, program operators, administration officials, congressional staffers, and reporters would have room to be optimistic that the evidence-based initiatives are achieving the results hoped for by the administration.

Programs Improve Based on Evidence

The great strength of RCTs is that they reliably indicate whether a program is producing impacts. Perhaps their greatest weakness is that they provide little information about why a program succeeds or fails. Even so, knowing that a program fails or produces only modest impacts tells program operators that they need to try something different. Perhaps the teachers are not trained well enough; perhaps the curriculum is ineffective; perhaps participants are not receiving an adequate dose of the intervention. Because an RCT usually does not provide information on which of these or other potential problems are at fault, improving programs is largely a trial and error process.

This weakness of RCTs has caused researchers to consider ways to make more effective use of RCTs in efforts to improve programs. One idea that is now receiving a great deal of attention is the possibility of conducting short-term, low-cost RCTs of social programs by using administrative data to reduce costs. Imagine that a school system wanted to test a new reading program. If the school system had the capacity, it could arrange a random assignment study within several elementary schools, administering the new program to one group and continuing the current program with the other. The school is likely to be collecting data already on various measures of reading ability that could serve as the outcome variables. By developing their own ability to design and conduct random assignment studies using administrative data, school systems, departments of social services, juvenile detention facilities, and other organizations could test their programs in a relatively economical way. Trial-and-error learning, as discussed by Jim Manzi in *Uncontrolled,*[19] would then be a realistic possibility for large and medium-size systems. The Coalition for Evidence-Based Policy, with funds from the Laura and John Arnold and the Annie E. Casey Foundations, is conducting a grant competition for organizations that want to conduct such quick, low-cost RCTs.[20]

Rather than conducting a long-term, expensive test of an entire program, program operators would be able to conduct many RCTs, each providing a rigorous test of modest changes, with relatively small investments of time, personnel, and money. Manzi uses the analogy of building a mountain of information about effective interventions one pebble at a time. There are now several examples of rapid, low-cost RCTs of social intervention programs, proof that such RCTs are possible.[21] It remains to be demonstrated, however, whether schools, departments of social services, medical systems, and other institutions that conduct social programs can make rapid, low-cost RCTs part of their normal operating procedures.

Issues

We can, of course, hope that two or three years from now there will be progress on the four signs of success discussed above. However, even if the initiatives achieve a measure of success, our study suggests that there are at least five perennial issues that will continue to play a significant role in the success or failure of the Obama or any other evidence-based initiatives. These issues are the role of RCTs, what to do when programs fail, the role of state and local governments, the tension between funding evidence-based or innovative programs, and a host of potential difficulties in implementing even evidence-based programs.

The Role of RCTs

There is much to learn from the problems that the Obama team encountered in implementing its six evidence-based initiatives. The first problem—the inevitable tension between a researcher's and a program operator's view of good evidence—is bound to be an issue for all six evidence-based initiatives. Some program operators as well as their board members and the politicians who support them seem to be satisfied with heartwarming anecdotes about children who have done well in their program. Other program operators think that simply collecting evidence of good outcomes—such as high test scores, high rates of school completion, or lower arrest rates—is enough to show that their program is effective. But effective compared with what? The RCT is the gold standard in the Obama evidence-based world—and also among many researchers and others who use the results of program evaluations to determine whether social programs are working. Other types of evidence can qualify for funding under the Obama initiatives, but the Obama gold standard is very similar to that of the National Academies, the Institute of Education Sciences, and other organizations that set standards for good evidence. Moreover, an implicit goal of the Obama initiatives is to encourage foundations, local education authorities, community-based programs, and other organizations conducting social programs to learn more about rigorous evidence and to use RCTs to evaluate programs when possible, while recognizing that innovative projects in their infancy may not be ready for an RCT. The Obama administration's vision is that with each passing year more and more federal dollars for social programs will go to programs that are backed by solid, preferably RCT, evidence and that funded programs will undergo continuous assessment, as often as possible by RCTs, to determine their ongoing effects.

Program operators cite a host of good reasons why they are hard pressed to use RCTs to evaluate their programs. Perhaps the most important is that they are so busy trying to run their program well that they have neither the time nor the resources to support expensive and time-consuming random assignment evaluations. This is a worthy criticism, and it is easy to sympathize with the many problems faced by program operators just to keep their programs going. Our interviews with both officials from the Corporation for National and Community Service (CNCS) and MDRC evaluators involved in several SIF programs revealed that many operators lacked knowledge about program evaluation and had never participated in a rigorous evaluation. We suspect that the same may be true of many local education authorities and the consultants and organizations that they work with. The CNCS solution as it administered the SIF initiative was to communicate with program operators for the specific purpose of teaching them about program evaluation and the use of rigorous designs. As part of that education process, CNCS developed an impressive manual to help programs develop their evaluation plans.[22] They also hired the research firm JBS to help programs develop and conduct high-quality evaluations. We did not interview program operators, but senior officials at CNCS told us that program operators understood the importance of evaluation and worked hard to create good evaluation plans for their own programs.

For what it might be worth, we think that the compromise reached by the Obama administration over RCTs and other forms of rigorous evaluation is about right. Sing the praises of RCTs, encourage (and pay for) their use wherever and whenever possible, but do not hold all programs to the RCT standard. There is and should remain a role for quasi-experimental designs in the funding of evidence-based programs. And there should remain a role for innovative programs that have good logic models but little or no data.

When a Program Fails, What's Next?

As we have seen, another problem with the evidence-based initiatives is that good evaluations are certain to show that many of the programs produce modest or no impacts.[23] The administration has hired reputable research companies to help programs improve the quality of their evaluations, and they almost certainly will do so. But the better the evaluation, the more likely it is to show that a program does not produce statistically significant impacts.

Our interviews with administration officials suggest that so far local programs are going along with the Obama emphasis on evaluation. However, at the moment, many—perhaps most—of the program developers, program operators, researchers, and politicians involved with social programs have become accustomed to thinking, on the basis of anecdotal and other unreliable evidence, that their programs are working well. Now, with the hundreds of evidence-based programs operating under the Obama initiatives—and with all the programs being subjected to rigorous evaluation—many program enthusiasts are going to face disappointment when the evaluations begin to show that a large majority of the programs produce modest or no impacts. At that point, a very important moment in the life of the Obama evidence-based initiatives will have arrived.

How will program directors and their staffs and boards respond when the evaluations show that their program is not producing significant impacts? This issue will play an important role in the success not just of the Obama evidence-based initiatives but of the evidence-based movement in general. If evaluation is to help programs improve, evaluations must provide continuous information to program officials so that they can make adjustments in their program in response to an evaluation's findings. At that point, one hopes that both the administration and the various evaluation experts that the administration and local programs have hired will help operators accept the results as an indication that they need to improve their programs and assure them that the administration will help them do so. An important part of a comprehensive, evidence-based strategy will be to continue funding programs that receive initially discouraging evaluations. Part of the federal evidence-based culture should be that federal agencies will work with programs and continue funding them as long as they are using evidence to improve their outcomes and are showing some progress. Only when operators with failing programs refuse to make recommended changes over a period of at least a year or two should the sponsoring agencies pull the plug.

The Role of State and Local Governments

During the old days, the answer to the question of who controls the federal evidence-based initiatives would have been obvious: the federal government has the authority and the money, so federal officials get to make the major decisions. But that answer is no longer always adequate. The states have become major players in social policy, in some respects more important than the federal government. Even the programs that are controlled in large part by federal statutes, such as No Child Left Behind, Medicaid, and the Child Care and Development Block Grant, are administered by the states. If the states administer the programs, it makes sense that they should have some voice in how the money is spent. Furthermore, it makes sense to shift more power over social spending from the federal government to the states because states are closer to the people that they represent and that closeness makes them better judges of what their populations need and what policies and programs can help them most.[24]

Moreover, states often are more flexible and venturesome than the federal government. As U.S. Supreme Court Justice Louis Brandeis argued in *New State Ice Co.* v. *Liebmann* (1932), states can, if their citizens so choose, serve as laboratories to try new laws and policies. In addition, although since passage of the Elementary and Secondary Education Act in 1965 the federal government can be seen as encroaching on state prerogatives in education policy, states are still by far the major actor in public K–12 education and even to a major extent in preschool education. These are strong arguments for giving states a broader role in improving the delivery of education and other social services. The Obama administration was wise, for example, to require states to develop a plan for conducting home visiting programs in areas of the state where they were most needed and to deliver the services using organizations selected by the states.

The Social Innovation Fund provides an even more remarkable example of decisionmaking about funding by entities other than the federal government. As discussed in chapter 5, a new type of nonprofit organization, the intermediary, has sprung up in recent years. These organizations, a key element of the social entrepreneurs movement, raise money to discover and support effective community-based organizations and help them expand. Recognizing the potential effectiveness of intermediary organizations, the SIF gives them federal dollars and lets them choose the winners. The twenty organizations currently involved as intermediaries in SIF include charities, foundations, and local government entities. They run their own grant competition under federal guidelines and provide support to the winning community-based organizations, helping them select and train staff members, consult with their boards, and plan and execute their evaluations. On paper, allowing nonfederal entities to allocate funds makes a lot of sense both philosophically and practically. Again, we will have to wait until impact data become available to evaluate the effectiveness of this innovative method of funding and providing assistance to community-based programs.

Innovation versus Evidence

No one with experience funding, operating, or studying social programs can believe that the nation now has enough model programs to solve its major social problems. As we have seen repeatedly, many of the nation's social programs— including almost the entire public school system and other large programs such as social services—are at best modestly effective. The nation therefore stands in dire need of better, more effective, and more efficient social programs. The need for innovation, as we note in chapter 5, is a major reason that the social entrepreneurs movement is so welcome.

At the beginning of the Obama administration, there appeared to be some conflict, especially in working out the details of the home visiting initiative, over whether the administration should concentrate its funds exclusively on programs that meet the highest evidence standards, like the Nurse-Family Partnership. But simply as a matter of logic, if all the money is spent on programs with strong evidence, where does that leave innovation? In order to mount a successful long-term attack on the nation's social problems, both proven programs and promising programs that develop new, possibly more effective, interventions are necessary. To allow for innovation, the tiered funding model was developed for the i3 initiative and eventually applied to the Workforce Innovation Fund, TAACCCT, and the Social Innovation Fund initiatives. Creating tiers of evidence and different levels of funding for each tier seems a useful and workable solution to the issue of where to invest government funds. For almost every social issue, model programs exist that are supported by evidence from rigorous evaluations. But for most social problems, intervention programs produce modest impacts. Funding programs at different stages of development, as is done in most of the Obama initiatives, therefore seems wise. Most of the funding is focused on programs with strong track records while new and innovative programs are simultaneously developed that can eventually join the ranks of evidence-based programs.

Implementation

A major assumption of the Obama evidence-based initiatives is that establishing programs shown to produce positive impacts in new settings is an effective way to attack the nation's social problems. However, the road from evidence-based program to social impacts is bumpy. If excellent programs are poorly implemented, the probability of producing impacts is close to zero. The growing field of implementation science shows that an effective implementation strategy has at least five elements:[25]

—Fidelity to the model. Although some aspects of a model program may need to be adapted to local conditions, research shows that the core components, defined as "the most essential and indispensable components of an intervention practice or program," must be well implemented if a replication is to succeed.[26] A problem with some model programs is that the program does not include a how-to guide that lists the core components that must be faithfully implemented.[27]

—Staff selection and training. A key to any social intervention program is having the right staff to deliver the program effectively. Organizations must make every effort to hire well-qualified people and train them carefully in how to use the program curriculum.

—Coaching. The idea of coaching is that an experienced expert practitioner can help teachers or others delivering a model program to improve their skills by working with them directly. An important element of good coaching is the ability of coaches to demonstrate the skills and practices that they believe are important to success while working with program participants. There is good evidence from both K–12 and preschool programs that coaching can have a significant impact on teacher success.[28]

—Administrative support. Program administrators have a huge range of responsibilities that must be met if the program is to be effective. Responsibilities include hiring personnel, selecting the curriculum, overseeing evaluation, fundraising, creating an effective parent program, and supervising and evaluating teachers. Good administrators also work to encourage collaboration and create a sense of mission among staff.

—Feedback. An effective program will continually monitor performance, report results, and adjust program activities accordingly.

Although we have not addressed implementation in this book, a thorough accounting of the Obama evidence-based initiatives will require a great deal of information on how the evidence-based programs are being implemented. The administration has wisely hired research firms with national reputations to evaluate and provide technical assistance to grantees carrying out evidence-based programs; hopefully the evaluations will provide extensive information about how the programs were implemented. In addition, it is to be hoped that many of the over 700 programs funded under the six evidence-based initiatives are being carefully studied by individual researchers and the research firms hired by many of the individual programs to record information about problems encountered during implementation, help evaluate teachers and administrators, and document the implementation of curriculum activities. If so, within a few years there will be a host of publications that provide valuable information about how the programs were implemented and why the programs succeeded or failed.

Moving the Needle

We think that the Obama experimental strategy of using federal dollars to support social intervention programs supported by rigorous evidence and to evaluate the programs as they are being conducted has the potential to become the most effective strategy yet for attacking the nation's social problems. We emphasize the word "potential." With over 700 projects sponsored under the six initiatives and with most of the projects being evaluated by rigorous designs, a broad test of the evidence-based strategy is well under way. In 2015 and 2016, most of the projects will have begun to report results, often from RCTs. But before making optimistic claims about how the evidence-based strategy can help the nation attack its most pressing social problems, we need proof that the evidence-based programs have had positive impacts on the social problems now being addressed by the initiatives—child rearing by poor mothers; teen pregnancy; several preschool and K–12 education issues; a host of community-level social problems; and employment and training issues. In addition, we need to see improvements over time as state and local programs use evaluation outcomes to improve their programs and increase their impacts. These are far from certain outcomes. But even if there are a number of program successes and improvements, that is still only a first step.

On a ten-point scale, with ten being fabulously effective in dramatically reducing one of the nation's major social problems, we would rate the nation's social intervention programs, taken as a whole, at two or three. Many programs score much higher, but to reduce the nation's social problems significantly, hundreds and potentially even thousands of programs must produce meaningful impacts. The Obama evidence-based approach holds real promise for producing those impacts at scale. We have a formidable weapon in the RCT because it can reliably tell us whether specific programs and practices work. And, if more and more program operators use evidence-based programs and practices shown by RCTs to work, it will be possible to increase the effectiveness of public spending on social programs. As many research groups are now trying to demonstrate, that will be possible especially if short-term, inexpensive RCTs using administrative data prove to be effective. And if program operators and their advisers become adept at using rigorous evaluations to improve their programs, the programs can produce even larger impacts. The vision of the evidence-based movement is that the nation will have thousands of evidence-based social programs that address each of the nation's most important social problems and that under the onslaught of these increasingly effective programs, the nation's social problems will at last recede.

Appendix A. Interviewees

Interview subjects are listed with the organization for which they worked when they were involved in the evidence-based initiative. Three subjects were interviewed for more than one initiative; they are listed as an interviewee under each initiative in which they were involved.

Teen Pregnancy Prevention

Ayers, Jacqueline, Planned Parenthood, interviewed by Greg Margolis, October 28, 2011.

Bernhardt, Lisa, Senate Appropriations Committee, interviewed by Greg Margolis, January 12, 2012.

Boonstra, Heather, Guttmacher Institute, interviewed by Greg Margolis, September 14, 2011.

Broman, Barbara, Department of Health and Human Services, interviewed by Ron Haskins and Greg Margolis, November 29, 2011.

Chamberlain, Seth, Department of Health and Human Services, interviewed by Ron Haskins and Greg Margolis, November 1, 2011.

Crane, Donna, NARAL Pro-Choice America, interviewed by Greg Margolis, October 28, 2011.

Drake, Jennifer (Fantroy), National Campaign to Prevent Teen and Unplanned Pregnancy, interviewed by Greg Margolis, August 25, 2011.

Dupre, Alicia, Planned Parenthood, interviewed by Greg Margolis, June 11, 2012.

Eelman, Emily, Office of Management and Budget, interviewed by Greg Margolis, October 28, 2011.

Gentile, Mike, House Appropriations Committee, interviewed by Greg Margolis, October 10, 2011.

Hamm, Katie, Office of Management and Budget, interviewed by Greg Margolis, August 31, 2011.

Hansell, David, Department of Health and Human Services, interviewed by Ron Haskins and Greg Margolis, March 15, 2012.

Heitel, Jennifer, SIECUS, interviewed by Greg Margolis, September 8, 2011.

Huber, Valerie, National Abstinence Education Association, interviewed by Greg Margolis, January 31, 2012.

Kane, Andrea, National Campaign to Prevent Teen and Unplanned Pregnancy, interviewed by Ron Haskins, Kent Weaver, and Greg Margolis, July 27, 2011.

Kappeler, Evelyn, Department of Health and Human Services, interviewed by Ron Haskins and Greg Margolis, November 28, 2011.

Kunko, Nicole, House Appropriations Committee, interviewed by Greg Margolis, September 28, 2011.

McCallum, Diana, Department of Health and Human Services, interviewed by Greg Margolis, November 14, 2011.

Monahan, John, Department of Health and Human Services, interviewed by Ron Haskins and Greg Margolis, September 9, 2011.

Parrott, Sharon, Department of Health and Human Services, interviewed by Ron Haskins and Greg Margolis, July 27, 2012.

Rubiner, Laurie, Planned Parenthood, interviewed by Ron Haskins and Greg Margolis, September 12, 2011.

Seiler, Naomi, Office of Representative Henry Waxman (D-Calif.), interviewed by Greg Margolis, September 6, 2011.

Smith, Bill, SIECUS, interviewed by Kent Weaver and Greg Margolis, January 5, 2012.

Taylor, Bettilou, Senate Appropriations Committee, interviewed by Greg Margolis, January 26, 2012.

Trenholm, Christopher, Mathematica Policy Research, interviewed by Greg Margolis, March 12, 2012.

Trivits, Lisa, Department of Health and Human Services, interviewed by Greg Margolis, November 17, 2011.

Wagoner, James, Advocates for Youth, interviewed by Ron Haskins and Greg Margolis, March 28, 2012.

Home Visiting

Allen, MaryLee, Children's Defense Fund, interviewed by Ron Haskins and Greg Margolis, June 19, 2012.

Baron, Jon, Coalition for Evidence-Based Policy, interviewed by Ron Haskins and Greg Margolis, October 5, 2011.

Bauer, Tamar, Nurse-Family Partnership, interviewed by Greg Margolis, September 23, 2011, and October 21, 2011.

Berntsen, Laura, Office of Representative Jim McDermott (D-Wash.), interviewed by Greg Margolis, October 14, 2011.

Birch, Tom, National Child Abuse Coalition, interviewed by Greg Margolis, April 6, 2012.

Bolger, Kerry, Office of Representative Diana DeGette (D-Colo.), interviewed by Greg Margolis, December 20, 2011.

Callahan, Jane, Parents as Teachers, interviewed by Greg Margolis, October 12, 2011.

Cha, Stephen, House Energy and Commerce Committee, interviewed by Greg Margolis, November 4, 2011.

Cooper, Hope, Child Trends, interviewed by Ron Haskins, December 5, 2011.

Coven, Martha, Domestic Policy Council, interviewed by Ron Haskins and Greg Margolis, September 15, 2011.

Freis, Farrah, Office of Management and Budget, interviewed by Greg Margolis, January 30, 2012.

Gavaghan, Bridget, Prevent Child Abuse America, interviewed by Greg Margolis, March 29, 2012.

Goldstein, Naomi, Department of Health and Human Services, interviewed by Ron Haskins and Greg Margolis, November 28, 2011.

Greenberg, Mark, Department of Health and Human Services, interviewed by Ron Haskins and Greg Margolis, February 3, 2012.

Gwyn, Nick, House Committee on Ways and Means, interviewed by Ron Haskins and Greg Margolis, August 23, 2011.

Henry-Spires, Diedra, Senate Finance Committee, interviewed by Ron Haskins and Greg Margolis, October 4, 2011.

Howard, Karen, Nurse-Family Partnership, interviewed by Greg Margolis, December 2, 2011.

Hughes, Dora, Staff of Senator Barack Obama, interviewed by Ron Haskins and Greg Margolis, September 6, 2012.

Hunter-Williams, Jill, Office of Representative Danny Davis (D-Ill.), interviewed by Greg Margolis, October 18, 2011.

Hutson, Rutledge, Center for Law and Social Policy, interviewed by Ron Haskins and Greg Margolis, March 12, 2012.

Jolly, Julie, Office of Senator Kit Bond (R-Mo.), interviewed by Greg Margolis, September 21, 2011.

Lesley, Bruce, First Focus, interviewed by Ron Haskins and Greg Margolis, August 29, 2012.

Lombardi, Joan, Department of Health and Human Services, interviewed by Ron Haskins and Greg Margolis, March 21, 2011.

Miller, Morna, House Budget Committee, interviewed by Greg Margolis, February 23, 2012.

Morancy, Jonathan, Congressional Budget Office, interviewed by Greg Margolis, January 31, 2012.

Nesbit, Sonja, House Committee on Ways and Means, interviewed by Greg Margolis, September 1, 2011.

Paulsell, Diane, Mathematica Policy Research, interviewed by Greg Margolis, March 29, 2012.

Pryor, Barbara, Office of Senator Jay Rockefeller (D-W.V.), interviewed by Ron Haskins and Greg Margolis, November 18, 2011.

Rodriguez, Roberto, Domestic Policy Council, interviewed by Ron Haskins and Greg Margolis, February 28, 2013.

Rollin, Miriam, Fight Crime: Invest in Kids, interviewed by Greg Margolis, November 3, 2011.

Rosenbaum, Dan, Office of Management and Budget, interviewed by Greg Margolis, October 12, 2011.

Schneider, Andy, Energy and Commerce Committee, interviewed by Ron Haskins and Greg Margolis, April 4, 2012.

Schneider, Audrey (Yowell), Department of Health and Human Services, interviewed by Greg Margolis, December 9, 2011.

Shea, Robert, Office of Management and Budget, interviewed by Ron Haskins and Greg Margolis, February 9, 2012.

Shipp, Becky, Senate Finance Committee, interviewed by Ron Haskins and Greg Margolis, August 30, 2011.

Smalligan, Jack, Office of Management and Budget, interviewed by Ron Haskins and Greg Margolis, November 1, 2011.

Stack, Kathy, Office of Management and Budget, interviewed by Ron Haskins and Greg Margolis, August 2, 2011.

Steiger, Douglas, Department of Health and Human Services, interviewed by Ron Haskins and Greg Margolis, November 2, 2011.

Stepleton, Susan S., Parents as Teachers, interviewed by Greg Margolis, October 17, 2011.

Supplee, Lauren, Department of Health and Human Services, interviewed by Greg Margolis, October 17, 2011.

Walzer, Sarah, Parent-Child Home Program, interviewed by Greg Margolis, March 30, 2012.

Weidinger, Matt, House Committee on Ways and Means, interviewed by Ron Haskins and Greg Margolis, March 13, 2012.

Wolfkiel, Rebeccah, Office of Representative Todd Platts (R-Pa.), interviewed by Greg Margolis, December 20, 2011.

Young, Kathryn, Office of Senator Patty Murray (D-Wash.), interviewed by Greg Margolis, February 27, 2012.

Investing in Innovation

Cain, Alice Johnson, House Committee on Education and Labor, interviewed by Greg Margolis, December 21, 2011.

Cole, Allison, Office of Management and Budget, interviewed by Greg Margolis, April 11, 2012.

Easton, John Q., Department of Education, interviewed by Ron Haskins and Greg Margolis, February 6, 2012.

Higginbottom, Heather, Domestic Policy Council, interviewed by Ron Haskins and Greg Margolis, October 4, 2011.

Immerman, Suzanne, Department of Education, interviewed by Greg Margolis, July 7, 2012.

Laisch, Mark, Senate Appropriations Committee, interviewed by Greg Margolis, June 19, 2012.

Martin, Carmel, Department of Education, interviewed by Ron Haskins and Greg Margolis, January 4, 2013.

Maynard, Rebecca, Department of Education, interviewed by Ron Haskins and Greg Margolis, September 30, 2011.

Mercer, Charmaine, House Appropriations Committee, interviewed by Greg Margolis, June 4, 2012.

Miller, Tony, Department of Education, interviewed by Ron Haskins and Greg Margolis, February 28, 2012.

Pestronk, Jefferson, Department of Education, interviewed by Ron Haskins and Greg Margolis, February 16, 2012.

Schnur, Jon, Education Adviser to President-Elect Obama, interviewed by Ron Haskins and Greg Margolis, May 8, 2012.

Shah, Shivam Mallick, Department of Education, interviewed by Ron Haskins and Greg Margolis, October 3, 2012.

Shelton, Jim, Department of Education, interviewed by Ron Haskins and Greg Margolis, April 19, 2012.

Smith, Cheryl, House Appropriations Committee, interviewed by Greg Margolis, November 30, 2011.

Social Innovation Fund

Baron, Jon, Coalition for Evidence-Based Policy, interviewed by Ron Haskins and Greg Margolis, June 28, 2012.

Berlin, Gordon, MDRC, interviewed by Ron Haskins, February 11, 2013.

Bradach, Jeff, Bridgespan Group, interviewed by Greg Margolis, March 29, 2012.

Carttar, Paul, Corporation for National and Community Service, interviewed by Ron Haskins and Greg Margolis, February 6, 2012.

Dorsey, Cheryl, Echoing Green, interviewed by Greg Margolis, September 19, 2012.

Hallett, Adrienne, Senate Appropriations Committee, interviewed by Greg Margolis, February 23, 2012.

Jolin, Michele, White House Office of Social Innovation and Civic Participation, interviewed by Ron Haskins and Greg Margolis, October 11, 2012, and February 8, 2013.

Kinneen, Kelly, Office of Management and Budget, interviewed by Greg Margolis, January 9, 2012.

Kunko, Nicole, House Appropriations Committee, interviewed by Greg Margolis, January 20, 2012.

McSwain, Kristin, Corporation for National and Community Service, interviewed by Greg Margolis, February 17, 2012.

Mitchell, Kent, Corporation for National and Community Service, interviewed by Greg Margolis, January 24, 2012.

Monje, Carlos, Domestic Policy Council, interviewed by Greg Margolis, November 29, 2011.

Potter, Lance, New Profit, interviewed by Greg Margolis, March 20, 2012.

Sagawa, Shirley, Office of the President-Elect, interviewed by Greg Margolis, April 16, 2012.

Senior Republican staffer in the Senate, interviewed by Greg Margolis, June 1, 2012.

Sheridan, Tom, Sheridan Group, interviewed by Greg Margolis, March 7 and March 29, 2012.

Silsby, Joscelyn, Corporation for National and Community Service, interviewed by Greg Margolis, June 15, 2012.

Spera, Christopher, Corporation for National and Community Service, interviewed by Ron Haskins and Greg Margolis, July 24, 2013.

Syman, Kim, New Profit, interviewed by Greg Margolis, March 15, 2012.

Urquilla, Marta, Corporation for National and Community Service, interviewed by Ron Haskins and Greg Margolis, April 10, 2012.

Vadehra, Emma, Senate Health, Education, Labor, and Pensions (HELP) Committee, interviewed by Greg Margolis, April 13, 2012.

Washburn, Susannah, Corporation for National and Community Service, interviewed by Greg Margolis, February 2, 2012.

Workforce Innovation Fund

Bomberger, Melissa, Office of Management and Budget, interviewed by Greg Margolis, October 26, 2011.

Cheney, Scott, Senate Health, Education, Labor, and Pensions (HELP) Committee, interviewed by Greg Margolis, March 8, 2012.

Colbert, John, Jobs for the Future, interviewed by Greg Margolis, May 17, 2012.

Kilbane, Grace A., Department of Labor, interviewed by Greg Margolis, April 6, 2012.

Lam, Livia, House Committee on Education and Labor, interviewed by Greg Margolis, June 25, 2012.

McCarthy, Mary Alice, Department of Labor, interviewed by Greg Margolis, April 12, 2012.

Oates, Jane, Department of Labor, interviewed by Ron Haskins and Greg Margolis, July 20, 2012.

Perkins-Cohen, Alison, Senate Appropriations Committee, interviewed by Greg Margolis, January 5, 2012.

Steigleder, Stephen, House Appropriations Committee, interviewed by Greg Margolis, February 29, 2012.

Wells, Gina, Department of Labor, interviewed by Greg Margolis, April 2, 2012.

Zinn, Rachel, Office of Management and Budget, interviewed by Greg Margolis, October 20, 2011.

TAACCCT

Ahlstrand, Amanda, Department of Labor, interviewed by Greg Margolis, January 27, 2012.

Baime, David, American Association of Community Colleges, interviewed by Ron Haskins and Greg Margolis, June 19, 2012.

Fiala, Gerri, Department of Labor, interviewed by Greg Margolis, March 14, 2012.

Grossman, Jean, Department of Labor, interviewed by Ron Haskins and Greg Margolis, October 20 and December 23, 2011.

Kanter, Martha, Department of Education, interviewed by Ron Haskins and Greg Margolis, May 22, 2012.

Laitinen, Amy, Department of Education, interviewed by Greg Margolis, December 21, 2011.

Liu, Sue, Department of Labor, interviewed by Greg Margolis, February 6, 2012.

Peller, Julie, House Committee on Education and Labor, interviewed by Greg Margolis, February 10, 2012.

Zinn, Rachel, Office of Management and Budget, interviewed by Greg Margolis, October 20, 2011.

Anonymous, interviewed by Greg Margolis, January 5, 2012.

General

Barnes, Melody, Domestic Policy Council, interviewed by Ron Haskins and Greg Margolis, June 22, 2012.

Cottingham, Phoebe, Department of Education, interviewed by Ron Haskins and Greg Margolis, March 27, 2012.

Gordon, Robert, Office of Management and Budget, interviewed by Ron Haskins and Greg Margolis, January 30 and December 21, 2012.

Harris, Seth, Department of Labor, interviewed by Ron Haskins and Greg Margolis, April 5, 2012.

Liebman, Jeffrey, Office of Management and Budget, interviewed by Ron Haskins and Greg Margolis, September 25, 2012.

Orszag, Peter, Office of Management and Budget, interviewed by Ron Haskins and Greg Margolis, May 30, 2012.

Rouse, Cecilia, Council of Economic Advisers, interviewed by Ron Haskins and Greg Margolis, October 3, 2012.

Whitehurst, Grover J. "Russ," Department of Education, interviewed by Ron Haskins and Greg Margolis, February 27, 2012.

Appendix B. Questionnaire

Name:

Position/agency during work on this initiative:

Initiative:

Interviewer:

Date:

Start time:

End time:

Introduction

We're studying the evidence-based initiatives being pushed by the Obama administration. We have identified you as a person who played some role in one or more of the initiatives. To find out more about your role and about the factors that you think might have influenced congressional approval of the initiatives, we want to ask you some questions. We will keep your responses confidential unless we get permission from you. *[For agencies: If you are concerned about a particular question for any reason, feel free to abstain from answering it.]* We might also want to do a follow-up interview with you at some point in the future; please indicate whether you would be willing to participate in a follow-up interview. We record the interview and then transcribe your answers to questions. Thanks so much for participating.

I. **General questions/initial proposal/getting it on the agenda**

1. How would you characterize your agency's general attitude towards evidence?

2. Did that change with the Obama administration?

3. Was the issue being addressed by this initiative a priority for your department before this initiative?

4. Was the idea of incorporating evidence into decisionmaking on grants a priority for your department before it was addressed by the administration? If so, how did it become a priority?

5. Before you became involved in this initiative, were you familiar with the evidence base on the particular problem or with the questions regarding using evidence in this field?

6. Did you learn more about the evidence while you worked on this initiative? How?

7. Give us a brief overview of the role you played in the formulation or enactment of this initiative.

8. What was the genesis of this particular initiative: where did the basic idea/structure for this initiative as it was originally conceived originate?

9. What was the motivating concern or set of concerns that caused this particular initiative rather than other initiatives to be a priority? Was it primarily a need to address a social problem, fiscal stress and government inefficiency, or some other factor or combination of factors?

10. How important was evidence in getting the initiative on the agenda and in the early conversations about the initiative?

11. Was there any dispute about what the evidence said or about the role that evidence would play in the original design of this initiative?

II. **The administration**

12. Who in the administration/agencies did you interact with directly in your work on this initiative?

13. Did you detect any tension between political appointees and career officials at OMB or the agencies? Between any other factions? If so, what was the source of this tension?

14. Did you believe that enactment of this initiative was important to the administration? If so, how was that conveyed to you?

15. When people from the administration went to Capitol Hill or talked to you about the initiative, did they ever stress that the president supported this initiative? Did they give a sense of how strong a priority it was for the president?

III. Congress

16. Did you meet with any members or staffers about this initiative?

17. If so, who? Describe your conversations with these members and/or staffers. What were the major points of contention?

18. Did you have discussions specifically about the evidence?

19. Were members/staffers aware of the evidence on this particular initiative?

20. Did the strength of the evidence matter to the members and staffers you met with?

21. What seemed to be the most persuasive line of argument with members and staffers for supporting this initiative?

22. Was the legislation modified as it went through Congress? If so, how and why?

IV. Advocacy groups

23. Did you meet with individuals or organizations outside the administration for advice about the initiatives?

24. Did the advocacy groups talk about the role of evidence to support their ideas for the initiative?

25. Did the outside advocacy groups you met with lobby for any particular program models? If so, which groups and which models?

26. What did you find to be the most persuasive line of argument from outside groups for supporting the initiative? Why was it persuasive?

27. Were there lines of argumentation that were less persuasive? If so, why?

V. Evidence review/development of funding announcement/grant solicitation

28. What were some of the major points of discussion on how the legislation would be implemented and the design of the program?

29. What were the conversations about evidence and how evidence would be built into the design of the program?

30. What were the biggest challenges you ran into when reviewing/creating the evidence standards or writing the grant solicitations/regulations?

31. Was there any tension between different camps over how the program would be designed—specifically over the role that evidence would play?

32. What particular lessons did you take from completing the first round of implementation? (How were those reflected in the second and third round competitions?)

VI. Evaluation

33. Give us a brief overview of the role you played.

34. Who did you work with directly in the crafting of the evaluation (inside and outside the government)?

35. What were some of the major design questions you faced in thinking about the evaluation component to this initiative?

VII. Background

36. Do you have any education or experience specifically in research methods or use of evidence in public policy?

37. How did this understanding of evidence influence your approach to legislation/policy?

38. Do you consider yourself a good consumer of evidence, and what does that mean to you?

39. Who else would it be useful for us to speak to regarding this initiative?

Appendix C. Share of Formula and Competitive Grant Funds in Six Evidence-Based Initiatives[a]

Dollars, millions

| Initiative | Type of grant | | Total |
	Competitive	Formula	
Home Visiting[b]	431.00	451.00	882.00
Teen Pregnancy[c]	398.00	0.00	398.00
i3[d]	1,100.00	0.00	1,100.00
SIF[e]	177.60	0.00	177.60
WIF[f]	147.00	0.00	147.00
TAACCCT[g]	1,300.00	144.80	1,444.80
Total	3,553.60	595.80	4,149.40
Percent	85.60	14.40	100.00

a. The table shows a breakdown of the funds awarded through competitive grants and formula grants (in millions of dollars) for each of the six evidence-based initiatives through 2013. Figures are approximate.

b. The amount for home visiting includes money that had been awarded in grants through 2013 rather than the total allocated by the statute, not all of which has been awarded and some of which was cut due to budget sequestration. For a full list of home visiting awards, see HRSA, "Home Visiting Grants and Grantees" (http://mchb.hrsa.gov/programs/homevisiting/grants.html). See also U.S. Department of Health and Human Services, "Justification of Estimates for Appropriations Committees," 2014 (www.hrsa.gov/about/budget/budgetjustification2015.pdf).

c. The amount for teen pregnancy includes only the Teen Pregnancy Prevention (TPP) initiative grants. This program has been funded at around $105 to $110 million annually since 2010. Of that amount, $100 million is dedicated to grants while the rest goes to program support and evaluation. In 2013, however, Congress cut the grant funds for TPP slightly, due to sequestration, appropriating only $98.4 million. U.S. Congress, "Consolidated Appropriations Act, 2010" (www.gpo.gov/fdsys/pkg/PLAW-111publ117/pdf/PLAW-111publ117.pdf); U.S. Congress, "Department of Defense and Full-Year Continuing Appropriations Act, 2011" (www.gpo.gov/fdsys/pkg/BILLS-112hr1473enr/pdf/BILLS-112hr1473enr.pdf); U.S. Congress, "Consolidated Appropriations Act, 2012" (www.gpo.gov/fdsys/pkg/BILLS-112hr2055enr/pdf/BILLS-112hr2055enr.pdf); Congressional Research Service, "Teenage Pregnancy Prevention: Statistics and Programs," 2014 (http://fas.org/sgp/crs/misc/RS20301.pdf).

d. U.S. Department of Education, " Investing in Innovation Fund (i3): Funding Status, FY 2014" (www2.ed.gov/programs/innovation/funding.html).

e. Corporation for National and Community Service, "Social Innovation Fund," 2014 (www.nationalservice.gov/sites/default/files/upload/SIFGeneralFactSheetJan2014.pdf).

f. U.S. Department of Labor, "Workforce Innovation Fund Grant Awards," 2014 (www.doleta.gov/workforce_innovation/grant_awards.cfm).

g. The figure for TAACCCT was estimated using the dollar amount of competitive awards made by the Department of Labor in 2011, 2012, and 2013, with an estimate of the formula portion based on $2.5 million for each state that did not have a fundable application (as specified in the legislation). U.S. Department of Labor, "Trade Adjustment Assistance Community College and Career Training Grant Program Grant Awards," 2013 (www.doleta.gov/taaccct/grantawards.cfm).

Appendix D. Abbreviations

ACA: Patient Protection and Affordable Care Act

ACC: adult career coaches

ACF: Administration for Children and Families

AGI: American Graduation Initiative

ARRA: American Recovery and Reinvestment Act

ASAP: Accelerated Study in Associate Programs

ASPE: Office of the Assistant Secretary for Planning and Evaluation

BART: Becoming a Responsible Teen

CAP: Center for American Progress

CBO: Congressional Budget Office

CBAE: Community-Based Abstinence Education

CBFRS: Community-Based Family Resource and Support Program

CDC: Centers for Disease Control and Prevention

CLASP: Center for Law and Social Policy

CMS: Centers for Medicare and Medicaid Services

CNCS: Corporation for National and Community Service

DOL: Department of Labor

DPC: Domestic Policy Council

EBHV: Supporting Evidence-Based Home Visiting

ED: Department of Education

EMCF: Edna McConnell Clark Foundation

FOA: Funding Opportunity Announcement

FY: Fiscal year

HELP: Senate Health, Education, Labor, and Pensions Committee

HFA: Healthy Families America

HHS: Department of Health and Human Services

HIPPY: Home Instruction for Parents of Preschool Youngsters

HRSA: Health Resources Services Administration

i3: Investing in Innovation

IES: Institute of Education Sciences

KIPP: Knowledge Is Power Program

LGBT: lesbian, gay, bisexual, and transgender

LEA: Local Educational Agency

NCLB: No Child Left Behind

NFP: Nurse-Family Partnership

NOFA: Notice of Funding Availability

OAH: Office of Adolescent Health

OECD: Organization for Economic Cooperation and Development

OMB: Office of Management and Budget

OPRE: Office of Planning, Research, and Evaluation

PAT: Parents as Teachers

PART: program assessment rating tool

PAVES: Partnership for Accelerated Learning through Visualization, Engagement, and Simulation

PREIS: Personal Responsibility Education Innovative Strategies

PREP: Personal Responsibility Education Program

QED: quasi-experimental design

RCT: randomized controlled trial

REAL: Responsible Education about Life

RFP: request for proposals

RTT: Race to the Top

SAFRA: Student Aid and Financial Responsibility Act

SCHIP: State Children's Health Insurance Program

SFA: Success for All

SGA: (Notice of Availability of Funds and) Solicitation for Grant Applications

SIF: Social Innovation Fund

SPRANS-CBAE: Special Projects of Regional and National Significance–Community-Based Abstinence Education

STEM: science, technology, engineering, and math

STI: sexually transmitted infection

TAA: Trade Adjustment Assistance

TAACCCT: Trade Adjustment Assistance Community College and Career Training

TANF: Temporary Assistance for Needy Families

TFA: Teach for America

TPP: Teen Pregnancy Prevention initiative

UC: unemployment compensation

WIA: Workforce Investment Act

WIB: Workforce Investment Board

WIF: Workforce Innovation Fund

Notes

Chapter 1

1. *New American Standard Bible,* Book of Daniel, chapter 1, verses 3-16.

2. Ron Haskins, Christina Paxson, and Jeanne Brooks-Gunn, "Social Policy Rising: A Tale of Evidence Shaping Social Policy," *Future of Children,* Policy Brief (Fall 2009).

3. Kimberly S. Howard and Jeanne Brooks-Gunn, "The Role of Home-Visiting Programs in Preventing Child Abuse and Neglect," *Future of Children,* vol. 19, no. 2 (Fall 2009), pp. 119–146; see especially table 2, p. 133.

4. See, for example, Richard M. Titmuss, *The Gift Relationship: From Human Blood to Social Policy* (New York: Vintage Books, 1971); Duncan MacRae Jr., *The Social Function of Social Science* (Yale University Press, 1976); Martin Rein, *Social Science and Public Policy* (New York: Penguin, 1976); Ron Haskins and James J. Gallagher, *Models of Analysis of Social Policy: An Introduction* (New York: Praeger, 1981).

5. I thank Robert Gordon for a tutorial on Title I contained in a written review of my book received from Robert on April 17, 2014.

6. U.S. Department of Education, *National Assessment of Title I: Final Report: Summary of Key Findings* (October 2007), see especially p. 2.

7. Ibid. The impact data are presented in exhibit 13, p. 29.

8. Dean L. Fixen and others, "Implementation Research: A Synthesis of the Literature" (University of South Florida, 2005).

9. Peter Orszag, "Building Rigorous Evidence to Drive Policy," Office of Management and Budget, June 8, 2009 (www.whitehouse.gov/omb/blog/09/06/08/Building RigorousEvidencetoDrivePolicy).

10. Evaluations of intervention programs for many types of social problems are either of low quality or have produced little evidence that the programs have successfully attacked those problems. The Obama administration was forced to deal with this fact in its two workforce initiatives (see chapters 6 and 7), its Social Innovation Fund (see chapter 5), and to some extent even its Investing in Innovation initiative with respect to education issues (see chapter 4).

11. Larry L. Orr, *Social Experiments: Evaluating Public Programs with Experimental Methods* (Thousand Oaks, Calif.: Sage Publications, 1999).

12. Jack Knott and Aaron Wildavsky, "If Dissemination Is the Solution, What Is the Problem?" *Science Communication,* vol. 1, no. 4 (June 1980), pp. 537–78.

13. Annie Lowrey, "Programs That Tie Funds to Effectiveness Are at Risk," *New York Times,* December 2, 2011 (www.nytimes.com/2011/12/03/us/politics/programs-tying-us-funds-to-effectiveness-are-at-risk.html?_r=0).

14. In addition to these three evidence-based initiatives, the other three covered in this book are the Teen Pregnancy Prevention initiative (TPP), the Investing in Innovation Fund (i3) initiative, and the Workforce Innovation Fund (WIF) initiative.

15. With the authorization and appropriation for the home visiting program set to expire at the end of fiscal year 2014, Congress passed a six-month extension of funding for the program on March 31, 2014. The extension means that home visiting will continue to be funded through March 31, 2015. See the Pew Charitable Trusts, "U.S. Congress Extends Funding for Vital Family Program" (Washington: March 2014) (www.pewstates.org/news-room/press-releases/us-congress-extends-funding-for-vital-family-program-85899542945?utm_campaign=2014-04-28%20HVN.html&utm_medium=email&utm_source=Eloqua).

16. In social science jargon, there are two types of validity: internal validity and external validity. According to a classic book on research design, internal validity is whether "in fact the experimental treatments [made] a difference in this specific experimental instance" while external validity raises the issue of "to what populations, settings, treatment variables can [the results of an experiment] be generalized?" See Donald T. Campbell and Julian C. Stanley, *Experimental and Quasi-Experimental Designs for Research* (Boston: Houghton Mifflin, 1963), pp. 5–6.

17. Annette Lareau, *Unequal Childhoods: Class, Race, and Family Life,* 2nd ed. (University of California Press, 2011).

18. Ariel Kalil, "Inequality Begins at Home: The Role of Parenting in the Diverging Destinies of Rich and Poor Children," in *Diverging Destinies: Families in an Era of Increasing Inequality,* edited by Paul Amato, Susan R. McHale, and Alan Booth (New York: Springer, 2014).

19. Jim Manzi, *Uncontrolled: The Surprising Payoff of Trial-and-Error for Business, Politics, and Society* (New York: Basic Books, 2012), pp. 72–73.

20. Donald T. Campbell and Julian Stanley cite McCall as giving the first thorough explanation of the uses of and justification for random assignment in their book *Experimental and Quasi-Experimental Designs for Research* (Cengage Learning, 1963), pp. 1–2.

21. William Anderson McCall, *How to Experiment in Education* (New York: Macmillan, 1923), p. 41.

22. One of the most interesting brief treatments of the historic importance of RCTs in medicine is Richard Doll, "Controlled Trials: The 1948 Watershed," *BMJ,* vol. 317 (October 1998), pp. 1217–20.

23. A facsimile of Dr. Bell's report is available at www.jameslindlibrary.org/illustrating/records/the-prevention-of-whooping-cough-by-vaccination/whole_articles.pdf. A detailed overview of the study, including pilot work and the outcomes of the study, can be found

in Iain Chalmers, "Joseph Asbury Bell and the Birth of Randomized Trials," *Journal of the Royal Society of Medicine,* vol. 100, no. 6 (June 2007), pp. 287–93.

24. Manzi, *Uncontrolled,* p. 79.

25. John Ionnidis wrote a provocative essay in which he argued that most findings published in medicine and other fields, even when good methods are used, are false. He posits that studies are less likely to be true when the sample size is small, when impacts (effect sizes) are small, when there is greater financial interest in the outcome, and when several research groups are competing to publish on the same issue, among other reasons. See John P. A. Ionnidis, "Why Most Published Research Findings Are False," *PLOS Medicine,* vol. 2, no. 8 (August 2005), pp. 696–701.

26. John P. A. Ioannidis, "Contradicted and Initially Stronger Effects in Highly Cited Clinical Research," *Journal of the American Medical Association,* vol. 294, no. 2 (July 13, 2005), pp. 218–28; Mohammad I. Zia and others, "Comparison of Outcomes of Phase II Studies and Subsequent Randomized Control Studies Using Identical Chemotherapeutic Regimens," *Journal of Clinical Oncology,* vol. 23, no. 28 (October 1, 2005), pp. 6982–91; John K. Chan and others, "Analysis of Phase II Studies on Targeted Agents and Subsequent Phase III Trials: What Are the Predictors for Success?" *Journal of Clinical Oncology,* vol. 26, no. 9 (March 20, 2008); for an overview of these studies, see Coalition for Evidence-Based Policy, "Randomized Controlled Trials Commissioned by the Institute of Education Sciences since 2002: How Many Found Positive versus Weak or No Effects?" (Washington: July 2013) (http://coalition4evidence.org/wp-content/uploads/2013/06/IES-Commissioned-RCTs-positive-vs-weak-or-null-findings-7-2013.pdf).

27. David H. Greenberg and Mark Shroder, *Digest of Social Experiments,* 3rd ed. (Washington: Urban Institute, 2004).

28. Gina Kolata, "Guesses and Hype Give Way to Data in Study of Education," *New York Times,* September 2, 2013 (www.nytimes.com/2013/09/03/science/applying-new-rigor-in-studying-education.html?_r=1&pagewanted=all&).

29. Manzi, *Uncontrolled,* especially Chapter 7.

30. See Coalition for Evidence-Based Policy, "Randomized Controlled Trials Commissioned by the Institute of Education Sciences since 2002," for a good example of the prevalence of modest impacts. In reviewing the results of all the RCTs conducted by the Institute of Education Sciences since 2002, the coalition found that of the 90 RCTs conducted, 12 percent found positive impacts while 88 percent found weak or no positive impacts.

31. For more on benefit-cost studies, see Harry Campbell and Richard Brown, *Benefit-Cost Analysis: Financial and Economic Appraisal Using Spreadsheets* (Cambridge University Press, 2003).

32. Judith M. Gueron and Howard Rolston, *Fighting for Reliable Evidence* (New York: Russell Sage, 2013).

33. Judgment is called for in deciding exactly when the impact of an experimental treatment has been proven. In medical research, preliminary experimentation often results in the finding that a treatment seems to be effective. However, when the treatment is then subjected to a full-scale RCT, the treatment does not produce the expected result. Our judgment is that a treatment has not been demonstrated to be effective until it has

been shown by a large-scale field trial, conducted under real-world conditions, to have significant impacts.

34. Gueron and Rolston, *Fighting for Reliable Evidence.*

35. The Florida experiment on welfare reform, which was covered by newspapers in Florida, Texas, and Washington, D.C., is explained in full in Gueron and Rolston, *Fighting for Reliable Evidence,* pp. 298–309. The Tuskegee experiment was conducted by the U.S. Public Health Service in Tuskegee, Alabama. A group of 600 black men, 399 of whom had syphilis, were followed from 1932 to 1972. The purpose of the study was to study the natural evolution of the disease. The men were not told that they had syphilis and were not given any treatment except aspirin for pain. By the end of the period, more than 100 of the men had died from syphilis and related causes. The study has now entered U.S. popular culture as an egregious example of racism in action and of science gone awry. See James H. Jones, *Bad Blood: The Tuskegee Syphilis Experiment: A Tragedy of Race and Medicine* (New York: Free Press, 1982).

36. National Research Council, *Preventing Mental, Emotional, and Behavioral Disorders among Young People: Progress and Possibilities* (Washington: National Academies Press, 2009). Also see the evidence guidelines issued by the Institute of Education Sciences and the National Science Foundation, "Common Guidelines for Education Research and Development" (Washington: August 2013).

37. Robert J. LaLonde, "Evaluating the Econometric Evaluations of Training Programs with Experimental Data," *American Economic Review,* vol. 76, no. 4 (September 1986), pp. 604–20; and Thomas Fraker and Rebecca Maynard, "The Adequacy of Comparison Group Designs for Evaluations of Employment-Related Programs," *Journal of Human Resources,* vol. 22, no.2 (Spring 1987), pp. 194–227.

38. MDRC, *Summary and Findings of the National Supported Work Demonstration* (Cambridge, Mass.: Ballinger, 1980).

39. Coalition for Evidence-Based Policy, "Which Comparison-Group ('Quasi-Experimental') Study Designs Are Most Likely to Produce Valid Estimates of a Program's Impact? A Brief Overview and Sample Review Form" (Washington: February 2012).

40. Here is how the coalition study explains what it means by "similar in motivation": "In this type of comparison-group study—sometimes called a 'cutoff-based' or 'regression-discontinuity' study—the program group is comprised of persons just above the threshold for program eligibility, and the comparison group is comprised of persons just below (e.g., families earning $19,000 per year versus families earning $21,000, in an employment program whose eligibility cutoff is $20,000). Because program participation is not determined by self-selection, and the two groups are very similar in their eligibility score, there is reason to believe they are also similar in motivation."

41. Roughly speaking, a quasi-experimental design is similar to an experimental design except that it lacks the most important feature—namely, random assignment. Thus, it is difficult (some would say impossible) to ensure that the treatment and control groups do not differ at the beginning of the experiment. Specific quasi-experimental designs include nonequivalent groups design and the regression-discontinuity design. For a succinct explanation, see Research Methods Knowledge Base, "Quasi-Experimental Design" (www.socialresearchmethods.net/kb/quasiexp.php).

42. There are at least 30 people, many of whom we had previously interviewed but some we had not, whom we called in order to check information, get additional sources, or confirm our interpretation of what interviewees had said during the interview. The people who gave us information that we used in the text can be found in our endnotes, usually preceded by "Personal communication with." These conversations are separate from the formal interviews that we conducted for the book, which were more standardized and used a questionnaire (see appendix B). The subjects who participated in formal interviews are listed in appendix A and are identified in the endnotes as having been interviewed. We gave the number of interviews as 133 in Ron Haskins and Greg Margolis, "Obama's Promise: Using Evidence to Fight the Nation's Social Problems," in *Using Research Evidence in Education: From the Schoolhouse Door to Capitol Hill,* edited by Kara S. Finnigan and Alan J. Daly (New York: Springer International Publishing, 2014). For this book, we reclassified one interview as "formal," bringing the total number of such interviews to 134.

43. See Patrick Biernacki and Dan Waldorf, "Snowball Sampling: Problems and Techniques of Chain Referral Sampling," *Sociological Methods Research,* vol. 10, no. 2 (November 1981), pp. 141–68; Oisín Tansey, "Process Tracing and Elite Interviewing: A Case for Non-Probability Sampling," *PS: Political Science and Politics,* vol. 40, no. 4 (October 2007), pp. 765–72.

44. Our interviews were promptly and ably transcribed by Melissa Heape of Ten Mile, Tennessee.

45. See the *Proposals to Provide Federal Funding for Early Childhood Home Visitation Programs: Hearing before the Subcommittee on Income Security and Family Support of the Committee on Ways and Means, United States House of Representatives,* 111th Cong. (2009).

46. The last step in passage of a law is the House-Senate conference, in which a compromise is struck on the House bill and the Senate bill in order to produce a single bill to be voted on by Congress before it is sent to the president for signature or veto. Before sending the enacted bill to the president, the conference committee produces an elaborate report that provides the text and summary of action on every provision in the bill that includes current law, the House provision, the Senate provision, and the conference agreement.

47. Thomas can be accessed at http://thomas.loc.gov/home/thomas.php.

48. Corporation for National and Community Service, "Social Innovation Fund: Content Requirements for Subgrantee Evaluation Plans" (Washington: February, 2012) (http://apps.legacyintl.org/wp-content/uploads/2012/04/SIF-SEP-Guidance_February-2012-Release.pdf).

49. The Trade Adjustment Assistance Community College and Career Training initiative did not require a third-party grantee-level evaluation the first year but did so in the following competitions, starting in the second year.

50. It is worth noting that even in fields in which there is a lack of good evidence about the effectiveness of intervention programs, federal agencies can still require rigorous evaluations, including RCTs, of the programs that they fund. Part of the Obama evidence-based vision is that many fields of social intervention will build up evidence about effective program over many years.

Chapter 2

1. Annette Lareau, *Unequal Childhoods: Class, Race, and Family Life*, 2nd ed. (University of California Press, 2003); Ariel Kalil, "Inequality Begins at Home: The Role of Parenting in the Diverging Destinies of Rich and Poor Children," in *Diverging Destinies: Families in an Era of Increasing Inequality*, edited by Paul R. Amato, Susan M. McHale, and Alan Booth (New York: Springer, 2014); Richard V. Reeves, Isabel Sawhill, and Kimberly Howard, "The Parenting Gap," *Democracy*, no. 30 (Fall 2013), pp. 40–50.

2. Ariel Kalil, "Inequality Begins at Home: The Role of Parenting in the Diverging Destinies of Rich and Poor Children," in *Diverging Destinies: Families in an Era of Increasing Inequality*, edited by Paul Amato and others (New York: Springer, 2014).

3. Jane Waldfogel and Elizabeth Washbrook, "Early Years Policy," *Child Development Research*, vol. 2011, Article ID 343016 (2011).

4. Betty Hart and Todd R. Risley, *Meaningful Differences in the Everyday Experience of Young American Children* (Baltimore: Paul H. Brookes, 1995).

5. Andrea J. Sedlak, Karla McPherson, and Barnali Das, *Fourth National Incidence Study of Child Abuse and Neglect (NIS-4): Supplementary Analysis of Race Difference in Child Maltreatment Rates in the NIS-4* (Washington: Westat, March 2010), p. 38.

6. Kassim Mbwana, Mary Terzian, and Kristin Moore, "What Works for Parent Involvement Programs for Children: Lessons from Experimental Evaluations of Social Interventions," *Child Trends Fact Sheet* (Washington: Child Trends, December 2009) (www.childtrends.org/wp-content/uploads/2009/12/What-Works-for-Parent-Involvement-Programs-for-Adolescents-February-2010.pdf).

7. For background on the Nurse-Family Partnership, see Nurse-Family Partnership, "About" (www.nursefamilypartnership.org/about/program-history).

8. David Olds and others, "Long-Term Effects of Nurse Home Visitation on Children's Criminal and Antisocial Behavior: 15-Year Follow-Up of a Randomized Controlled Trial," *Journal of the American Medical Association*, vol. 280, no. 14 (October 1998), pp. 1238–44; Andy Goodman, "The Story of David Olds and the Nurse Home Visiting Program" (Princeton, N.J.: Robert Wood Johnson Foundation, July 2006).

9. Personal communication from David Olds, April 22, 2014.

10. John Eckenrode and others, "Long-Term Effects of Prenatal and Infancy Nurse Home Visitation on the Life Course of Youths: 19-Year Follow-Up of a Randomized Controlled Trial," *Archives of Pediatrics and Adolescent Medicine*, vol. 164, no. 1 (January 2010), pp. 9–15.

11. For more information about the NFP model, see Nurse-Family Partnership (www.nursefamilypartnership.org/).

12. For a review of the evidence-based home visiting model programs, see Kimberly S. Howard and Jeanne Brooks-Gunn, "The Role of Home-Visiting Programs in Preventing Child Abuse and Neglect," *Future of Children*, vol. 19, no. 2 (Fall 2009), pp. 119–46.

13. Barack Obama, "Remarks to the Hampton University Annual Ministers' Conference in Hampton, Virginia," speech, June 5, 2007, available on the website of the American Presidency Project, University of California, Santa Barbara (www.presidency.ucsb.edu/ws/?pid=77002).

14. Barack Obama and Joe Biden, "Blueprint for Change: Obama and Biden's Plan for America," p. 57 (http://arsiv.setav.org/ups/dosya/28460.pdf).

15. Olds and others, "Long-Term Effects of Nurse Home Visitation." For the Denver trial, see David Olds and others, "Effects of Home Visits by Paraprofessionals and by Nurses: Age 4 Follow-Up Results of a Randomized Trial," *Pediatrics*, vol. 114, no. 6 (December 2004), pp. 1560–68; for the Memphis trial, see David Olds and others, "Effects of Nurse Home-Visiting on Maternal Life Course and Child Development: Age 6 Follow-Up Results of a Randomized Trial," *Pediatrics*, vol. 114, no. 6 (December 2004), pp. 1550–59.

16. The original legislation was S. 2412, the Education Begins at Home Act, and was introduced in May 2004. Bond later worked with Representative Danny Davis (D-Ill.) in the House on the Education Begins at Home Act. Davis introduced a version of the bill in 2007, the Education Begins at Home Act of 2008 (H.R. 2343). In the various iterations of the Education Begins at Home Act (EBAH), the funds would be allotted by formula. While Bond helped create the Parents as Teachers program in Missouri, the EBAH did not focus exclusively on Parents as Teachers (PAT). The language was geared more toward child educational development and school readiness. EBAH requires that state plans include "a description of the State's strategy to establish or expand PAT programs, or other quality programs of early childhood home visitation, to serve all eligible families in the state." We interviewed several members of the home visiting coalition and others who worked on various versions of the Bond and Davis bills, including Jane Callahan, policy director for Parents as Teachers; Sarah Walzer, CEO of the Parent-Child Home Program; Bridget Gavaghan, senior director of public policy for Prevent Child Abuse America; Tom Birch, former legislative counsel for the National Child Abuse Coalition; and MaryLee Allen, director of child welfare and mental health at the Children's Defense Fund.

17. Bond now serves on the board of directors of Parents as Teachers. His biography on the website describes how he enrolled his son in the pilot phase of PAT; see Parents as Teachers, "About" (www.parentsasteachers.org/about/leadership-directory/board).

18. See the Parents as Teachers website (www.parentsasteachers.org); see also "Parents as Teachers Welcomes Former Senator Kit Bond to Board of Directors," *St. Louis Post-Dispatch,* June 30, 2012 (http://interact.stltoday.com/pr/non-profits/PR06301104216450).

19. Mary Wagner and Serena Clayton, "The Parents as Teachers Program: Results from Two Demonstrations," *Future of Children*, vol. 9, no. 1 (Spring/Summer 1999), pp. 91–115.

20. Home Instruction for Parents of Preschool Youngsters (HIPPY) is a widely respected home visiting program with evidence of success from good evaluation research; see www.hippyusa.org/.

21. Parents as Teachers targets all families with children, beginning during pregnancy and continuing through preschool (age 3) or kindergarten. PAT features hour-long home visits and group meetings; its goals are to increase parent knowledge of early childhood development; detect developmental delays; prevent child abuse and neglect; and increase school readiness and success. The program costs, on average, $1,400–$1,500 per family annually. See Emilie Stoltzfus and Karen Lynch, "Home Visitation for Families

with Young Children" (Congressional Research Service, October 23, 2009) (www.prevent childabusesb.org/crshomevisitreportoct2009.pdf).

22. HIPPY is geared toward low-income families without much education; the program costs, on average, $1,250 per child annually. Home visitors are paraprofessionals and work to promote school readiness and early literacy through parental involvement. Children are 3 to 5 years of age. The program consists of half-hour biweekly home visits along with two-hour biweekly group meetings over a three-year period. See Stoltzfus and Lynch, "Home Visitation for Families with Young Children."

23. Healthy Families America (HFA) targets families with children ages 0 to 5 years or pregnant women who are identified as "at risk." The average cost of the program is $3,348 per family annually. It begins during pregnancy or within two weeks of birth and continues through preschool or kindergarten enrollment. Visits are weekly for the first six months and then twice a month. The program focuses on preventing child abuse and neglect, enhancing child health and development, and promoting positive parenting. See Stoltzfus and Lynch, "Home Visitation for Families with Young Children."

24. Kit Bond first introduced the Education Begins at Home Act (S. 2412) in 2004; for the text and summary of that legislation, see http://thomas.loc.gov/cgi-bin/bdquery/ D?d108:9:./temp/~bdIcPi:@@@D&summ2=m&. Danny Davis later introduced a companion bill in the House, the Education Begins at Home Act of 2008 (H.R. 2343); for the text and summary of that legislation, see https://www.govtrack.us/congress/bills/110/ hr2343.

25. Jane Callahan, interviewed by Greg Margolis, October 12, 2011.

26. See Sec. 3(a)(2) and (b)(3) of Healthy Children and Families Act of 2007, H.R. 3024, 110th Cong. (2007).

27. In accord with long-standing policy not to release materials used by OMB before policy decisions were made, OMB officials did not share the memo with us. However, Fries described the memo during our interview with her. Farrah Freis, interviewed by Greg Margolis, January 30, 2012.

28. Even natural sciences have their internal disputes about both theory and evidence. Some of these disputes can get personal and result in serious conflicts and even invective between different camps. See Thomas S. Kuhn, *The Structure of Scientific Revolutions* (University of Chicago Press, 1970).

29. Barack Obama, "A New Era of Responsibility: Renewing America's Promise" (Office of Management and Budget, February 26, 2009).

30. Ibid., p. 23.

31. Discretionary funding refers to money that is appropriated by Congress annually. Mandatory funding is money automatically appropriated every year as part of authorizing legislation. Mandatory funding is usually authorized for a specific number of years, often five years. After those five years, funding must be reauthorized or the spending authority lapses. Entitlement funding is a type of mandatory funding in which individuals, states, or other entities are provided with a specific benefit, often cash. The earned income tax credit, Supplemental Nutrition Assistance Program, Medicaid, Social Security, and Medicare are entitlements to individuals or families; housing and child care are discretionary appropriations and do not convey an entitlement to individuals.

32. Tamar Bauer, interviewed by Greg Margolis, September 23, 2011, and October 21, 2011.

33. Tom Birch, interviewed by Greg Margolis, April 6, 2010.

34. On January 24, two days before the January 26 meeting, Baron sent Gordon and others an e-mail containing a short paper exploring ideas for implementing the Social Innovation Fund (see chapter 5). One of the ideas was to create different levels of funding for programs supported by different levels of evidence. The Baron memo may be obtained by writing to Jon Baron at the Coalition for Evidence-Based Policy in Washington, DC.

35. Tom Birch interview.

36. Kathy Stack, interviewed by Ron Haskins and Greg Margolis, August 2, 2011.

37. Personal communication from Deborah Daro, senior fellow at Chapin Hall, University of Chicago, February 6, 2014.

38. The William T. Grant Foundation provided most of the funding for this study of the Obama evidence-based initiatives.

39. Robert Granger, "The Big Why: A Learning Agenda for the Scale-Up Movement," *Pathways Magazine* (Winter 2011), pp. 28–32. Bob Granger is a former president of the Grant Foundation.

40. Martha Coven, interviewed by Ron Haskins and Greg Margolis, September 15, 2011.

41. Tamar Bauer interview.

42. Tom Birch interview.

43. Barack Obama, "Analytical Perspectives: Budget of the U.S. Government, Fiscal Year 2010" (Office of Management and Budget, May 11, 2009) (www.gpo.gov/fdsys/pkg/BUDGET-2010-PER/pdf/BUDGET-2010-PER.pdf).

44. Ibid., p. 92.

45. Ibid.

46. Reserve funds are not binding; they simply indicate the intent of a committee to take a legislative action at some point in the future. They are more or less a way to open discussion on a topic that is related to future legislation. See Bill Heniff Jr. and Justin Murray, "Congressional Budget Resolutions: Historical Information" (Congressional Budget Office, March 13, 2012) (www.fas.org/sgp/crs/misc/RL30297.pdf).

47. Taken from e-mailed comments on this volume by Robert Gordon, received on April 17, 2014.

48. "Deficit-Neutral Reserve Fund for Home Visiting," Sec. 311, in House Committee on the Budget, *Concurrent Resolution*, H. CON. RES. 85 (March 27, 2009) (www.gpo.gov/fdsys/pkg/BILLS-111hconres85rh/pdf/BILLS-111hconres85rh.pdf).

49. Ibid.

50. "Deficit-Neutral Reserve Fund for Home Visitation Programs," Sec. 227, in *Concurrent Resolution*, S. CON. RES. 13 (April 2, 2009) (www.gpo.gov/fdsys/pkg/BILLS-111sconres13es/pdf/BILLS-111sconres13es.pdf).

51. "Deficit-Neutral Reserve Fund for Home Visiting," Sec. 331, in *Concurrent Resolution*, S. CON. RES. 13. (April 29, 2009) (www.gpo.gov/fdsys/pkg/BILLS-111sconres13enr/pdf/BILLS-111sconres13enr.pdf).

52. Obama, "Analytical Perspectives," p. 92.

53. See "Bill Summary and Status, 111th Congress (2009–2010), H.R. 2667, All Congressional Actions" (http://thomas.loc.gov/cgi-bin/bdquery/z?d111:HR02667:@@@X).

54. Nick Gwyn, interviewed by Ron Haskins and Greg Margolis, August 23, 2011.

55. Sec. 2 of the Early Support for Families Act, H.R. 2667, 111th Cong. (2009).

56. Ibid. From section 440 of H.S. 2667: "Priority funding for programs with strongest evidence—(A) In general—The expenditures, described in paragraph (1), of a State for a fiscal year that are attributable to the cost of programs that do not adhere to a model of home visitation with the strongest evidence of effectiveness shall not be considered eligible expenditures for the fiscal year to the extent that the total of the expenditures exceeds the applicable percentage for the fiscal year of the allotment of the State under subsection (c) for the fiscal year."

57. *Hearing on Proposals to Provide Federal Funding for Early Childhood Home Visitation Programs*, Hearing before the Subcommittee on Income Security and Family Support of the Committee on Ways and Means, U.S. House of Representatives, 111 Cong., 1st sess., June 9, 2009 (www.gpo.gov/fdsys/pkg/CHRG-111hhrg52502/html/CHRG-111hhrg52502.htm).

58. Andy Schneider, interviewed by Ron Haskins and Greg Margolis, April 4, 2012.

59. Karen Howard, one of NFP's lobbyists, was a former staffer for Senator Ken Salazar (D-Colo.) and continued to work closely with staffers in the House and Senate as the DeGette-Salazar legislation was being written.

60. The Energy and Commerce Committee's provision on home visiting amended Title XIX of the Social Security Act (the title that contains the Medicaid program). This title is generally under the jurisdiction of the Energy and Commerce Committee in the House. By contrast, the House Ways and Means home visiting provision amended Title IV of the Social Security Act, which was generally under the jurisdiction of the Ways and Means Committee.

61. Our interviews showed that many Senate offices weighed in as the bill was being written. Usually the offices weighed in through staff-to-staff contacts between the Senate offices and the Finance Committee staffers who were drafting the bill. The offices involved included, among others, those of Patty Murray (D-Wash.), Ted Kennedy (D-Mass.), Tom Harkin (D-Iowa), Kit Bond (R-Mo.), Chris Dodd (D-Conn.), Orrin Hatch (R-Utah), Robert Menendez (D-N.J.), and Robert Casey (D-Penn.). Chairman Baucus was making a deliberate attempt to consult widely to gather support for his bill.

62. Much of this section is based on our interviews with Diedra Henry-Spires, interviewed by Ron Haskins and Greg Margolis, October 4, 2011, and Becky Shipp, interviewed by Ron Haskins and Greg Margolis, August 30, 2011. Henry-Spires was the Democratic staffer responsible for drafting Chairman Baucus's home visiting legislation; Shipp was the senior Republican staffer participating in the drafting.

63. In the House, Minority Leader John Boehner did take notice of the home visiting provision, arguing sarcastically during the House floor debate on the ACA that the government was now "going to put $750 million into a program to help legislate how parents should parent." A transcript of Boehner's comments can be found at the website of Project Vote Smart (http://votesmart.org/public-statement/469094/

affordable-health-care-for-america-act); a video recording can be found on YouTube at the 14-minute mark of www.youtube.com/watch?v=9FGuYpMI6iI . Further indicating the scorn some conservatives had for home visiting programs, the conservative actor Chuck Norris wrote an op-ed on the Townhall website claiming that the home visiting initiative, which was eventually passed as part of the Patient Protection and Affordable Care Act ("Obamacare") was one of the "dirty secrets" of the Obamacare legislation. Norris claimed that the home visiting provision was "buried deep within" the legislative text and that it allowed the government to "come into homes and usurp parental rights over child care and development." Norris did not mention that the Ways and Means Committee had held a public hearing on the home visiting provision. See Chuck Norris, "Dirty Secret No. 1 in Obamacare," *Townhall*, August 11, 2009 (http://townhall.com/columnists/chucknorris/2009/08/11/dirty_secret_no_1_in_obamacare). According to Julie Jolly, a former Bond staffer, the senator, who supported the home visiting provision in the ACA without supporting the ACA itself, worked behind the scenes to ensure that conservative opposition to the provision did not gain too much momentum. Julie Jolly, interviewed by Greg Margolis, September 21, 2011.

64. Sheryl Gay Stolberg and Robert Pear, "Obama Signs Health Care Overhaul Bill, with a Flourish," *New York Times*, March 23, 2010 (www.nytimes.com/2010/03/24/health/policy/24health.html).

65. See Sec. 2951 of Subtitle L of the Patient Protection and Affordable Care Act (www.gpo.gov/fdsys/pkg/BILLS-111hr3590enr/pdf/BILLS-111hr3590enr.pdf).

66. See Title V Section 511(d)(3)(A)(iii) of the Social Security Act, as amended by the Patient Protection and Affordable Care Act, Pub. L No. 111-148, 124 Stat. 119 (2010).

67. This section is based largely on Sarah Avellar and Diane Paulsell, "Lessons Learned from the Home Visiting Evidence of Effectiveness Review" (Princeton, N.J.: Mathematica, January 31, 2011), and on our interviews with several people who participated in the systematic evidence review, especially Lauren Supplee, the project officer from HHS for the Mathematica portion of the evidence review, interviewed by Greg Margolis, October 17, 2011.

68. Judy Gueron and Howard Rolston, *Fighting for Reliable Evidence* (New York: Russell Sage Foundation, 2013).

69. Diane Paulsell and others, "Home Visiting Evidence of Effectiveness Review: Executive Summary" (Office of Planning Research and Evaluation, Administration for Children and Families, U.S. Department of Health and Human Services, November 2010) (http://homvee.acf.hhs.gov/HomVEE_Executive_Summary.pdf).

70. A quasi-experimental study was defined by the review team as "a study design in which sample members (children, parents, or families) are selected for the program and comparison conditions in a nonrandom way," including matched comparison group designs, single case designs, and regression discontinuity designs. See Paulsell and others, "Home Visiting Evidence of Effectiveness Review," p. 4.

71. The model programs included Early Head Start—Home Visiting, Family Check-Up, Healthy Families America, Healthy Start—Home Visiting, Healthy Steps, Home Instruction for Parents of Preschool Youngsters, Nurse-Family Partnership, Parent-Child

Home Program, Parents as Teachers, Resource Mothers Program, and SafeCare. To be responsive to the needs of the states, the first funding announcement gave states the opportunity to request that a specific model program that had not yet been selected by HHS as evidence based be included in the review.

72. See Department of Education, "What Works Clearinghouse: Procedures and Standards Handbook, Version 2.0" (December 2008) (http://ies.ed.gov/ncee/wwc/pdf/reference_resources/wwc_procedures_v2_standards_handbook.pdf).

73. See Home Visiting Evidence of Effectiveness, "Oklahoma's Community-Based Family Resource and Support (CBFRS) Program: In Brief," updated October 2012 (http://homvee.acf.hhs.gov/document.aspx?sid=50&rid=1&mid=1).

74. See the HHS website for the information on implementation of the designated home visiting model programs (http://homvee.acf.hhs.gov/implementations.aspx).

75. The legislation specifies that no more than 25 percent of the funds awarded may be spent on programs that are "promising" rather than evidence based.

76. For information on the state home visiting programs at the outset of the Obama home visiting initiative (2009–10), see Pew Charitable Trusts, "States and the New Federal Home Visiting Initiative: An Assessment from the Starting Line" (www.pewstates.org/research/reports/states-and-the-new-federal-home-visiting-initiative-85899377168?p=2).

77. Prevent Child Abuse North Dakota received a grant to implement home visiting in the state after the legislature declined to participate in the program. Personal communication with Arvy Smith, deputy state health officer in the North Dakota Department of Health, January 16, 2014. Subsequently, nonprofit organizations in both Florida and Wyoming received grants.

78. Personal communication with Arvy Smith.

79. See Sec. 511(g) of Title V of the Social Security Act as amended by the Patient Protection and Affordable Care Act, Pub. L. No. 111-148, 124 Stat. 119 (2010) (www.gpo.gov/fdsys/pkg/PLAW-111publ148/pdf/PLAW-111publ148.pdf).

80. See Sec. 511(d)(1)(A) of Title V of the Social Security Act as amended by the Patient Protection and Affordable Care Act, Pub. L. No. 111-148, 124 Stat. 119 (2010).

81. Charles Michalopoulos and others, "Revised Design for the Mother and Infant Home Visiting Program Evaluation" (Washington and New York: Office of Planning, Research, and Evaluation and MDRC, April 2013) (www.acf.hhs.gov/sites/default/files/opre/mihope_full_report_april_17_3.pdf).

82. As an example, Baron's testimony notes that HHS identified the Parents as Teachers home visiting model as evidence based because on a total of 208 outcome measures across four randomized evaluations of the programs, five statistically significant positive effects and six statistically significant adverse effects were found. But given the large number of tests, eleven statistically significant effects (out of 208 tests) could be expected on the basis of chance alone. Thus, a reasonable interpretation of these findings, according to Baron, was that the program produced no important effects.

83. Home visiting differs from several of the other Obama evidence-based initiatives because home visiting is a mode of service delivery and not a goal or outcome measure like teen pregnancy reduction, work force participation, and educational improvement.

Chapter 3

1. Katy Suellentrop, "What Works 2011–2012: Curriculum-Based Programs that Help Prevent Teen Pregnancy" (Washington: National Campaign to Prevent Teen and Unplanned Pregnancy, 2011); Douglas Kirby, "Emerging Answers 2007: Research Findings on Programs to Reduce Teen Pregnancy and Sexually Transmitted Diseases" (Washington: National Campaign to Prevent Teen and Unplanned Pregnancy, November 2007) (http://files.eric.ed.gov/fulltext/ED456171.pdf); Mathematica Policy Research and Child Trends, "Identifying Programs That Impact Teen Pregnancy, Sexually Transmitted Infections, and Associated Sexual Risk Behaviors, Review Protocol: Version 1.0" (Princeton, N.J.: Mathematica, 2010) (www.hhs.gov/ash/oah/oah-initiatives/tpp/eb-programs-review.pdf).

2. John S. Santelli and others, "Explaining Recent Declines in Adolescent Pregnancy in the United States: The Contribution of Abstinence and Improved Contraceptive Use," *American Journal of Public Health,* vol. 97, no. 1 (2007), pp. 150–56.

3. Joyce A. Martin and others, "Births: Final Data for 2012," *National Vital Statistics Reports,* vol. 62, no. 9 (December 2013).

4. Brady E. Hamilton and Stephanie J. Ventura, "Birth Rates for U.S. Teenagers Reach Historic Lows for All Age and Ethnic Groups," *NCHS Data Brief* 89 (April 2012), p. 3.

5. Ibid.

6. World Bank, "Adolescent Fertility Rate (Births per 1,000 Women ages 15–19)" (http://data.worldbank.org/indicator/SP.ADO.TFRT).

7. National Campaign to Prevent Teen and Unplanned Pregnancy, "Counting It Up: The Public Costs of Teen Childbearing: Key Data" (Washington: December 2013) (http://thenationalcampaign.org/resource/counting-it-key-data-2013).

8. Section 510 of Title V of the Social Security Act, as amended by Title IX, Section 912 of the Personal Responsibility and Work Opportunity Act of 1996, P. L. 104-193, 110 Stat. 2105 (1996).

9. Carmen Solomon-Fears, "Teenage Pregnancy Prevention: Statistics and Programs" (Congressional Research Service, June 19, 2013), p. 10.

10. In 1995, at the time of the welfare reform debate, 66 percent of high school seniors had had sex; in 2011, 63 percent had had sex. See "Youth Risk Behavior Surveillance System (YRBSS)," 1991–2011 surveys (www.cdc.gov/healthyyouth/yrbs/index.htm).

11. National Campaign to Prevent Teen and Unplanned Pregnancy, "Briefly . . . Some Thoughts on Abstinence" (Washington: January 2009) (http://thenationalcampaign.org/resource/briefly-some-thoughts-abstinence).

12. National Campaign to Prevent Teen and Unplanned Pregnancy, "With One Voice 2012: America's Adults and Teens Sound Off about Teen Pregnancy" (Washington: August 2012) (http://thenationalcampaign.org/sites/default/files/resource-primary-download/wov_2012.pdf).

13. Potential federal funding sources for family planning include Teen Pregnancy Prevention, the Centers for Disease Control and Prevention, Personal Responsibility Education Program, Medicaid, Title X of the Public Health Service Act, State Abstinence

Education Grants, the Pregnancy Assistance Fund, and federal block grant programs such as the Social Services Block Grant, the Maternal and Child Health Block Grant, and Temporary Assistance to Needy Families.

14. The program was also known as Special Projects of Regional and National Significance–Community-Based Abstinence Education (SPRANS-CBAE).

15. After Democrats won the presidency in 2008, to go along with their existing control of both the House and the Senate, they ended the Community-Based Abstinence Education program; for estimates of spending on abstinence-only programs, see Solomon-Fears, "Teenage Pregnancy Prevention."

16. Associated Press, "States Refusing Grants for Abstinence Education," June 24, 2008 (www.nbcnews.com/id/25354119/ns/health-childrens_health/t/states-refusing-grants-abstinence-education/#.U16yAj8odnU); see also P. J. Huffstutter, "Abstaining from Federal Sex-Ed Funds," *Los Angeles Times*, April 8, 2007 (http://articles.latimes.com/2007/apr/08/nation/na-abstinence8).

17. See Balanced Budget Act of 1997, P.L. 105-33, 111 Stat. 251 (1997), which added technical corrections to the 1996 Welfare Reform law and funded the abstinence education evaluation.

18. Personal communication from Matthew Stagner, Mathematica Policy Research, July 7, 2014; in 2007 Stagner was the director of the Division of Child and Youth Policy at HHS and in charge of the abstinence-only evaluation.

19. Elaine Bennett had developed a highly regarded abstinence-only program called "Best Friends." HHS did its best to get Bennett to allow a program following her model to participate in the evaluation, but Bennett refused. The programs that participated were "My Choice, My Future" in Powhatan, Virginia; "ReCapturing the Vision" in Miami; "Families United to Prevent Teen Pregnancy" in Milwaukee; and "Teens in Control" in Clarksdale, Mississippi. After visiting 28 program sites, HHS selected eleven programs for further study and four of those for random assignment evaluation. For details of sample selection, see Christopher Trenholm and others, "Impacts of the Four Title V, Section 510 Abstinence Education Programs: Final Report" (Princeton, N.J.: Mathematica, April 2007), pp. 7–10.

20. U.S. House of Representatives, Committee on Government Reform, Minority Staff Special Investigations Division, "The Content of Federally Funded Abstinence-Only Education Programs" (Washington: December 2004) (www.apha.org/apha/PDFs/HIV/The_Waxman_Report.pdf).

21. U.S. House of Representatives, Committee on Energy and Commerce, "A Better Approach to Teenage Pregnancy Prevention: Sexual Risk Avoidance" (July 2012) (http://energycommerce.house.gov/sites/republicans.energycommerce.house.gov/files/analysis/20120706riskavoidance.pdf).

22. Ibid., p.1.

23. Ibid.

24. The Office of Adolescent Health eventually developed a list of 28 (and later 31) programs that are supported by rigorous evidence indicating that they reduce teen sexual activity, STIs, or teen pregnancy. Several of the programs on this list are comprehensive in the sense that they emphasize both abstinence and birth control; examples are Becoming a Responsible Teen (BART) and Teen Health Project. For the current list

of 31 effective teen pregnancy prevention programs, see the Office of Adolescent Health (www.hhs.gov/ash/oah/oah-initiatives/teen_pregnancy/db/programs.html).

25. National Campaign to Prevent Teen and Unplanned Pregnancy, "Briefly . . . A Summary of Effective Interventions" (Washington: December 2011) (http://thenational campaign.org/resource/briefly-summary-effective-interventions); Kirby, "Emerging Answers 2007."

26. These include HR 4737, S1443, and S657, all in 2002.

27. For information on the Heritage Keepers evidence-based program, see Heritage Community Services, "Proven Effective and Evidence-Based" (www.heritageservices. org/research/); for the quasi-experimental study judged to be rigorous by HHS standards, see Stan E. Weed and others, "Testing a Predictive Model of Youth Sexual Intercourse Initiation," unpublished paper, Brigham Young University, 2011.

28. Larry Rohter, "Ad on Sex Education Distorts Obama Policy," *New York Times,* September 10, 2008 (www.nytimes.com/2008/09/11/us/politics/11checkpoint.html).

29. Dan Gilgoff, "Obama Seeks Common Ground on Abortion," *U.S. News and World Report,* June 16, 2009 (www.usnews.com/news/religion/articles/2009/06/16/obama-seeks-common-ground-on-abortion); John Gehring, "What Ever Happened to the Common Ground on Abortion Reduction?" *Religion and Politics,* April 16, 2013 (http://religionandpolitics.org/print/?pid=5270).

30. President's statement, "President-Elect Obama Commemorates 20th Annual World AIDS Day" (http://change.gov/newsroom/entry/president_elect_obama_commemorates_20th_annual_world_aids_day/).

31. James Wagoner, interviewed by Ron Haskins and Greg Margolis, March 28, 2012.

32. Barack Obama, "A New Era of Responsibility: Renewing America's Promise" (Office of Management and Budget, February 26, 2009), p. 70.

33. Kirby, "Emerging Answers."

34. The president's nominee for Secretary of Health and Human Services, Kathleen Sebelius, was not sworn in until April 28, 2009.

35. Barack Obama, "Analytical Perspectives: Budget of the U.S. Government, Fiscal Year 2010" (Office of Management and Budget, May 11, 2009), p. 92 (www.gpo.gov/fdsys/pkg/BUDGET-2010-PER/pdf/BUDGET-2010-PER.pdf).

36. Department of Health and Human Services, Administration for Children and Families, "Justification of Estimates for Appropriations Committees" (May 7, 2009), p. 94 (http://wayback.archive-it.org/3920/20131028125635/http://archive.acf.hhs.gov/programs/olab/budget/2010/cj2010.html).

37. Trenholm and others, "Impacts of the Four Title V, Section 510 Abstinence Education Programs: Final Report."

38. Sharon Jayson, "Obama Budget Cuts Funds for Abstinence-Only Sex Education," *USA Today,* May 11, 2009 (http://usatoday30.usatoday.com/news/health/2009-05-11-abstinence-only_N.htm?csp=34).

39. From notes taken at the meeting by Andrea Kane of the National Campaign to Prevent Teen and Unplanned Pregnancy.

40. See Kirby, "Emerging Answers 2007"; Trenholm, "Impacts of the Four Title V, Section 510 Abstinence Education Programs: Final Report."

41. Robert Rector, "The Effectiveness of Abstinence Education Programs in Reducing Sexual Activity among Youth" (Washington: Heritage Foundation, April 8, 2002) (www. heritage.org/research/reports/2002/04/the-effectiveness-of-abstinence-education-programs). Of the programs described in this report, only the evaluation of Project Taking Charge uses random assignment. In 2010, Rector and Christine C. Kim published an update on effective abstinence programs that cites three random assignment studies showing positive results for abstinence programs: Christine C. Kim and Robert Rector, "Evidence on the Effectiveness of Abstinence Education: An Update" (Washington: Heritage Foundation, February 19, 2010) (www.heritage.org/research/reports/2010/02/evidence-on-the-effectiveness-of-abstinence-education-an-update). In one of the studies cited by Kim and Rector, John B. Jemmott III and his colleagues published what most scholars regard as the first random assignment study to show that abstinence-only programs can have an impact on teen sexual behavior—in this case, on the likelihood of ever having sexual intercourse up to 24 months after the end of the intervention; see John B. Jemmott III, Loretta S. Jemmott, and Geoffrey T. Fong, "Efficacy of a Theory-Based Abstinence-Only Intervention over 24 Months," *Archives of Pediatric and Adolescent Medicine,* vol. 164, no. 2 (2010), pp. 152–59.

42. U.S. House of Representatives, Committee on Government Reform, Minority Staff Special Investigations Division, "The Content of Federally Funded Abstinence-Only Education Programs," p. 2.

43. Preventing Unintended Pregnancies, Reducing the Need for Abortion, and Supporting Parents Act, H.R. 3312, 111th Cong. (2009) (http://thomas.loc.gov/cgi-bin/bdquery/z?d111:HR03312:@@@D&summ2=m&).

44. Responsible Education about Life, H.R. 1551, 111th Cong. (2009) (www.gpo.gov/fdsys/pkg/BILLS-111hr1551ih/pdf/BILLS-111hr1551ih.pdf).

45. Sec. 2526, Healthy Teen Initiative to Prevent Teen Pregnancy of the Affordable Health Care for America Act, H.R. 3962, 111th Cong. (2009) (www.gpo.gov/fdsys/pkg/BILLS-111hr3962ih/pdf/BILLS-111hr3962ih.pdf).

46. As we pointed out in chapter 2 on the home visiting initiative, the president always puts new proposals in his annual budget, as President Obama did in the case of teen pregnancy. However, Congress writes the text of the law, often after hearings and a lot of negotiation and amendments. In this case, the House and Senate were controlled by Democrats so they were happy to work with their new president and write a proposal to his liking.

47. Andrea Kane, interviewed by Ron Haskins and Greg Margolis, October 11, 2011.

48. Departments of Labor, Health and Human Services, and Education, and Related Agencies Appropriations Act, H.R. 3293, 111th Cong. (2009) (www.gpo.gov/fdsys/pkg/BILLS-111hr3293rh/pdf/BILLS-111hr3293rh.pdf).

49. For a video of Aderholt and Wamp defending their amendment, see www.youtube.com/watch?v=uyHbwIciyys.

50. H.R. 3293, the Labor-HHS-Education Departments appropriations bill, was later rolled into another bill (H.R. 3288) that passed the House in its final form on December 10 and the Senate on December 13. The bill, including the appropriation for the teen pregnancy program, became law on December 16.

51. The Personal Responsibility Education Program is a formula and competitive grant program funded with mandatory money from the Affordable Care Act. The money is to be used for states to operate comprehensive approaches to teen pregnancy prevention that include both instruction in abstinence and contraception to prevent pregnancy and STIs. The program also includes instruction on "adulthood preparation" by teaching about healthy relationships, adolescent development, financial literacy, parent-child communication, education and career success, and healthy life skills. States must certify that PREP funds are spent on programs that address both abstinence and contraception and that incorporate at least three of the adult preparation topics. The law also requires states to replicate evidence-based programs or at least incorporate elements of programs that are evidence based. For a more thorough explanation, see Solomon-Fears, "Teenage Pregnancy Prevention," pp. 13–14.

52. For details of how the evidence review was conducted, see Mathematica and Child Trends, "Identifying Programs That Impact Teen Pregnancy, Sexually Transmitted Infections, and Associated Sexual Risk Behaviors, Review Protocol."

53. Officials at HHS assumed that once the new teen pregnancy prevention programs were enacted by Congress, the existing abstinence-only education staff at HHS would switch over and become teen pregnancy prevention staff. Stan Koutstaal, who headed the Family Youth Services Bureau, pointed out that HHS might soon be responsible for this new program and would need a list of all the evidence-based programs that had been checked for quality. This information is based on our interview with Seth Chamberlain, interviewed by Ron Haskins and Greg Margolis, November 1, 2011.

54. Mathematica was already on a contract with HHS on a different pregnancy prevention program called Prevention Approaches, funded by the Public Health Services Act. When officials at HHS saw that the teen pregnancy prevention legislation would likely call for identifying successful, evidence-based teen pregnancy prevention programs, they were able to extend the existing contract to cover the systematic review. A detailed explanation of the evidence review can be found in Mathematica and Child Trends, "Identifying Programs That Impact Teen Pregnancy, Sexually Transmitted Infections, and Associated Sexual Risk Behaviors, Review Protocol."

55. Chris Trenholm, interviewed by Greg Margolis, March 12, 2012.

56. National Abstinence Education Association, "Abstinence Works 2013: Sexual Risk Avoidance (SRA) Abstinence Education Programs Demonstrating Improved Teen Outcomes" (Washington: July 2013) (http://www.thenaea.org/docs/Abstinence-Works.pdf).

57. Chris Trenholm interview.

58. Ibid.

59. A quasi-experimental design is one in which the experimental and comparison groups are formed by some method other than random assignment. Program effects can be assessed with some confidence to the extent that the experimental and control groups can be matched on characteristics or their characteristics can be statistically adjusted to resemble each other. However, it is generally agreed that a quasi-experimental design results in less confidence in program impacts than random assignment designs. See Peter H. Rossi, Mark W. Lipsey, and Howard E. Freeman, *Evaluation: A Systematic Approach,* 7th ed. (Thousand Oaks, Calif.: Sage, 2004), pp. 274–97.

60. Mathematica Policy Research and Child Trends, "Identifying Programs That Impact Teen Pregnancy, Sexually Transmitted Infections, and Associated Sexual Risk Behaviors, Review Protocol."

61. Susan Philliber and others, "Preventing Pregnancy and Improving Health Care Access among Teenagers: An Evaluation of the Children's Aid Society-Carrera Program," *Perspectives on Sexual and Reproductive Health,* vol. 34, no. 5 (2002), pp. 244–51.

62. See Office of Adolescent Health, "Evidence-Based Programs" (www.hhs.gov/ash/oah/oah-initiatives/teen_pregnancy/db/programs.html).

63. For a list of the programs, including three added in the subsequent reviews, see TPP Resource Center, "Evidence-Based Programs (31 Programs)" (www.hhs.gov/ash/oah/oah-initiatives/teen_pregnancy/db/programs.html).

64. Office of Adolescent Health, "Teenage Pregnancy Prevention: Replication of Evidence-Based Programs: Funding Opportunity Announcement and Application Instructions" (Department of Health and Human Services, April 1, 2010) (www.hhs.gov/ash/oah/grants/assets/funding_announcement_04012010.pdf).

65. Ibid.

66. More information on LGC is available at http://lcginc.com/.

67. Office of Adolescent Health, "Teen Pregnancy Prevention Replication of Evidence-Based Program Models" (www.hhs.gov/ash/oah/oah-initiatives/tpp/grantees/). See the National Campaign to Prevent Teen and Unplanned Pregnancy, press release, "New Federal Investment in Preventing Teen Pregnancy Applauded," *PRNewswire,* September 30, 2010 (www.prnewswire.com/news-releases/new-federal-investment-in-preventing-teen-pregnancy-applauded-104099773.html).

68. PREP, as enacted by the Affordable Care Act (ACA) is mostly formula funds. However, much as with the home visiting initiative, if a state chooses not to apply for PREP formula funds, HHS will hold a competition among nonprofits in that state for those funds. There is a separate program, specified in the ACA section on PREP, called "Innovative Strategies," or PREIS (Personal Responsibility Education Innovative Strategies) that provides $10 million in competitive grants to target at-risk populations. HHS combined the FOA for the PREIS $10 million pot and the tier 2 pot of funding. For a brief summary of all the various funding streams, see the National Campaign to Prevent Teen and Unplanned Pregnancy, "Federal Funding Streams for Teen Pregnancy Prevention."

69. For a complete list of the funded TPP projects, see the Teen Pregnancy Prevention website (www.hhs.gov/ash/oah/oah-initiatives/tpp). For an overview of the community-based programs, see Office of Adolescent Health, "TPP Communitywide Initiative" (www.hhs.gov/ash/oah/oah-initiatives/teen_pregnancy/about/communitywide.html).

70. Information in this section is based on descriptions on the Office of Adolescent Health's website of evaluation of teen pregnancy prevention programs (www.hhs.gov/ash/oah/oah-initiatives/for-grantees/evaluation/) and on two e-mails from Seth Chamberlain of HHS received on July 16, 2014, and July 18, 2014.

71. But after Republicans won back the House in the elections of 2010, they eventually funded a new abstinence-only education program as part of the appropriations process; see Administration for Children and Families, "Competitive Abstinence Education

Grant Program" (www.acf.hhs.gov/grants/open/foa/view/HHS-2012-ACF-ACYF-AR-0553), and Solomon-Fears, "Teenage Pregnancy Prevention."

72. For more information, see the National Campaign to Prevent Teen and Unplanned Pregnancy, "U.S. House of Representatives Proposes Cuts to Teen Pregnancy Prevention Programs: A Statement from the National Campaign to Prevent Teen and Unplanned Pregnancy" (Washington: February 2011) (https://thenationalcampaign.org/press-release/us-house-representatives-proposes-cuts-teen-pregnancy-prevention-programs#). The program was eventually included in the Senate's continuing resolution and then agreed to in the House and passed into law.

73. Rector, "The Effectiveness of Abstinence Education Programs in Reducing Sexual Activity among Youth"; Weed and others, "Testing a Predictive Model of Youth Sexual Intercourse Initiation."

74. Our count is based on the outcome information given in the summaries of each of the 31 evidence-based programs on the Office of Adolescent Health's website (www.hhs.gov/ash/oah/oah-initiatives/teen_pregnancy/db/programs.html).

75. The i3 and Teen Pregnancy Prevention initiatives differ in an interesting way. In the case of the i3 field (roughly speaking, education agencies), there were many programs but few of them had been shown by rigorous evaluations to be effective; in the case of teen pregnancy, there were many programs and evaluations but few studies had shown impacts on what are arguably the two most important outcome measures, teen pregnancy and frequency of STIs.

76. Personal communication from Seth Chamberlain, HHS, April 30, 2014. For more information on ongoing evaluations related to teen pregnancy prevention, see the Teen Pregnancy Prevention website at (www.hhs.gov/ash/oah/oah-initiatives/tpp).

Chapter 4

1. For a detailed version of how a faction within the Democratic Party focused on improving American education, in part by overcoming union opposition to teacher evaluation based on improved student performance, see Steven Brill, *Class Warfare: Inside the Fight to Fix America's Schools* (New York: Simon and Schuster, 2011).

2. See Innovation Districts for School Improvement Act, S. 2441, 109th Cong. (2006) (https://www.govtrack.us/congress/bills/109/s2441).

3. Quoted in Gerald Seib, "In Crisis, Opportunity for Barack Obama," *Wall Street Journal*, November 21, 2008 (http://online.wsj.com/article/SB122721278056345271.html).

4. The context of the Emanuel comment, which was made at a conference of corporate chief executives sponsored by the *Wall Street Journal* shortly after Obama had been elected, shows that he was referring to items that might have been on the Republican agenda as well. But that was not the way that Republicans saw the ARRA; many Republicans called it a Christmas tree for the Democratic agenda. See the Factcheck.org blog, *The Wire*, "Bum Rap for Rahm," January 13, 2011 (www.factcheck.org/2011/01/bum-rap-for-rahm/).

5. Much of this section is based on Jon Schnur, interviewed by Ron Haskins and Greg Margolis, May 8, 2012.

6. Innovation Districts for School Improvement Act.

7. See section 1117 of Miller-McKeon Discussion Draft, Title I: Amendments to Title 1, 110th Cong. (2007); *Reauthorization of the Elementary and Secondary Education Act of 1965: Hearing before the Committee on Education and Labor,* U.S. House of Representatives, 110th Cong. (2007).

8. Brill, *Class Warfare,* p. 5.

9. Race to the Top was the centerpiece of the Obama education agenda. Enacted as part of the ARRA, it made $4.35 billion available to states on a competitive basis to reform their education systems. State applications were scored on the basis of several factors related to quality of teachers and principals, state progress in closing achievement gaps, standards and assessments, progress in turning around the most poorly performing schools, the state data system to support instruction, and other factors. Some of the more controversial features of the legislation were awarding points to states if they adopted policies such as merit pay for teachers; allowing an unlimited number of charter schools, making it easy for students in failing schools to switch to charter schools; and adopting the Common Core curriculum. These policies were and are opposed by various organized groups such as teacher unions, civil rights organizations, and organizations of educators. Some states had to change their laws to comply with the federal incentives. Forty states and the District of Columbia applied for funding in three rounds of funding. In the first three rounds, two, nine (plus D.C.), and seven states respectively were awarded funds; see Brill, *Class Warfare;* Michele McNeil, "Bill Comes Due on Race to Top's Varied Goals," *Education Week,* September 28, 2011 (www.edweek.org/ew/articles/2011/09/28/06rttt_ep.h31.html).

10. American Recovery and Reinvestment Act of 2009, P.L. 111-5, 123 Stat. 115 (2009).

11. Information came from, among others, Alice Johnson Cain, then the senior education policy adviser on the House Committee on Education and Labor, interviewed by Greg Margolis, December 11, 2012.

12. Obey later told the media that he wanted to switch funds out of RTT and i3 into the part of the stimulus bill that provided cash to school systems around the country so they would not need to lay off teachers. However, after discussions with Miller and Emanuel, he agreed to leave both RTT and i3 as they were. Nick Anderson, "Lawmaker Wants to Shift Some 'Race to the Top' Funds to Prevent Teacher Layoffs," *Washington Post,* June 30, 2010 (www.washingtonpost.com/wp-dyn/content/article/2010/06/30/AR2010063002732.html).

13. Section 14007 of American Recovery and Reinvestment Act of 2009, P.L. 111-5, 123 Stat. 115 (2009).

14. Jim Shelton, interviewed by Ron Haskins and Greg Margolis, April 19, 2012.

15. Under the rules of the House of Representatives, the majority party gets to appoint a majority of the members of the Rules Committee. That allows the majority to decide which amendments requested by members of the minority party will be debated and voted on during floor debate on the underlying bill. The majority can kill amendments that they don't like by simply refusing to allow them to come to the floor. In the case of the ARRA, the Democrat-controlled Rules Committee allowed 11 amendments to be debated on the floor, but none of them proposed major changes in the

bill. See Christopher M. Davis, "The Amending Process in the House of Representatives" (Congressional Research Service, November 2012) (www.senate.gov/CRSReports/crs-publish.cfm?pid=%26*2%3C4R\%3F%3E%0A). See also K. J. Hertz, "Consideration of the American Recovery and Reinvestment Act of 2009: How This Landmark Bill Made Its Way through a Divided Congress," *New Voices in Public Policy,* vol. 4, no. 1 (Fall 2009) (http://digilib.gmu.edu/dspace/bitstream/1920/6533/1/101-536-1-PB.pdf).

16. See, for example, Department of Education, "Investing in Innovation Fund (i3): Overview of the i3 Review Process" (Department of Education, July 26, 2010) (www2.ed.gov/programs/innovation/2010/applicant.html).

17. When Miller left the department, Shelton was promoted to deputy secretary and confirmed in March 2014.

18. These include Allison Cole, interviewed by Greg Margolis, April 11, 2012; Rebecca Maynard, interviewed by Ron Haskins and Greg Margolis, September 30, 2011; Jim Shelton, interviewed by Ron Haskins and Greg Margolis, April 19, 2012; Robert Gordon, interviewed by Ron Haskins and Greg Margolis, January 30, 2012 and December 21, 2012; Shivam Mallick Shah, interviewed by Ron Haskins and Greg Margolis, October 3, 2012; Suzanne Immerman, interviewed by Greg Margolis, July 12, 2012; Jefferson Pestronk, interviewed by Ron Haskins and Greg Margolis, February 16, 2012; Carmel Martin, interviewed by Ron Haskins and Greg Margolis, January 3, 2013; Tony Miller, interviewed by Ron Haskins and Greg Margolis, February 28, 2012.

19. Institute of Education Sciences, "What Works Clearinghouse: Procedures and Standards Handbook Version 2.0" (Washington: 2008) (http://ies.ed.gov/ncee/wwc/pdf/reference_resources/wwc_procedures_v2_standards_handbook.pdf).

20. National Research Council, "Improving Student Learning: A Strategic Plan for Education Research and Its Utilization" (Washington: 1999) (www.nap.edu/catalog.php?record_id=6488).

21. Full disclosure: Russ Whitehurst is now the Herman and George R. Brown Chair and director of the Brown Center on Education Policy at Brookings; we work with him frequently.

22. Gina Kolata, "Guesses and Hype Give Way to Data in Study of Education," *New York Times,* September 2, 2013 (www.nytimes.com/2013/09/03/science/applying-new-rigor-in-studying-education.html?_r=0).

23. See Department of Education, Office of Innovation and Improvement, "Overview Information: Investing in Innovation Fund; Notice Inviting Applications for New Awards for Fiscal Year (FY) 2010," *Federal Register,* vol. 75, no. 48 (March 12, 2010), p. 12074 (www2.ed.gov/legislation/FedRegister/announcements/2010-1/031210d.pdf).

24. The exception to the evidence requirement was the first round of the Trade Adjustment Assistance Community College and Career Training grant program, although even this program required each program to conduct an evaluation starting with the second year of grants.

25. See Department of Education, Office of Innovation and Improvement, "Overview Information," p. 12081.

26. Personal communication with Beth Boulay, principal associate, Abt Associates, October 13, 2013.

27. Department of Education, "Investing in Innovation," *Federal Register,* vol. 74, no. 195 (October 9, 2009), pp. 52214–28.

28. Department of Education, "Investing in Innovation," *Federal Register,* vol. 75, no. 48 (March 12, 2010), pp. 12004-12071.

29. Kim Smith and Julie Petersen, "Supporting and Scaling Change: Lessons from the First Round of the Investing in Innovation (i3) Program" (Washington: Bellwether Education Partners, June 2011) (www.edweek.org/media/belwetherreport-37i3.pdf).

30. Bill and Melinda Gates Foundation, "12 Major Foundations Commit $500 Million to Education Innovation in Concert with U.S. Department of Education's $650 Million 'Investing in Innovation' Fund" (2010) (www.gatesfoundation.org/Media-Center/Press-Releases/2010/04/12-Foundations-Commit-to-Education-Innovation-with-US-Department-of-Education).

31. Reviewers for the scale-up grants were from IES.

32. During the second stage of the proposal scoring process, outside experts in evaluation scored these two criteria; when the proposals that were still in consideration reached the third stage, these criteria were scored by well-trained evaluation experts from the Department of Education and IES.

33. Michele McNeil, "49 Applicants Win 'i3' Grants," Politics K–12 blog, *Education Week,* August 4, 2010 (http://blogs.edweek.org/edweek/campaign-k-12/2010/08/49_applicants_win_i3_grants_1.html).

34. Sara Mead, "How Did Parents as Teachers Win an i3 Grant?" Sara Mead's Policy Notebook blog, *Education Week,* September 7, 2010 (http://blogs.edweek.org/edweek/sarameads_policy_notebook/2010/09/how_did_parents_as_teachers_win_an_i3_grant.html).

35. Smith and Petersen, "Supporting and Scaling Change."

36. Rick Hess, "i3 Winners: Long on Talent, Execution, and 'Best Practices'—Not Transformation," Rick Hess Straight Up blog, *Education Week,* August 6, 2010 (http://blogs.edweek.org/edweek/rick_hess_straight_up/2010/08/i3_winners_long_on_talent_execution_best_practices--not_transformation.html).

37. It could be argued that Investing in Innovation is a misleading name for the initiative given what the administration wanted to accomplish. Their original, less catchy, more cumbersome title, "Grow What Works and Invest in Innovation Fund," seems to describe the true goals better than "Investing in Innovation" and may have led to less confusion and criticism of the lack of innovation.

38. Department of Defense and Full-Year Continuing Appropriations Act, 2011, P.L. 112-10, 125 Stat. 38 (2011) (www.gpo.gov/fdsys/pkg/PLAW-112publ10/pdf/PLAW-112publ10.pdf).

39. Department of Education, "Investing in Innovation (i3) 2011 Competition: Summary Document" (Washington: June 2011), under "FY 2011 i3 Competition Overview Slides and Summary Document" (www2.ed.gov/programs/innovation/2011/applicant.html).

40. For a short summary of the evaluations, see Coalition for Evidence-Based Policy, "Can Using Rigorous Evidence to Guide Federal Education Funds Improve Student Achievement?" (Washington: January 2014) (http://coalition4evidence.org/

wp-content/uploads/2014/01/i3-Fund-new-evaluation-findings-for-the-scale-up-grants-Jan-2014.pdf).

41. Henry May and others, "Evaluation of the i3 Scale-up of Reading Recovery: Year One Report, 2011–12" (Newark, N.J.: Consortium for Policy Research and Education and the Center for Research in Education and Social Policy, August 2013) (http://reading recovery.org/images/pdfs/Reading_Recovery/Research_and_Evaluation/RRi3_Year1 Eval_Report.pdf).

42. Janet C. Quint and others, "The Success for All Model of School Reform: Early Findings from the Investing in Innovation (i3) Scale-Up" (New York: MDRC, October 2013) (www.mdrc.org/sites/default/files/The_Success_for_All_Model_FR_0.pdf).

43. Melissa A. Clark and others, "The Effectiveness of Secondary Math Teachers from Teach for America and the Teaching Fellows Program" (Washington: Institute of Education Sciences, September 2013) (http://ies.ed.gov/ncee/pubs/20134015/ pdf/20134015.pdf).

44. Jim Manzi, *Uncontrolled: The Surprising Payoff of Trial-and-Error for Business, Politics, and Society* (New York: Basic Books, 2012).

45. Coalition for Evidence-Based Policy, "Randomized Controlled Trials Commissioned by the Institute of Education Sciences since 2002: How Many Found Positive versus Weak or No Effects" (Washington: 2013) (http://coalition4evidence.org/ wp-content/uploads/2013/06/IES-Commissioned-RCTs-positive-vs-weak-or-null-findings-7-2013.pdf).

46. Manzi, *Uncontrolled;* Jim Manzi, "Science Knowledge and Freedom," speech presented at Harvard's Program on Constitutional Government, Cambridge, Massachusetts, December 8, 2012.

47. Personal communication with Beth Boulay, principal associate, Abt Associates, October 13, 2013.

48. National Center for Education Statistics, *Education Digest: 2012,* table 98: "Number of Public School Districts and Public and Private Elementary and Secondary Schools: Selected Years, 1869–70 through 2010–11" (http://nces.ed.gov/programs/digest/d12/ tables/dt12_098.asp).

Chapter 5

1. See Amy S. Blackwood, Katie L. Roeger, and Sarah L. Pettijohn, "The Non-Profit Sector in Brief: Public Charities, Giving, and Volunteering, 2012" (Washington: Urban Institute, 2012) (www.urban.org/UploadedPDF/412674-The-Nonprofit-Sector-in-Brief.pdf); see also National Center for Charitable Statistics, "Quick Facts about Nonprofits" (http://nccs.urban.org/statistics/quickfacts.cfm).

2. See Urban Institute, "Human Service Nonprofit-Government Contracting" (www.urban.org/nonprofitcontracting.cfm).

3. "Americans of all ages, all stations in life, and all types of disposition . . . are forever forming associations. There are not only commercial and industrial associations in which all take part, but others of a thousand different types—religious, moral,

serious, futile, very general and very limited, immensely large and very minute." Alexis de Tocqueville, *Democracy in America* (New York: Penguin Classics, 2003).

4. See Teach for America (www.teachforamerica.org/); KIPP (www.kipp.org/); Steven Brill, *Class Warfare* (New York: Simon and Schuster, 2011); and Stephan Thernstrom and Abigail Thernstrom, *No Excuses: Closing the Racial Gap in Learning* (New York: Simon and Schuster, 2004).

5. However, good social programs can save money by reducing or avoiding future problems in health, mental health, education, or crime. One interesting example of how social programs might save money and produce a profit for investors is social impact bonds: investors pay for the cost of an intervention up front and then may earn a profit as part of the savings (if any) in government spending that result from a successful intervention. As a general rule, in any case in which government pays for social services for a person (foster care, mental health services, incarceration), the potential to save money through more effective prevention or treatment programs does raise the possibility of investor returns from reduced government spending. For an overview of the concept of social impact bonds, see Jeffrey B. Liebman, "Social Impact Bonds: A Promising New Financing Model to Accelerate Social Innovation and Improve Government Performance" (Washington: Center for American Progress, February 2011) (http://community-wealth.org/sites/clone.community-wealth.org/files/downloads/paper-liebman.pdf).

6. David Bornstein, *How to Change the World: Social Entrepreneurs and the Power of New Ideas,* updated ed. (Oxford University Press, 2007), especially chapters 1 and 2.

7. See Ashoka, "About Us" (www.ashoka.org/about).

8. The Congressional Research Service estimates that the federal government spent about $750 billion on programs for low-income families in 2011. The states spent around $250 billion on these programs, bringing the total to around $1 trillion. See Congressional Research Service, "Spending for Federal Benefits and Services for People with Low Income, FY2008–2011," Memo to the Senate Budget Committee (October 16, 2012) available at (www.budget.senate.gov/republican/public/index.cfm/files/serve/?File_id=0f87b42d-f182-4b3d-8ae2-fa8ac8a8edad); and Ron Haskins, "Testimony before the Committee on the Budget, U.S. House of Representatives," presented April 17, 2012 (www.brookings.edu/~/media/research/files/testimony/2012/4/17%20means%20testing%20haskins/0417_means_testing_haskins.pdf).

9. See New Profit, "Our Story" (http://newprofit.com/cgi-bin/iowa/about/3.html).

10. Ibid.

11. The Monitor Group was an international management consulting group founded by several people with close ties to the Harvard Business School. It was hit especially hard by the economic crisis in 2008 and eventually filed for chapter 11 bankruptcy in 2012. In 2013, Monitor Group was bought by Deloitte.

12. Teach for America describes its mission as "growing the movement of leaders who work to ensure that kids growing up in poverty get an excellent education" (www.teachforamerica.org/our-mission).

13. City Year describes itself as "an education-focused, nonprofit organization founded in 1988 that partners with public schools to help keep students in school and on track to graduate. In 24 communities across the United States and through two international

affiliates, this innovative public-private partnership brings together teams of young AmeriCorps members who commit to a year of full-time service in schools. Corps members support students by focusing on attendance, behavior, and course performance through in-class tutoring, mentoring, and after school programs" (www.cityyear.org).

14. Kim Syman, interviewed by Greg Margolis, March 15, 2012.

15. Ibid.

16. After we sent an early draft of this section of the chapter to Syman, she sent us an e-mail elaborating her views on the impact of Gergen's talk. These quotes are taken from that e-mail, sent to Haskins on May 19, 2014.

17. The term "Social Innovation Fund" was not coined for several years, but we use it here consistently to reduce the confusion that would result from using different names to label a single movement.

18. See America Forward (www.americaforward.org/).

19. See "The Hill's 2012 Top Lobbyists," *The Hill* (http://thehill.com/business-a-lobbying/264987-2012-top-lobbyists).

20. Tom Sheridan, interviewed by Greg Margolis, March 7 and March 29, 2012.

21. The America Forward policy coalition produced many policy proposals that it planned to present to the various presidential campaigns. The organization's leadership had numerous ideas for national service and nonprofit programs, which it attempted to sell to the campaigns. We concentrate here on the coalition's effort to obtain funds for what ultimately became the Social Innovation Fund, with federal funds going to intermediary organizations that would in turn fund community-based organizations.

22. According to Tom Sheridan, they met with all of the presidential candidates' campaigns; the reactions of only the most important campaigns are discussed here.

23. Tom Sheridan interviews.

24. Michele Jolin, interviewed by Ron Haskins and Greg Margolis, October 11, 2012 and February 8, 2013.

25. Mark Green and Michele Jolin, *Change for America: A Progressive Blueprint for the 44th President* (New York: Basic Books, 2009).

26. Michele Jolin, "Innovating the White House: How the Next President of the United States Can Spur Social Entrepreneurship," *Stanford Social Innovation Review,* vol. 6, no. 2 (Spring 2008), pp. 23–24; see also Michele Jolin, "Investing in Social Entrepreneurship and Fostering Social Innovation" (Washington: Center for American Progress, December 2007).

27. Jolin, "Innovating the White House," p. 23.

28. Nicholas Kristof, "How to Change the World," *New York Times,* October 20, 2010 (http://kristof.blogs.nytimes.com/2010/10/20/how-to-change-the-world/).

29. David Bornstein, *How to Change the World,* p. 5.

30. Department of Education, Institute of Education Sciences, "What Works Clearinghouse: Procedures and Standards Handbook, Version 2.1" (September 2011). It should be emphasized that SIF evidence standards permit quasi-experimental evidence as well as RCTs to be considered "strong" evidence.

31. Jim Shelton, interviewed by Ron Haskins and Greg Margolis, April 19, 2012; Tony Miller, interviewed by Ron Haskins and Greg Margolis, February 28, 2012.

32. Jon Baron and Isabel Sawhill, "Federal Programs for Youth: More of the Same Won't Work" (Brookings, May 1, 2010) (www.brookings.edu/research/opinions/2010/05/01-youth-programs-sawhill).

33. The bill that eventually passed both the House and Senate as the Edward M. Kennedy Serve America Act was originally called the "Generations Invigorating Volunteerism and Education Act (Give Act)" in the House. That bill, which eventually became law, was renamed in March 2009 in honor of Senator Kennedy, who was gravely ill at the time. He died in August of that year. Kennedy introduced the companion legislation in the Senate; he had also introduced the Serve America Act in 2008. A summary is available at www.nationalservice.gov/about/legislation/edward-m-kennedy-serve-america-act.

34. President Bush requested $8.5 million for the transition to the next administration, even before the presidential election; as it turned out, Obama used $5.3 million in public funds and around $6.7 million in private funds to pay for his transition. See FactCheck.org, "Cost of Obama's Transition," December 16, 2008 (http://www.factcheck.org/2008/12/cost-of-obamas-transition/), and Fox News, "Despite Bells and Whistles, 'Office of President-Elect' Holds No Authority," November 25, 2008 (www.foxnews.com/politics/2008/11/25/despite-bells-whistles-office-president-elect-holds-authority/).

35. One of the biggest and most immediate tasks is to get the administration's budget in place; the budget is usually made public within a few weeks of the inauguration.

36. See the Office of the President-Elect, "Policy Working Groups" (http://change.gov/learn/policy_working_groups).

37. Michele Jolin, "A New Office of Social Entrepreneurship," in *Change for America: A Progressive Blueprint for the 44th President,* edited by Green and Jolin.

38. The office was not officially announced until May 2009. See, for example, Pam Fessler, "White House Creates Office of Social Innovation," NPR, May 28, 2009 (www.npr.org/templates/story/story.php?storyId=104648050).

39. Eduardo Perez-Giz, "Notorious G.I.Z. (Senior Swan Song)," *Harvard Crimson,* March 3, 1999 (http://www.thecrimson.com/article/1999/3/3/notorious-giz-senior-swan-song-it/).

40. The Senate version continued to be known as the Serve America Act, while the House version was the Generations Invigorating Volunteerism and Education Act (GIVE Act). The final version of these service bills eventually became "The Edward M. Kennedy Serve America Act."

41. Personal communication with Michele Jolin, May 13, 2014.

42. The original Kennedy bill, the Serve America Act (S. 3487), introduced in 2008 during the 110th Congress, is available at https://www.govtrack.us/congress/bills/110/s3487/text. The law as passed, the Edward M. Kennedy Serve America Act, P.L. 111-13 123 Stat. 1460 (2009), is available at http://www.gpo.gov/fdsys/pkg/PLAW-111publ13/pdf/PLAW-111publ13.pdf.

43. See sections 198K (f)(4) and (j)(3)(D) of the final bill.

44. Appropriations bills, like other bills, must pass both houses of Congress. Differences between the House and Senate bills must be reconciled by a conference committee, and the final bill must be passed by both houses. The versions of the appropriation bills passed by the House and Senate must be identical. If both houses cannot agree on every provision in each of the 12 appropriations bills for the upcoming fiscal year, both houses

must pass a law, called a continuing resolution, that retains the exact provisions from the appropriations bill for the previous year. If both houses cannot agree on even a continuing resolution, the authority to spend money expires on the first day of the new fiscal year (always October 1) and any agency or government activity funded by the expired provisions must close down. Sometimes, as in 1995–96 and 2013, major portions of the government close down because Congress and the president cannot agree on a budget for many agencies. Fortunately, in both 2009 and 2010, the House and Senate enacted budget resolutions and regular order was maintained.

45. Adrienne Hallett, interviewed by Greg Margolis, February 23, 2012.

46. For overview of the bill's progress through Congress, see "Bill Summary and Status, 111th Congress (2009–2010), H.R.3288, Major Congressional Actions" (http://thomas.loc.gov/cgi-bin/bdquery/z?d111:HR03288:@@@R).

47. Quoted in Rachel L. Swarns, "Mrs. Obama Announces New Fund to Aid Nonprofits," *New York Times,* May 6, 2009 (www.nytimes.com/2009/05/06/us/politics/06michelle.html).

48. Barack Obama, "Remarks by the President on Community Solutions Agenda," speech, Washington, June 30, 2009 (www.whitehouse.gov/the_press_office/Remarks-by-The-President-on-Community-Solutions-Agenda-6-30-09).

49. For more information, see the Mayor's Fund to Advance New York City (www.NYC.gov/fund).

50. See Melody Barnes, "Innovation with Crawfish Sauce: What a New Orleans Nonprofit Can Teach the Rest of the Country," White House Office of Social Innovation and Civic Participation blog post, October 30, 2009 (www.whitehouse.gov/blog/2009/10/30/innovation-with-crawfish-sauce-what-a-new-orleans-nonprofit-can-teach-rest-country).

51. Susannah Washburn, interviewed by Greg Margolis, February 2, 2012.

52. Kent Mitchell, interviewed by Greg Margolis, January 24, 2012.

53. Suzanne Perry, "Social Innovation Fund Issues Call for Grant Proposals," *Chronicle of Philanthropy,* February 16, 2010 (http://philanthropy.com/article/Social-Innovation-Fund-Issues/64218/?sid=&utm_source=&utm_medium=en).

54. Corporation for National and Community Service, "Notice of Federal Funds Availability" (February 2010) (www.nationalservice.gov/sites/default/files/nofa/10_0219_sif_nofa_final.pdf).

55. Ibid., p. 3.

56. Ibid., p. 16.

57. Issue-based applicants have to focus their programs on addressing one of the three program target areas of SIF: healthy futures, economic and educational development, or youth development. The geography-based applicants have to focus on serving "low-income communities within a specific local geographic area, and propose to focus on improving measureable outcomes" related to the three program issue areas.

58. Corporation for National and Community Service, "2010 Social Innovation Fund Grant Reviewing and Scoring Process" (www.nationalservice.gov/sites/default/files/documents/10_0910_grant_reviewing_scoring_process.pdf).

59. Ibid. For information about the announcement of grant awards, see Corporation for National and Community Service, "Social Innovation Fund" (July 2010) (www.nationalservice.gov/sites/default/files/documents/10_0722_sif_factsheet.pdf).

60. How the Edna McConnell Clark Foundation selected its nine subgrantees for 2010 and their characteristics are thoroughly described in Edna McConnell Clark Foundation, "A Summary of EMCF's 2010–2011 Selection of SIF Grantees" (March 2011) (www.emcf.org/fileadmin/media/PDFs/emcf_sifreport2011.pdf).

61. Ron Haskins is a member of the board of directors of MDRC.

62. See the Edna McConnell Clark Foundation, "The True North Fund" (http://www.emcf.org/capital-aggregation/true-north-fund/).

63. Gordon Berlin, interviewed by Ron Haskins, February 11, 2013.

64. Paul Light, "Stonewalling at the Social Innovation Fund," Light on Leadership Blog, *Washington Post* (http://views.washingtonpost.com/leadership/light/2010/08/stonewalling-at-the-social-innovation-fund.html); see also Tactical Philanthropy, "Transparency Controversy at the Social Innovation Fund," August 20, 2010 (www.tacticalphilanthropy.com/2010/08/transparency-controversy-at-the-social-innovation-fund/).

65. Stephanie Strom, "Nonprofit Fund Faces Questions about Conflicts and Selection Procedures," *New York Times*, August 21, 2010 (http://www.nytimes.com/2010/08/22/us/22nonprofit.html?pagewanted=all&_r=0).

66. Suzanne Perry, "Amid Concerns of Favoritism, Federal Officials Disclose New Details on Selection Process," *Chronicle of Philanthropy*, August 23, 2010 (http://philanthropy.com/article/Social-Innovation-Fund-Acts-to/124100/).

67. Ruth McCambridge, "Office of Inspector General at CNCS to Review SIF Selection Process," *Nonprofit Quarterly*, Friday, November 12, 2010 (www.nonprofitquarterly.org/index.php?option=com_content&view=article&id=7221:office-of-inspector-general-at-cncs-to-review-sif-selection-process&Itemid=336).

68. Howard Bloom, James A. Riccio, and Nandita Verma, "Promoting Work in Public Housing: The Effectiveness of Jobs-Plus" (New York: MDRC, March 2005).

69. Michael Smith, "Innovation to Impact: Obama's Social Innovation Fund at Four," blog, *Stanford Social Innovation Review*, March 3, 2014 (www.ssireview.org/blog/entry/innovation_to_impact_obamas_social_innovation_fund_at_four). The "Fact Sheet" about SIF posted on the CNCS website says that 221 nonprofit organizations are receiving SIF funds not the 217 organizations cited in the *Stanford Social Innovation Review* blog by Michael Smith. Corporation for National and Community Service, "Social Innovation Fund" (January 2014) (www.nationalservice.gov/sites/default/files/documents/SIF_Fact_Sheet_1_22_2014.pdf).

70. Corporation for National and Community Service, "Notice of Funding Opportunity" (2011), p. 8 (www.nationalservice.gov/sites/default/files/nofa/11_0228_sif_nofo.pdf).

71. Corporation for National and Community Service, "Social Innovation Fund: 2012 Competition" (www.nationalservice.gov/programs/social-innovation-fund/previous-competitions/2012).

72. See Corporation for National and Community Service, "Social Innovation Fund Grants FY 2014" (http://www.nationalservice.gov/build-your-capacity/grants/funding-opportunities/2014/social-innovation-fund-grants-fy-2014).

73. A number of intermediaries are conducting the same program with several subgrantees.

74. Corporation for National and Community Service, "Social Innovation Fund: Content Requirements for Subgrantee Evaluation Plans" (February 2013) (http://apps. legacyintl.org/wp-content/uploads/2012/04/SIF-SEP-Guidance_February-2012-Release.pdf).

Chapter 6

1. Gertrude Himmelfarb, *The Idea of Poverty: England in the Early Industrial Age* (New York: Knopf, 1983).

2. Sheldon Danziger, Robert Haveman, and Robert Plotnick, "How Income Transfers Affect Work, Savings, and the Income Distribution: A Critical Review," *Journal of Economic Literature,* vol. 19, no. 3 (1981), pp. 975–1028; Rebecca M. Blank, *It Takes a Nation: A New Agenda for Fighting Poverty* (Princeton University, 1997).

3. Ron Haskins, *Work Over Welfare: The Inside Story of the 1996 Welfare Reform Law* (Brookings, 2006).

4. Employers pay the unemployment tax in the same manner as Social Security and Medicare taxes, but most economists agree that the tax is paid out of money that would have gone to workers in the form of wages. For a more detailed analysis, see Chad Stone and William Chen, "Introduction to Unemployment Insurance" (Washington: Center on Budget and Policy Priorities, February 6, 2013) (www.cbpp.org/cms/index. cfm?fa=view&id=1466).

5. National Association of Workforce Boards, "Our 12,000 Business Members Making Workforce Investments Work" (www.nawb.org/about_us.asp).

6. For a detailed and readable description of the nation's workforce system, see David Bradley, "The Workforce Investment Act and the One-Stop Delivery System" (Congressional Research Service, June 2013) (http://digitalcommons.ilr.cornell.edu/cgi/ viewcontent.cgi?article=2151&context=key_workplace).

7. One of the officials at OMB that we spoke to in 2014 shortly before the book went to the printer told us that there were now only about 2,500 One-Stop Centers. We could not find a citation for the 2,500 figure.

8. See the American Job Center website (http://jobcenter.usa.gov/). For an explanation, see Jane Oates, "Training and Employment Guidance Letter No. 36-11" (Employment and Training Administration, U.S. Department of Labor, June 24, 2012) (http:// wdr.doleta.gov/directives/attach/TEGL/TEGL_36_11.Acc.pdf).

9. Bradley, "The Workforce Investment Act," p. 6.

10. Vee Burke, "Cash and Noncash Benefits for Persons with Limited Income: Eligibility Rules, Recipient and Expenditure Data, FY2000-FY2002" (Congressional Research Service, November 2003). Expenditures on jobs and training for 1978, 1979, and 1980 were $27,178 billion, $23,533 billion, and $19,285 billion respectively, in 2002 dollars. The average is $23,332 billion in 2002 dollars. Converting 2002 to 2012 dollars using the GDP implicit price deflator yields $29,375 billion.

11. Congressional Research Service, "Spending for Federal Benefits and Services for People with Low Income, FY 2008-FY2011: An update of Table B-1 from CRS

Report R41625, Modified to Remove Programs for Veterans" (October 2012) (www. budget.senate.gov/republican/public/index.cfm/files/serve/?File_id=0f87b42d-f182-4b3d-8ae2-fa8ac8a8edad).

12. For a review of all the expansions of unemployment compensation benefits, see Julie M. Whittaker and Katelin P. Isaacs, "Extending Unemployment Compensation Benefits during Recessions" (Congressional Research Service, October 2012) (http://greenbook.waysandmeans.house.gov/sites/greenbook.waysandmeans.house.gov/files/2012/documents/RL34340%20v2_gb.pdf). For the cost estimate, see Congressional Budget Office, "Unemployment Insurance in the Wake of the Recent Recession" (November 2012), p. 1(www.cbo.gov/sites/default/files/cbofiles/attachments/11-28-Unemployment Insurance_0.pdf).

13. For a succinct overview of the WIA, see Department of Labor, "The 'Plain English' Version of the Workforce Investment Act of 1998" (www.doleta.gov/usworkforce/wia/Runningtext.cfm).

14. Formula money is funding that is divided up among the states based on a formula; the formula is usually based on population and other factors, such as poverty. By contrast, competitive grants provide funds to the states or other entities that submit high-quality proposals, usually proposals that are superior to other submitted proposals. With formula grants, every state gets a share of the funds; with competitive grants, only states that compete well obtain funding.

15. Melissa Bomberger, interviewed by Greg Margolis, October 26, 2011.

16. Parts of this section are based on Seth Harris, interviewed by Ron Haskins and Greg Margolis, April 5, 2012.

17. A logic model is used to organize the thinking behind why a new program or policy might have its expected effects. The model is generally composed of at least three parts: resources, activities, and outputs. The purpose is to portray the relationships between the elements of a program or policy, leading to a kind of "If this, then that" progression showing that if resources are available to conduct a specified activity, the desired outcomes can be expected. See, for example, "W.K. Kellogg Foundation Logic Model Development Guide" (Battle Creek, Mich.: January 2004) (www.wkkf.org/resource-directory/resource/2006/02/wk-kellogg-foundation-logic-model-development-guide).

18. U.S. Government Accountability Office, "Opportunities to Reduce Potential Duplication in Government Programs, Save Tax Dollars, and Enhance Revenue" (GAO-11-318SP) (March 2011), pp. 140–43.

19. For spending on the various Workforce Investment Act programs, see "Department of Labor," pp. 813–14 (www.whitehouse.gov/sites/default/files/omb/budget/fy2013/assets/lab.pdf).

20. Sectoral training programs focus on a particular sector of the local economy in which jobs are known to be available and in which job growth is expected. Examples of sector jobs are computer technician, medical assistant, welder, and business services jobs.

21. The Senate Health, Education, Labor, and Pensions (HELP) Committee released copies of its discussion draft to various stakeholders, including the National Skills Coalition, which posted the bill, dated June 8, 2011, on its website.

22. Melissa Maynard, "States Want More Control over Workforce Development Funds," *Stateline*, August 15, 2013 (www.lowellsun.com/todaysheadlines/ci_23867842/ states-seek-more-control-over-federal-workforce-development-dollars).

23. Title VIII, Sec. 1801(a)(3) of the Department of Defense and Full-Year Continuing Appropriations Act, 2011, P.L. 112-10 125 Stat. 38 (2011) (http://www.gpo.gov/fdsys/ pkg/PLAW-112publ10/pdf/PLAW-112publ10.pdf).

24. The administration proposed $380 million for the Workforce Innovation Fund in its fiscal year 2012 budget, released in February 2011. But after congressional negotiations over the 2012 appropriations, the administration was able to secure only $50 million for the Fund, in the Consolidated Appropriations Act, 2012, which was passed in December 2011.

25. Gina Wells, interviewed by Greg Margolis, April 2, 2012.

26. See National Career Pathways Network, "Career Pathways" (https://www.cord. org/career-pathways/).

27. See Washington State Board for Community and Technical Colleges, "Integrated Basic Education and Skills Training (I-BEST)" (www.sbctc.ctc.edu/college/e_integrated basiceducationandskillstraining.aspx).

28. See, for example, Peter Schochet, John Burghardt, and Sheena McConnell, "National Job Corps Study and Longer-Term Follow-Up Study: Impact and Benefit-Cost Findings Using Survey and Summary Earnings Records Data: Final Report" (Princeton: Mathematica Policy Research, August 2006), available at (http://wdr.doleta. gov/research/FullText_Documents/National%20Job%20Corps%20Study%20and%20 Longer%20Term%20Follow-Up%20Study%20-%20Final%20Report.pdf).

29. Fred Doolittle and others, "The Design and Implementation of the National JTPA Study: A Summary" (New York: MDRC, August 1993) (www.upjohninst.org/sites/ default/files/erdc/reports/njtpareport.pdf).

30. See, for example, Douglas Besharov and Phoebe Cottingham, *The Workforce Investment Act: Implementation Experiences, and Evaluation Findings* (Kalamazoo, Mich.: Upjohn Institute Press, 2011); Kevin Hollenbeck, "Using Administrative Data for Workforce Development Program Evaluation," Working Paper 04-103 (Kalamazoo, Mich.: W.E. Upjohn Institute for Employment Research, August 2004) (http://research.upjohn. org/cgi/viewcontent.cgi?article=1120&context=up_workingpapers); Paul Osterman, "Employment and Training Policies: New Directions for Less-Skilled Adults," in *Reshaping the American Workforce in a Changing Economy,* edited by Harry J. Holzer and Demetra Smith Nightingale (Washington: Urban Institute, 2007).

31. Gina Wells interview.

32. Grace A. Kilbane, interviewed by Greg Margolis, April 6, 2012.

33. Mary Alice McCarthy, interviewed by Greg Margolis, April 12, 2012.

34. Ibid.

35. Employment and Training Administration, Department of Labor, "Notice of Availability of Funds and Solicitation for Grant Applications for Workforce Innovation Fund Grants" (December 22, 2011) (www.doleta.gov/grants/pdf/SGA-DFA-PY-11-05.pdf).

36. A recent survey by the Organization for Economic Cooperation and Development (OECD) found that the basic literacy and numeracy skills of U.S. workers were below the

average of all the countries surveyed. See OECD, "Time for the U.S. to Reskill? What the Survey of Adult Skills Says" (2013) (http://skills.oecd.org/Survey_of_Adult_Skills_US.pdf).

37. Gina Wells interview.

38. Ibid.

39. As used in the SGA, "ideas" refers to the intervention program or strategy the applicant is proposing to test.

40. Ohio Department of Job and Family Services, "Abstract: Workforce Innovation Fund Application" (March 2012) (www.doleta.gov/workforce_innovation/pdf/grantees/OhioDeptofJFS_abstract.pdf).

41. "A Special Issue on the U.S. Department of Labor Symposium," edited by Lawrence M. Kahn, *ILR Review,* vol. 67, Supplement (Spring 2014).

Chapter 7

1. Technically, President Obama's speech to a joint session of Congress on February 24, 2009, was not considered an official State of the Union address. His first such speech did not occur until 2010.

2. Barack Obama, "Address to Joint Session of Congress," February 24, 2009 (www.whitehouse.gov/the_press_office/Remarks-of-President-Barack-Obama-Address-to-Joint-Session-of-Congress).

3. Martha Kanter, interviewed by Ron Haskins and Greg Margolis, May 22, 2012.

4. See American Association of Community Colleges, "2014 Fact Sheet" (Washington: 2014) (www.aacc.nche.edu/AboutCC/Documents/Facts14_Data_R2.pdf).

5. For an overview of the state of remedial education in the nation's community colleges, see Elizabeth Zachry Rutschow and Emily Schneider, "Unlocking the Gate: What We Know about Improving Developmental Education" (New York: MDRC, June 2011) (www.mdrc.org/sites/default/files/full_595.pdf).

6. Julie Peller, interviewed by Greg Margolis, February 20, 2012.

7. Congressional Budget Office, "Cost Estimate: H.R. 3221, Student Aid and Fiscal Responsibility Act of 2009" (July 24, 2009) (www.cbo.gov/sites/default/files/cbofiles/ftpdocs/104xx/doc10479/hr3221.pdf).

8. Barack Obama, "Remarks by the President on the American Graduation Initiative," July 14, 2009 (www.whitehouse.gov/the_press_office/Remarks-by-the-President-on-the-American-Graduation-Initiative-in-Warren-MI).

9. See, for example, the president's speech in the East Room of the White House on his Social Investment Fund initiative: Barack Obama, "Remarks by the President on the Community Solutions Agenda," June 30, 2009 (www.whitehouse.gov/the-press-office/remarks-president-community-solutions-agenda-6-30-09).

10. Obama, "Remarks by the President on the American Graduation Initiative."

11. For an overview of SAFRA and an explanation of the cost estimate, see Cassandria Dortch, David P. Smole, and Shannon M. Mahan, "The SAFRA Act: Education Reconciliation in the 111th Congress" (Congressional Research Service, March 19, 2010) (www.clhe.org/documents/crssafrareport.pdf).

12. Student Aid and Fiscal Responsibility Act, H.R. 3221, 111th Cong. (2009) (www. gpo.gov/fdsys/pkg/BILLS-111hr3221ih/pdf/BILLS-111hr3221ih.pdf).

13. Ibid.

14. Alex Isenstadt, "Town Halls Gone Wild," *Politico,* August 3, 2009 (www.politico. com/news/stories/0709/25646.html); Kimberly Kindy, "Tea Party Protest Organizers Target Health-Care Reform," 44: The Obama Presidency, *Washington Post,* August 22, 2009 (http://voices.washingtonpost.com/44/2009/08/22/tea_party_protest_organizers_t. html).

15. U.S. House of Representatives, Committee on Rules, "Basic Training: The Reconciliation Process" (http://rules-republicans.house.gov/Educational/Read.aspx?ID=28).

16. The Committee on Finance and Committee on Health, Education, Labor and Pensions in the Senate; the Committee on Ways and Means, Committee on Education and Labor, and the Committee on Energy and Commerce in the House.

17. Judd Gregg (R-N.H.) and Blanche Lincoln (D-Ark.) quoted in Lori Montgomery, "President's Budget Strategy under Fire," *Washington Post,* March 18, 2009 (www. washingtonpost.com/wp-dyn/content/article/2009/03/17/AR2009031703798.html).

18. Quoted in Shailagh Murray and Lori Montgomery, "Obama Calls for Reconciliation to Prevent Filibuster on Health-Care Reform," *Washington Post,* March 4, 2010 (www.washingtonpost.com/wp-dyn/content/article/2010/03/03/AR2010030302213_ pf.html); David M. Herszenhorn, "Obama's Student Loan Overhaul Endangered," *New York Times,* March 10, 2010 (www.nytimes.com/2010/03/11/us/politics/11loans.html).

19. This quote comes from John Boehner, then the House minority leader, as quoted in Murray and Montgomery, "Obama Calls for Reconciliation to Prevent Filibuster on Healthcare Reform."

20. Paul Basken, "Student-Loan Bill's Windfall Shrinks in New Estimate from Congressional Budget Office," *Chronicle of Higher Education,* March 7, 2010 (http://chronicle. com/article/Student-Loan-Bills-Windfall/64546/); Congressional Budget Office, "An Analysis of the President's Budgetary Proposals for Fiscal Year 2011" (March 24, 2010) (www.cbo.gov/ftpdocs/112xx/doc11280/03-24-apb.pdf).

21. For a detailed analysis and description of CBO's scoring of the House's reconciliation bills and its effect on the AGI and SAFRA, see Dortch, Smole, and Mahan, "The SAFRA Act: Education Programs in the FY2010 Budget Reconciliation," and Congressional Budget Office, "An Analysis of the President's Budgetary Proposals for Fiscal Year 2011."

22. William Branigin, "Obama Signs Higher-Education Measure into Law," 44: Politics and Policy in Obama's Washington, *Washington Post,* March 30, 2010 (http://voices. washingtonpost.com/44/2010/03/obama-signs-higher-education-m.html).

23. Martha Kanter interview.

24. Amanda Ahlstrand, interviewed by Greg Margolis, January 27, 2012.

25. For example, the evidence-based Career Pathways approach focuses on skills development, postsecondary education and career-technical content but does not specifically target the population of trade-displaced workers. See Dan M. Hull and Richard "Dick" Hinckley, *Adult Career Pathways: Providing a Second Chance in Public Education* (Waco, Tex.: Cord, 2007).

26. Amanda Ahlstrand interview.

27. Jean Grossman, interviewed by Ron Haskins and Greg Margolis, October 20, 2011, and December 23, 2011.

28. Here is how the SGA defined the three tiers: strong—the evidence includes a study or multiple studies whose design can support strong causal conclusions and studies that demonstrate the strategy to be effective with multiple populations and/or in multiple sites; moderate—evidence from a study or studies that include multiple sites and/or populations that support weaker causal conclusions or that support strong causal conclusions that are not yet generalizable; and preliminary—conclusions are based on research findings or reasonable hypotheses, including related research or theories of change in education, training, and other sectors. The SGA also had an attachment about evidence that was taken from i3. See U.S. Department of Labor, "Notice of Availability of Funds and Solicitations for Grant Applications for Trade Adjustment Assistance Community College and Career Training Grants Program" (January 2011) (www.doleta.gov/grants/pdf/SGA-DFA-PY-10-03.pdf).

29. "Employment retention rate" is defined as follows in the SGA: Of those who are employed in their first quarter after leaving the program, the percentage employed in both the second and third quarters after exiting.

30. According to its website, I-Best is a "model that quickly boosts students' literacy and work skills so that students can earn credentials, get living wage jobs, and put their talents to work for employers." The model features two classroom instructors, one for professional and technical content, and the other for basic skills, including reading, writing, and math. The idea is to integrate both the technical content and the developmental skills into one comprehensive classroom experience, using job training to reach basic skills and vice versa. For more information, see Integrated Basic Education and Skills Training (www.sbctc.ctc.edu/college/e_integratedbasiceducationandskillstraining.aspx).

31. Davis Jenkins, Matthew Zeidenberg, and Gregory Kienzl, "Educational Outcomes of I-BEST, Washington State Community and Technical College System's Integrated Basic Education and Skills Training Program: Findings from a Multivariate Analysis," CCRC Working Paper 16 (Community College Research Center, Columbia University, May 2009).

32. Full technical proposals from most of the first round of TAACCCT grant awards (and subsequent rounds) are available on the Department of Labor website (www.doleta.gov/taaccct/pdf/TACT_Winning_Applications_2011.pdf).

33. Virginia's Community Colleges, "Achieve 2015: A Strategic Plan for Virginia's Community Colleges" (www.nvcc.edu/about-nova/directories--offices/administrative-offices/college-planning/planning/achieve2015.pdf).

34. Scott Kemp, Wendy Kang and Carrie Douglas, "Impact of the Career Coach Program 2009-2010," Annual Report, Virginia's Community Colleges (http://old.vccs.edu/Portals/0/ContentAreas/Workforce/CCPerformancesReport200910.pdf).

35. Henry M. Levin and Emma Garcia, "Cost-Effectiveness of Accelerated Study in Associate Programs (ASAP) of the City University of New York (CUNY)"(New York: Center for Benefit-Cost Studies in Education, Columbia University, September 2012) (www.cuny.edu/academics/programs/notable/asap/Levin_Report_WEB.pdf).

36. Virginia's Community Colleges, "Reengineering Progress Report: Automate Student Success Solutions and Develop Public-Private Partnerships for Student Success," 2014 (http://rethink.vccs.edu/progress/automate-student-success-solutions/).

37. Veronica A. Lotkowski, Steven B. Robbins, and Richard J. Noeth, "The Role of Academic and Non-Academic Factors in Improving College Retention: ACT Policy Report" (Iowa City, Iowa.: ACT, 2004) (www.act.org/research/policymakers/pdf/college_retention.pdf).

38. Complete College America, "A Working Model for Student Success: The Tennessee Technology Centers, Preliminary Case Study" (Washington, 2011) (www.complete college.org/docs/Tennessee%20Technology%20Centers-%20A%20Preliminary%20 Case%20Study%281%29.pdf).

39. Phuong T. Do, John R. Moreland, and Dennis P. Korchek, "The Influence of Multimodal 3D Visualizations on Learning Acquisition," in *Advances in Visual Computing*, edited by Richard Boyle and others (New York: Springer, 2010), pp. 484–93 (http://link. springer.com/chapter/10.1007%2F978-3-642-17277-9_50).

40. Council for Adult and Experiential Learning, "Fueling the Race to Postsecondary Success: A 48-Institution Study of Prior Learning Assessment and Adult Student Outcomes" (Chicago: March 2010) (www.cael.org/pdfs/PLA_Fueling-the-Race).

41. Eric Bettinger and Rachel Baker, "The Effects of Student Coaching in College: An Evaluation of a Randomized Experiment in Student Mentoring," Working Paper 16881 (Cambridge, Mass.: National Bureau of Economic Research, March 2011) (www.nber. org/papers/w16881).

42. Complete College America, "Transform Remediation" (Washington: September 2011) (www.completecollege.org/docs/CCA%20Essential%20Steps%20Remediation %20Sept%202011%20Update%20high%20res.pdf).

43. Bureau of Labor Statistics, "The Employment Situation: July 2014" (USDL-14-1391) (www.bls.gov/news.release/pdf/empsit.pdf).

44. Bill McBride, "March Employment Report: 192,000 Jobs, 6.7% Unemployment Rate," April 4, 2014 (www.calculatedriskblog.com/2014/04/march-employment-report-192000-jobs-67.html).

45. Organization for Economic Cooperation and Development, "OECD Skills Outlook 2013: First Results from the Survey of Adult Skills" (2013); Center on International Education Benchmarking, "PIAAC Skills Outlook 2013 from OECD" (www.ncee.org/ cieb/piaac-skills-outlook-2013-from-oecd/).

46. For an example of a random assignment study of a community college program on learning communities, see Michael J. Weiss and others, "A Random Assignment Evaluation of Learning Communities at Kingsborough Community College" (New York: MDRC, 2014) (http://www.mdrc.org/publication/random-assignment-evaluation-learning-communities-kingsborough-community-college); for an overview of research on learning community research in community colleges, see MDRC, "What Have We Learned about Learning Communities at Community Colleges?" (July 2012) (www.mdrc.org/ publication/what-have-we-learned-about-learning-communities-community-colleges).

Chapter 8

1. Esther Duflo and others, "Saving Incentives for Low- and Middle-Income Families: Evidence from a Field Experiment with H&R Block," Brookings Institution, Retirement Security Project, No. 2005-5, 2005.

2. Gordon had a steep learning curve about experimental design in the social sciences. Of course, at OMB he was surrounded by great experts in experimental design, including both career officials such as Stack and political appointees such as Orszag and Liebman, who could advise him. In addition, there were experts outside the administration to advise him, especially Jon Baron of the Coalition for Evidence-Based Policy. For example, in November 2009, as negotiations proceeded between OMB and the Corporation for National and Community Service about the funding announcement for the Social Innovation Fund, Baron sent Gordon a thoughtful memo about some of Gordon's concerns with random assignment designs.

3. For more information about the role that Robert Gordon played in the Democratic education reform movement, see Steven Brill, *Class Warfare: Inside the Fight to Fix America's Schools* (New York: Simon and Schuster, 2011).

4. Robert Gordon, "Criminal Intent: An Agenda for Reducing Crime and Imprisonment," *New Republic,* March 25, 2008 (www.newrepublic.com/article/politics/criminal-intent); Robert Gordon, "Going from B to A: How to Fix the No Child Left Behind Act," *Slate,* September 24, 2007 (www.slate.com/articles/news_and_politics/jurisprudence/2007/09/going_from_b_to_a.html); Robert Gordon, Thomas J. Kane, and Douglas O. Steiger, "Identifying Effective Teachers Using Performance on the Job," Discussion Paper 2006-01 (Hamilton Project, Brookings, April 2006) (www.brookings.edu/~/media/Research/Files/Papers/2006/4/education%20gordon/200604hamilton_1.PDF).

5. House minority leader John Boehner mocked the home visiting provision of the Affordable Care Act on the House floor, saying that it would "put $750 million into a program to help legislate how parents should parent." A transcript of Boehner's comments can be found at "Affordable Health Care for America Act" (http://votesmart.org/public-statement/469094/affordable-health-care-for-america-act); a video record can be found at the 14-minute mark at "Boehner: Speaker Pelosi's Government Takeover of Health Care Will Dim the Light of Freedom" (w ww.youtube.com/watch?v=9FGuYpMI6iI).

6. Individuals who meet the qualifications for an entitlement program such as Medicaid or the Supplemental Nutrition Assistance Program have a legal right to the benefit. By contrast, discretionary programs like housing and child care programs provide benefits only up to the amount of the annual appropriation by Congress. In the entitlement case, everyone who qualifies and applies for the benefits receives them; in the case of discretionary programs, many who are qualified do not receive the benefits because not enough money was appropriated by Congress to cover all qualified individuals. This difference can have a significant impact on CBO scoring. If a social intervention program results in fewer people receiving benefits from an entitlement program, spending on the entitlement program is reduced because fewer people qualify to receive the benefit. The Nurse-Family Partnership (NFP), for example, showed in randomized controlled

trials that hospital admissions of infants and children were reduced, saving money in Medicaid. If CBO decides that the evidence of reduced hospital admissions is strong enough, it can score savings in Medicaid, thereby reducing the net cost of the NFP. But if an intervention program results in reducing the number of individuals who are qualified for a discretionary benefit such as housing, the money will simply be spent on another qualified individual who previously could not receive the benefit.

7. Office of the President, "Paying for Success," Federal Budget: Fiscal Year 2012. The Pay for Success website (www.payforsuccess.org) has abundant information about Pay for Success programs and theory as well as a calendar of upcoming events.

8. MDRC, "Financing Promising Evidence-Based Programs: Early Lessons from the New York City Social Impact Bond" (New York: December 2013).

9. Maria Cancian and Ron Haskins, "Changes in Family Composition: Implications for Income, Poverty, and Public Policy," *Annals of the American Academy of Political and Social Science*, vol. 654 (July 2014), pp. 31–47.

10. According to the Census Bureau's 2012 American Community Survey, the median age at first marriage is 27.1 for women and 29.1 for men; see Census Bureau, "American Fact Finder" (http://factfinder2.census.gov/faces/tableservices/jsf/pages/productview.xhtml?pid=ACS_12_1YR_B12007&prodType=table).

11. See Title V, Section 511(d)(1)(A) of the Social Security Act, as amended by the Patient Protection and Affordable Care Act, P.L. 111-148, 124 Stat. 119 (2010).

12. Kimberly S. Howard and Jeanne Brooks-Gunn, "The Role of Home-Visiting Programs in Preventing Child Abuse and Neglect," *Future of Children*, vol. 19, no. 2 (Fall 2009), pp. 95–118 (http://futureofchildren.org/publications/journals/article/index.xml?journalid=71&articleid=514).

13. Jim Manzi, *Uncontrolled: The Surprising Payoff of Trial-and-Error for Business, Politics, and Society* (New York: Basic Books, 2012).

14. National Research Council and Institute of Medicine, *Preventing Mental, Emotional, and Behavioral Disorders among Young People: Progress and Possibilities*, edited by Mary Ellen O'Connell, Thomas Boat, and Kenneth E. Warner (Washington: National Academies Press, 2009), p. 371 (www.nap.edu/catalog.php?record_id=12480).

15. As discussed in chapter 7, in attempting to create a community college initiative, the administration found money in the 2010 reconciliation bill that was designed to accompany the Affordable Care Act. The savings were produced by reforms in the student loan program. But under the rules of a reconciliation bill, no new programs can be authorized. Thus, to take advantage of the available money to create its community college initiative, the administration was forced to use a program that had already been authorized. It turned out, purely by coincidence, that a program had been authorized in 2009 to help workers displaced by trade changes get job training at community colleges. So the administration put $2 billion over four years into that program and then worked with the Department of Labor to create the TAACCCT evidence-based initiative.

16. Manzi, *Uncontrolled*.

17. Coalition for Evidence-Based Policy, "Randomized Controlled Trials Commissioned by the Institute of Education Sciences since 2002: How Many Found Positive

versus Weak or No Effects" (Washington: 2013) (http://coalition4evidence.org/wp-content/uploads/2013/06/IES-Commissioned-RCTs-positive-vs-weak-or-null-findings-7-2013.pdf).

18. Two of these evaluated projects that were funded with an i3 grant in 2010. The third evaluation, of Teach for America, was for a separate project, although the organization did receive an i3 scale-up grant in 2010. Henry May and others, "Evaluation of the i3 Scale-Up of Reading Recovery: Year One Report, 2011–12" (Newark, N.J.: Consortium for Policy Research and Education and the Center for Research in Education and Social Policy, August 2013) (http://readingrecovery.org/images/pdfs/Reading_Recovery/Research_and_Evaluation/RRi3_Year1Eval_Report.pdf), and Janet C. Quint and others, "The Success for All Model of School Reform: Early Findings from the Investing in Innovation (i3) Scale-Up," (New York: MDRC, October 2013) (www.mdrc.org/sites/default/files/The_Success_for_All_Model_FR_0.pdf).

19. Manzi, *Uncontrolled.*

20. Coalition for Evidence-Based Policy, "Demonstrating How Low-Cost Randomized Controlled Trials Can Drive Effective Social Spending" (Washington: 2013) (http://coalition4evidence.org/low-cost-rct-competition/).

21. The Coalition on Evidence-Based Policy, with funds from the Laura and John Arnold Foundation and the Annie E. Casey Foundation, sponsored a competition to award funds to program evaluators to conduct rapid, low-cost RCTs; the coalition ultimately awarded grants to three evaluators. For a summary of the coalition's grant process and the winning proposals, see the report by Jon Baron, president of the coalition, to its board of advisers, at http://coalition4evidence.org/wp-content/uploads/2014/07/Coalition-Update-July-2014.pdf. See also David Leonhardt, "The Quiet Movement to Make Government Fail Less Often," *New York Times,* July 15, 2014 .

22. Corporation for National and Community Service, "Social Innovation Fund: Content Requirements for Subgrantee Evaluation Plans" (Washington: May 2013) (http://apps.legacyintl.org/wp-content/uploads/2012/04/SIF-SEP-Guidance_February-2012-Release.pdf).

23. Manzi, *Uncontrolled;* Coalition for Evidence-Based Policy, "Randomized Controlled Trials Commissioned by the Institute of Education Sciences since 2002."

24. Larry N. Gerston, *American Federalism: A Concise Introduction* (Armonk, N.Y.: M. E. Sharpe, 2007); Joseph F. Zimmerman, *Contemporary American Federalism: The Growth of National Power* (Westport, Conn.: Greenwood, 1992).

25. Dean L. Fixsen and others, *Implementation Research: A Synthesis of the Literature* (University of South Florida, 2005); Stuart M. Butler and David B. Muhlhausen, "Can Government Replicate Success?" *National Affairs* 19 (Spring 2014).

26. Fixsen and others, *Implementation Research,* p. 24.

27. Sidney G. Winter and Gabriel Szulanski, "Replication as Strategy," *Organization Science,* vol. 12, no. 6 (2001), pp. 730–43.

28. Bruce R. Joyce and Beverly Showers, *Student Achievement through Staff Development,* 3rd ed. (Alexandria, Va.: Association for Supervision and Curriculum Development, 2002); B. E. Hanft, D. D. Rush, and M. L. Shelden, *Coaching Families and Colleagues in Early Childhood* (Baltimore, Md.: Paul H. Brookes, 2004).

Index

Note: page numbers followed by t and f refer to tables and figures respectively.

Center for American Progress (CAP), 138, 218

Center on Law and Social Policy (CLASP), 37

Centers for Disease Control and Prevention (CDC), 67, 76, 85, 96

Centers for Medicare and Medicaid Services (CMS), 63

Chamberlain, Seth, 86

Change for America (Jolin and Green, eds.), 138, 144–45

Child Care and Development Block Grant, 235

Children's Aid Society, 22t, 136

Children's Defense Fund, 37

Child Trends, 85, 88–89

Child Welfare League of America, 37

Citizen Schools, 135

City University of New York (CUNY), 205

City Year, 135

CLASP. *See* Center on Law and Social Policy

Clinton, Hillary, 137

CMS. *See* Centers for Medicare and Medicaid Services

CNCS. *See* Corporation for National and Community Service

Coaching, value of, 237

Coalition for Evidence-Based Policy, 19, 33, 41, 63–64, 128, 217, 232

Cole, Allison, 111, 112

CollegeYes program, 122t

Collins, Susan, 108

Committee jurisdiction: as frequent sticking point in negotiations, 44; over home visiting programs, 44–45, 50

"Common ground" initiative for teen pregnancy reduction, 73, 74

Community-Based Abstinence Education (CBAE) grant program, 70, 80, 81, 99, 100

Community-based Family Resource and Support Program (Oklahoma), 57

Community College and Career Training Grant Program, transformation into TAACCCT, 196, 211

Community college initiative: administration interest in, 188; evidence-based focus of, 190, 191, 211; funding for, 190; legislative struggle over health care reform and, 192–96. *See also* American Graduation Initiative (AGI); Trade Adjustment Assistance Community College and Career Training initiative (TAACCCT)

Community college system: Great Recession and, 189; increasing interest in good evidence in, 211–12; number of students in, 189; student demographics in, 189

Community Services Block Grant, 170

Community Solutions Fund, 143–44, 146

Community Solutions Tour, 150, 151

Competitive funding: in Investing in Innovation Initiative (i3), 109–10, 215; as key component in evidence-based initiatives, 26–28, 29, 214, 221–27; in Maternal, Infant, and Early Childhood Home Visiting initiative, 58, 59–60; in Teen Pregnancy Prevention initiative, 94; value of, 211; in Workforce Innovation Fund initiative, 172

Complete College America, 208

Concentric Research and Evaluation, 88–89

Conflicts of interest: elimination of, in home visiting programs, 58; policy on, intermediary granting organizations in SIF and, 156

Congress: American Recovery and Reinvestment Act and, 105–08; budget resolutions, importance of, 44; and Bush evidence-based pilot programs, 33–34; and debate on funding of home visiting programs, 36–38, 43; debate on Teen Pregnancy Prevention initiative,